Blackstone's

Police Investigators'

Q&A 2022

Blackstone's
Police Investigators'
Q&A
2022

Paul Connor

Great Clarendon Street, Oxford, OX2 6DP,
United Kingdom

Oxford University Press is a department of the University of Oxford. It furthers the University's objective of excellence in research, scholarship, and education by publishing worldwide. Oxford is a registered trade mark of Oxford University Press in the UK and in certain other countries

First Edition published in 2021

Impression: 1

Published in the United States of America by Oxford University Press
198 Madison Avenue, New York, NY 10016, United States of America

British Library Cataloguing in Publication Data
Data available

Library of Congress Control Number
Data available

ISBN 978–0–19–284761–4

DOI: 10.1093/law/9780192847614.001.0001

Printed in Great Britain by
Ashford Colour Press Ltd, Gosport, Hampshire

Contents

Introduction

The aim of this book is to assist Trainee Investigators who are studying and revising for the NIE.

Every answer is followed by a paragraph reference to *Blackstone's Police Investigators' Manual*. This means that once you have attempted a question and looked at an answer, the Manual can immediately be referred to for help and clarification.

Each question and answer has the same unique number. This should ensure that there is no confusion as to which question is linked to which answer. For example, Question 2.1 is linked to Answer 2.1.

At the back of the book you will find a checklist. This has been designed to help you keep track of your progress when answering the multiple-choice questions. If you fill in the checklist after attempting a question, you will be able to check how many you got right on the first attempt and will know immediately which questions need to be looked at a second time.

I have included chapters on studying and revising for the NIE and taking the NIE to assist students in their efforts to pass the examination.

I know how hard students have to work to pass the NIE and I applaud your efforts. I sincerely hope that this book will help you in your study and contribute to your successful performance in your forthcoming examination.

Acknowledgements

The primary purpose of this book is to provide advice and direction for students taking the National Investigators' Examination and to enable them to test their knowledge against multiple-choice questions based on the *Police Investigators' Manual*.

I could not have accomplished this task without the assistance of many officers from West Midlands Police, West Mercia Constabulary, Essex Police and West Yorkshire Police (Rob Waite). I wish to thank all the officers who have provided me with feedback about their examination experiences.

Thanks must also go to all the team at Oxford University Press for their continued professional support of my work.

Most of all I would like to thank my wife, Kate, whose encouragement, patience and understanding are the reason these words are in print.

Acknowledgements

PART ONE

General Principles, Police Powers and Procedures

1 *Mens Rea* (State of Mind)

QUESTIONS

Question 1.1

LLOYD is involved in an argument with GOUGH at a bowling alley. LLOYD picks up a 14 lb bowling ball and throws it at GOUGH, intending to cause him an injury. GOUGH ducks and the bowling ball hits DOOGAN, causing her an injury. The ball then drops onto a table smashing several glasses in the process.

Considering the doctrine of transferred *mens rea*, which of the following statements is correct?

A LLOYD would only be liable for the injury to DOOGAN.

B LLOYD would only be liable for the damage to the glasses.

C LLOYD would be liable for the injury to DOOGAN and the damage to the glasses.

D LLOYD would not be liable for the injury to DOOGAN or the damage to the glasses.

Question 1.2

When considering *mens rea*, offences may fall into the categories of specific and basic intent. The distinction between such offences is important when considering defences.

Which of the following comments is correct?

A An offence of maliciously wounding or inflicting grievous bodily harm (contrary to s. 20 of the Offences Against the Person Act 1861) would be a crime of 'specific' intent.

B An offence of burglary (contrary to s. 9(1)(a) of the Theft Act 1968) would be a crime of 'basic' intent.

C An offence of murder (contrary to common law) would be a crime of 'basic' intent.

D An offence of taking a conveyance without consent (contrary to s. 12(1) of the Theft Act 1968) would be a crime of 'basic' intent.

Question 1.3

TI GERMAIN is investigating an offence of s. 18 wounding/grievous bodily harm (contrary to the Offences Against the Person Act 1861) and has the offender, MANLEY, in custody. The offence took place in a pub and involved MANLEY picking up a glass, smashing it on a bar and shouting loudly *'I'm going to cut you to ribbons!'*, driving the glass a dozen times into the face of the victim. This has resulted in wounds requiring hundreds of stitches and reconstructive surgery. TI GERMAIN interviews MANLEY who states that he did not intend to wound the victim of the offence. After the interview, TI GERMAIN speaks to her supervisor about the offence and in particular the need to prove that MANLEY intended to cause the wounds/ grievous bodily harm.

Considering the mental element of 'intent', which of the following comments is correct?

A The intention required to prove a s. 18 wounding is defined by statute.

B Even though MANLEY denies the offence, a court could infer the necessary intent.

C The only way to prove intent for such an offence is by obtaining a confession from MANLEY.

D Whether to infer intent from the defendant's actions is a question of law to be decided by the magistrates or judge as appropriate.

Question 1.4

DC OGRILL is assisting in an enquiry into an incident where a self-employed boiler engineer botched a routine boiler service leading to an escape of carbon monoxide gas; that leak killed a family of four who owned the house where the boiler was situated. As a result of those deaths the possibility of prosecuting the boiler engineer for manslaughter (by gross negligence) is being considered by the enquiry team.

Thinking only about the mental element of 'negligence', which of the following statements is correct?

A Negligence is concerned with the defendant's compliance with the standards of reasonableness of ordinary people.

B Negligence is similar to strict liability as there is little to prove beyond the act itself and the state of mind of the defendant is immaterial.

C Negligence involves a subjective element, i.e. the standards of the defendant are important.

D It is the conduct of the defendant which is all important when considering negligence.

Question 1.5

TI CARTER is dealing with SPARROW who has been arrested in connection with an incident that occurred at a public house. It appears that HARDWARE had a disagreement with SPARROW who lost his temper with HARDWARE. SPARROW picked up a wooden chair and threw it at HARDWARE intending to cause grievous bodily harm to HARDWARE but the chair missed HARDWARE and hit GROUCOTT in the face causing her a broken jaw and very serious facial cuts. The chair fell to the floor and in the process smashed a vase standing on the floor.

Considering the doctrine of transferred *mens rea*, which of the following statements is correct?

A SPARROW is not liable for any offences in relation to HARDWARE.

B SPARROW is only liable for the injury received by GROUCOTT.

C SPARROW is liable for the attempted s. 18 (Offences Against the Person Act 1861) against HARDWARE and a s. 18 (Offences Against the Person Act 1861) against GROUCOTT only.

D SPARROW is liable for the attempted s. 18 (Offences Against the Person Act 1861) against HARDWARE, a s. 20 (Offences Against the Person Act 1861) against GROUCOTT and the criminal damage to the vase (s. 1 of the Criminal Damage Act 1971).

Question 1.6

BIRD, TAYLOR and HALL are in the sitting room of BIRD's flat where they have met in order to have a chat and a drink. BIRD and TAYLOR are drinking whisky but HALL is only drinking orange juice as alcohol has an adverse effect on him if he drinks it. BIRD and TAYLOR think it will be funny to 'spike' HALL's drink and during the evening they pour increasingly large amounts of vodka into HALL's drink. HALL is oblivious to this as he gets more and more drunk. BIRD and TAYLOR drink a large amount of whisky and they too become drunk. In fact, the three men are so drunk that they could only be described as completely intoxicated. Later in the evening, a fight occurs between the three men resulting in TAYLOR and HALL attacking BIRD and killing him. Both men are later charged with the offence of murder but claim that they were intoxicated at the time the offence took place and could not, therefore, have formed the necessary *mens rea* for murder.

In relation to the issues of voluntary and involuntary intoxication and the offence of murder, which of the following comments is correct?

A The fact that both men were intoxicated has no bearing in respect of a charge of murder.

B HALL's intoxication is relevant as it was involuntary; TAYLOR's intoxication is irrelevant as he was voluntarily intoxicated.

C As both men were intoxicated, they could raise this as an issue in relation to a charge of murder.

D Intoxication is only relevant to an offence of 'basic' intent and as murder is a 'specific' intent offence, the fact that both men were intoxicated is irrelevant.

Question 1.7

MINCHER and DUDLEY are old friends who used to be at university together. They meet in a pub for a reunion drink—MINCHER drinks a couple of pints of lager but DUDLEY is driving so she is only drinking lemonade. During their conversation, MINCHER reminds DUDLEY of the fun they used to have when they took drugs together and states that he has some LSD with him and asks DUDLEY if she would like some for 'old times' sake'. DUDLEY politely refuses. DUDLEY visits the toilet of the pub and while she is away MINCHER places a 'tab' of LSD in her lemonade. He swallows some LSD himself and when DUDLEY returns from the toilet she drinks her lemonade, swallowing the LSD in the process. The drug intoxicates MINCHER and DUDLEY who both begin to behave in an extremely erratic fashion resulting in GALLON (the landlord of the pub) requiring the two to leave the premises. MINCHER and DUDLEY attack GALLON causing him actual bodily harm (s. 47 of the Offences Against the Person Act 1861). The police are called and MINCHER and DUDLEY are arrested.

In relation to the law regarding intoxication and its use as a 'general defence', which of the following comments is correct?

A Intoxication is only relevant when the source of the intoxication is alcohol.

B As a s. 47 assault is a 'basic' intent offence, intoxication (whether it be from drink or drugs) would have no relevance for either of the accused.

C As DUDLEY was involuntarily intoxicated, she would be able to raise 'intoxication' in defence to a charge of s. 47 assault.

D It does not matter that MINCHER was voluntarily intoxicated as a result of taking the LSD—he could still raise the issue of intoxication in defence to a charge of s. 47 assault.

ANSWERS

Answer 1.1

Answer **A** — The doctrine of transferred *mens rea* only operates if the crime remains the same. In *R* v *Latimer* (1886) 17 QBD 359, the defendant lashed out with his belt at one person but missed, striking a third party instead. As it was proved that the defendant had the required *mens rea* when he swung the belt, the court held that the same *mens rea* could support a charge of wounding against any other victim injured by the same act. Therefore, LLOYD is liable for the assault on DOOGAN, making answers B and D incorrect. If the nature of the offence changes, then the doctrine will not operate. LLOYD's *mens rea* to injure will not transfer into the *mens rea* for an offence of criminal damage, making answer C incorrect.

Investigators' Manual, para. 1.1.11

Answer 1.2

Answer **D** — A crime of 'specific' intent is only committed where the defendant is shown to have had a particular intention to bring about a specific consequence at the time of the criminal act. Answers B and C are examples of such offences—they are not 'basic' intent offences and these answers are therefore incorrect. Answer A is incorrect as the offence of maliciously wounding or inflicting grievous bodily harm (contrary to s. 20 of the Offences Against the Person Act 1861) is a crime of 'basic' intent, not 'specific' intent. Answer D (taking a conveyance without consent contrary to s. 12(1) of the Theft Act 1968) is a 'basic' intent offence.

Investigators' Manual, para. 1.1.2.1

Answer 1.3

Answer **B** — Intention can be inferred in two ways (i) by virtue of s. 8 of the Criminal Justice Act 1967 or (ii) by the body of case law that has developed around the subject. There is no requirement for a confession to exist (otherwise very few intention-based offences would be proved), making answer C incorrect. Answer A is incorrect as the word 'intent' is not defined by any statute and intent means different things for different offences. Answer D is incorrect as whether a defendant intends a particular consequence will be a question of fact left to the jury or magistrate(s) as appropriate.

Investigators' Manual, para. 1.1.2

Answer 1.4

Answer **A** — Negligence is concerned with the defendant's compliance with the standards of reasonableness of ordinary people (answer A) and not the standards of the defendant, making answer C incorrect. Like strict liability, the concept focuses on the consequences (not the conduct) of the defendant rather than demanding proof of a particular state of mind at the time, making answer D incorrect. However, negligence does not have such a close relationship with strict liability so as to mean that only the act needs to be proved—there is still the requirement to illustrate 'fault' or 'blame' of the defendant who must be shown to have acted in a way that runs contrary to the expectations of the reasonable person (making answer B incorrect).

Investigators' Manual, para. 1.1.9

Answer 1.5

Answer **C** — The doctrine of transferred *mens rea* will only apply if the nature of the offence remains the same. When SPARROW throws a chair at HARDWARE he intends to cause *someone* harm and that is the end result when the chair hits GROUCOTT. So SPARROW is liable for the attempted injury to HARDWARE (the attempted s. 18) and the actual injury caused to GROUCOTT (a s. 18 offence), making answers A and B incorrect. SPARROW is not liable for the damage to the vase as the nature of the offence (assault to criminal damage) has changed, making answer D incorrect.

Investigators' Manual, para. 1.1.11

Answer 1.6

Answer **C** — Intoxication can be divided into two categories; voluntary intoxication (you got yourself in that condition) and involuntary intoxication (you are not responsible for getting in that condition). The distinction is important when considering whether the offence alleged is one of 'specific' or 'basic' intent (terms discussed in Chapter 1 of your *Investigators' Manual*). Where an offence is a specific intent offence such as murder, defendants who were voluntarily intoxicated at the time the offence was committed (in this question TAYLOR) may be able to show that they were so intoxicated that they were incapable of forming the *mens rea* required for the offence. An individual who is voluntarily intoxicated *would not* be able to say this if accused of an offence of basic intent as the courts have accepted that a defendant is still capable of forming basic intent even when completely inebriated (*DPP* v *Majewski* [1977] AC 443). So TAYLOR's intoxication is relevant to these circumstances and intoxication is relevant to 'basic' or 'specific' intent offences meaning that answers A and D are incorrect. This information also rules out answer B. In addition, where the offence is a basic intent offence, such as s. 47 assault, defendants who were involuntarily intoxicated (perhaps because their drinks had been spiked, i.e. HALL) at the time of the offence may be able to say that they lacked the *mens rea* for that basic intent offence. Therefore, voluntary intoxication can be raised in answer to a charge of an offence of specific intent but not basic intent; involuntary intoxication can be raised in answer to a charge of both specific *and* basic intent.

Investigators' Manual, paras 1.1.2.1 to 1.1.2.2

Answer 1.7

Answer **C** — Answer A is incorrect as the source of the intoxication can be drink or drugs. Intoxication is not a 'general defence' as such—what intoxication does is potentially remove the necessary *mens rea* required for a defendant to commit an offence. Intoxication can be divided into two categories: voluntary intoxication (you got yourself in that condition—MINCHER) and involuntary intoxication (you are not responsible for getting in that condition—DUDLEY). The distinction is important when considering whether the offence alleged is one of 'specific' or 'basic' intent. Where an offence is a specific intent offence such as murder, defendants who were voluntarily intoxicated at the time the offence was committed may be able to show that they were so intoxicated that they were incapable of forming the *mens rea* required for the offence. An individual who is voluntarily intoxicated *would not* be able to say this if accused of an offence of basic intent (MINCHER) as the courts have accepted that a defendant is still capable of forming basic intent even when completely inebriated (*DPP* v *Majewski* [1977] AC 443), making answer D incorrect. Where the offence is a basic intent offence such as s. 47 assault, defendants who were involuntarily intoxicated (perhaps because their drink had been spiked) at the time of the offence may be able to say that they lacked the *mens rea* for that basic intent offence. So 'intoxication' is relevant as far as DUDLEY is concerned making answer B incorrect. As involuntary intoxication can be raised in answer to a charge of basic intent (s. 47 assault), answer C is correct.

Investigators' Manual, paras 1.1.2.1, 1.1.2.2

2 *Actus Reus* (Criminal Conduct)

QUESTIONS

Question 2.1

MASTERS is evicted from her home and moves in with her next-door neighbour OXFORD. The two are unrelated. OXFORD is housebound and extremely ill and needs constant attention otherwise she will die. MASTERS tells OXFORD that she will look after her and that OXFORD can dismiss the full-time nurse OXFORD has employed to perform this duty; OXFORD agrees. MASTERS looks after OXFORD for six months but then becomes bored by the constant care OXFORD requires. MASTERS totally ignores OXFORD for over four days and as a result, OXFORD dies.

Would MASTERS be criminally liable for her omission to act?

A No, MASTERS is under no duty to act under a statute, a public office or under the terms of a contract.

B Yes, MASTERS has taken it upon herself to carry out a duty and has then failed to do so.

C No, MASTERS must have some sort of relationship with OXFORD such as a parent with a child.

D Yes, MASTERS has created a dangerous situation and has taken no action to counteract the danger she created.

Question 2.2

MEREDITH assaults PERK by pushing her through a glass window. This causes several deep cuts to PERK's wrists. PERK manages to escape and seek medical attention at a hospital where she is left waiting for some four hours before being told that her injuries are not life-threatening as long as she has a blood transfusion. PERK is a Jehovah's Witness and refuses to have the transfusion because of her religious beliefs. As a result of her refusal to have the transfusion, PERK dies from the injuries. Apart from the initial waiting period, hospital staff carried out their duties carefully.

Which of the following is correct with regard to MEREDITH's criminal liability?

A MEREDITH is liable for PERK's death, as defendants must take their victims as they find them. PERK's refusal to have the blood transfusion on religious grounds would not affect MEREDITH's liability.

B MEREDITH is not liable for PERK's death as her refusal to have a blood transfusion breaks the causal link between the assault and PERK's death.

C MEREDITH would not be liable for PERK's death because the negligent treatment PERK received on her arrival at the hospital would be classed as an 'intervening act', breaking the causal link.

D MEREDITH is liable for the death of PERK as under no circumstances could negligent medical treatment ever break the chain of causation from MEREDITH's assault to PERK's death.

Question 2.3

BULL is homeless and breaks into an abandoned house looking for shelter. He goes upstairs into the back bedroom and lies down on a mattress. BULL lights a cigarette and then falls asleep. He wakes up several minutes later to find that the mattress is on fire. BULL does not put out the fire; instead he gets up and goes into another room and goes to sleep. The mattress continues to burn, causing serious damage to the bedroom. The only reason BULL survives is because of the rapid attendance of the fire brigade.

Which of the following comments is correct regarding BULL's criminal liability?

A BULL is not liable as a defendant can only be punished for his/her positive conduct; an omission cannot be punished by criminal law.

B BULL is liable for the criminal damage as he has created a dangerous situation and has a duty to act.

C Unless BULL is under a duty to act under a statute, a contract or because of a public office, he will not be liable for an omission to act.

D BULL is not liable, as criminal law will only punish an omission if the defendant has taken it upon him/herself to carry out a duty and then fails to do so.

Question 2.4

During an argument in a pub, McCLEOD attacks RUMLEY causing him serious brain damage. RUMLEY is already suffering from a serious stomach ulcer when McCLEOD attacks him. RUMLEY is taken to hospital but the brain damage caused in the assault prevents doctors from operating on the stomach ulcer, which eventually ruptures and kills RUMLEY.

What is McCLEOD's criminal liability in these circumstances?

A McCLEOD will not be liable for the death of RUMLEY as it is the lack of medical treatment that is the cause of RUMLEY's death.

B McCLEOD has no liability for the death of RUMLEY as the ultimate and actual cause of death was an untreated ulcer.

C McCLEOD would be liable for manslaughter, as his criminal conduct has made a significant contribution to RUMLEY's death.

D McCLEOD would not be liable for RUMLEY's death, as the ruptured ulcer would be viewed as an intervening act.

Question 2.5

PYE agrees to accompany his friend BASRAN to an isolated farm where BASRAN intends to steal the farm owner's car. PYE is fully aware of BASRAN's intention and has agreed to act as a 'look out' while BASRAN steals the car. PALFREY, the owner of the car, confronts them as BASRAN is breaking into the car. Unexpectedly, BASRAN produces a knife and stabs PALFREY, causing her a serious injury. PYE had no idea that BASRAN was carrying a knife and only accompanied BASRAN in order to steal the car.

Considering the law relating to principals and accessories, would PYE be liable with regard to the wounding against PALFREY?

A PYE is an accessory present at the scene of a crime when it is committed. His presence may amount to encouragement that would support a charge of aiding, abetting, counselling or procuring the wounding offence.

B PYE is an accessory who has helped in the commission of an offence. A court will treat him in the same way as the principal offender (BASRAN) for the wounding of PALFREY.

C PYE did not physically assist BASRAN in the wounding of PALFREY. Unless this element forms part of the offence, PYE can never be liable as an accessory to the wounding offence.

D Although PYE and BASRAN are part of a joint enterprise, BASRAN has gone beyond what had been agreed. As such, PYE could not be held liable for the consequences of such an 'unauthorised' act by BASRAN.

Question 2.6

SUTTON is a drug dealer and regularly supplies BOND with heroin. SUTTON visits BOND at her home address and sells her £200 worth of heroin before leaving. Several hours after SUTTON has left, BOND prepares the heroin for injection, applies a tourniquet to her arm and injects all of the heroin. She dies several minutes later of an overdose.

With regard to the chain of causation and intervening acts, which of the following comments is correct?

A SUTTON supplied BOND with the heroin and is therefore the direct cause of her death and would be liable for her murder.

B BOND exercised her free will and has brought about her own death by injecting the heroin; SUTTON is not liable for her death.

C Although SUTTON is not the direct cause of BOND's death, the fact that he supplied her with the heroin makes him guilty of her manslaughter.

D Even if SUTTON actually prepared the heroin and injected BOND with it, bringing about her death, he would not commit an offence.

Question 2.7

TI GARRETT and TI DESULT are discussing a case where a number of offenders have been charged as accessories to the primary offence. The officers make a number of comments in respect of the law surrounding principals and accessories.

Which is the only comment to show a correct understanding of the law?

A TI GARRETT states that if an accessory 'aids, abets, counsels or procures' an indictable offence then their sentence is punishable by a term of imprisonment that will be half the length of a principal offender.

B TI DESULT states that when an accessory is charged, it must be made clear on the charge what form the accessory has taken, i.e. have they aided, abetted, counselled or procured the offence?

C TI GARRETT states that, generally speaking, aiding or abetting an offence will usually involve the presence of the accessory at the scene of the offence.

D TI DESULT states that if you are trying to show that a defendant procured an offence there is no need to show a causal link between the conduct of the accessory and the offence.

Question 2.8

LATIF approaches ENLY in a street intending to rob him. LATIF holds a knife towards ENLY and tells ENLY that unless he hands over his wallet he will be stabbed. ENLY panics in the face of such a violent threat and turns away from LATIF and runs across a nearby road to escape. As ENLY does so he is hit by a car and is seriously injured as a consequence.

Is LATIF responsible for the serious injury received by ENLY?

A Yes, as ENLY's reaction is one that could reasonably be anticipated from any victim in such a situation.

B No, the car striking ENLY would be interpreted as an intervening act, breaking the chain of causation.

C Yes, but LATIF could not be held accountable for the death of ENLY should he die from the serious injury.

D No, as ENLY's reaction is one carried out entirely of his own volition.

Question 2.9

Companies which are 'legally incorporated' have a legal personality of their own, that is they can own property, employ people and bring law suits: they can therefore commit offences, giving us the concept of 'corporate liability'.

Considering companies and 'corporate liability', which of the following comments is true?

A Legally incorporated companies can only be prosecuted for offences of strict liability.

B A legally incorporated company cannot be convicted as an accessory to an offence, i.e. it cannot aid, abet, counsel or procure the commission of an offence.

C There are occasions where the courts will accept that the knowledge of certain employees will be extended to the company.

D Companies cannot be prosecuted for offences that require a state of mind, i.e. *mens rea*.

Question 2.10

In order to prove the *actus reus* (criminal conduct) of an offence, the prosecution are required to prove two elements.

What are those two elements?

A That the defendant's conduct was voluntary and that he/she realised the consequences of his/her actions.

B That the defendant brought about a consequence as a result of his/her actions and that this consequence was a realistic possibility when the act took place.

C That the defendant's conduct was voluntary and that it occurred while the defendant still had the requisite *mens rea* .

D That the defendant knew what was likely to occur and he/she had the requisite *mens rea* for the act at the time of the offence.

Question 2.11

MINACK and LORIMER agree to carry out a burglary at a house owned by OXFORD; the house is in the middle of a row of houses and the two men agree that they will gain access to the house via a service road at the rear of the premises. MINACK leads the way but makes a mistake when he chooses the house to be broken into, accidentally selecting a house belonging to ATHERTON who is a neighbour of OXFORD. MINACK and LORIMER enter the house and as they do so they are confronted by ATHERTON. MINACK produces a knife and stabs ATHERTON causing him serious injury in the process. LORIMER did not know that MINACK had a knife with him.

Considering the law in relation to joint enterprise, which of the following comments is correct?

A LORIMER is liable for the burglary at ATHERTON's house and for the injury to ATHERTON.

B LORIMER is only liable for the burglary at ATHERTON's house.

C LORIMER is only liable for the injury received by ATHERTON.

D LORIMER is not liable for the burglary or the injury to ATHERTON.

ANSWERS

Answer 2.1

Answer **B** — Criminal liability usually arises as a result of a defendant's action. However, in some cases a defendant can be criminally liable because of an omission or a failure to act. The section on omissions gives specific examples of when such a liability may arise, one of those being when a defendant has taken it upon him/herself to carry out a duty and then fails to do so (*R* v *Stone* [1977] QB 354). Although answers A, C and D all relate to criminal liability via omissions, they are still incorrect. MASTERS is liable for her inaction. Answer D is incorrect as the creation of a dangerous situation involves the doing of some act and then a failure to prevent the harm in question occurring. MASTERS has not 'done' an act.

Investigators' Manual, para. 1.2.5

Answer 2.2

Answer **A** — This question relates to the 'but for' test applied to the principles surrounding the causation. The simple way to deal with this question is to ask, 'But for MEREDITH's actions, would PERK have died?' The answer is 'No'. The next step is to ask if there has been an intervening act that breaks the chain of causation. Again the answer is 'No'. Defendants must take their victims as they find them, so refusing a blood transfusion on religious grounds will not break the chain of causation (*R* v *Blaue* [1975] 1 WLR 1411), making answer B incorrect. Negligent treatment has to be grossly negligent to break the chain of causation, making answer C incorrect. Answer D is incorrect because although negligent medical treatment will not normally break the chain of causation, there are exceptions where this has been the case (*R* v *Jordan* (1956) 40 Cr App R 152).

Investigators' Manual, paras 1.2.6, 1.2.7

Answer 2.3

Answer **B** — Criminal conduct is generally associated with the actions of the defendant; however, there are certain circumstances where an omission will attract criminal liability, making answer A incorrect. Such a duty can arise from a number of circumstances including where the defendant is under a duty to act under a statute (answer C), where the defendant has taken it upon him/herself to carry out a duty and then fails to do so (answer D), where the defendant is in a parental relationship with a child or young person or where the defendant creates a situation of danger (answer B and based on the case of *R* v *Miller* [1983] 2 AC 161). This makes answers C and D incorrect.

Investigators' Manual, para. 1.2.5

Answer 2.4

Answer **C** — There must be a causal link (or chain of causation) between the act of the defendant and the consequences; this is generally called the 'but for' test, e.g. if McCLEOD had not assaulted RUMLEY would he have died? The answer must be 'No'. If the assault had not taken place then the ulcer could have been operated on and RUMLEY may have lived. This question is based on the circumstances in the case of *R* v *McKechnie* [1992] Crim LR 194, where the court held that the defendant's actions had made a significant contribution to the victim's death (answer C). Answer A is incorrect as the lack of medical treatment was caused by McCLEOD's assault. Answer B is incorrect as although the ulcer is the *actual* cause of death, it ruptured because of a lack of medical treatment, which could not be given because of the brain damage caused by the assault. Answer D is incorrect as the ruptured ulcer is not an intervening act.

Investigators' Manual, paras 1.2.6, 1.2.7

Answer 2.5

Answer **D** — Whether an accessory will be liable for the actions of the principal offender will depend on the nature and extent of the offence that was initially agreed to and contemplated by the accessory. The offence agreed to in this scenario was the theft of a car; this is entirely different to the wounding that BASRAN commits. In these circumstances, PYE will not be liable because BASRAN has gone 'beyond what has been tacitly agreed as part of the common enterprise' (*R* v *Anderson* [1966] 2 QB 110). In addition, there need be no physical assistance by the accessory to attract liability.

Investigators' Manual, paras 1.2.8 to 1.2.8.2

Answer 2.6

Answer **B** — If a drug dealer supplies drugs to another person who then kills him/herself by overdose, the dealer cannot, without more, be said to have caused the death. Death would have been brought about by the deliberate exercise of free will by the user, making answers A and C incorrect. Answer D is incorrect as the Court of Appeal has accepted that, under certain circumstances, where a person buys a controlled drug from another and immediately injects it, resulting in his/her death, the supplier can attract liability for the person's death.

Investigators' Manual, para. 1.2.5

Answer 2.7

Answer **C** — Answer A is incorrect as if an accessory 'aids, abets, counsels or procures' an offence then he/she will be treated by a court in the same way as a principal offender for an indictable offence (s. 8 of the Accessories and Abettors Act 1861). Answer B is incorrect as the expression 'aid, abet, counsel or procure' is generally used in its entirety when charging a defendant, without separating out the particular element that applies. Answer D is incorrect as if you are trying to show that a defendant 'procured' an offence, you *must* show a causal link between his/her conduct and the offence.

Investigators' Manual, paras 1.2.8, 1.2.8.1

Answer 2.8

Answer **A** — Although actions by the victim will sometimes be significant in the chain of causation, the victim's behaviour will not necessarily be regarded as a new intervening act. If the victim's actions are those which might reasonably be anticipated from any victim in such a situation, there will be no new and intervening act and the defendant will be responsible for the consequences flowing from them, i.e. being hit by a car in escaping. If you threaten someone with a knife telling them they will be stabbed if they do not hand over their wallet it is a thoroughly understandable reaction from the victim to try to escape from such a threat. Therefore, LATIF is responsible for the injury to ENLY, making answers B and D incorrect. Answer C is incorrect as if ENLY did die from the injury received then LATIF would be liable for his death—a simple example of the chain of causation in action.

Investigators' Manual, paras 1.2.6, 1.2.7

Answer 2.9

Answer **C** — Companies have been prosecuted for offences of strict liability (*Alphacell Ltd* v *Woodward* [1972] AC 824) but they have also been prosecuted for offences involving *mens rea* (*Tesco Supermarkets Ltd* v *Nattrass* [1972] AC 153) and also as accessories (*R* v *Robert Millar (Contractors) Ltd* [1970] 2 QB 54), making answers A, B and D incorrect. There are occasions where the courts will accept that the knowledge of certain employees will be extended to the company (see, e.g. *Tesco Stores Ltd* v *Brent Borough Council* [1993] 1 WLR 1037).

Investigators' Manual, para. 1.2.9

Answer 2.10

Answer **C** — When proving *actus reus* you must show that the defendant's conduct was voluntary and that it occurred while the defendant still had the required *mens rea*.

Investigators' Manual, para. 1.2.1

Answer 2.11

Answer **B** — MINACK and LORIMER have embarked on the commission of an offence and have a common goal (to break into a house)—that is a joint enterprise. As the parties to a joint enterprise share a combined purpose, each will be liable for the consequences of the actions of the other in the pursuit of the joint enterprise. This is the case even if the consequences of the joint enterprise are a result of a mistake (as in the question). Here, MINACK and LORIMER have agreed to carry out a burglary—the fact that MINACK goes to the wrong house will not prevent LORIMER being liable for burglary. This makes answers C and D incorrect. However, where the nature of the offence changes liability will not exist. LORIMER did not know that MINACK had a knife and the stabbing of the occupier of the house is a clear departure from the nature and type of crime that was envisaged by LORIMER. It is so fundamentally different that LORIMER would not be liable for the injury, making answer A incorrect.

Investigators' Manual, paras 1.2.8 to 1.2.8.2

3 Incomplete Offences

QUESTIONS

Question 3.1

A travel company employs LUCAS and KIRK as coach staff; amongst other duties, the two sell refreshments to customers travelling by coach. LUCAS suggests to KIRK that they make their own sandwiches and sell these to people using the coach instead of the sandwiches supplied by the travel firm. KIRK agrees to the suggestion.

Would this constitute an offence of conspiracy to defraud (contrary to common law)?

A No, because this offence involves deceiving another into acting in a way that is contrary to his/her duty.

B Yes, but you must show that the defendants were dishonest.

C No, at least three people must be involved in the conspiracy.

D Yes, but only as long as you prove that the end result would amount to the commission of an offence.

Question 3.2

McEVOY is due to be a contestant on a 'live' general knowledge TV show. When McEVOY takes part in the show his wife will be watching at home. Before the show begins husband and wife devise a plan so that when McEVOY is asked a question by the host of the show, McEVOY's wife will send him a text message via his mobile phone that will contain the correct answer. If all goes according to plan, the two will win up to £50,000.

Does this amount to a statutory conspiracy (contrary to s. 1 of the Criminal Law Act 1977)?

A Yes, the two have agreed on a course of conduct that will amount to the commission of an offence.

B No, McEVOY cannot commit statutory conspiracy if the only other party to the agreement is his wife.

C No, for there to be a conspiracy there must be an agreement with at least three people involved.

D Yes, unless the plan is later abandoned by the two.

Question 3.3

WISEDALE plans to falsely imprison a schoolboy and sexually assault him. He plans to gain access to a local school and commit the offence in the school toilets. WISEDALE buys a rucksack and places a kitchen knife, some rope and masking tape into the rucksack. He gains entry to the school and hides in the toilets waiting for his chance to commit the offence. The school caretaker catches him before the offence is committed.

Considering the law relating to attempts under s. 1 of the Criminal Attempts Act 1981, at what stage, if at all, does WISEDALE commit the offence of attempted false imprisonment?

A When he plans to gain access to the school and commit the offence in the toilets.

B When he buys the rucksack and places the kitchen knife, rope and masking tape into the rucksack.

C When he gains entry to the school and hides in the toilets waiting for a chance to commit the offence.

D The offence of attempted false imprisonment is not made out in these circumstances.

Question 3.4

KRAY arranges to handle a container load of electrical goods stolen in the course of a robbery. Unknown to KRAY, the container full of goods has been intercepted by the police who arrest the driver, return the contents to the rightful owner and substitute a container full of boxes containing old newspapers for the original container. A police officer drives the substituted container to the arranged meeting point and KRAY arrives shortly after, driving a large goods vehicle. KRAY backs the goods vehicle up to the container, opens the container doors and begins to load the worthless boxes into his goods vehicle when he is arrested.

Does KRAY attempt to handle stolen goods in these circumstances?

A No, in these circumstances the goods have ceased to be stolen and as the goods are not stolen the offence cannot be committed.

B Yes, although it is physically impossible to handle goods that are not stolen, this impossibility would not preclude such a charge under the Criminal Attempts Act 1981.

C No, this offence does not exist and would be a legal impossibility.

D Yes, but the prosecution would have to show that KRAY intended to dispose of the goods in order to show he had 'embarked on the crime proper'.

Question 3.5

PINTER is a paedophile who wants to carry out a sexual assault against his next-door neighbour's 11-year-old child. He plans to kidnap her when she is playing in a nearby park and take her to his lock-up garage where the assault will be committed. PINTER's problem is that he only has one arm and does not think he will be able to restrain the child. He approaches SANDY (who PINTER thinks would be interested in these types of offence if asked to join in) and asks him to help out in the kidnap and sexual assault. PINTER believes that his request will encourage SANDY to commit the offences and if he says 'Yes' the two men will commit the offences. SANDY is utterly horrified by PINTER's suggestion and refuses to have anything to do with PINTER's suggested plan.

With regard to offences under ss. 44 to 46 of the Serious Crime Act 2007 (encouraging or assisting crime), which of the following comments is correct?

A An offence has not been committed as PINTER's encouragement did not have the effect that he desired (that SANDY would join the venture).

B To prove encouragement, PINTER would need to approach SANDY or another person on a second occasion.

C PINTER has not committed an offence as he would need to intend that his act will encourage or assist the commission of an offence (he only believes that it will).

D PINTER has committed the offence in these circumstances.

Question 3.6

ARUN (aged 14 years) has a 'crush' on FLATLEY (aged 25 years) who is ARUN's school teacher. ARUN watches the car park of the school where FLATLEY has parked his car and when FLATLEY appears and is just about to open the door of his car ARUN intercepts him. ARUN strikes up a conversation with FLATLEY about a lesson she took part in that day but all the while she is intending to persuade him to let her have oral sex with him (FLATLEY's penis to her mouth). Moments into the conversation, ARUN states *'I'd do anything for you, absolutely anything'*. FLATLEY quickly becomes concerned about the tone of the conversation when ARUN states, '*Take me back to your place and I'll give you a "blow-job"*'. FLATLEY tells ARUN that this is not going to happen and he immediately returns to the school to report the incident.

At what point, if at all, does ARUN commit the offence of encouraging or assisting an offence (contrary to s. 44 of the Serious Crime 2007)?

A When she initially strikes up the conversation with FLATLEY.
B When she tells FLATLEY she would do anything for him.
C When she asks FLATLEY to take her back to his home for oral sex.
D ARUN does not commit the offence in these circumstances.

Question 3.7

BULLMAN wishes to commit a robbery at a supermarket. He originally intended to commit the offence alone, but realises that to escape capture he needs somebody to act as his getaway driver. He approaches FLINTOFF and suggests that he assists him as the getaway driver; FLINTOFF does not want to get involved in the offence and refuses BULLMAN's request.

In relation to offences under the Criminal Attempts Act 1981 alone, which of the following statements is correct?

A BULLMAN is guilty of attempting to conspire with FLINTOFF.
B BULLMAN is guilty of attempting to counsel FLINTOFF to commit the offence.
C BULLMAN commits no offence under this legislation.
D BULLMAN is guilty of attempting to procure the commission of an offence.

Question 3.8

PATAVAN and CRADDOCK are chatting in a pub. PATAVAN tells CRADDOCK that he is having a hard time meeting all of his monthly bills and that he is extremely short of cash. CRADDOCK informs PATAVAN that a nearby jeweller's shop has a problem with its CCTV and alarm system and that neither will be working for the rest of the week. CRADDOCK encourages PATAVAN to go into the jeweller's shop and steal as much jewellery as he can. CRADDOCK believes that his advice will assist PATAVAN to commit the offence but does not actually believe PATAVAN will commit the offence as he has a very timid nature. PATAVAN tells CRADDOCK he will commit the offence of theft and leaves the pub and makes his way to the jeweller's intending to commit the offence of theft. However, he has a change of heart during the journey and decides not to commit any offence.

Considering the offences associated with encouraging or assisting an offence (under s. 45 of the Serious Crime Act 2007), which of the following comments is correct?

A No offence under this legislation has been committed as PATAVAN did not actually commit the offence of theft from the jeweller's shop.

B The offence is committed when CRADDOCK provides information about the jeweller's shop believing it will assist PATAVAN to commit an offence.

C No offence is committed because CRADDOCK does not believe that PATAVAN will commit the offence.

D The offence is committed when PATAVAN tells CRADDOCK that he will commit the offence of theft.

Question 3.9

PCs SUTTER and HANNON are discussing the Criminal Attempts Act 1981 with regard to their revision programme for their forthcoming National Investigators' Examination.

PC SUTTER makes the following statements to test HANNON's knowledge.

With regards to the Criminal Attempts Act 1981, which of the following statements made by PC SUTTER is correct?

A A person can be guilty of attempting low-value theft, even though it is triable summarily.

B A person can be found guilty of attempting to assist an offender contrary to s. 4 of the Criminal Law Act 1967.

C A person cannot be found guilty of attempting an offence if it is impossible to commit the substantive offence.

D A person who attempts an offence that is triable only on indictment can be tried either way.

Question 3.10

POTOLI and VERRITT are civil partners who have been having problems with ROSS (who frequents a pub that POTOLI and VERRITT visit). ROSS constantly directs abuse at POTOLI and VERRITT about their sexuality and the pair have had enough. They decide that ROSS needs to be taught a lesson and agree that they will attack him (although they do not intend to cause him any more than very minor harm, i.e. a common battery). The two plan the offence so that there will be no witnesses and so that ROSS will not be able to identify them as the offenders. On the night of the planned offence, they leave their house and wait for ROSS in an alleyway at the side of the pub. Whilst waiting, POTOLI has second thoughts about committing the offence and tells VERRITT that he does not want to go through with their plan. VERRITT states that he understands and that they should forget their plan. The two men return to their home and ROSS is not subject to any harm by the pair. As it turns out, ROSS could not possibly have been assaulted as he was not drinking in the pub that evening—he was on holiday in Poland.

Considering only the offence of statutory conspiracy (contrary to s. 1 of the Criminal Law Act 1977), which of the following comments is correct?

A A conspiracy offence does not exist as you can only conspire to commit an indictable offence and an offence of 'common battery' under s. 39 of the Criminal Justice Act 1988 is an offence that is triable summarily.

B A conspiracy offence has not been committed as there was never any 'end product' as a consequence of the agreement between the two men.

C A conspiracy offence has not been committed as it was impossible for ROSS to be assaulted as he was in Poland at the time the two men planned to assault him.

D No conspiracy offence has been committed as the two participants are civil partners.

ANSWERS

Answer 3.1

Answer **B** — Answer A is incorrect as the offence of conspiracy to defraud can take two forms—one is as per answer A, and the other is an agreement by two or more persons, by dishonesty, to deprive a person of something which is his or to which he is or would or might be entitled [or] an agreement by two or more by dishonesty to injure some proprietary right [of the victim] (Viscount Dilhorne in *Scott* v *Metropolitan Police Commissioner* [1975] AC 819). This definition means that answers C and D are incorrect.

Investigators' Manual, para. 1.3.3.2

Answer 3.2

Answer **B** — Although there has been an agreement that if carried out in accordance with the conspirators' intentions will involve the commission of an offence, the offence of statutory conspiracy is not made out. This is because a defendant cannot be convicted of statutory conspiracy if the *only* other party to the agreement is his/her spouse, a child/children under 10 years of age or the intended victim.

Investigators' Manual, para. 1.3.3.1

Answer 3.3

Answer **D** — The defendant's actions must be shown to have gone beyond mere preparation towards the commission of the substantive offence. The courts have accepted an approach of questioning whether the defendant had 'embarked on the crime proper' (*R* v *Gullefer* [1990] 1 WLR 1063), although there is no requirement for the defendant to have passed a point of no return if the intention of the defendant can be ascertained. Up to point C, WISEDALE has not 'embarked on the crime proper'. In *R* v *Geddes* [1996] Crim LR 894, G was found in a boys' toilet of a school in possession of articles that suggested his reason for being there was to kidnap a child. His conviction for attempted false imprisonment was quashed. Even clear evidence of what he had in mind 'did not throw light on whether he had begun to carry out the commission of the offence'.

Investigators' Manual, para. 1.3.4

Answer 3.4

Answer **B** — You may consider that the offence cannot be committed because the goods from the container have been recovered by the police and returned to their rightful owner. Under s. 24(3) of the Theft Act 1968 this would mean that the goods shall no longer be regarded as stolen goods. However, s. 1(2) of the Criminal Attempts Act 1981 states: 'A person may be guilty of attempting to commit an offence to which this section applies even though the facts are such that the commission of the offence is impossible.' This makes answer A incorrect and also answer C as the offence is not a legal impossibility. Answer D is incorrect as KRAY has already 'embarked on the crime proper' by moving the boxes from one vehicle to another.

Investigators' Manual, paras 1.3.4, 1.3.5

Answer 3.5

Answer **D** — The offence under s. 46 of the Act is committed when a person does an act (the request by PINTER to SANDY) capable of encouraging or assisting the commission of one or more of a number of offences (kidnap and sexual assault) and he *believes* that one or more of those offences will be committed and that his act will encourage or assist in the commission of one or more of them. One conversation is ample, making answer B incorrect. Only a *belief* is required (not intention—that is under s. 44 of the Act and makes answer C incorrect). Answer A is incorrect as the offence can be committed regardless of whether the encouragement or assistance has the effect the defendant intended or believed it would have.

Investigators' Manual, para. 1.3.2

Answer 3.6

Answer **D** — The first thing to consider here is what kind of offence is ARUN trying to encourage FLATLEY to commit? The answer to that would be an offence under s. 9 of the Sexual Offences Act 2003—sexual activity with a child. That offence exists to protect children under 16 from this kind of sexual activity. So ARUN is encouraging FLATLEY to commit an offence that exists for her own protection. Section 51 of the Act limits the liability of the offence by setting out in statute the common law exception established in *R* v *Tyrell* [1894] 1 QB 710. A person cannot be guilty of an offence under s. 44, 45 or 46 if, in relation to the offence, it is a 'protective' offence and the person who does the act capable of encouraging or assisting that offence (ARUN in this question) falls within the category of persons that the offence was designed to protect and would be considered a victim.

Investigators' Manual, para. 1.3.2

Answer 3.7

Answer **C** — This question checks whether you know the exceptions regarding the Criminal Attempts Act 1981. You cannot attempt to conspire, making answer A incorrect. You cannot attempt to counsel, making answer B incorrect and you cannot attempt to procure the commission of an offence, making answer D incorrect.

Investigators' Manual, para. 1.3.4

Answer 3.8

Answer **C** — The offence under s. 45 of the Serious Crime Act 2007 will be committed if a person does an act capable of encouraging or assisting in the commission of an offence and he believes that the offence will be committed and that his act will encourage or assist its commission. CRADDOCK does not believe that PATAVAN will commit the offence and therefore the offence under s. 45 is not committed, making answers B and D incorrect. The fact that PATAVAN does not go on to commit an offence (if all the other elements were present) would not prevent CRADDOCK committing the offence, making answer A incorrect.

Investigators' Manual, para. 1.3.2

Answer 3.9

Answer **A** — Answer B is incorrect as s. 4 of the Criminal Law 1967 is specified in the Criminal Attempts Act 1981 list of offences that cannot be attempted. Answer C is incorrect as you can attempt an offence that is impossible to commit. Answer D is incorrect as if the offence attempted is triable only on indictment, the attempt will be triable only on indictment. Answer A is correct because even though low-value theft is triable summarily, it is only because of the statutory limit, meaning the offence can still be attempted.

Investigators' Manual, para. 1.3.4

Answer 3.10

Answer **D** — A defendant cannot be convicted of statutory conspiracy if the only other party to the agreement is:

- his/her spouse or civil partner;
- a person under 10 years of age;
- the intended victim (s. 2(2) of the Criminal Law Act 1977).

You can conspire to commit offences that are indictable only, triable either way or summary only, making answer A incorrect. Answer B is incorrect as although there must be a 'meeting of minds' for a conspiracy to be committed, the whole purpose of the offence is to catch behaviour leading up to the commission of the offence. Any failure to bring about the end result or abandoning of the agreement will not prevent the offence being committed. The fact that the commission of the offence is impossible as the victim is in Poland will not prevent the offence being committed (s. 1(1)(b)), making answer C incorrect.

Investigators' Manual, para. 1.3.3.1

4 General Defences and Issues in Evidence

QUESTIONS

Question 4.1

TI GARRETT is investigating an offence of fraud by false representation (contrary to s. 2 of the Fraud Act 2006) and is interviewing the suspect, NOCTOR, regarding the offence. During the interview NOCTOR states that the reason he committed the offence was because he made a mistake—he told the purchaser of a painting that he was selling that the painting was by a well-known artist when in fact it was not.

Considering the general defence of 'mistake', which of the following statements is correct?

A For the defence to be valid, the magistrates or jury would have to consider that the mistake made was 'reasonable' in the circumstances.

B The defence has no application in these circumstances as the defence of 'mistake' is only relevant to offences involving negligence.

C For the defence to be valid, the 'mistake' made would have to be one relating to the law and not to facts.

D NOCTOR's claim that he made a 'mistake' would only be an effective defence if it negated the *mens rea* for the offence.

Question 4.2

PASKIN is a member of a gang of thieves who specialise in pickpocket thefts. The leader of the gang is GIBSON who tells the gang who to target when they are out on the streets. While the gang are on the streets, GIBSON sees KENWORTHY (who is not part of the gang) stealing from several pedestrians. GIBSON is outraged by what he sees as an 'invasion of his turf' and tells PASKIN that he needs to prove his loyalty to the gang by stabbing KENWORTHY and he gives PASKIN a knife. PASKIN does not want to stab KENWORTHY and says so to GIBSON, who responds, *'Stab him or I'll break your little girl's arm tomorrow when she leaves school!'* GIBSON has a history of violent behaviour and PASKIN genuinely believes he will seriously injure his child if he does not do as GIBSON has said. He stabs KENWORTHY who is seriously injured as a result. PASKIN is arrested and charged with an offence of s. 18 wounding (under the Offences Against the Person Act 1861).

Considering the general defence of duress, which of the following comments is correct?

A PASKIN could not use the defence as it is only available to a charge of murder or attempted murder.

B PASKIN could not use the defence as the serious physical injury that was threatened was threatened to his child rather than to PASKIN himself.

C PASKIN could not use the defence as it is only available when the person concerned was threatened with death.

D PASKIN could not use the defence because he would have an opportunity to neutralise the effect of the threat.

Question 4.3

ASPELL and GOLD have both been arrested in connection with an offence of murder. It is alleged that ASPELL is the person directly responsible for the offence (as a principal offender) and that GOLD helped ASPELL commit the offence by aiding him (as an accessory to the offence). In interview ASPELL and GOLD both state that the reason they carried out the offence was because the other had threatened him with serious physical injury unless he carried out the offence.

Would either person be able to utilise the general defence of duress in this situation?

A Yes, ASPELL alone would be able to utilise the defence.

B No, the defence is not available in answer to a charge of murder.

C Yes, GOLD alone would be able to utilise the defence.

D No, as the defence is not available to offences involving injury or death to a person.

Question 4.4

WHITLEY is a disqualified driver and is running behind time in her preparations for getting to work. WHITLEY is of an extremely nervous disposition and is genuinely concerned that she will be late for work and honestly believes that if she is late she will be sacked and consequently lose her home as she will not be able to pay her mortgage. This is not the case at all and WHITLEY's belief is wholly unfounded. She makes the decision to drive to work and is driving along a road when she is stopped by the police. She is charged with driving whilst disqualified (under s. 103(1)(b) of the Road Traffic Act 1988).

Would WHITLEY be able to claim the general defence of duress of circumstances (necessity) in this situation?

A No, because the consequences do not involve death or serious injury.

B Yes, as WHITLEY held an honest belief that she would lose her job.

C No, the defence of duress of circumstances is not available in answer to charges under the Road Traffic Act 1988.

D Yes, if the court finds that a sober person of reasonable firmness and sharing the same characteristics as WHITLEY would have responded to the situation as WHITLEY did.

Question 4.5

DCs COATE and DRANSKI are investigating an offence of causing grievous bodily harm. EGLINTON (the person allegedly responsible for the offence) is a householder who used force on BARBER who broke into EGLINTON's house. The officers make a number of comments in relation to the use of force by EGLINTON.

Considering the law under s. 76 of the Immigration Act 2008, which of the comments below is correct?

A DC COATE states that if EGLINTON used force merely in order to protect his property then the use of force would always be unacceptable.

B DC DRANSKI states that the use of disproportionate force can, in 'householder' cases, be justified in certain circumstances.

C DC COATE states that EGLINTON could use force against BARBER but only for the purpose of self-defence or in defence of another.

D DC DRANSKI states that in rare 'householder' cases, the use of grossly disproportionate force can be justified.

Question 4.6

Even though evidence may be admissible in criminal cases, at common law the trial judge has a general discretion to exclude legally admissible evidence tendered by the prosecution. In addition, evidence may be excluded for a variety of reasons.

Which of the following statements is correct in respect of a reason for excluding admissible evidence?

A In deciding whether the evidence should be admitted, the question the judge has to ask is whether the evidence was obtained fairly or by unfair means.

B Evidence could not be excluded because of the incompetence of a witness.

C The judge generally has discretion to exclude relevant admissible evidence on the ground that it was obtained improperly.

D Evidence may be excluded if it is non-expert opinion evidence.

Question 4.7

The 'facts in issue' of a case are those which must be proved by the prosecution in order to establish the defendant's guilt, or in exceptional circumstances those facts which are the essential elements of a defence, where the burden of proof is on the defendant to prove a defence.

Which of the following comments is correct is respect of these 'facts in issue'?

A 'Facts in issue' would not include the identity of the defendant.

B The relevant criminal conduct (*actus reus*) and state of mind (*mens rea*) will always be facts in issue.

C The standard of proof for the defence is the same as the prosecution, i.e. 'beyond all reasonable doubt'.

D It is only when attempting to utilise a statutory defence that the burden of proof will shift to the defence.

Question 4.8

A number of police officers are attending a training course as part of their development in their role as investigators. They are asked to plan an operation involving the arrest of a violent offender who is known to possess firearms and who has declared a willingness to use them. Consequently the officers are considering the involvement of firearms trained officers in the arrest. One of the aspects of the planning of the operation is the impact of Article 2 of the European Convention on Human Rights (the Right to Life) and the use of lethal force if absolutely necessary to do so.

In relation to the use of such force, which of the following comments is correct?

A TI ABERNATHY states that the use of lethal force is forbidden in any circumstances by Article 2.

B TI LAMPING states that lethal force is allowed under Article 2 but this is only when the force is used for the purpose of quelling a riot or insurrection.

C TI DODDS states that lethal force could be used in order to effect a lawful arrest or to prevent the escape of a person lawfully detained.

D TI SCHIMMEL states that lethal force can be used in a variety of situations including those where the only thing being protected is property.

ANSWERS

Answer 4.1

Answer **D** — There are occasions where a defendant makes a mistake about some circumstance or consequence, however, claims that a defendant 'made a mistake' or did something 'inadvertently' will only be an effective defence if they negate the *mens rea* for that offence (correct answer D). Answer A is incorrect as it does not matter whether the mistake was 'reasonable' (*DPP* v *Morgan* [1976] AC 182). The appropriate test is whether the defendant's mistaken belief was an honest and genuine one. A defence of mistake has to involve a mistake of fact, not a mistake of law, making answer C incorrect (note that s. 2 of the Theft Act 1968 provides an exception to this). The defence is applicable to a wide variety of offences, not just those involving negligence, making answer B incorrect.

Investigators' Manual, para. 1.4.2

Answer 4.2

Answer **D** — Where a person is threatened with death or *serious physical injury* unless he/she carries out a criminal act, he/she may have a defence of duress (*R* v *Graham* [1982] 1 WLR 294). This means that answer C is incorrect. It would seem that the threat need not be made solely to the person who goes on to commit the relevant offence; there are authorities to suggest that threats of death/serious harm to loved ones may allow a defence of duress, meaning that answer B is incorrect. The defence is not available in respect of an offence of murder (*R* v *Howe* [1987] AC 417) or attempted murder (*R* v *Gotts* [1992] 2 AC 412), as a principal or secondary offender. It is, however, available in *other offences* even in offences of strict liability, meaning that answer A is incorrect. Duress is not available as a defence if it is proved that the defendant failed to take advantage of an opportunity to neutralise the effects of the threat (perhaps by escaping from it), which a reasonable person of a similar sort to the defendant would have taken in the same position. An example of this approach is the case of *R* v *Heath* [2000] Crim LR 109, where the defendant alleged that he had been pressurised into transporting drugs. Because the defendant had more than one safe avenue of escape (going to the police, which he did not do because he was scared and because he was a drug addict, and going to his parents in Scotland, which he did not do because he did not want them to know about the position he was in) the defence failed. Whether a defendant could be expected to take such an opportunity of rendering the threat ineffective, e.g. by seeking police protection, will be a matter for the jury. Therefore, a defendant who is ordered to steal from a shop in 24 hours' time or suffer a serious physical injury for failing to do so might be unable to utilise the defence as a jury may consider that the defendant had ample opportunity to take evasive action and avoid the threat.

Investigators' Manual, para. 1.4.3

Answer 4.3

Answer **B** — The defence is not available in respect of an offence of murder (*R* v *Howe* [1987] AC 417) or attempted murder (*R* v *Gotts* [1992] 2 AC 412), as a principal (ASPELL) or secondary (GOLD) offender.

Investigators' Manual, para. 1.4.3

Answer 4.4

Answer **A** — The defence of duress of circumstances will only be available if the person concerned committed the offence because he/she reasonably believed that he/she had good cause to fear he/she would suffer death or serious injury if he/she did not do so.

Investigators' Manual, para. 1.4.4

Answer 4.5

Answer **B** — There are circumstances where the use of force against a person or property will be permissible. This aspect of criminal law is dealt with by s. 76 of the Criminal Justice and Immigration Act 2008. The law can be formulated quite simply along the following lines.

A person may use such force as is reasonable in the circumstances as he believes them to be for the purpose of:

(a) self-defence; or
(b) defence of another; or
(c) defence of property; or
(d) prevention of crime; or
(e) lawful arrest.

So there are a variety of circumstances where the use of force may be permissible, making answer C incorrect. This includes the use of force to protect property, making answer A incorrect.

Section 43 of the Crime and Courts Act 2013 amends s. 76 of the Criminal Justice and Immigration Act 2008 so that the use of *disproportionate* force can be regarded as reasonable in the circumstances as the accused believed them to be when householders are acting to protect themselves or others from trespassers in their homes (self-defence). The use of *grossly* disproportionate force would still not be permitted, making answer D incorrect.

Investigators' Manual, paras 1.4.5.2 to 1.4.5.4

Answer 4.6

Answer **D** — In deciding whether the evidence should be admitted, the question the judge asks him/herself is whether it is fair to allow the evidence, *not* whether it is obtained fairly or by unfair means, making answer A incorrect. The judge generally *has no discretion* whether to exclude relevant admissible evidence on the ground that it was obtained improperly, making answer C incorrect. Evidence may be excluded for a number of reasons amongst which is the incompetence of a witness, making answer B incorrect.

Investigators' Manual, para. 1.5.2.2

Answer 4.7

Answer **B** — 'Facts in issue' will include the *identity of the defendant*, the *actus reus* and the *mens rea* of an offence (making answer A incorrect). The standard of proof for the defence is 'on the balance of probabilities', making answer C incorrect. The evidential burden may shift to the defence in a variety of situations; statute (e.g. diminished responsibility) or common law (e.g. the defence of insanity), making answer D incorrect.

Investigators' Manual, paras 1.5.3 to 1.5.4.2

Answer 4.8

Answer **C** — Article 2 of the Convention states:

1. Everyone's right to life shall be protected by law. No one shall be deprived of his life intentionally save in the execution of a sentence of a court following his conviction of a crime for which this penalty is provided by law.
2. Deprivation of life shall not be regarded as inflicted in contravention of this Article when it results from the use of force which is no more than absolutely necessary:
   (a) in defence of any person from unlawful violence;

(b) in order to effect a lawful arrest or to prevent the escape of a person lawfully detained;
(c) in action lawfully taken for the purpose of quelling a riot or insurrection.

So there are a number of situations where lethal force would be permissible making answers A and B incorrect. Answer D is incorrect as, according to Article 2, defending property is not included in the circumstances where property alone is being protected. The correct answer is given at C (para. 2(b) of Article 2 allows lethal force in order to effect a lawful arrest or to prevent the escape of a person lawfully detained).

Investigators' Manual, para. 1.4.5.1

5 Entry, Search and Seizure

QUESTIONS

Question 5.1

DS GRETTEN carries out a search of a house along with DC WALKER (who has 10 years' police service) and PC LOWE (a probationary constable with 11 months' police service). The search is being carried out as a result of a long investigation and subsequent arrest carried out by DC WALKER, who is extremely familiar with the facts of the case.

Considering Code B of the Codes of Practice, which of the following comments is correct in respect of who should be in charge of the search?

A The officer in charge of the search must be the most senior officer present (DS GRETTEN).

B DS GRETTEN should normally be in charge of the search but as DC WALKER is more conversant with the facts of the case, DS GRETTEN may appoint him as the officer in charge.

C DS GRETTEN or DC WALKER could be in charge of the search. PC LOWE could not be in charge of the search in any circumstances as she is a probationary constable.

D In normal circumstances any one of the three officers could be in charge of the search.

Question 5.2

DC BENTLEY wishes to make an application for a search warrant to search two sets of premises in respect of drug-related offences.

Which of the following statements is correct with regard to the officer's application?

A The application for a search warrant must be made with the written authority of an officer of the rank of superintendent or above.

B The application for a search warrant must be made with the written authority of an officer of the rank of inspector or above.

C The application for a search warrant must be made with the authority of an officer of the rank of inspector or above. The authority can be oral or written.

D An application for a search warrant must be made with the written authority of a magistrate.

Question 5.3

DC EMERY receives intelligence which indicates that HALL has committed an offence of handling stolen goods (contrary to s. 22 of the Theft Act 1968). DC EMERY's intelligence indicates that there are stolen goods located at HALL's home address and also in a lock-up garage belonging to HALL, the location of which is unknown. DC EMERY makes an application for an all-premises search warrant under s. 8 of the Police and Criminal Evidence Act 1984 (PACE).

Which of the following comments is correct?

A The application will be refused because handling stolen goods is not an indictable only offence.

B If the application is granted then the warrant must be executed within one month from the date of its issue.

C If an all-premises warrant is granted then premises which are not specified in it may only be entered and searched if an officer of the rank of inspector or above authorises the search in writing.

D An all-premises warrant can only authorise entry to premises on one occasion.

Question 5.4

HANSON is in a cafe when it is raided by the police and he is arrested by DC KHAN for an offence of possessing a controlled drug. HANSON breaks down on arrest and tells the officer that there are several dozen stolen Sony PlayStation game consoles at his home address that were stolen from an electrical store by his flatmate three weeks ago. He tells the officer he is unlikely to find them as they are well hidden and his flatmate may well dispose of them if he hears of HANSON's arrest.

Which of the following statements is correct?

A DC KHAN could take HANSON to his home address and search the address before HANSON is taken to a police station under the powers of s. 18 of the Police and Criminal Evidence Act 1984 (PACE).

B DC KHAN could take HANSON to his home address and search it by virtue of s. 32 of PACE.

C DC KHAN could search HANSON's home address under s. 17 of PACE.

D DC KHAN could not utilise his powers under s. 17, 18 or 32 to search HANSON's home address in these circumstances.

Question 5.5

In certain circumstances it is permissible to search premises with the consent of a person entitled to grant entry to the premises. Code B of the Codes of Practice details the practice and procedure for such searches.

In respect of such a search, which of the following statements is correct?

A In a lodging house, a search of a lodger's room can be made solely on the basis of the landlord's consent.

B A search based on the consent of a person entitled to grant entry cannot be made unless an officer of the rank of inspector or above authorises it.

C If it is proposed to search premises with the consent of a person entitled to grant entry then that consent should, if practicable, be given in writing on the Notice of Powers and Rights before the search.

D If an occupier has given his consent to a search but then withdraws that consent before the search is complete, the search may continue until it is completed.

Question 5.6

DC EASTWOOD is the officer in charge of a search carried out under a warrant granted by virtue of s. 8 of the Police and Criminal Evidence Act 1984. The search is being carried out at the home address of GRAINGER. GRAINGER demands that his friend, ORTON, be allowed to witness the search. ORTON lives three hours away from the scene of the search.

Which of the following comments is correct?

A ORTON may be allowed to witness the search but this will not stop the search beginning immediately.

B GRAINGER does not have the right to have a friend, neighbour or other person witness the search of his house.

C DC EASTWOOD can refuse to allow ORTON to witness the search but only if he believes ORTON's presence will endanger officers or other people.

D The search must be delayed until ORTON arrives at GRAINGER's address to witness the search.

Question 5.7

DS CHILDS is the officer in charge of a search where seize and sift powers were utilised (under s. 50 of the Criminal Justice and Police Act 2001) due to the fact that it was going to take a lengthy period of time and a large number of officers to separate material relevant to the offence and other material. The material seized was a large amount of papers contained in over 50 crates.

Which of the following statements is correct in relation to those seize and sift powers?

A Section 50 allows for the seizure of material that is reasonably believed to be legally privileged where it is not reasonably practicable to separate it.

B Section 50 provides for extended seizure of materials found on people who are being lawfully searched.

C Section 50 provides a freestanding power to seize property.

D Section 50 should not have been used by DS CHILDS as the power is only relevant to material stored on computers.

Question 5.8

DC KIRK has arrested OPLINGTON for numerous offences of handling stolen goods and has brought him to a designated police station. OPLINGTON gives the custody officer his home address and after being processed is placed in a cell. DC KIRK has reasonable grounds for suspecting there is evidence at OPLINGTON's home address regarding handling offences. The officer makes further enquiries regarding OPLINGTON and discovers that he owns a lock-up garage near to his home address. He carries out intelligence checks on OPLINGTON and finds out that the lock-up garage has been linked with a separate criminal enterprise of OPLINGTON's, namely the supply of drugs. Intelligence also suggests that OPLINGTON has been linked with a shop (as he is supposed to own it) where the stolen goods are sold. All of the intelligence is of a good quality and causes the officer to suspect OPLINGTON controls the shop premises and that there are drugs in the lock-up garage. DC KIRK wishes to search all three premises (house, lock-up and shop) using s. 18 of the Police and Criminal Evidence Act 1984 to do so.

Which of the following statements is correct in respect of the use of the power?

A Only OPLINGTON's home address can be searched under s. 18.

B Only OPLINGTON's home address and the lock-up garage can be searched under s. 18.

C All three premises can be searched under s. 18.

D Only OPLINGTON's home address and the shop can be searched under s. 18.

Question 5.9

PC DRAPER is called to the scene of a robbery. The property stolen in the offence consists of a gold ring and a gold watch. The victim identifies BROWN as the offender and provides a description of BROWN to PC DRAPER. BROWN's details are circulated along with a warning that BROWN is known to be a violent drug dealer who has attempted to stab officers with hypodermic needles in the past. Shortly after the circulation, DCs HEMMINGWAY and LE FORT see BROWN standing outside a busy shopping centre. The officers stop BROWN and arrest him for the robbery offence. The officers propose to search BROWN at the location of the arrest under s. 32 of the Police and Criminal Evidence Act 1984.

Which of the following statements is correct in respect of this power?

A The officers could search BROWN but only for the stolen property.
B This power would not authorise the search of BROWN's mouth.
C Such a search could involve BROWN being required to take off his shoes.
D The officers could search the location where BROWN was arrested.

Question 5.10

PC ROSE (a uniformed officer) has arrested MARKOU for an offence of theft and is transporting him to a police station. While being transported to the police station, he manages to escape from custody. A search for MARKOU takes place but he is not found. Two days later, DC GOWER (who is working in plain clothes) hears about the incident and remembers that he dealt with MARKOU six months ago for a theft and at that time he was living with a girlfriend at an address nearby. DC GOWER believes that MARKOU is at the address and contacts PC ROSE and together the two officers visit the address. The officers knock on the front door which is answered by DELPH (MARKOU's girlfriend). DELPH tells the officers that she no longer has anything to do with MARKOU and has not seen him for three months.

Can the officers enter the address under s. 17 of the Police and Criminal Evidence Act 1984?

A No, as MARKOU is not an escaped HMP prisoner.
B Yes, but the power is only available to an officer in uniform.
C No, because they are not in 'fresh' pursuit of MARKOU.
D Yes, the power is available to either police officer, in uniform or not.

Question 5.11

DC JACKS is making enquiries regarding an armed robbery at an electrical store where a large amount of TV/audio equipment was stolen. He is in the process of visiting houses near to the store to try and locate witnesses and sees that a house opposite the store, belonging to LOMAS, has a security camera system which might possibly have captured the robbery. DC JACKS visits LOMAS who invites the officer into her house. Whilst chatting to LOMAS in the lounge of the house, DC JACKS notices some documentation on a coffee table that appears to be useful intelligence regarding crime in the area and decides to seize it. When LOMAS asks what is going on, DC JACKS tells her, to which she responds, '*Well you can fuck off then!*' DC JACKS is ushered towards the front door by LOMAS but before he leaves he sees the recording device for the security cameras and seizes the recording device as he suspects it may contain evidence of the armed robbery.

Taking into account the powers under s. 19 of the Police and Criminal Evidence Act 1984 only, which of the following comments is true?

A DC JACKS has legitimately seized the intelligence material and the recording device.

B DC JACKS has legitimately seized the intelligence but not the recording device as he was a trespasser at this point.

C DC JACKS has legitimately seized the recording device but not the intelligence.

D DC JACKS has no power to seize either item.

Question 5.12

TI ROBERT wishes to apply for a warrant under s. 8 of PACE 1984 to search a house belonging to GRISHAM who is suspected of involvement in a burglary (contrary to s. 9(1)(a) of the Theft Act 1968).

Which of the following comments is correct?

A If the application is successful, the warrant can only authorise entry on one occasion.

B A s. 8 warrant can authorise an unlimited number of entries to GRISHAM's house.

C A s. 8 warrant will only permit a search of one specific premises, which must be clearly identified in the warrant.

D A s. 8 warrant permits the large-scale seizure of all material found on premises to be 'sifted' at another location.

Question 5.13

DC KIDBY receives information that WESTGATE is in possession of a significant quantity of stolen property from a burglary that occurred two days ago. The information states that WESTGATE is a traveller and moves around the country in a car and is at present camped in a tent in a field in DC KIDBY's police area. The stolen property is being kept inside the tent and also in WESTGATE's car.

Considering s. 15 of PACE 1984 (in respect of an application for a warrant), which of the following comments is correct?

A A warrant could not be granted to search a car or a tent.

B A warrant could be granted to search both the car and the tent.

C A warrant could be granted to search the car but not the tent.

D A warrant could be granted to search the tent but not the car.

Question 5.14

DS BAKER is in charge of an investigation looking into the activities of OLNEY who owns a business selling high-quality watches. OLNEY is suspected of handling stolen watches and using the business as a 'front' to cover his illegal activities. A warrant under s. 8 of the Police and Criminal Evidence Act 1984 is obtained to search OLNEY's business address for stolen watches. Accompanied by DCs DRUMMOND and TISHVALI, DS BAKER executes the warrant and, in a storage room at the premises, several hundred watches are found along with documentation relating to the watches. OLNEY is present during the search and maintains that the watches are legitimate purchases. DS BAKER believes some of the watches are stolen but as it is wholly impractical to examine every watch and connected documentation, she decides to use her powers under the Criminal Justice and Police Act 2001 to seize all the watches and documentation and examine them at a police station. OLNEY states that the documentation contains letters from his solicitors and cannot be seized as it is subject to 'legal privilege'.

In respect of the seize and sift power, which of the following comments is correct?

A The property seized must be examined within 72 hours of the initial seizure.

B OLNEY (or his representative) must be present when the seized watches are examined.

C DS BAKER cannot seize the property unless an officer of the rank of inspector or above has attended the premises and authorises the use of the seize and sift power.

D Documentation that is reasonably believed to be legally privileged can be seized where it is not reasonably practicable to separate it.

Question 5.15

Section 17 of the Police and Criminal Evidence Act 1984 provides a power under which an officer may enter and search premises without a warrant.

In which of the following circumstances would the power be used correctly?

A PC GRAHAM (an officer in uniform) enters premises for the purpose of arresting a person for an offence under s. 163 of the Road Traffic Act 1988 (failure to stop when required to do so by a constable in uniform).

B DC PATEL (an officer in plain clothes) enters premises for the purposes of arresting a person for an offence under s. 9A of the Misuse of Drugs Act 1971 (supplying articles for administering or preparing controlled drugs).

C PC JENKINS (an officer in uniform) enters premises for the purpose of arresting a person for an offence under s. 2(2) of the Firearms Act 1968 (failing to comply with the conditions of a shotgun certificate).

D DC LIN (an officer in plain clothes) enters premises for the purpose of arresting a person for an offence under s. 1(1) of the Malicious Communications Act 1988 (sending a malicious communication).

Question 5.16

PC VICKERS and PC MOORE attend 25 Trent Street, the dwelling of HENRY SEARS who is suspected of a street robbery that occurred this morning. The officers wish to search the house to see if he has returned home. JOAN SEARS, his mother who rents the address with her son, invites the officers into the house and tells them to feel free to search the house for her son as she tells them he is 100 per cent not in the house. PC VICKERS and PC MOORE search the living room and then the kitchen. In the walk-in pantry, the officers see in the corner a box of mobile phones and believing that these may be the subject of a robbery the officers seize them. As the officers seize the phones, JOAN says to the officers '*Fuck off*'; however, they continue to search and in HENRY's bed room find a blank credit card on the window sill and seize it. JOAN then says to the officers, '*Henry is not here, you must leave now.*' The officers then leave the house.

Which of the following statements is correct with regard to the actions of PC VICKERS and PC MOORE?

A The officers had no power to seize the phones or the credit card as they were searching for HENRY SEARS.

B The officers could seize the mobile phones but not the credit card because when told to 'Fuck off' they were then trespassing and should have left the dwelling.

C The officers had no power to enter or search the dwelling in these circumstances even with consent, as they would need a premises warrant.

D The officers' actions were correct as they had consent to enter and search; they can seize property unconnected to the original offence with consent and saying 'Fuck off' is not classed as a full removal of permission to remain lawfully.

ANSWERS

Answer 5.1

Answer **B** — Code B states that the officer in charge of a search should *normally* be the most senior officer present (DS GRETTEN), making answers A and D incorrect. However, an exception to this is when the supervising officer who attends or assists at the scene of the premises appoints an officer of lower rank as officer in charge (OIC) of the search because that officer is more conversant with the facts (answer B). The senior officer could appoint any officer to be in charge of the search if that officer is a more appropriate officer to be in charge of the search, making answer C incorrect.

Investigators' Manual, para. 1.6.3.1

Answer 5.2

Answer **B** — Applications for all search warrants must be made with the written authority of an officer of at least the rank of inspector (Code B, para. 3.4). However, in cases of urgency where no such officer is 'readily available', the senior officer on duty may authorise the application.

Investigators' Manual, para. 1.6.4

Answer 5.3

Answer **C** — A s. 8 warrant must relate to the fact that an indictable offence has been committed. Handling stolen goods is an either-way offence, which means that it is indictable and would qualify (it does not have to be indictable only), making answer A incorrect. Entry and search under a warrant must be within three months from the date of issue, making answer B incorrect. An all-premises warrant may authorise entry and search on more than one occasion if, on the application, the justice of the peace is satisfied that it is necessary to authorise multiple entries in order to achieve the purpose for which he issues the warrant, therefore answer D is incorrect.

Investigators' Manual, para. 1.6.3.7

Answer 5.4

Answer **D** — Section 18 cannot be utilised unless DC KHAN is searching for evidence that relates to the offence which HANSON is under arrest for or to some other indictable offence which is connected with or similar to that offence, making answer A incorrect. Section 32 searches can only take place to find evidence relating to the offence for which the person was arrested, making answer B incorrect. Section 17 of PACE is a power of entry rather than a power of search, making answer C incorrect.

Investigators' Manual, para. 1.6.5.3

Answer 5.5

Answer **C** — A lodger's room should not be searched based solely on the permission of the landlord unless the situation is urgent and the lodger is unavailable, making answer A incorrect. Answer B is incorrect as the authority of an inspector is not required when carrying out a search by consent. If an occupier gives his/her consent but then withdraws it the search must stop at that point, making answer D incorrect.

Investigators' Manual, paras 1.6.5.3 to 1.6.6.1

Answer 5.6

Answer **A** — Code B allows a friend, neighbour or other person to witness a search, making answer B incorrect. That can be refused if the OIC of the search has reasonable grounds for believing that this would seriously hinder the investigation or endanger officers or others, making answer C incorrect. A search need not be unreasonably delayed for this purpose, making answer D incorrect.

Investigators' Manual, para. 1.6.7

Answer 5.7

Answer **A** — Section 50 of the Act relates to material at the scene of the search and not on individuals (this is s. 51 of the Act), making answer B incorrect. Answer C is incorrect as these powers can only be used to extend the scope of an existing power and do not allow for seizure as a freestanding power. Answer D is incorrect as these powers can be utilised in a variety of situations and considerations relating to the use of the power would include the length of time and the number of people that would be required to separate the material on the premises (s. 50(3)).

Investigators' Manual, paras 1.6.8.6, 1.6.8.7

Answer 5.8

Answer **A** — Section 18 searches can only take place at premises occupied or controlled by the arrested person; suspicion that the person occupies or controls the premises is not sufficient and therefore the lock-up garage and shop are eliminated, making answers B, C and D incorrect. Further, the premises searched must be searched because the officer has reasonable grounds to suspect that there is evidence on the premises of that offence (the offence the person has been arrested for) or to some other indictable offence which is connected with or similar to that offence. The suspected drug dealing is entirely separate from the handling so the lock-up garage is further eliminated.

Investigators' Manual, para. 1.6.5.3

Answer 5.9

Answer **D** — A search under s. 32 allows a constable to search for anything that may present a danger to himself or others, that the person might use to assist him to escape from lawful custody, or that might be evidence relating to an offence. The officers can therefore search for the stolen property and the needles, making answer A incorrect. Such a search will not authorise the removal, in public, of more than the jacket, outer coat and gloves of the person, so answer C is incorrect. Such a search does authorise the search of a person's mouth, making answer B incorrect. The power under s. 32 authorises a search to take place where the person was arrested (other than at a police station).

Investigators' Manual, para. 1.6.5.2

Answer 5.10

Answer **C** — Section 17 provides a power of entry in a large variety of situations. One of those is to recapture a person who is 'unlawfully at large'. This term is not defined and could include someone who has escaped from custody, making answer A incorrect. Wearing a uniform is irrelevant to the power of entry for such a purpose, making answer B incorrect. However, the pursuit of the person unlawfully at large must be 'fresh'—calling at an address two days after the event is not and makes answer D incorrect.

Investigators' Manual, para. 1.6.5.1

Answer 5.11

Answer **D** — The power under s. 19 allows an officer who is legitimately, i.e. lawfully, on premises to seize anything which the officer reasonably *believes* is evidence of an offence or has been obtained in consequence of an offence to prevent it being lost, altered, damaged or destroyed. This is not a power to seize property purely for the purposes of intelligence so answers A and B are incorrect. Telling the officer to 'fuck off' does not turn him into a trespasser (you need to be more explicit and clearly communicate that fact) but the officer only suspects the recording device is evidence, making answer C incorrect.

Investigators' Manual, para. 1.6.8.1

Answer 5.12

Answer **B** — Answer A is incorrect as a s. 8 warrant can permit entry on a number of occasions. Answer C is incorrect as the warrant may be a 'specific premises' warrant or an 'all premises' warrant. Answer D is incorrect as possession of a warrant under s. 8 does not authorise police officers to seize all material found on relevant premises to be taken away and 'sifted' somewhere else (*R* v *Chesterfield Justices, ex parte Bramley* [2000] 2 WLR 409).

Investigators' Manual, para. 1.6.3.7

Answer 5.13

Answer **B** — The 'premises' that are referred to in the legislation include any place, and in particular (a) any vehicle, vessel, aircraft or hovercraft; (b) any offshore installation; (c) any renewable energy installation; (d) any tent or movable structure (s. 23 of the Act). The car and the tent can be searched under the terms of a warrant, making answers A, C and D incorrect.

Investigators' Manual, para. 1.6.3.4

Answer 5.14

Answer **D** — Answer A is incorrect as an initial examination of the property seized under s. 50 or s. 51 of the Act should be carried out as soon as practicable. Answer B is incorrect, although all reasonable steps should be taken to accommodate an interested person's request to be present (provided the request is reasonable and subject to the need to prevent harm to, interfere with or unreasonably delay the investigative process). The authorisation of an inspector or above is not required to utilise the seize and sift power, making answer C incorrect. Section 50 allows for seizure of material that is reasonably believed to be legally privileged where it is not reasonably practicable to separate it (correct answer D).

Investigators' Manual, paras 1.6.8.6 to 1.6.8.11

Answer 5.15

Answer **A** — Section 17 of the Police and Criminal Evidence Act 1984 provides a wide variety of conditions in which an officer may enter and search premises without a warrant. All of the offences mentioned in A, B, C and D are summary-only offences but only one of them is specifically mentioned in s. 17 (s. 17(1)(c)(iiia)) and that is the offence under s. 163 of the Road Traffic Act 1988 (failure to stop when required to do so by an officer in uniform) meaning that answer A is correct. The officers entering premises in the circumstances described in answers B, C and D have no power to do so under s. 17 of PACE.

Investigators' Manual, para. 1.6.5.1

Answer 5.16

Answer **D** — Where the police officers enter premises *lawfully*, including when they are there by invitation/consent, they are on the premises for *all lawful purposes*. So when they are at 25 Trent Street by consent of JOAN SEARS they can seize other crime property making answer A incorrect. If an invitation is terminated, the person needs to communicate that clearly to the officer: it has been held that merely telling officers to 'fuck off' is not necessarily sufficient (*Snook* v *Mannion* [1982] RTR 321) making answer B incorrect. A premises warrant is not required in these circumstances making answer C incorrect, making answer D the correct option.

Investigators' Manual, para. 1.6.1

6 Detention and Treatment of Persons by Police Officers

QUESTIONS

Question 6.1

DC MANLER arrests DAWSON for an offence of theft. Due to the circumstances surrounding the arrest, DC MANLER takes DAWSON to a non-designated police station where DC ROBERTS (who is not involved in the investigation) performs the role of custody officer.

As the acting custody officer, whom, if anyone, should DC ROBERTS inform of these circumstances?

A There is no requirement for DC ROBERTS to inform anyone of the circumstances.
B The custody officer at a designated police station.
C An officer of the rank of inspector or above at a designated police station.
D An officer of the rank of superintendent or above at a designated police station.

Question 6.2

DC JOPLIN has arrested FARROW for an offence of aggravated burglary. In the custody block, FARROW requests that he be allowed to telephone his girlfriend, ROWE. ROWE lives with FARROW and DC JOPLIN is concerned that if ROWE speaks to FARROW, she will dispose of any property relating to the aggravated burglary before he searches the home address of FARROW.

In these circumstances, can FARROW be prevented from making the telephone call to ROWE?

A Yes, with the authorisation of an officer of the rank of superintendent or above.
B No, this right cannot be withheld in any circumstances.

C Yes, if an officer of the rank of inspector or above authorises it.

D No, because FARROW has not been arrested for a drug trafficking offence.

Question 6.3

MULLAN is in custody for an offence of kidnapping and requests that TURNER (a solicitor friend of MULLAN) represents him whilst he is in police custody. DC SAUL is in charge of the investigation and is genuinely concerned that if MULLAN is allowed to use TURNER as a solicitor, TURNER will, inadvertently or otherwise, act in a way that will interfere with evidence connected to the kidnapping.

Which of the following statements is correct?

A DC SAUL should seek a superintendent's authority to deny MULLAN access to legal advice from TURNER.

B MULLAN should be allowed to speak with TURNER, but to ensure that TURNER acts ethically, his consultations with MULLAN can be monitored by a police officer.

C Once the decision to deny MULLAN his legal advice has been taken, the authorisation applies to all solicitors or legal advisers and lasts up to a maximum of 36 hours.

D MULLAN cannot be denied access to legal advice from TURNER in these circumstances.

Question 6.4

PARRISH voluntarily attends at a police station in your force area to be dealt with for an offence of theft; he arrives at the police station at 10.00 hrs and is arrested at 10.15 hrs. You have circulated PARRISH as wanted for an offence of rape and you are informed of his detention. You travel to the police station where PARRISH is detained and arrest him for the offence at 13.00 hrs. At no stage has PARRISH been questioned in relation to the offence of rape. You escort PARRISH back to your police station and arrive at 14.00 hrs.

From what time will PARRISH's 'relevant time' be calculated?

A 10.00 hrs.

B 10.15 hrs.

C 13.00 hrs.

D 14.00 hrs.

Question 6.5

DYTHAM is arrested for murder and has been in custody for 20 hours. DS KNIBBS, the officer in charge of the case, considers that the investigating and interviewing officers need more time to carry out their enquiries and realises that this will take more than the 24-hour basic period of detention. DS KNIBBS believes that it is unlikely that more than 36 hours will be needed to conclude matters.

Who will approve the 12-hour extension required by DS KNIBBS?

A The custody officer.

B An officer of the rank of inspector or above.

C An officer of the rank of superintendent or above.

D A magistrates' court.

Question 6.6

MURPHY (aged 15 years) is arrested for burglary. Due to problems with MURPHY's family, SERCOMBE (a responsible adult aged over 18 years) is called out to act as the appropriate adult during MURPHY's interview. MURPHY requests that he be allowed to consult a solicitor and HEMSTOCK (a solicitor) attends the police station. MURPHY asks for a consultation with HEMSTOCK but demands that SERCOMBE be excluded from the consultation.

Which of the following statements is correct?

A SERCOMBE will not be excluded as otherwise she cannot advise and assist MURPHY in her role as an appropriate adult.

B If SERCOMBE were related to MURPHY she could not be excluded but as she has no relationship with MURPHY, she can be excluded.

C The solicitor, HEMSTOCK, will make the decision as to whether SERCOMBE will be allowed into the consultation.

D If MURPHY wishes to have a private consultation with HEMSTOCK without SERCOMBE being present, he must be permitted to do so.

Question 6.7

At 10.00 hrs DC HEATHCOCK arrests DEBNEY (aged 15 years) for an offence of supplying a controlled drug (contrary to s. 4(3) of the Misuse of Drugs Act 1971). DEBNEY arrives at a police station at 11.00 hrs and as well as his father he requests that his friend, GRUNDY, be informed of his arrest. DC HEATHCOCK is concerned that if GRUNDY is contacted it will lead to interference with evidence relating to the offence.

With regard to DEBNEY's right to have someone informed (s. 56 of the Police and Criminal Evidence Act 1984), which of the following comments is correct?

A This right cannot be delayed in any circumstances.

B In these circumstances, DEBNEY's right can be delayed and this delay can continue until 23.00 hrs the following day.

C An officer of the rank of superintendent or above may authorise the delay in DEBNEY having someone informed of his arrest.

D DEBNEY's rights can be delayed with the authority of an inspector but cannot be delayed after 10.00 hrs the following day.

Question 6.8

Section 118 of the Police and Criminal Evidence Act 1984 defines the meaning of 'police detention'.

In which of the following circumstances would the named person not be classed as being in 'police detention'?

A OGDEN is arrested at a police station after attending voluntarily at the station.

B DUNKLEY is arrested by PC WEST and is sitting with the officer in a police livery vehicle waiting to go into a custody block.

C PELHAM is being escorted from the scene of her arrest to a police station by HALSETT (a designated escort officer).

D KHAN is in court after being charged with burglary and is in the charge of PC WYATT.

Question 6.9

DC BAKER arrests ZAFAR for an offence of theft and takes him to a designated police station. On arrival it becomes apparent that there is no custody officer readily available to deal with ZAFAR. PC CHARLES is allocated to perform the role of custody officer and begins to deal with ZAFAR in the custody block. Several minutes later Sergeant EDEN telephones PC CHARLES to see how he is doing. Sergeant EDEN is supervising a road check one mile away from the designated police station.

Considering the law with regard to the provision of custody officers, which of the following statements is correct?

A A constable can only perform the role of custody officer at a non-designated police station.

B PC CHARLES cannot perform the role of custody officer as an officer of at least the rank of sergeant must perform it.

C As a sergeant is not readily available, then PC CHARLES can perform the role of custody officer.

D Sergeant EDEN would be considered available to carry out the role of custody officer and allowing PC CHARLES to continue in the role would be unlawful.

Question 6.10

DC MOHAMMED arrests WALSH in connection with an offence of aggravated burglary. When WALSH arrives at a police station he indicates that he wishes to have a solicitor to represent him. Due to the circumstances surrounding the offence, DC MOHAMMED wants to take non-intimate samples for evidential purposes from WALSH and also carry out an urgent interview without a solicitor being present (under the provisions of Code C, para. 6.6). WALSH tells DC MOHAMMED that he will not consent to the taking of the non-intimate samples or answer questions in any interview.

Which of the following statements is correct in these circumstances?

A As WALSH has requested a solicitor, any evidence gained from an interview carried out in such circumstances will be inadmissible because no solicitor was present.

B If WALSH refuses to answer any questions during the course of the urgent interview it may lead to a court drawing an inference from that failure.

C DC MOHAMMED can take non-intimate samples without consent even if WALSH has not consulted his solicitor.

D If an officer of the rank of inspector or above authorises it, an urgent interview can take place.

Question 6.11

BAXTER has been detained under the Terrorism Act 2000.

When should BAXTER's first review of detention take place?

A As soon as reasonably practicable after his arrest.

B 6 hours after his arrest.

C 12 hours after his arrest.

D 24 hours after his arrest.

Question 6.12

FERRY is arrested for an offence of burglary and is charged with the offence. Seven months after being charged the CPS decide to take no further action against FERRY and the case is dropped. After hearing that it has been decided to take no further action against him, FERRY attends the police station where he was detained for the offence and asks for a copy of his custody record.

Is FERRY entitled to a copy of his custody record?

A No, as the entitlement does not exist when it is decided that no further action will be taken against an individual.

B Yes, as the entitlement lasts for 12 months after his release from custody.

C No, as the entitlement only lasts for 6 months after his release from custody.

D Yes, but this request must be made by FERRY's legal representative.

Question 6.13

COURTNEY is a juvenile and has been arrested for an offence of robbery. COURTNEY is taken to a designated police station and booked into custody by PS BARNES. The custody block is extremely busy and there is a shortage of space for persons in custody meaning there is no secure accommodation available for COURTNEY; PS BARNES is considering what to do with COURTNEY.

With regard to the Codes of Practice and in particular issues surrounding conditions of detention, which of the following comments is correct?

A PS BARNES could place COURTNEY in a cell with HUCK, an adult who has been detained in respect of an offence of theft.

B COURTNEY cannot be placed in a cell under any circumstances.

C COURTNEY can be placed in a cell if PS BARNES considers it is not practicable to supervise him otherwise.

D COURTNEY can be placed in a cell if an officer of the rank of inspector or above authorises it.

Question 6.14

DC WHITTAKER has arrested HENDERSON for supplying a controlled drug (contrary to s. 4(3) of the Misuse of Drugs Act 1971). As HENDERSON was being arrested he swallowed a small amount of what DC WHITTAKER suspected was a controlled drug. This information was passed to the custody officer, PS SADRETTIN, when HENDERSON was brought into custody.

Considering Code C of the Codes of Practice, which of the following comments is correct?

A HENDERSON should be visited and roused every 15 minutes.

B HENDERSON should be visited and roused every 30 minutes.

C HENDERSON should be visited and roused every 60 minutes.

D HENDERSON should be visited and roused every 90 minutes.

Question 6.15

ATWAL has been arrested for an offence of assault (contrary to s. 20 of the Offences Against the Person Act 1861) and has been brought to a designated police station where the facts of the arrest are related to the custody officer, PS WEBSTER. ATWAL complains that he is suffering pain in his stomach as a consequence of the fight that led to his arrest. PS WEBSTER tells ATWAL that a health care professional will be called out to examine him regarding the pain but ATWAL is not happy with this and insists that his local doctor, Dr SCOTT, also examine him.

Which of the following statements is correct in respect of the action to be taken?

A PS WEBSTER should call out a health care professional; ATWAL's wishes to be examined by Dr SCOTT should be ignored.

B PS WEBSTER should have ATWAL examined by a health care professional and also by Dr SCOTT. Dr SCOTT's examination will be funded by the police.

C PS WEBSTER can choose between having ATWAL examined by a health care professional or Dr SCOTT.

D ATWAL should be examined by a health care professional and Dr SCOTT. However, ATWAL will fund the examination by Dr SCOTT.

Question 6.16

HUMBER (a juvenile aged 15 years) has been arrested in connection with an offence of murder. HUMBER has been in custody for a number of hours and her second review is due.

In respect of this review, which of the following comments is correct?

A The review must take place in person.

B The review can take place either in person or by telephone.

C The review can take place either in person or by video conferencing.

D The review can take place in person, by telephone or by video conferencing.

Question 6.17

WARDALE has been arrested for an offence of s. 20 wounding by DC HERRIOT. During the course of the audio-recorded interview, WARDALE replied '*No comment*' to all the questions put to him apart from the question '*Who was responsible for the assault?*', to which WARDALE replied, '*It wasn't me.*' WARDALE is charged with the offence and, after the custody officer charges and cautions him, WARDALE replies, '*I can tell you who committed the assault if you want me to.*'

Could WARDALE be interviewed about his comments?

A No, a detainee may not be interviewed about an offence after they have been charged with it, or informed they will be prosecuted for it.

B Yes, to clear up any ambiguity in a previous answer or statement.

C No, this can only be done to prevent or minimise harm or loss to some other person, or the public.

D Yes, as long as WARDALE agrees in writing to be re-interviewed regarding his comments.

Question 6.18

Sections 38 and 39 of the Police Reform Act 2002 allow persons employed by the Local Policing Body or persons employed by a contractor of the Local Policing Body (in relation to detention officers and escort officers) to be designated as investigating officers, detention officers and escort officers. Schedule 4 to the Police Reform Act 2002 outlines the powers of these individuals.

In relation to the powers of detention officers and escort officers, which of the following statements is correct?

A A detention officer can carry out an examination of a person detained at a police station in order to identify the person concerned via marks on their body (such as a tattoo).

B An escort officer cannot conduct an non-intimate search of a detainee.

C A detention officer cannot carry out an intimate search of a detained person.

D An escort officer can photograph detained persons in the same way as constables.

Question 6.19

Section 30 of the Police and Criminal Evidence Act 1984 requires that persons who have been arrested must be taken to a police station as soon as practicable after arrest. A prisoner who will be detained (or is likely to be detained) for a certain period of time must go to a 'designated' police station.

What is that time period?

A A prisoner who will be detained (or is likely to be detained) for more than six hours must go to a 'designated' police station.

B A prisoner who will be detained (or is likely to be detained) for more than 12 hours must go to a 'designated' police station.
C A prisoner who will be detained (or is likely to be detained) for more than 18 hours must go to a 'designated' police station.
D A prisoner who will be detained (or is likely to be detained) for more than 24 hours must go to a 'designated' police station.

Question 6.20

STUBBS (who is 15 years old) is brought to a police station by HAWTHORNE (the 30-year-old uncle of STUBBS) and ADEY (who is 25 years old and a friend of the family). HAWTHORNE has discovered that STUBBS had stolen £2,000 from him and he wants STUBBS dealt with by the police. When they arrive at the police station, they speak to PC BUTCHER about the matter. PC BUTCHER asks ADEY why he has come along and ADEY responds, '*I know he's stolen the money as he told me he has, but I want to help out.*' After hearing the facts, PC BUTCHER arrests STUBBS for the offence of theft.

Who, if anyone, could act as an appropriate adult for STUBBS?
A HAWTHORNE only.
B ADEY only.
C HAWTHORNE or ADEY.
D HAWTHORNE and ADEY could not be appropriate adults for STUBBS.

Question 6.21

WIDMER is 17 years old and has been arrested for an offence of burglary and taken to a designated police station. The custody officer, PS DETMER, is dealing with WIDMER.

Considering Code C of the Codes of Practice in relation to detained persons, which of the following comments is correct?
A PS DETMER would not require an appropriate adult to look after WIDMER's welfare as he is 17 years old.
B PS DETMER must ascertain the identity of a person responsible for WIDMER's welfare and as soon as practicable inform that person of the place and time that WIDMER was arrested.
C WIDMER should be informed that an appropriate adult will look after his welfare and that he can consult privately with such an appropriate adult at any time.

D Contact should be made with an appropriate adult; however, whether the custody officer informs the appropriate adult of the grounds for WIDMER's detention is a matter of choice for the custody officer.

Question 6.22

RASBAND has been arrested on suspicion of committing an offence of burglary and is transported to a designated police station. At the station he is presented to PS BOX (the custody officer), and the arresting officer, TI GRAVLIN, informs PS BOX of the circumstances of the arrest. PS BOX then considers the issues in relation to RASBAND's property.

Considering s. 54 of the Police and Criminal Evidence Act 1984 and Code C of the Codes of Practice, which of the following comments is correct?

A Section 54 imposes an absolute requirement that RASBAND must be searched on his arrival at the designated police station.

B If PS BOX authorises a search of RASBAND it must be carried out by a constable who is the same sex as RASBAND.

C An intimate search can be authorised by PS BOX under s. 54 of PACE.

D As soon as RASBAND arrives at the designated police station, TI GRAVLIN can search him under s. 54 of PACE as the use of this power does not require the approval of the custody officer.

Question 6.23

STRIKER, a citizen of Australia (an independent Commonwealth country), is out drinking with COWEE (who is a citizen of the Republic of Ireland). The two men become involved in a brawl resulting in both men being arrested for assault and public order offences. The custody officer, PS WEATHER, is dealing with the two men and is considering what Code C states about citizens of independent Commonwealth countries and foreign nationals.

Which of the following comments is correct?

A STRIKER and COWEE can, on request, consult with the appropriate High Commission, Embassy or Consulate at any time.

B STRIKER could consult with his High Commission, Embassy or Consulate at any time; COWEE (as a citizen of the Republic of Ireland) does not have this facility available.

C STRIKER and COWEE have the right to contact their High Commission, Embassy or Consulate on one occasion only and that is after their detention has been authorised by PS WEATHER.

D If either STRIKER or COWEE asks to communicate with their High Commission, Embassy or Consulate this should be acted upon immediately.

Question 6.24

AUBUCHON (who is a citizen of France) has been arrested for an offence of robbery and has been brought to a designated police station. AUBUCHON can speak some English but his command of the English language is not particularly good and so the custody officer, PS BAGGERLEY, calls an interpreter to assist in communication whilst AUBUCHON is at the police station. PIERRON is called to the station as an interpreter to facilitate communication. AUBUCHON is interviewed regarding the offence but the interview does not last long as AUBUCHON claims that PIERRON is a poor quality interpreter. AUBUCHON tells PS BAGGERLEY that he wants a different interpreter.

Which of the following statements is correct in respect of this situation?

A PS BAGGERLEY must arrange for a different interpreter to attend the police station.

B PS BAGGERLEY is responsible for deciding whether a different interpreter should be called to the police station.

C If PS BAGGERLEY decides that a different interpreter should not be called, and AUBUCHON challenges the decision, the matter should be reported to an officer of the rank of superintendent or above.

D A police officer or a member of police staff could be used to assist in communication in the interview.

Question 6.25

SMITH is wanted by West Midlands Police for an offence of attempted murder. He is arrested in Glasgow by Scottish police officers for an unrelated burglary offence that took place in Glasgow. West Midlands Police are notified of the arrest of SMITH and DCs TRAINER and LOWBRIDGE travel to Scotland to pick up SMITH and transport him back to the West Midlands. The officers arrive in Glasgow at 11.00 hrs and pick SMITH up. They leave Glasgow immediately and cross the border between Scotland and England at 12.45 hrs the same day. Later in the day, they arrive in the West Midlands force area at 16.45 hrs and arrive at the first police station in the West Midlands at 17.15 hrs (all on the same day).

What time will SMITH's 'relevant time' begin in relation to the attempted murder offence?

A 11.00 hrs.

B 12.45 hrs.

C 16.45 hrs.

D 17.15 hrs.

Question 6.26

HANE has been arrested on suspicion of murder. Due to the complex nature of the offence and the large-scale enquiries connected with it, HANE has spent 27 hours in police custody (a superintendent lawfully authorised an extension of HANE's detention). The Senior Investigating Officer is considering her options regarding obtaining a further extension of HANE's detention by way of a warrant of further detention.

In respect of such a warrant of further detention, which of the following comments is correct?

A A warrant of further detention can only be made with the written authorisation of an officer of the rank of superintendent or above.

B An application for a warrant of further detention must be made by an officer of the rank of inspector or above.

C An application for a warrant of further detention is made in the Crown Court.

D An application for a warrant of further detention can be made at any time, even before a superintendent's review has been carried out.

Question 6.27

NOREM has been arrested on suspicion of being a terrorist (under s. 41 of the Terrorism Act 2000) and a large-scale investigation is under way regarding his activities.

In relation to warrants of further detention and terrorism cases, which of the following statements is correct?

A A court could extend NOREM's period of detention up to a total of 14 days (starting at the time NOREM was arrested).

B NOREM could be held for a period of 96 hours without charge before an application must be made to issue or extend a warrant of further detention.

C An extension of detention in such a matter will normally be for a five-day period.

D An application for a warrant of further detention in a terrorism case can only be made by a Crown Prosecutor.

Question 6.28

At 06.00 hrs today, PALER is arrested for an offence of rape. He is escorted to a designated police station by the arresting officer, DC FULLWOOD, and they arrive at the station at 06.30 hrs. PALER's detention is authorised by PS MOSES at 06.50 hrs. PALER remains in police custody while the investigation progresses—he has not yet been charged with any offence.

Considering any review of PALER's detention, which of the following statements is correct?

A As PALER has not been charged with an offence, the 'review officer' will be the custody officer.

B The first review of PALER's detention shall be no more than six hours after his arrival at a designated police station.

C The first review of PALER's detention shall be no more than six hours after his detention was first authorised.

D The first review of PALER's detention shall be no more than nine hours after his detention was first authorised.

Question 6.29

CHARNOCK is an extremely violent 14-year-old child who has been arrested for an offence of s. 18 wounding which was committed using a razor blade of some description. He is brought into custody by DC ALMACK and, when the circumstances of the arrest are provided, CHARNOCK states, *'The blade is right up my arse where you can't get it!'* Inspector KEYS is in the custody block when this exchange takes place and consequently has reasonable grounds for believing that CHARNOCK may have concealed upon himself something which he could and might use to cause physical injury to himself or others at the station.

Could an intimate search of CHARNOCK be authorised?

A Yes, but it would have to be carried out by a registered medical practitioner or a registered nurse.

B No, as CHARNOCK has not been arrested for supplying a Class A drug.

C Yes, as long as an officer of the rank of inspector or above authorised it to take place.

D No, not unless an appropriate adult has given their consent to the search taking place.

Question 6.30

BALLARD (aged 13 years) and EDGAR (aged 15 years) have both been arrested in connection with an offence of burglary and brought to a designated police station by the arresting officers. They are presented to the custody officer who provides them with their notice of rights, including the right to legal advice. BALLARD states that he wants a solicitor; EDGAR states that he does not need one. The custody officer, PS CHIN, makes contact with appropriate adults for both juveniles. BALLARD's mother states that she will make her way to the station but will be at least an hour in getting there, whilst EDGAR's father states he will be at the police station within 5 minutes. EDGAR's father asks if his son has requested the services of a solicitor and is told that he has not.

Considering Code C of the Codes of Practice and the right to legal advice, which of the following comments is correct?

A PS CHIN should make the appropriate arrangements regarding legal advice for BALLARD; this action should not be delayed purely to await the arrival of BALLARD's mother.

B EDGAR's father does not have the right to ask for a solicitor to attend the police station on behalf of his son.

C Even if EDGAR is adamant that he does not want to see a solicitor, if his father thinks it is in his best interests then his son must see the solicitor.

D As EDGAR has declined the right to legal advice, his father need not consider whether legal advice from a solicitor is required.

Question 6.31

YATES, an adult male, has been arrested for an offence of murder and authorisation has been given for him to be held incommunicado. TI HAYES approaches DC TRUMP and asks him the maximum time that YATES can be held incommunicado if all the relevant authorities have been obtained.

To comply under s. 5 or s. 6 or both of PACE 1984, rights may be delayed if the person is in police detention, as in s. 118(2) of PACE for an indictable offence, and has not been charged. Which of the following is correct for DC TRUMP to tell TI HAYES?

A 12 hours.

B 24 hours.

C 36 hours.

D 48 hours.

Question 6.32

FRANKLIN is arrested in Glasgow for an offence of theft and is dealt with. Officers dealing with the enquiry ascertain that FRANKLIN is circulated as wanted by officers at Plymouth Police Station, in the Devon and Cornwall Police area, for an offence of rape. Officers travel from Plymouth to Glasgow by car and arrive at the station FRANKLIN is detained in at 13:00 hours. They do not question FRANKLIN and start their return journey at 13:30 hours. They cross the border into England at 15:30 hours and continue their journey. At 18:00 hours, they stop at Stafford Police Station (in the Staffordshire Police area) to use the toilet and canteen facilities. They then continue their journey and at 21:00 hours they stop at Exeter Police Station (a police station in the force area of Devon and Cornwall Police) to use the toilet and the canteen facilities. Continuing their journey, they arrive at Plymouth Police Station at 22:00 hours.

With regards to the offence of rape in Plymouth, when does the relevant time commence?

A When they stop at Exeter Police Station at 21:00 hours in the force area where FRANKLIN is wanted.

B When they arrive at Plymouth Police Station at 22:00 hours at the police station where FRANKLIN is wanted.

C When they cross the border into England and Wales area at 15:30 hours.

D When they stop at Stafford Police Station at 18:00 hours, the first police station in England and Wales area.

ANSWERS

Answer 6.1

Answer **C** — Where an officer performs the duties of a custody officer in the circumstances described in the question, that officer shall inform an officer, who (a) is attached to a designated police station and (b) is of at least the rank of inspector, that he has done so.

Investigators' Manual, para. 1.7.2

Answer 6.2

Answer **C** — Code C, para. 5.6 states that the detained person shall, on request, be given writing materials and/or be allowed to telephone one person for a reasonable time. This privilege may be denied or delayed if an officer of the rank of inspector or above considers sending the letter or making the telephone call may result in any of the consequences set out in Annex B, paras 1 and 2 of Code C (making answer B incorrect). One of those consequences is that the inspector believes the exercise of the right will hinder the recovery of property obtained in consequence of the commission of such an offence.

Investigators' Manual, paras 1.7.9, 1.7.9.1

Answer 6.3

Answer **A** — If an authorising officer, of superintendent rank or above, considers that access to a solicitor will interfere with evidence relating to an indictable offence, then access to that solicitor may be delayed, making answer D incorrect. This authorisation to delay access is not a 'blanket' authorisation to deny access to *all* legal advisers and in the example given in the question, the authorising officer should consider offering the detained person access to another solicitor on the Duty Solicitor scheme, making answer C incorrect. The consultation with a solicitor must be in private (Code C, para. 6.1). In *Brennan* v *United Kingdom* (2001) 34 EHRR 507, the court held that a suspect's right to communicate confidentially with a solicitor 'is part of the basic requirements of a fair trial'. The court found that there had been a breach of Article 6(3)(c) because a police officer had been present during a suspect's first interview with his solicitor, making answer B incorrect.

Investigators' Manual, paras 1.7.10, 1.7.10.1

Answer 6.4

Answer **B** — Section 41(2)(c) of the Police and Criminal Evidence Act 1984 states that in the case of a person who attends voluntarily at a police station or accompanies a constable to a police station without having been arrested, and is arrested, the 'relevant time' will begin at the time of his/her arrest. In situations where a person is arrested at one police station and has been circulated as wanted by another police station in the same force area, the detention clock for the second offence (in this case for the offence of rape) starts at the same time as for the original offence for which they were arrested.

Investigators' Manual, para. 1.7.16.1

Answer 6.5

Answer **C** — Section 42(1) of the Police and Criminal Evidence Act 1984 permits an officer of superintendent rank or above who is responsible for the station at which the person is detained to authorise detention beyond 24 hours and up to a maximum of 36 hours (Code C, para. 15.2). The offence investigated must be an indictable offence and the senior officer must be satisfied that there is not sufficient evidence to charge, that the investigation is being conducted diligently and expeditiously and that the person's detention is necessary to secure or preserve evidence relating to the offence or to obtain such evidence by questioning that person.

Investigators' Manual, para. 1.7.16

Answer 6.6

Answer **D** — The right to have a private consultation with a solicitor also applies to juveniles (Code C). If a juvenile wishes to have a private consultation without the presence of an appropriate adult, they must be permitted to do so.

Investigators' Manual, paras 1.7.10, 1.7.10.1

Answer 6.7

Answer **B** — The right under s. 56 of the Act can be delayed (making answer A incorrect). The delay can be authorised by an officer of the rank of inspector or above, making answer C incorrect. Answer D is incorrect as although the authorisation level is correct, the right can only be delayed up to a maximum of 36 hours (48 in cases involving terrorism) and this 36-hour period is calculated from the 'relevant time'. The 'relevant time' is the time that DEBNEY arrives at the police station, i.e. 11.00 hrs, and so the right could be delayed up to 23.00 hrs on the following day, making answer B correct.

Investigators' Manual, paras 1.7.9, 1.7.9.1

Answer 6.8

Answer **D** — Section 118 states that a person will be in police detention for the purposes of the Act if (i) he has been taken to a police station after being arrested for an offence or after being arrested under s. 41 of the Terrorism Act 2000, or (ii) he is arrested at a police station after attending voluntarily at the station (answer A) or accompanying a constable to it, or is detained there or is detained elsewhere in the charge of a constable (answer B), except that a person who is at court after being charged *is not* in police detention for those purposes (answer D). In addition, where a person is in another's lawful custody by virtue of para. 22, 34(1) (a designated escort officer and answer C) or 35(3) of sch. 4 to the Police Reform Act 2002, he shall be treated as being in police detention.

Investigators' Manual, para. 1.7.5.2

Answer 6.9

Answer **C** — Section 36(3) states that a custody officer must be an officer of at least the rank of sergeant (answer B); however, s. 36(4) allows an officer of any rank to perform the functions of a custody officer if a sergeant is not readily available to perform them (answer C). An officer of any rank can perform the role at a designated or non-designated police station, making answer A incorrect. The effect of these sections is that the practice of allowing an officer of any rank to perform the role of custody officer where a sergeant (*who has no other role to perform*) is in the police station must therefore be unlawful. Answer D has Sergeant EDEN (i) performing another role and (ii) *out* of the police station.

Investigators' Manual, para. 1.7.2

Answer 6.10

Answer **C** — As long as the interview under Code C, para. 6.6 can be justified at court, the interview will be admissible, making answer A incorrect. Where a suspect is in an authorised place of detention and fails to answer questions, no inference will be drawn from that failure if he/she has not been allowed the opportunity to consult a solicitor prior to being questioned, making answer B incorrect. Answer D is incorrect as an interview under Code C, para. 6.6 can only take place if an officer of the rank of superintendent or above authorises it. It is not necessary to await the arrival of a solicitor to take a non-intimate sample without consent for evidential purposes.

Investigators' Manual, paras 1.7.10, 1.7.10.1

Answer 6.11

Answer **A** — In cases where the person has been detained under the Terrorism Act 2000, the first review should be conducted as soon as reasonably practicable after his/her arrest. It must be conducted by a superintendent after the 24-hour period.

Investigators' Manual, para. 1.7.16.13

Answer 6.12

Answer **B** — When a detainee leaves police detention or is taken before a court they, their legal representative or appropriate adult shall be given, on request, a copy of the custody record as soon as practicable. This entitlement lasts for 12 months after release.

Investigators' Manual, para. 1.7.6

Answer 6.13

Answer **C** — A juvenile may not be placed in a cell with a detained adult, making answer A incorrect. COURTNEY can be placed in a cell (making answer B incorrect) if there is no other secure accommodation available and the custody officer considers it is not practicable to supervise him if he is not placed in a cell or that the cell provides more comfortable accommodation than other secure accommodation in the station (Code C, para. 8.8). This does not require the authority of an inspector, making answer D incorrect.

Investigators' Manual, para. 1.7.12

Answer 6.14

Answer **B** — Detainees should be visited every hour but if it is suspected that they are intoxicated through drink or drugs or have swallowed a drug or there are concerns about a detainee's level of consciousness, they should be visited and roused at least every half hour (Code C, para. 9.3).

Investigators' Manual, para. 1.7.13

Answer 6.15

Answer **D** — The custody officer must make sure a detainee receives appropriate clinical attention as soon as reasonably practicable if the person is injured. The detainee may also be examined by a medical practitioner of their choice at their expense (Code C, para. 9.8).

Investigators' Manual, para. 1.7.13

Answer 6.16

Answer **D** — The decision on whether the review takes place in person or by telephone or by video conferencing (video conferencing is subject to the introduction of regulations by the Secretary of State) is a matter for the review officer.

Investigators' Manual, para. 1.7.16.12

Answer 6.17

Answer **B** — Answer A is incorrect as Code C, para. 16.5 details the occasions when it is permissible to re-interview a suspect after they have been charged or informed that they will be prosecuted for an offence. There is no requirement for the suspect to agree in writing to this taking place, making answer D incorrect. The re-interviewing of a suspect can take place if it is necessary to (i) prevent or minimise harm or loss to some other person or the public, or (ii) clear up any ambiguity in a previous answer or statement, or (iii) in the interests of justice for the detainee to have put to them, and have an opportunity to comment on, information concerning the offence which has come to light since they were charged or informed that they might be prosecuted. The reasons for re-interviewing could be any one of these, making answer C incorrect.

Investigators' Manual, para. 1.7.17

Answer 6.18

Answer **A** — A detention officer can carry out an examination of a person detained at a police station in order to identify the person concerned via marks on their body (such as a tattoo). Answers B and C are incorrect as these are all powers available to detention officers and escort officers. The power to photograph a detained person is not available to an escort officer, making answer D incorrect.

Investigators' Manual, paras 1.7.3.2, 1.7.3.3

Answer 6.19

Answer **A** — A prisoner who will be detained (or is likely to be detained) for more than six hours must go to a 'designated' police station.

Investigators' Manual, para. 1.7.4

Answer 6.20

Answer **D** — HAWTHORNE and ADEY could both potentially act as an appropriate adult for STUBBS; however, a person should not be an appropriate adult if he/she is the victim of an offence (HAWTHORNE) or has received admissions prior to attending to act as an appropriate adult (ADEY).

Investigators' Manual, para. 1.7.5.4

Answer 6.21

Answer **C** — Code C, para. 3.13 states that if a person is a juvenile, the custody officer must, if it is practicable, ascertain the identity of a person responsible for their welfare. Paragraph 1.5 states that anyone who appears to be under 18 shall, in the absence of clear evidence that they are older, be treated as a juvenile for the purposes of Code C and any of the other Codes of Practice, making answer A incorrect. Paragraph 3.15 states that the custody officer must, as soon as practicable, inform the appropriate adult of the grounds for the juvenile's detention (making answer D incorrect) and their whereabouts. It does not require the custody officer to inform the appropriate adult of the time and place of the juvenile's arrest (making answer B incorrect). Paragraph 3.18 points out that the juvenile should be informed that they can consult privately with the appropriate adult at any time.

Investigators' Manual, para. 1.7.7

Answer 6.22

Answer **B** — Not all detained persons need to be searched; s. 54(1) and para. 4.1 of Code C require a detainee to be searched when it is clear that the custody officer will have continuing duties in relation to the detainee or when that detainee's behaviour or offence makes an inventory appropriate. They do not require every detainee to be searched, making answer A incorrect. Answer C is incorrect as although a custody officer can authorise a strip search, an intimate search can only be authorised by an officer of the rank of inspector or above. Answer D is incorrect as the custody officer must first authorise any search and the extent of the search—officers should not search a person until the authority has been given. Section 54(9) states that such a search is a same-sex process (answer B).

Investigators' Manual, paras 1.7.8, 1.7.8.1

Answer 6.23

Answer **A** — You may consider this a strange question for a Trainee Investigator to consider, but the reason it is asked is that s. 7 of Code C, which deals with citizens of independent Commonwealth countries and foreign nationals, has been questioned in a number of examinations. Code C, para. 7.1 states that a detainee who is a citizen of an independent Commonwealth country or a national of a foreign country, including the Republic of Ireland (so answer B is incorrect), has the right, upon request, to communicate at any time (making answer C incorrect) with the appropriate High Commission, Embassy or Consulate. Such a request should be acted upon as soon as practicable (making answer D incorrect).

Investigators' Manual, para. 1.7.11

Answer 6.24

Answer **B** — Code C, para. 13.9 states that a police officer or any other police staff cannot be used for the purpose described in the question, making answer D incorrect. Paragraph 13.10A states that if a detainee complains that they are not satisfied with the quality of the interpretation, the custody officer or (as the case may be) the interviewer is responsible for deciding whether a different interpreter should be called (this makes answer A incorrect). Paragraph 13.10D states that if a suspect challenges the decision of the custody officer (or interviewer) not to provide a different interpreter, that matter should be reported to an inspector to deal with as a complaint (making answer C incorrect).

Investigators' Manual, para. 1.7.14

Answer 6.25

Answer **D** — This scenario has long been an exam favourite. Section 41(2)(b) states that where a person is arrested outside England and Wales, the 'relevant time' shall be the time at which that person arrives at the first police station to which he/she is taken in the police area in England and Wales in which the offence for which he/she was arrested is being investigated or the time 24 hours after the time of that person's entry into England and Wales, whichever is the sooner. Therefore, the time of arrival at the first police station in the West Midlands is the 'relevant time', i.e. 17.15 hrs. This makes answers A, B and C incorrect.

Investigators' Manual, para. 1.7.16.1

Answer 6.26

Answer **D** — There is no requirement for the written authorisation of a superintendent in order to apply for a warrant of further detention, nor is there a need for the application to be made by an officer of the rank of inspector or above, making answers A and B incorrect. The application for the warrant is made in the magistrates' court, making answer C incorrect.

Investigators' Manual, paras 1.7.16.7, 1.7.16.8

Answer 6.27

Answer **A** — The court can extend the period of detention of a person up to a total of 14 days—this will start at the time of arrest when a person is arrested under s. 41 of the Terrorism Act 2000 (correct answer A). A person detained in these circumstances may only be held for a maximum of 48 hours without charge before an application must be made (making answer B incorrect). Answer C is incorrect as extensions by the court will normally be for a seven-day period. Answer D is incorrect as applications to the court can be made by a superintendent or a Crown Prosecutor.

Investigators' Manual, para. 1.7.16.11

Answer 6.28

Answer **C** — In the case of a person arrested but not charged, the 'review officer' will be an officer of at least inspector rank not directly involved in the investigation, making answer A incorrect. Answers B and D are incorrect as the first review shall not be later than six hours after detention was first authorised (not nine hours and not calculated from the time of arrival at the designated police station).

Investigators' Manual, para. 1.7.16.12

Answer 6.29

Answer **C** — Answer A is incorrect as an intimate search may only be carried out by a registered medical practitioner or a registered nurse, unless an officer of the rank of at least inspector considers that this is not practicable, in which case a police officer could carry out the search (very much a last resort—see Code C, paras 3 and 3A of Annex A). Answer B is incorrect as whilst an intimate search could be authorised in connection with Class A drugs, it can also be authorised if an officer of the rank of inspector or above has reasonable grounds for believing that the person may have concealed upon themselves anything which they could and might use to cause physical injury to themselves or others at the station. Answer D is incorrect as consent is not required for an intimate search to take place in the circumstances described.

Investigators' Manual, para. 1.7.19

Answer 6.30

Answer **A** — Paragraph 6.5A of Code C of the Codes of Practice states that in the case of a person who is a juvenile or is mentally disordered or otherwise mentally vulnerable, an appropriate adult should consider whether legal advice from a solicitor is required (making answer D incorrect). If such a detained person wants to exercise the right to legal advice, the appropriate action should be taken and should not be delayed until the appropriate adult arrives (correct answer A). If the person indicates that they do not want legal advice, the appropriate adult has the right to ask for a solicitor to attend if this would be in the best interests of the person, making answer B incorrect. However, the person cannot be forced to see the solicitor if they are adamant that they do not wish to do so, making answer C incorrect.

Investigators' Manual, para. 1.7.10

Answer 6.31

Answer **C** — The rights may be delayed only for as long as grounds exist and in no case beyond 36 hours after the relevant time as in s. 41 of PACE.

Investigators' Manual, para. 1.7.20

Answer 6.32

Answer **A** — Where a person has been arrested outside England and Wales the relevant time is calculated under s. 41(2)(b) of PACE and states:

(b) in the case of a person arrested outside England and Wales, shall be—
- (i) the time at which that person arrives at the first police station to which he is taken in the force area in England or Wales in which the offence for which he was arrested is being investigated; or
- (ii) the time 24 hours after the time of that person's entry into England and Wales.

This clearly makes A the correct answer. Relevant time has been tested in the NIE so a good knowledge is important in your preparation.

Investigators' Manual, para 1.7.16.1

7 Identification

QUESTIONS

Question 7.1

SALISBURY is looking out of her bedroom window when she sees COX attempting to break into her neighbour's house. SALISBURY watches COX for a continuous period of five minutes and then telephones the police to tell them what she has seen. SALISBURY describes the approximate age of COX and the clothes he is wearing. The police arrive and COX is arrested. In interview, COX disputes being the person responsible for the offence but does not request an identification parade.

Considering the law with regard to identification, which of the following statements is correct?

A A suspect's failure to request an identification parade means that the police may proceed without one.

B This would not be classed as an identification within the terms of the Codes of Practice as SALISBURY has only described the clothing and approximate age of COX.

C The Codes of Practice are clear; where a witness is available and the suspect disputes being the person responsible for the offence, an identification procedure shall be held.

D Following the decision in *R* v *Forbes*, if the police are in possession of sufficient evidence to justify an arrest of a suspect and any identification is disputed then an identification procedure should be held.

Question 7.2

PITCHER commits a robbery and is filmed on a town centre CCTV system carrying out the offence. DC THORPE wishes to trace witnesses to the offence and obtains a still image from the CCTV and places this in the local newspaper. MAYBURY recognizes

PITCHER from the still image and contacts DC THORPE, who subsequently arrests PITCHER.

Considering Code D of the Codes of Practice, which of the following statements is correct?

A There is no requirement for PITCHER or his solicitor to view the material released to the media before any identification procedure is carried out.

B As MAYBURY has recognised PITCHER from a still image placed in a newspaper, she would not be allowed to take part in any further identification procedures.

C DC THORPE may keep a copy of the material released to the media for the purposes of recognising or tracing the suspect.

D The fact that MAYBURY identified PITCHER from a still image in a newspaper would not stop her taking part in any further identification procedures.

Question 7.3

You have arrested TRAVIS on suspicion of committing 30 bogus-official type burglaries. Descriptions of the offender have been obtained for every incident and there is a reasonable chance that each victim would be able to identify the offender. During her interview, TRAVIS denies any involvement in the offences. TRAVIS states that she will stand on an identification parade to prove her innocence.

What action will you take?

A As TRAVIS disputes her involvement, there is an identification issue. In these circumstances you must arrange an identification in the first instance.

B As there is an identification issue, you must initially offer TRAVIS the choice between taking part in a video identification or standing on an identification.

C You should, initially, invite TRAVIS to take part in a video identification.

D As the officer in the case you may choose freely between a video identification and an identification parade.

Question 7.4

CHURCH is involved in large-scale crowd violence at a football match during which he takes part in a violent disorder. The incident is caught on CCTV film. As well as the CCTV film of the incident, an E-fit is released to the public to identify CHURCH, who is recognised from the E-fit by DRAPER. As a result, CHURCH is later arrested, charged and bailed for the offence. On his release, CHURCH makes a series of threatening telephone calls to DRAPER, who records the threats.

Considering the law relating to photographs, images and sound, which of the following statements is correct?

A The interpretation of images on film is a matter for the jury; expert evidence would not be admitted to interpret such images.

B The Codes of Practice preclude the use of aural identification procedures.

C A police officer familiar with the CCTV of the crowd violence may be allowed to assist the court in interpreting and explaining events shown within the film.

D DRAPER would not be allowed to give evidence identifying CHURCH's voice.

Question 7.5

GROUCOTT (aged 21 years) admits to an offence of theft (a recordable offence) and is cautioned. At the time of her caution she had an injury to her left hand that meant no fingerprints relating to that hand could be taken.

Considering the powers to take fingerprints under s. 61 of the Police and Criminal Evidence Act 1984, which of the following statements is correct?

A GROUCOTT cannot be required to provide any further fingerprints in connection with a case for which she was cautioned.

B Section 61 of the Act is only applicable if the person has been convicted of a recordable offence.

C The authority of an inspector would be required to take further fingerprints from GROUCOTT.

D The custody officer must authorise the taking of such prints from GROUCOTT.

Question 7.6

You are investigating a s. 20 wounding where the blood of the offender has been found on the clothing of the victim. You strongly suspect that HARPER is responsible for the offence but you have no direct evidence to implicate him. A colleague suggests obtaining an intimate sample (of blood) for DNA analysis from HARPER for elimination purposes.

Is this possible?

A Yes, with an inspector's authorisation and the consent of HARPER.

B No, an intimate sample could only be obtained from HARPER if he was in police detention.

C Yes, with a superintendent's authorisation and the consent of HARPER.

D No, because this is not an indictable offence.

Question 7.7

Section 62 of the Police and Criminal Evidence Act 1984 sets out police powers to take intimate samples.

Which of the following comments is correct with regard to those powers?

A An intimate sample cannot be taken by a police officer in any circumstances.

B Intimate samples can only be obtained from a suspect who is in police detention.

C Where an intimate sample is taken from a child under 14 years of age consent must be obtained from the child and also from his/her parents or guardian.

D An intimate sample can only be obtained with the consent of the suspect and this consent must be in writing.

Question 7.8

SMALLWOOD has been arrested on suspicion of burglary. A scenes of crime examination of the scene of the offence led to the recovery of several samples of head hair. DC FELLOWS, the officer in the case, wants to obtain samples of head hair from SMALLWOOD. No samples have been obtained from SMALLWOOD at this stage of the enquiry.

Which of the following statements is correct in respect of obtaining those head hair samples?

A Head hair samples cannot be obtained from SMALLWOOD unless he provides his consent, which must be in writing.

B Head hair samples can be obtained from SMALLWOOD by force if necessary as long as an inspector authorises the taking of the sample.

C The authority of an inspector is not required as SMALLWOOD is in police detention for a recordable offence and has not had a non-intimate sample of the same type and from the same part of the body taken in the course of the investigation.

D Head hair samples should only be obtained from SMALLWOOD if an inspector believes that the sample will tend to prove or disprove his involvement in the commission of the offence.

Question 7.9

HILL has been arrested for an offence of rape. His alleged victim has provided a witness statement detailing HILL's description. The victim states that HILL had a tattoo of a snake on his stomach. The officer in the case, DS BARRY, wishes to examine HILL's stomach to establish if he has such a tattoo.

With regard to any examination of HILL under s. 54A(1) of the Police and Criminal Evidence Act 1984, which of the following statements is correct?

A An inspector must give an authorisation for HILL's stomach to be examined regardless of whether HILL provides his consent to the examination.

B If HILL refuses, then an officer of the rank of inspector or above can orally authorise that HILL be examined.

C HILL cannot be examined for the tattoo under this section as it can only be used to establish the identity of the person examined.

D HILL can be examined for the tattoo but not with the use of force.

Question 7.10

OAKMOOR (aged 12 years) has been arrested for an offence of burglary. DC COPELAND wishes to obtain impressions of OAKMOOR's footwear to compare against marks found at the scene. OAKMOOR has not had an impression of his footwear taken in connection with the investigation of the offence.

Which of the following comments is correct?

A As OAKMOOR is under 14 years of age, his footwear impressions cannot be obtained unless an appropriate adult has given their permission for them to be taken.

B OAKMOOR must consent to the taking of a footwear impression.

C If OAKMOOR does not consent, then an inspector must authorise the obtaining of footwear impressions.

D PACE allows footwear impressions to be taken without consent in such circumstances.

Question 7.11

TI ORPINGDON is discussing a case of robbery with her supervisor, DS FRIEND. The issue of identification is raised and TI ORPINGDON asks DS FRIEND what the term 'available' means in respect of Code D of the Codes of Practice.

In respect of that term, which of the following comments is correct?

A 'Available' means that a suspect is immediately available or will be within a reasonably short time, in order that they can be invited to take part in at least one of the eye-witness identification procedures (video identification, an identification parade or a group identification) and it is practicable to arrange an effective procedure.

B 'Available' means that the location of the suspect is known to the police.

C 'Available' means that a suspect has been arrested by the police in connection with the offence and has indicated that they are willing to take an effective part in a video identification or identification parade.

D 'Available' means that the suspect has informed the police that they will take part in an identification parade, a video identification or a group identification.

Question 7.12

Annex A of Code D governs the rules relating to a video identification.

With regard to the number of images in a video identification parade, which of the following statements is true?

A The set of images must include the suspect and at least seven other people who, so far as possible, resemble the suspect in age, general appearance and position in life.

B The set of images must include the suspect and at least eight other people who, so far as possible, resemble the suspect in age, general appearance and position in life.

C The set of images must include the suspect and at least nine other people who, so far as possible, resemble the suspect in age, general appearance and position in life.

D The set of images must include the suspect and at least twelve other people who, so far as possible, resemble the suspect in age, general appearance and position in life.

Question 7.13

DC GUDDEN and TI INCE are working alongside uniform colleagues whilst policing a large-scale demonstration against the building of an airport in a rural area. Intelligence suggests that the protesters plan to cause damage and use violence and it is anticipated that a significant number of arrests will be made in respect of public order and other offences. In a briefing it is suggested that persons who are arrested should have their photograph taken with the arresting officer. TI INCE asks DC GUDDEN about this idea and whether it complies with the Police and Criminal Evidence Act 1984 and the Codes of Practice.

Which of the following responses is correct?

A Photographs cannot be taken of an arrested person unless that person is at a police station.

B Photographs of an arrested person can be taken elsewhere than a police station if that person has been arrested by a constable for an offence.

C An arrested person can be photographed elsewhere than at a police station but the photograph must be obtained with that person's consent.

D Photographs of arrested persons can be obtained if an officer of the rank of inspector or above authorises them to be taken.

Question 7.14

CLEVE and O'SULLIVAN both live in a small village where a murder takes place. The Senior Investigating Officer in charge of the murder investigation decides to ask all village residents for a set of their fingerprints for elimination purposes as part of intelligence-led screening to assist in the investigation of the offence. When an officer calls at CLEVE's house, he refuses to participate. When an officer calls at O'SULLIVAN's house, O'SULLIVAN agrees to provide his fingerprints but only on the strict understanding that they will be destroyed after the investigation has been concluded. O'SULLIVAN has a set of prints taken and signs a consent form which specifically states his prints will be destroyed at the end of the case and that they will only be compared to fingerprints from the murder enquiry. Unfortunately, nobody is ever convicted or even arrested in connection with the murder.

Considering Code D of the Codes of Practice, which of the following comments is correct?

A A set of prints for elimination purposes may be obtained from CLEVE (at the time of their request) by force if necessary.

B Regardless of the form that O'SULLIVAN signed, his fingerprints could be retained to be used in the investigation of other offences.

C Fingerprints obtained in such a mass screening exercise must always be destroyed at the end of the investigation.

D O'SULLIVAN volunteers his fingerprints but his consent for them to be used in the investigation may be withdrawn at any time.

Question 7.15

DC SERSAN and TI MITCHUM are discussing the taking of intimate and non-intimate samples from persons in custody.

Which of the following statements is correct?

A DC SERSAN states that a dental impression is a non-intimate sample.

B TI MITCHUM states that a sample of saliva is an intimate sample.

C DC SERSAN states that a sample of urine is an intimate sample.

D TI MITCHUM states that a sample of tissue fluid is a non-intimate sample.

Question 7.16

Code D of the Codes of Practice concerns the principal methods used by the police to identify people in connection with the investigation of offences.

In relation to that Code, which of the following comments is correct?

A The phrase 'known' means that the identity (name) of the person concerned is 'known' to the police.

B Code D is wholly concerned with visual identification processes.

C The eye-witness procedures dealt with by Code D are limited to video identification, identification parades and group identification.

D Aural identification procedures would be permitted under the provisions of Code D.

Question 7.17

GRANTLEY has been arrested for an offence of s. 47 assault (contrary to the Offences Against the Person Act 1861) committed against NAILER. NAILER provided a statement in which he gave a description of the person responsible for the assault and expressed an ability to be able to identify the person responsible for the offence. In interview, GRANTLEY denied the offence, disputing that he was the person responsible. Due to the unusual physical features of GRANTLEY, DC KNOWLES (the officer in charge of the investigation) considers that a group identification would be the most appropriate identification procedure to take place.

What does Code D of the Codes of Practice state about such a situation?

A GRANTLEY should not be invited to take part in a group identification in the first instance—the procedure GRANTLEY should be invited to take part in should be a video identification or an identification parade if it is more practicable and suitable.

B The decision as to what identification procedure should take place is not one that has anything to do with DC KNOWLES as the officer in the case—this is a decision made entirely by the 'identification officer'.

C GRANTLEY may initially be invited to take part in a group identification if DC KNOWLES considers it is more suitable than a video identification or an identification parade and the identification officer considers it practicable to arrange.

D A 'group identification' procedure is not available as a first option—it is only available when a suspect has refused to take part in a video identification or an identification parade.

Question 7.18

STOCKMAN has been arrested for an offence of armed robbery. The officer in charge of the case is DS WINGFIELD who interviewed STOCKMAN with another officer involved in the investigation, DC REID. STOCKMAN denied the offence, disputing the identification evidence of several witnesses who saw him carry out the offence and gave a description of him. It is proposed to keep STOCKMAN in police detention whilst an identification parade is carried out and there is concern that waiting for an inspector to act as an 'identification officer' would cause unreasonable delay to the investigation.

With regard to the role of the 'identification officer' in such circumstances, which of the comments below is correct?

A The explanation of the identification procedure and notice in relation to it could be provided to STOCKMAN by DS WINGFIELD or DC REID.

B The explanation of the identification procedure and notice in relation to it could be provided to STOCKMAN by the custody officer (who is not involved in the investigation).

C The explanation of the identification procedure and the notice in relation to it must be provided to STOCKMAN by an officer of the rank of inspector or above who is not involved in the investigation.

D The explanation of the identification procedure and the notice in relation to it could be provided to STOCKMAN by DS WINGFIELD but not by DC REID.

Question 7.19

TIPPING was arrested and interviewed regarding an offence of sexual touching. TIPPING denied the offence and disputed the identification evidence of McCABE (an eye-witness to the offence). This has resulted in a video identification procedure being arranged. FINLAY (who is a solicitor representing TIPPING) has been notified of the time and place of the video identification procedure by the identification officer and has made a request to the identification officer that she be present when the procedure takes place.

Considering Annex A of Code D (dealing with video identification procedures), which of the statements below is correct?

A If the identification officer is satisfied that FINLAY's presence will not deter or distract McCABE from viewing the images and making an identification, then FINLAY can be present when the video identification procedure takes place.

B If FINLAY requests it and the identification officer authorises it, TIPPING may also be present when the video identification procedure takes place.

C During the identification procedure FINLAY would not be allowed to communicate with McCABE or the identification officer.

D A supervised viewing of the recording of the video identification procedure by TIPPING and/or FINLAY may be arranged on request, at the discretion of the identification officer.

Question 7.20

HANNA is detained at a police station in consequence of being arrested for an offence of burglary (a recordable offence) and has not had his fingerprints taken in the course of the investigation of the offence.

Considering the Police and Criminal Evidence Act 1984 and Code D of the Codes of Practice, which of the statements below is correct?

A Fingerprints may be taken from HANNA with his consent; that consent can be provided in writing or orally.

B A constable may use reasonable force to take fingerprints from HANNA without his consent.

C Fingerprints cannot be taken from HANNA unless an officer of the rank of inspector or above has authorised it.

D Fingerprints cannot be taken from HANNA unless he has been charged with the offence of burglary.

Question 7.21

FROST, aged 14 years, has been the victim of a sexual assault, whereby she was dragged into some bushes in the local park and digitally penetrated by the offender whilst he masturbated. The offender was wearing a balaclava so there is no possibility of using facial identification procedures. The scene has not been identified as the victim cannot be sure where the attack took place and from the medical examination of FROST, although there is evidence of such abuse, no DNA of the offender has been found. However, the victim's statement states that the offender had shaved off his pubic hair and had a small cut above his penis. PACEY has been arrested in connection with this offence and DC TRANTER, the officer in the case, wants to take a photograph of PACEY's genital region to prove or disprove his involvement in the offence, also knowing full well that PACEY's pubic hair will have grown by the time the matter gets to court. PACEY will not consent to the photograph being taken.

To comply with s. 54A(1) of PACE 1984, which of the following statements is correct?

A Authority can be given by a superintendent or above for a photograph to be taken and if the suspect still refuses reasonable force can be used to take it.

B Authority can be given by a superintendent or above for a photograph to be taken and if the suspect still refuses a warning will be given that the court can draw an inference from his refusal.

C Authority can be given by an officer of at least inspector rank or above for a photograph to be taken and if the suspect still refuses reasonable force can be used to take it.

D Authority can be given by an officer of at least inspector rank or above for a photograph to be taken, and if the suspect still refuses a warning will be given that the court can draw an inference from his refusal.

Question 7.22

JAKEMAN, an adult male, has been arrested for an offence of burglary (a recordable offence) and is in police detention having been taken to the custody block of a designated police station. At the scene of the burglary there is a footprint made by trainer-style footwear. JAKEMAN has trainer-style footwear on when documented by the custody officer and you wish to take impressions of his trainers but JAKEMAN has refused.

Under s. 61A of PACE 1984 footwear impressions can be taken, but which of the statements below is correct?

A Authority is required from an officer of the rank of inspector or above and force can be used.

B Authority is required from an officer of the rank of inspector or above and force cannot be used but a warning can be given that a court can draw an inference from a refusal.

C Authority can be given by the custody sergeant and force can be used.

D A police officer can take an impression of JAKEMAN's footwear and force can be used.

ANSWERS

Answer 7.1

Answer **B** — Answer A is incorrect as a suspect's failure to request an identification parade does not mean the police may proceed without one (*R* v *Graham* [1994] Crim LR 212). Answer C is incorrect as (under Code D, para. 3.12) an identification procedure does not need to be held if it is not practicable or would serve no useful purpose in proving or disproving whether the suspect committed the offence. Answer D is incorrect as the exceptions that apply for answer C also apply to decisions when considering *R* v *Forbes*. This question is based on the case of *D* v *DPP* (1998) The Times, 7 August, where it was held that an identification had not been made (as per answer B). An identification parade would have served no useful purpose since the clothing would have changed and those persons used for the parade would have been the same approximate age.

Investigators' Manual, paras 1.8.4.4, 1.8.4.5

Answer 7.2

Answer **D** — Code D, paras 3.38 to 3.41 govern identification when the media has been used. When a broadcast or publication is made, a copy of the relevant material released to the media for the purposes of recognising or tracing the suspect must be kept, making answer C incorrect. The suspect or their solicitor must be allowed to view the material released to the media prior to any identification procedure, provided it is practicable and would not unreasonably delay the investigation, making answer A incorrect. The fact that MAYBURY has recognised PITCHER would not preclude her participation in any future identification procedure, therefore answer B is incorrect. However, each witness will be asked, after they have taken part, whether they have seen any broadcast or published films or photographs relating to the offence and any description of the suspect and their replies shall be recorded.

Investigators' Manual, para. 1.8.4.16

Answer 7.3

Answer **C** — The circumstances of this question would mean that an identification would be held (Code D, para. 3.12). Under Code D, para. 3.14, where an identification is to be held, the suspect shall initially be invited to take part in a video identification.

Investigators' Manual, paras 1.8.4.6, 1.8.4.8

Answer 7.4

Answer **C** — Expert evidence may be admitted to interpret images on film (*R* v *Stockwell* (1993) 97 Cr App R 260), making answer A incorrect. The Codes of Practice do not preclude the police making use of aural identification procedures, making answer B incorrect. Answer C is correct as police officers who are familiar with a particular film clip (e.g. crowd violence at a football match) may be allowed to assist the court in interpreting and explaining events shown within it (*R* v *Clare and Peach* (1995) 2 Cr App R 333). Generally, a witness (DRAPER) may give evidence identifying the defendant's voice (*R* v *Robb* (1991) 93 Cr App R 161), making answer D incorrect.

Investigators' Manual, paras 1.8.4.12, 1.8.4.14

Answer 7.5

Answer **C** — Section 61(6) of the Police and Criminal Evidence Act 1984 provides that a person who has been given a caution (making answers A and B incorrect) in respect of a recordable offence which, at the time of the caution, the person admitted, may be required to provide fingerprints if, since their caution, their fingerprints have not been taken or their fingerprints which have been taken do not constitute a complete set or some, or all, of the fingerprints are not of sufficient quality to allow satisfactory analysis, comparison or matching. In either case, an officer of the rank of inspector (making D incorrect) or above must be satisfied that taking the fingerprints is necessary to assist in the prevention or detection of crime and authorise the taking.

Investigators' Manual, para. 1.8.5

Answer 7.6

Answer **A** — The Criminal Justice and Police Act 2001, s. 80(1) provides that the authorisation level required to obtain an intimate sample is that of an inspector or above, making answer C incorrect. Section 62(2)(a) of the Police and Criminal Evidence Act 1984 states that the type of offence for which an intimate sample may be taken need only be a recordable offence and not an indictable offence, making answer D incorrect. Code D recognises that an intimate sample may be taken from a person not in police detention, for the purposes of elimination, providing his/her consent is given, making answer B incorrect.

Investigators' Manual, paras 1.8.7 to 1.8.7.3

Answer 7.7

Answer **D** — Urine (an intimate sample) can be obtained by a police officer, making answer A incorrect. An intimate sample may be taken from a person not in police detention, making answer B incorrect. An intimate sample taken from a child under the age of 14 years requires the consent of his/her parents alone, making answer C incorrect. Answer D is correct as the consent of a suspect must be given in writing (Code D, para. 6.2).

Investigators' Manual, para. 1.8.7.2

Answer 7.8

Answer **C** — The authority of an inspector to take a non-intimate sample from SMALLWOOD is not required in these circumstances, making answers B and D incorrect. SMALLWOOD's consent will be sought (answer A) and it should be in writing; however, if he will not provide it then the sample can be taken by force as per answer C.

Investigators' Manual, paras 1.8.7, 1.8.7.4

Answer 7.9

Answer **B** — If HILL refuses then an inspector can provide oral authorisation that he be examined, although this will have to be confirmed in writing as soon as practicable (Code D, para. 5.8). HILL's consent is not required but if it is given then an inspector's authority is not required, making answer A incorrect. The power can be used to establish the identity of an individual or to identify them as a person involved in the commission of an offence, making answer C incorrect. Force can be used if necessary, making answer D incorrect.

Investigators' Manual, para. 1.8.6

Answer 7.10

Answer **D** — Section 61A of the Police and Criminal Evidence Act 1984 provides a power for police officers to take footwear impressions without consent from any person over the age of ten who is detained at a police station in consequence of being arrested for a recordable offence and they have not had an impression of their footwear taken in the course of the investigation of the offence.

Investigators' Manual, para. 1.8.5.3

Answer 7.11

Answer **A** — A suspect being 'available' means the suspect is immediately available or will be within a reasonably short time, in order that they can be invited to take part in at least one of the eye-witness procedures (video identification, identification parade or group identification) and it is practicable to arrange an effective procedure. This makes answers B, C and D incorrect.

Investigators' Manual, para. 1.8.4.2

Answer 7.12

Answer **B** — The set of images for a video identification must include the suspect and at least *eight* other people who, so far as possible, resemble the suspect in age, general appearance and position in life. Only one suspect shall appear in any set unless there are two suspects of roughly similar appearance, in which case they may be shown together with at least twelve other people.

Investigators' Manual, para. 1.8.8

Answer 7.13

Answer **B** — Section 64A of the Police and Criminal Evidence Act 1984 governs the taking of photographs of persons. Such photographs will be taken of a person whilst they are detained at a police station but can also be taken elsewhere, making answer A incorrect. Neither the consent of the person being photographed nor the authority of an officer of the rank of inspector or above is required to do so, making answers C and D incorrect.

Investigators' Manual, para. 1.8.6

Answer 7.14

Answer **D** — Force cannot be used to obtain elimination prints, making answer A incorrect. Fingerprints obtained in mass screening exercises do not always have to be destroyed if they were taken for the purposes of an investigation for which a person has been convicted and fingerprints were also taken from the convicted person for the purposes of the investigation, making answer C incorrect. This is further the case as the person from whom the prints were obtained may sign a form allowing the prints to be used in the prevention or detection of crime. Answer B is incorrect as fingerprints may not be used in the investigation of any offence or in evidence against a person who is, or would be, entitled to its destruction. Consent for the fingerprints to be used can be withdrawn at any time.

Investigators' Manual, paras 1.8.13, 1.8.13.1

Answer 7.15

Answer **C** — A dental impression is an intimate sample, making answer A incorrect. A sample of saliva is a non-intimate sample, making answer B incorrect. A sample of tissue fluid is an intimate sample, making answer D incorrect.

Investigators' Manual, para. 1.8.7

Answer 7.16

Answer **D** — The phrase 'known' does not relate to identity—para. 3.1A(a) of Code D states that 'known' means there is sufficient information known to the police to establish, in accordance with Code G (Arrest), that there are reasonable grounds to suspect a particular person of involvement in the offence, making answer A incorrect. Code D not only deals with visual identification processes but also those involving other forms of identification (e.g. intimate and non-intimate samples), making answer B incorrect. Answer C is incorrect as eye-witness procedures also include 'confrontation' situations (see Annex D). While Code D concentrates on visual identification procedures, it does not prevent the police from making use of aural identification procedures such as a 'voice identification parade', where they judge that appropriate (correct answer D).

Investigators' Manual, paras 1.8.2, 1.8.3, 1.8.4.2

Answer 7.17

Answer **C** — Paragraph 3.14 of Code D states that if an identification procedure is to be held, the suspect shall initially be invited to take part in a video identification unless:

(a) a video identification is not practicable; or
(b) an identification parade is both practicable and more suitable than a video identification; or
(c) paragraph 3.16 applies.

The identification officer and the officer in charge of the investigation shall consult each other to determine which option is to be offered (making answer B incorrect). Paragraph 3.16 of Code D states that a suspect may initially be invited to take part in a group identification if the officer in charge of the investigation considers it is more suitable than a video identification or an identification parade and the identification officer considers it practicable to arrange (correct answer C). This means that GRANTLEY can be invited to participate in a group identification in the first instance (making answers A and D incorrect).

Investigators' Manual, para. 1.8.4.6

Answer 7.18

Answer **B** — Paragraph 3.11 of Code D states that no officer or any other person involved with the investigation of the case against the suspect may take any part in these procedures or act as the identification officer, meaning that answers A and D are incorrect. Paragraph 3.11 also states that arrangements for, and conduct of, the eye-witness identification procedures in paras 3.5 to 3.10 and circumstances in which any such identification procedure must be held shall be the responsibility of an officer not below inspector rank who is not involved with the investigation ('the identification officer'). This would appear to mean that answer C is correct; however, para. 3.19 states that in the case of a detained suspect, the duties under paras 3.17 and 3.18 (providing an explanation of the identification procedure and the notice in relation to it) may be performed by the custody officer or by another officer or police staff not involved in the investigation as directed by the custody officer, if:

(a) it is proposed to release the suspect in order that an identification procedure can be arranged and carried out and an inspector is not available to act as the identification officer, before the suspect leaves the station; or

(b) it is proposed to keep the suspect in police detention whilst the procedure is arranged and carried out and waiting for an inspector to act as the identification officer would cause unreasonable delay to the investigation.

The officer concerned shall inform the identification officer of the action taken and give them the signed copy of the notice. Therefore answer B is the correct option.

Investigators' Manual, paras 1.8.4.4, 1.8.4.6

Answer 7.19

Answer **A** — The suspect is not allowed to be present when the images are shown to an eye-witness, making answer B incorrect. Answer C is incorrect as although the solicitor is not allowed to communicate with the witness, he/she would be allowed to communicate with the identification officer. A supervised viewing of the recording of the video identification procedure by the suspect and/or their solicitor may be arranged on request, at the discretion of the *investigating* officer not the identification officer, making answer D incorrect. Answer A is correct as a suspect's solicitor may only be present at the video identification on request and with the prior agreement of the identification officer, if the officer is satisfied that the solicitor's presence will not deter or distract any eye-witness from viewing the images and making an identification.

Investigators' Manual, para. 1.8.8

Answer 7.20

Answer **B** — A person's fingerprints may be taken with their consent but if they are at a police station then that consent will be in writing, making answer A incorrect. Section 61(3) of the Police and Criminal Evidence Act 1984 states that fingerprints may be taken without the consent of the person (who is over the age of ten years) from a person detained at a police station in consequence of being arrested for a recordable offence, if they have not had their fingerprints taken in the course of the investigation of the offence unless those previously taken fingerprints are not a complete set or some or all of those fingerprints are not of sufficient quality to allow satisfactory analysis, comparison or matching, making answer D incorrect. No authorisation from an officer of the rank of inspector or above is required, making answer C incorrect. Paragraph 4.6 of Code D states that reasonable force may be used, if necessary, in the execution of the power (s. 117 of the Police and Criminal Evidence Act 1984) (correct answer B).

Investigators' Manual, para. 1.8.5

Answer 7.21

Answer **C** — Section 54A(1) of PACE allows a detainee at a police station to be searched or examined or both, to establish:

(a) whether they have any marks, features or injuries that would tend to identify them as a person involved in the commission of an offence and to photograph any identifying marks,
(b) their identity.

A search/examination to find marks under s. 54A(1)(a) may be carried out without the detainee's consent only if authorised by an officer of at least inspector rank when consent has been withheld or it is not practicable to obtain consent. Reasonable force can be used in the exercise of this power.

Investigators' Manual, para. 1.8.6

Answer 7.22

Answer **D** — Section 61A of PACE provides a power for a police officer to take footwear impressions without consent from any person over the age of 10 years who is detained at a police station:

(a) in consequence of being arrested for a recordable offence.

Reasonable force can be used, if necessary to take footwear impressions from a detainee without consent. Therefore D is the correct answer.

Investigators' Manual, para. 1.8.5.3

8 Interviews

QUESTIONS

Question 8.1

JENKINS (aged 15 years) has stolen several bottles of concentrated acid from his school chemistry laboratory and has hidden them in an unknown location on the school premises. The principal of the school has detained JENKINS and contacted the police to deal with the matter. PC McATEER attends the school and is concerned that if the acid is not located immediately it will lead to physical harm to other people. PC McATEER wishes to interview JENKINS regarding the location of the stolen acid and believes that contacting JENKINS's parents would cause an unreasonable delay in the circumstances.

Which of the following statements is correct?

A The principal cannot act as an appropriate adult because JENKINS is suspected of an offence against his educational establishment.

B Under no circumstances can PC McATEER interview JENKINS at his place of education.

C Regardless of the circumstances, JENKINS's parents must be notified of the interview and be present when the interview is carried out.

D If waiting for JENKINS's parents to attend would cause an unreasonable delay, the principal can act as an appropriate adult.

Question 8.2

DC BUTLIN is interviewing FLATMAN in relation to the kidnapping of his ex-wife. Before the kidnapping took place, FLATMAN told HARLOWE (a civilian witness) that he had considered kidnapping his ex-wife to teach her a lesson after she retained possession of their marital home in the divorce settlement between them. HARLOWE has provided DC BUTLIN with a witness statement to this effect.

Considering the Codes of Practice in relation to significant statements, what action should DC BUTLIN take with regard to FLATMAN's comment to HARLOWE?

A DC BUTLIN should introduce the comment made to HARLOWE at the start of the interview after caution, as it is a significant statement.

B DC BUTLIN may introduce the comment made to HARLOWE at any time during the interview, as unless the comment is a direct admission of guilt it is not a significant statement.

C DC BUTLIN may introduce the comment made to HARLOWE at any time during the course of the interview, even though the comment is a significant statement.

D DC BUTLIN may introduce the comment made to HARLOWE at any time during the course of the interview, as it would not be classed as a significant statement.

Question 8.3

DCs CHURCHLEY and RAY are conducting an audio-recorded interview with HOLLAND for an offence of robbery. Also present in the interview is HOLLAND's solicitor, MASPERO. Thirty minutes after the interview has started, HOLLAND asks for a short two-minute break in the interview while he gathers his thoughts. During the short break, DCs CHURCHLEY and RAY will remain in the interview room with HOLLAND and MASPERO.

Considering Code E of the Codes of Practice, what action should the interviewing officers take?

A The Codes of Practice do not allow for short breaks to be taken. The officers should stop the recording media and vacate the interview room.

B The officers should remove the recording media from the audio recorder and follow the procedures as if the interview had been concluded.

C As this is only a short break, the officers may turn off the audio recorder and when the interview recommences, continue the interview on the same tapes.

D The officers should leave the audio machine running for the duration of the short break and then continue the interview on the same recording media.

Question 8.4

CROXTON is arrested for an offence of supplying a Class A controlled drug and on arrival in the custody block he requests the presence of his solicitor, Mr JONES. Mr JONES is contacted but tells the custody officer it will be ten hours before he can get to the police station. The arresting officer, DC ROACH, speaks to her duty superintendent who authorises an interview without the presence of Mr JONES on the grounds that to await his arrival would cause an unreasonable delay to the process of the investigation. During the course of this interview, CROXTON's reply to all the questions put to him is, *'No comment'*.

Considering only s. 34 of the Criminal Justice and Public Order Act 1994, what effect will CROXTON's *'No comment'* response have on the case?

A A court could draw an inference from CROXTON's failure to provide an answer to DC ROACH's questions.

B A court will draw no inference unless there is additional evidence produced by the prosecution to prove the case.

C Should a court draw an inference from CROXTON's failure to answer questions, CROXTON can be convicted on that inference alone.

D A court will draw no inference, as CROXTON was not allowed to consult a solicitor prior to being questioned.

Question 8.5

VOWLES makes a statement to the police complaining that THOMAS assaulted him with a knuckle-duster. VOWLES states that during the assault he managed to punch THOMAS on his left cheek. The next day, DCs STOKOE and McCROW visit THOMAS's home address and arrest him for a s. 20 grievous bodily harm (contrary to the Offences Against the Person Act 1861) on VOWLES. On his arrest, DC STOKOE notices that THOMAS has a large bruise on his left cheekbone. During the arrest, DC McCROW seizes a knuckle-duster from THOMAS's living room. In interview, THOMAS tells DC STOKOE that he got the bruised cheekbone playing football the previous day but refuses to answer any questions relating to the knuckle-duster. DC STOKOE believes that THOMAS's bruised cheekbone and the knuckle-duster are attributable to THOMAS taking part in the offence.

Considering only s. 36 of the Criminal Justice and Public Order Act 1994, which, if any, of the following would DC STOKOE be able to give THOMAS a special warning for?

A THOMAS's bruised cheekbone.

B The knuckle-duster recovered at THOMAS's home address.

C THOMAS's bruised cheekbone and the knuckle-duster recovered at THOMAS's home address.

D Special warnings are not applicable for either the bruised cheekbone or the knuckle-duster.

Question 8.6

DCs KENT and TORBIN are interviewing SPONDEN in respect of an arson offence and associated offences of witness intimidation. The interview is being audio-recorded. SPONDEN is a particularly violent suspect and has a history of violent behaviour towards witnesses and also towards police officers. DC KENT believes that if she discloses her name during the course of interviewing SPONDEN it will put her in danger; DC TORBIN believes that if he discloses his name during the course of interviewing SPONDEN it will put his family in danger.

Considering Code E of the Codes of Practice, which of the following statements is correct?

A Both officers must provide their names in the interview as the case does not involve enquiries into the investigation of terrorism.

B DC KENT may use her warrant number and police station as a means of identification in interview; DC TORBIN must use his name.

C DC TORBIN may use his warrant number as a means of identification; DC KENT must use her name.

D Both officers may withhold their names and use their warrant numbers and police stations as a means of identification.

Question 8.7

DC ENGLISH and TI JONES are in the process of interviewing HAY on audio recording media regarding an offence of burglary. Thirty minutes into the interview, the audio recording machine malfunctions and stops. Despite the interviewing officers' best efforts, the machine cannot be fixed. No other interviewing room or recording facility is available.

According to Code E of the Codes of Practice, what should occur?

A The interview must be suspended until an appropriate interviewing room or device becomes available.

B The interview may be continued without being audio-recorded but the officers will need to seek the authority of an officer of the rank of inspector or above to do so.

C The interview may be continued without being audio-recorded but the officers will need to seek the authority of the custody officer to do so.

D The interview may be continued without being audio-recorded. No particular authority is required in such a situation.

Question 8.8

DC MORRIN (who has 10 years' police service) and TI EDMOND (who has 12 years' police service) are interviewing YOUNG about an allegation of fraud. At the conclusion of the interview DC MORRIN seals the master recording of the interview, signs the master recording label and asks YOUNG to sign the label. YOUNG refuses to do so.

Which of the following comments is correct in such a situation?

A The senior police officer in the interview (TI EDMOND) should sign the label to the effect that YOUNG would not sign the seal.

B Either DC MORRIN or TI EDMOND can sign the label to the effect that YOUNG would not sign the seal.

C The custody officer should be called into the interview room and he/she should sign the label.

D An officer of the rank of inspector or above should be called into the interview room and sign the label.

Question 8.9

TI DIOLA is the officer in charge of an investigation into a series of burglaries. The suspect, BOURNE, was interviewed on audio recording media and released on bail. A record of the interview with BOURNE is required for the court file but the working copy of the audio recording media is accidentally destroyed. The only remaining audio recording media is the master recording which has been sealed according to the rules governing such matters. TI DIOLA needs to access the master recording to create a record of the interview.

Can TI DIOLA break the seal on the master recording?

A Yes, but this can only be done with the authority of an officer of the rank of superintendent or above.

B No, unless TI DIOLA arranges for the seal to be broken in the presence of a representative of the Crown Prosecution Service.

C Yes, but the seal must be broken in a magistrates' court.

D No, unless TI DIOLA obtains an authorisation from the Crown Court.

Question 8.10

DUCLIN has been arrested for an offence of rape and is in his cell awaiting interview. DCs HUTTON and PAGE tell the custody officer they are ready to interview DUCLIN but when the custody officer assistant attempts to get DUCLIN out of his cell, he refuses to attend and shouts that he will not leave his cell. DUCLIN is spoken to by the custody officer but continues to refuse to leave his cell.

Could DUCLIN be interviewed in his cell?

A Yes, as long as the custody office considers, on reasonable grounds, that the interview should not be delayed the interview can be conducted in DUCLIN's cell using portable recording equipment.

B No, interviews must not take place in cells.

C Yes, if an officer of the rank of inspector or above believes that it will cause an unreasonable delay to act otherwise, the interview can be recorded using portable recording equipment.

D No, because of the seriousness of the allegation (an offence of rape) the interview must be conducted in an interview room.

Question 8.11

DC NUMAN is working on an enquiry into the activities of PROSSER who is suspected of working for an organised crime syndicate as an 'enforcer'. PROSSER is arrested for several offences of s. 18 grievous bodily harm/wounding and DC NUMAN is asked to take part in the visually recorded interview of PROSSER. Due to certain elements of DC NUMAN's personal life, the officer reasonably believes that to provide his name during the course of the interview would put him in danger.

Considering the guidance provided by Code F of the Codes of Practice on such matters, which of the following comments is correct?

A The interview should take place as normal but DC NUMAN should only provide his warrant number (instead of his name).

B As DC NUMAN would be recognised in a visually recorded interview, he cannot take part in it.

C If an officer of the rank of at least inspector certifies that it is necessary for the officer's safety, DC NUMAN should give his warrant number (instead of his name) and also state the police station to which he is attached.

D DC NUMAN can take part in the interview but should have his back to the camera and give his warrant number (not his name) and the name of the police station to which he is attached.

Question 8.12

DC BOLTON has arrested PIKE (who is 19 years old and profoundly deaf) and DAPSON (who is 15 years old) for an offence of robbery. PIKE and DAPSON are taken to a custody block where an interpreter is called out for PIKE and an appropriate adult called for DAPSON. Several interview rooms in the custody block have the ability to visually record interviews with suspects; there are also interview rooms in the custody block that only record sound.

Considering Code F of the Codes of Practice, which of the following statements is correct?

A DC BOLTON must interview PIKE using a visual recording interview room; it does not matter what type of interview recording is used for DAPSON.

B DAPSON must be interviewed in a visual recording interview room; it does not matter what type of interview recording is used for PIKE.

C As PIKE is deaf and DAPSON is a juvenile, Code F states that both suspects must be interviewed in a visual recording interview room if one is available.

D There is no requirement for either suspect to be interviewed in a visual recording interview room.

Question 8.13

PRIEST has been arrested in connection with an offence of rape and is being interviewed by DCs ROWLEY and SKILLEN. The officers decide to give PRIEST a special warning under s. 36 of the Criminal Justice and Public Order Act 1994.

Which of the following is correct with regard to the delivery of the special warning?

A PRIEST does not need to be told what offence is being investigated.

B PRIEST does not need to be told what fact he is being asked to account for.

C PRIEST does not need to be told that a record is being made of the interview and that it may be given in evidence at any subsequent trial.

D PRIEST does not need to be cautioned at the conclusion of the special warning.

Question 8.14

SIMPSON is a civilian authorised investigating officer and is dealing with TAYLOR for offences of burglary of a building; TAYLOR has been stealing power tools and lawn mowers from garden sheds. SIMPSON will be interviewing TAYLOR on her own. From the file it is evident that if TAYLOR fails to answer certain questions there would be a potential to give him a special warning (under s. 36 of the Criminal Justice and Public Order Act 1994).

With regard to authorised investigators, which of the following statements is correct in relation to SIMPSON's powers to give a special warning in an interview?

A Civilian investigators cannot give a special warning.

B Civilian investigators can only give a special warning if they interview a suspect in the company of a police officer.

C Civilian investigators can give a special warning, but need a police officer to warn the suspect of the inference a court may draw from their silence.

D Civilian investigators can give a special warning and also warn the suspect of the inference a court may draw from their silence.

ANSWERS

Answer 8.1

Answer **A** — Code C, para. 11.16 states that a juvenile can be interviewed at his/her place of education in exceptional circumstances and with the agreement of the principal or the principal's nominee, making answer B incorrect. The parents of the juvenile should be notified and allowed a reasonable time to attend unless waiting for the appropriate adult would cause an unreasonable delay in which case the principal or his/her nominee can act as an appropriate adult, making answer C incorrect. However, if the juvenile is suspected of an offence against the educational establishment then the principal or his/her nominee cannot act as an appropriate adult, making answer D incorrect.

Investigators' Manual, para. 1.9.3.2

Answer 8.2

Answer **D** — Code C, para. 11.4A states that a significant statement is one that appears capable of being used in evidence against the suspect, in particular a direct admission of guilt, making answer B incorrect. FLATMAN's comment to HARLOWE would appear to be a significant statement on that basis. However, para. 11.4 states that a significant statement is a statement that occurred in the presence and hearing of a police officer or a civilian interviewer before the start of the interview and this is not the case with the comment made to a civilian witness. Therefore, the comment is not a significant statement, making answers A and C incorrect. Answer C is further incorrect as a significant statement should be put to the suspect at the beginning of the interview after caution.

Investigators' Manual, para. 1.9.3

Answer 8.3

Answer **C** — Code E, para. 4.13 allows for short breaks to be taken during an audio-recorded interview, making answer A incorrect. This paragraph states that if the break is to be a short one and both the suspect and the interviewer are to remain in the room, then the audio-recorder may be turned off. There is no need to remove the tapes and when the interview recommences the tape recording should continue on the same tapes, making answers B and D incorrect.

Investigators' Manual, para. 1.9.10

Answer 8.4

Answer **D** — Section 34(2A) states that if the defendant has not been allowed an opportunity to consult a solicitor prior to being questioned then no inference will be drawn by the court on the defendant's silence, refusal or failure to give an account. This section was introduced because of the judgment of the European Court of Human Rights in the case of *Murray* v *United Kingdom* (1996) 22 EHRR 29. The court held that inferences being drawn from the silence of the accused when denied access to legal advice constituted a breach of Article 6(1) in conjunction with Article 6(3) of the European Convention on Human Rights (right to a fair trial).

Investigators' Manual, para. 1.9.2.3

Answer 8.5

Answer **B** — Special warnings under s. 36 of the Act are applicable if a person is arrested by a constable and there is (i) on his person, or (ii) in or on his clothing or footwear, or (iii) otherwise in his possession or (iv) in any place in which he is at the time of his arrest, any object, substance or mark, or there is any mark on any such object which the officer reasonably believes may be attributable to the participation of the arrested person in the commission of an offence. This would mean that both the bruised cheekbone (a mark on the person) and the knuckle-duster (an object in any place in which the person is at the time of the arrest) could form part of a special warning. However, the special warning should only be given if the defendant fails or refuses to account for the fact. THOMAS has answered the question relating to the bruised cheekbone, making answers A and C incorrect. He refuses to answer questions relating to the knuckle-duster and so a special warning may be given regarding this item, making answer D incorrect.

Investigators' Manual, paras 1.9.2.4, 1.9.2.5

Answer 8.6

Answer **B** — Nothing in Code E requires the identity of officers or police staff conducting interviews to be recorded or disclosed:

(a) in the case of enquiries linked to the investigation of terrorism; or
(b) if the interviewer reasonably believes recording or disclosing their name might put them in danger.

In these cases interviewers should use warrant or other identification numbers and the name of their police station.

Therefore, answer A is incorrect as it is not only in terrorism cases where this facility exists. Answers C and D are incorrect as DC TORBIN believes disclosing his name will put his family *and not him* in danger. Answer C is additionally incorrect as identification must be a warrant number *and* the individual's police station.

Investigators' Manual, para. 1.9.7

Answer 8.7

Answer **C** — Where there is a failure of the recording media and it is not possible to continue recording on that recorder and no replacement recorder is readily available, the interview may continue without being audio-recorded (making answer A incorrect). Should this occur, authority to continue the interview without it being audio-recorded is required from the custody officer (making answers B and D incorrect).

Investigators' Manual, para. 1.9.9.4

Answer 8.8

Answer **D** — Answers A, B and C are incorrect as if a suspect or a third party present during the interview refuses to sign the master recording label an officer of at least inspector rank, or if not available the custody officer, shall be called into the interview room and asked (subject to para. 2.3 of Code E) to sign it.

Investigators' Manual, para. 1.9.9

Answer 8.9

Answer **B** — No actual 'authorisation' is required to break the seal on a master recording, making answers A and D incorrect. There are also no rules as to where the seal should be broken, making answer C incorrect. However, if the seal is to be broken it must be broken in the presence of a representative of the Crown Prosecution Service.

Investigators' Manual, para. 1.9.9

Answer 8.10

Answer **A** — Interviews can take place in cells, making answer B incorrect. This is the case regardless of the seriousness of the offence the suspect is to be interviewed for, making answer D incorrect. The decision as to whether this takes place is at the discretion of the custody officer, making answer C incorrect. Such an interview can take place if the custody officer considers, on reasonable grounds, that the interview should not be delayed. It can be conducted using portable recording equipment or, if none is available, recorded in writing (Code E, para. 3.4).

Investigators' Manual, para. 1.9.8

Answer 8.11

Answer **D** — Code F, para. 2.5 states that nothing in the Code requires the identity of the officer to be recorded or disclosed if the interview or record relates to a person detained under the Terrorism Act 2000 or otherwise where the officer reasonably believes that recording or disclosing their name might put them in danger. In these cases, the officer will have their back to the camera and shall use their warrant number or other identification number and the name of the police station to which they are attached.

Investigators' Manual, para. 1.9.13

Answer 8.12

Answer **D** — Code F does not enforce the use of visually recorded interviews but offers advice on when such use '*might be appropriate*'. Two examples are where the interview is with a deaf person or with anyone who requires the presence of an 'appropriate adult'.

Investigators' Manual, para. 1.9.13

Answer 8.13

Answer **D** — Answers A, B and C are all incorrect as all of these are requirements when delivering a special warning to a suspect. Answer D is correct, as the suspect *does not have* to be cautioned at the conclusion of the special warning.

Investigators' Manual, para. 1.9.2.4

Answer 8.14

Answer **D** — An authorised civilian investigator is allowed to question an arrested person under ss. 36 and 37 of the Criminal Justice and Public Order Act 1994 about facts which may be attributable to the person's participation in an offence. The designated person may also give the suspect the necessary warning about the capacity of a court to draw inferences from a failure to give a satisfactory account in response to questioning.

Investigators' Manual, para. 1.7.3.1

9 Release of Person Arrested

QUESTIONS

Question 9.1

LOVETT has a previous conviction for attempted rape for which he served three years' imprisonment. LOVETT is arrested and charged in connection with a s. 18 wounding.

Considering the bail restrictions under s. 25 of the Criminal Justice and Public Order Act 1994, which of the following statements is correct?

A This section only applies to defendants who have a previous conviction for murder, attempted murder or manslaughter and would not affect the granting of bail for LOVETT.

B A previous conviction for attempted rape is covered by this section, as is the charge of s. 18 wounding; bail should only be granted to LOVETT if there are exceptional circumstances which justify it.

C This section only applies to defendants if they have previously been convicted by or before a court in the United Kingdom of culpable homicide and so LOVETT's previous conviction will not affect the granting of bail.

D Although LOVETT's previous conviction for attempted rape is relevant, a s. 18 wounding is not and so will not alter the decision to grant bail.

Question 9.2

DC WRAGG arrests SYMONS for three robberies and tells the custody officer that SYMONS has carried out the offences with PARTINGTON who has yet to be arrested. The custody officer asks for SYMONS's name and address to which SYMONS replies, '*I'll never say.*' DC WRAGG tells the custody officer that SYMONS has failed to answer bail on two previous occasions. Several hours later SYMONS is charged with the offences of robbery although DC WRAGG still has some further enquiries to make regarding the offences. The issue of bail is now being considered.

For which one of the following reasons could the custody officer refuse to bail SYMONS?

A SYMONS has failed to comply with s. 38(1) of the Police and Criminal Evidence Act 1984 as he has refused to provide his name and address.

B If released, SYMONS will interfere with the administration of justice, as the police have still to arrest PARTINGTON.

C There is a risk that SYMONS will abscond and this is evidenced by his previous failure to answer bail.

D SYMONS will interfere with the administration of justice because there are still further enquiries to make regarding the offences.

Question 9.3

You are the officer in charge of a case involving MOUNTFORD. You arrested MOUNTFORD for a fraud-related offence and charged him at your police station. MOUNTFORD was bailed to appear at your local magistrates' court and the custody officer at the time of his charging, PS GLEDHILL, granted bail on the condition that MOUNTFORD would report to your police station on a daily basis at 18.00 hrs. MOUNTFORD contacts you and asks if it is possible for his bail conditions to be modified as he has injured his leg and will have difficulty getting to the police station every day at the appointed time.

What will you tell MOUNTFORD?

A MOUNTFORD should make the request to any custody officer at your police station.

B Once bail conditions have been imposed, only a magistrates' court can alter them.

C Only PS GLEDHILL can alter the bail conditions.

D MOUNTFORD can make his request to any custody officer serving at any police station in your force.

Question 9.4

BOON is arrested for burglary. The custody officer decides to give him bail on the condition that he obtains a surety to secure his surrender to custody. BOON suggests that his cousin, MAGEE, will stand as a surety. MAGEE is contacted by the police for this purpose.

Which of the following statements is true?

A MAGEE would have a liability if BOON committed any further offences or interfered with witnesses whilst on bail.

B MAGEE cannot be a surety for BOON because they are related to each other.

C MAGEE would be required to forfeit the entire sum in which he stood surety.

D In order for MAGEE to forfeit the sum in which he stood surety, it would be necessary to prove that he had some involvement in BOON's non-appearance.

Question 9.5

You have arrested MILBURN (aged 13 years) on suspicion of burglary. During interview, MILBURN tells you that he has committed at least 30 other burglaries and wants to confess to them. You are considering charging MILBURN with the burglary that he has been arrested for and requesting a remand in police custody under s. 128 of the Magistrates' Courts Act 1980 with a view to interviewing MILBURN for the other 30 offences.

Will such a request be successful?

A Yes, the court can remand MILBURN into local authority accommodation for a period not exceeding three days.

B No, such a remand can only be given if MILBURN has attained the age of 15 and the offences are of a violent or sexual nature.

C Yes, MILBURN may be remanded to police custody for a period not exceeding 24 hours.

D No, such a remand may only be sought if its purpose is to make enquiries into the offence for which MILBURN has been charged.

Question 9.6

Sergeant ANDERSON is acting as a custody officer and is considering granting bail to FRAZER. It appears necessary to impose bail conditions on FRAZER in order to prevent him from failing to surrender to custody and to prevent him committing an offence whilst on bail.

Which of the following conditions would Sergeant ANDERSON be unable to impose on FRAZER?

A A requirement that FRAZER resides in a bail hostel or probation hostel.

B A requirement that FRAZER surrenders his passport.

C A requirement restricting FRAZER from entering a certain area or building or to go within a specified distance of a specified address.

D A requirement that FRAZER provides a surety or security.

Question 9.7

PC CROWTHER arrests JONES in relation to a minor offence of theft and decides to grant JONES 'street bail' (as per s. 30A of the Police and Criminal Evidence Act 1984).

In relation to the granting of bail in these circumstances, which of the following statements is correct?

A 'Street bail' granted in such circumstances will normally be for a period of 28 days from the day after arrest.

B PC CROWTHER may require JONES to provide a surety in order to ensure that he surrenders himself at a police station.

C PC CROWTHER may grant JONES 'street bail' but only after she has obtained permission to do so from a custody officer serving within the relevant area in which JONES was arrested.

D PC CROWTHER may grant JONES 'street bail' but cannot attach any conditions to such bail.

Question 9.8

EBBY was arrested and charged with an offence of theft and bailed (without conditions) to appear back at the same police station to enable further enquiries to be made in respect of the offence. Due to an administrative error, the custody officer forgot to provide EBBY with a copy of the record of the decision to bail him. Several weeks later, EBBY is at home thinking that he has to attend the police station the following morning then suddenly remembers that he was supposed to attend the police station that morning—when he looks at his watch, he sees he is three hours late. He drives to the police station but on the way decides to have a couple of drinks at his local pub as he thinks it does not matter now that he is already late. EBBY stays in the pub for two hours and then attends the police station.

Considering the offence of absconding (contrary to s. 6 of the Bail Act 1976), which of the following statements is correct?

A No offence has been committed by EBBY as the custody officer failed to provide him with a record of the decision to bail him.

B EBBY has committed the offence which, in this form, is a summary-only offence.

C No offence has been committed by EBBY as the offence does not apply to bail granted to a suspect to appear at a police station.

D EBBY would have a reasonable excuse for committing the offence as he was mistaken about the day on which he should have appeared.

Question 9.9

PERCIVAL has been arrested for an offence of robbery. There are numerous enquiries to make in relation to the case and the custody officer, PS ADAMS, has determined that there is insufficient evidence to charge PERCIVAL with the offence. PS ADAMS is satisfied that it is necessary and proportionate to bail PERCIVAL under s. 47(3)(c) of the Police and Criminal Evidence Act 1984.

Considering the law in respect of pre-conditions for bail and limits on the period of bail without charge, which of the following comments is correct?

A PS ADAMS (as the custody officer) authorises PERCIVAL's release on bail; the 'applicable bail period' will be the period of 7 days beginning with the person's bail start date.

B An officer of the rank of inspector or above authorises PERCIVAL's release on bail; the 'applicable bail period' will be the period of 14 days beginning with the person's bail start date.

C An officer of the rank of inspector or above authorises PERCIVAL's release on bail; the 'applicable bail period' will be the period of 28 days beginning with the person's bail start date.

D An officer of the rank of superintendent or above authorises PERCIVAL's release on bail; the 'applicable bail period' will be the period of 3 months beginning with the person's bail start date.

Question 9.10

The amendments to the Police and Criminal Evidence Act 1984 brought about by the Policing and Crime Act 2017 include a regime of time limits and extensions introduced in respect of pre-charge bail.

With regard to those time limits, which of the following statements is correct?

A The 'applicable bail period', in relation to a person, means in a Serious Fraud Office (SFO) case, the period of three months beginning with the person's bail start date; that 'bail start date' will commence on the day the person was arrested for the relevant offence.

B The 'applicable bail period', in relation to a person, means in a Serious Fraud Office (SFO) case, the period of three months beginning with the person's bail start date; that 'bail start date' will commence on the day after the day on which the person was arrested for the relevant offence.

C The 'applicable bail period', in relation to a person, means in a Serious Fraud Office (SFO) case, the period of six months beginning with the person's bail start date; that 'bail start date' will commence on the day the person was arrested for the relevant offence.

D The 'applicable bail period', in relation to a person, means in a Serious Fraud Office (SFO) case, the period of six months beginning with the person's bail start date; that 'bail start date' will commence on the day after the day on which the person was arrested for the relevant offence.

Question 9.11

DC EWART is dealing with CROTHER in relation to a complex fraud offence involving numerous lines of enquiry. CROTHER was bailed from the police station under s. 47(3) (c) of the Police and Criminal Evidence Act 1984 in order to allow further enquiries and investigation to be made in relation to the case. Even though DC EWART has been pursuing the investigation diligently and expeditiously, it is obvious that far more work needs to be carried out. DC EWART speaks to Superintendent MAXWELL about the case and asks about the possibility of extending CROTHER's bail period.

Could Superintendent MAXWELL extend CROTHER's bail period?

A Yes, as an officer of the rank of superintendent or above could authorise an extension of CROTHER's bail from 28 days to 3 months if the correct conditions are met.

B Yes, as an officer of the rank of superintendent or above could authorise an extension of CROTHER's bail from 28 days to 6 months if the correct conditions are met.

C No, only an officer of the rank of assistant chief constable (or Commander in the Metropolitan or City of London forces) could extend CROTHER's bail period.

D No, only a magistrates' court could extend CROTHER's bail period.

Question 9.12

In certain exceptional circumstances it is possible to extend the period of pre-charge bail to a period of six months where certain conditions have been met and the case has been designated as 'exceptionally complex' by a designated senior prosecutor from the DPP.

In such circumstances, who would authorise the applicable bail period to be extended so that it ends at the end of the period of six months beginning with the person's bail start date?

A An officer of the rank of superintendent or above.

B An officer of the rank of assistant chief constable (Commander in the Metropolitan or City of London Forces) or above.

C An officer of the rank of chief constable (or Commissioner in the Metropolitan or City of London forces).

D The designated senior prosecutor from the DPP.

Question 9.13

LEER has been arrested in respect of an offence of burglary. The pre-conditions relating to bailing LEER are satisfied but LEER is also on bail for another separate offence of theft. Bail for the theft offence was granted one week ago. It is suggested that it would be appropriate to align LEER's attendance in relation to both offences.

Which of the statements below is correct in relation to this suggestion?

A This cannot be done as the bail dates must remain separate.

B This can be done but only if LEER provides his written consent to such an alignment.

C This cannot be done as the offences LEER is bailed in respect of are not serious fraud offences.

D This can be done if the custody officer believes that a decision as to whether to charge LEER with the burglary offence would be made before the end of the applicable bail period in relation to the person.

Question 9.14

CAVANAGH, DAVEY and JONES have all been arrested and charged with an offence of rape (contrary to s. 1 of the Sexual Offences Act 2003). CAVANAGH has a previous conviction for attempted murder, DAVEY has a previous conviction for a s. 18 wounding and JONES has a previous conviction for an offence of assault by penetration (contrary to s. 2 of the Sexual Offences Act 2003). The custody officer, PS PARDOE, is considering the issue of bail.

Considering s. 25 of the Criminal Justice and Public Order Act 1994 only, who could be granted bail (there are no exceptional circumstances relating to any of the detainees)?

A Only JONES could be granted bail.

B Only DAVEY could be granted bail.

C DAVEY and JONES could be granted bail.

D CAVANAGH, DAVEY and JONES could be granted bail.

Question 9.15

WILSON is standing surety of £5,000 to secure the attendance on bail to the court of JONES for offences of burglary. WILSON has found out from a friend that JONES is making plans to leave the area and will not attend court. WILSON believes that JONES will not appear and wishes to relinquish his surety for securing JONES's attendance.

To comply with the Bail Act 1976, as he believes JONES will not attend court, which of the following is correct in order that WILSON can be relieved of his obligation as a surety?

A WILSON must attend the police station where bail was granted and inform any custody sergeant of his wish to be removed as a surety.

B WILSON must attend the police station where bail was granted and inform any constable of his wish to be removed as a surety.

C WILSON must notify a constable in writing that JONES is unlikely to surrender to custody and for that reason he wishes to be relieved of his obligations as a surety.

D WILSON must notify the custody sergeant (in writing) who granted bail to JONES that JONES is unlikely to surrender to custody and for that reason he wishes to be relieved of his obligations as a surety.

Question 9.16

MONROE is being investigated for child sexual offences. MONROE has been interviewed about some of the offences that are known but there is further investigation needed before a decision to charge can be made. DC HARRIS wants the bail to be extended from the initial period of 28 days to three months owing to the complexities of the case.

If all the conditions required are met, what is the rank of the officer that can authorise this extension?

A An officer of superintendent rank or above.

B An officer of the rank of chief inspector or above who is not involved in the case.

C An officer of the rank of inspector or above.

D An officer of the rank of inspector or above who is not involved in the case.

ANSWERS

Answer 9.1

Answer **D** — Section 25 of the Criminal Justice and Public Order Act 1994 states that bail will only be granted to a defendant who is affected by it in the most exceptional circumstances. A defendant will be subject to this section if he/she has a previous conviction for murder, attempted murder, manslaughter, rape or attempted rape; this makes answers A and C incorrect. LOVETT's previous conviction for attempted rape is, therefore, relevant. However, the defendant must not only have a previous conviction for one of the stated offences but also be charged with one of those offences. LOVETT is charged with a s. 18 wounding which is not covered by the legislation; this makes answer B incorrect.

Investigators' Manual, para. 1.10.5

Answer 9.2

Answer **C** — The fact that SYMONS refuses to give his name and address does not satisfy the grounds on which bail can be refused under s. 38 of the Police and Criminal Evidence Act 1984; this is only so if the name and address *cannot be ascertained*, making answer A incorrect. Although refusing bail on the grounds that the defendant will interfere with the administration of justice is a reason for refusing bail, this ground would not apply for the purposes of the police making further enquiries or where other suspects are still to be arrested, making answers B and D incorrect.

Investigators' Manual, para. 1.10.6

Answer 9.3

Answer **A** — Section 3A of the Bail Act 1976 applies to bail granted by a custody officer and amends s. 3 of the Act. Section 3A(4) states that where a custody officer has granted bail in criminal proceedings *he or another* custody officer serving *at the same police station* may, at the request of the person to whom it was granted, vary the conditions of bail and in doing so he may impose conditions or more onerous conditions.

Investigators' Manual, para. 1.10.7.3

Answer 9.4

Answer **C** — A surety has no responsibility or liability should the defendant commit further offences or interfere with witnesses whilst on bail, making answer A incorrect. The decision as to whether a surety is suitable rests with the custody officer. The fact that there is a relationship between the two is a consideration but not a bar, making answer B incorrect. It is not necessary to prove that the surety has any involvement in the defendant's non-appearance (*R* v *Warwick Crown Court, ex parte Smalley* [1987] 1 WLR 237), making answer D incorrect.

Investigators' Manual, para. 1.10.7.4

Answer 9.5

Answer **C** — Section 128 of the Magistrates' Courts Act 1980 provides that a magistrates' court may remand a person to *police custody* for a period not exceeding three days (*24 hours for a person under 18*) for the purposes of enquiries into other offences (*other than the offence for which he/she appears before a court*).

Investigators' Manual, para. 1.10.11

Answer 9.6

Answer **A** — Section 3A of the Bail Act 1976 applies to bail granted specifically by a custody officer. Section 3A(5) provides for the occasions when a custody officer can consider imposing bail conditions. Answers B, C and D are all conditions that can be imposed. However, there is no authority under s. 3A to bail a defendant to a bail hostel or a probation hostel as this has been omitted from this part of the Act.

Investigators' Manual, paras 1.10.7.1, 1.10.7.2

Answer 9.7

Answer **A** — Section 30A(3A)(c) states that where a constable releases a person on 'street bail', the person shall not be required to provide a surety or sureties for his/her surrender to custody, making answer B incorrect. Answer C is incorrect as the authority of an officer of the rank of inspector or above is required to grant 'street bail'. Answer D is incorrect as s. 30A(3B) states that a constable may impose conditions when granting 'street bail'. A written bail notice must be given to the person bailed. The notice must, in addition to the existing requirements, set out the date, time and place at which bail must be answered. The date is required to be 28 days from the day after arrest (correct answer A).

Investigators' Manual, para. 1.10.2

Answer 9.8

Answer **B** — Section 6 applies where:

- the police grant bail to a suspect to appear at the police station (making answer C incorrect);
- the police grant bail to a defendant to appear at court on the first appearance;
- the court grants bail to the defendant to return to court at a later date.

The burden of proof in relation to showing 'reasonable cause' (s. 6(1)) is a matter for the accused (s. 6(3)). A person who has 'reasonable cause' still commits the offence if he/she fails to surrender 'as soon after the appointed time as is reasonably practicable'. Where an accused was half an hour late in appearing at court it was held that he/she had absconded (*R* v *Scott* [2007] EWCA Crim 2757). In *Laidlaw* v *Atkinson* (1986) The Times, 2 August, it was held that being mistaken about the day on which one should have appeared was not a reasonable excuse (making answer D incorrect). Failure to give to a person granted bail in criminal proceedings a copy of the record of the decision does not constitute reasonable cause for that person's failure to surrender to custody (s. 6(4)), making answer A incorrect. The offence in this form is a summary offence and the decision to initiate proceedings is for the police/prosecutor using the written charge and requisition procedure (answer B).

Investigators' Manual, para. 1.10.10

Answer 9.9

Answer **C** — There is an array of MCQ possibilities from the question writer's perspective regarding time limits and authorisation levels. It is exceptionally important in the practical world of policing and so it is very reasonable to expect questions may focus on this area in your exam. In this question the answer is C. The preconditions of bail are, under s. 50A of the Police and Criminal Evidence Act 1984:

(a) that the custody officer is satisfied that releasing the person on bail is necessary and proportionate in all the circumstances (having regard, in particular, to any conditions of bail which would be imposed), and

(b) that an officer of the *rank of inspector or above* authorises the release on bail (having considered any representations made by the person or the person's legal representative).

So straight away answers A and D are incorrect—the officer authorising a release on bail in these circumstances is an officer of the rank of inspector or above.

When the custody officer is releasing a person on bail to attend at a police station under s. 47(3)(c), he or she must appoint a time on the day on which the 'applicable bail period' in relation to the person ends (s. 47ZA(1) and (2)). The 'applicable bail period', in relation to a person, means in a Serious Fraud Office (SFO) case, the period of three months beginning with the person's bail start date, or in a Financial Conduct Authority (FCA) case or any other case, *the period of 28 days beginning with the person's bail start date.* A person's bail start date is the day after the day on which the person was arrested for the relevant offence (s. 47ZB). So the 'applicable bail period' will be the period of 28 days beginning with the person's bail start date, making answer B incorrect and answer C correct.

Investigators' Manual, paras 1.10.3.1, 1.10.3.2

Answer 9.10

Answer **B** — A person's bail start date is the day after the day on which the person was arrested for the relevant offence (s. 47ZB). This makes answers A and C incorrect. The 'applicable bail period', in relation to a person, means in a Serious Fraud Office (SFO) case, the period of *three months* beginning with the person's bail start date, making answer D incorrect.

Investigators' Manual, para. 1.10.3.2

Answer 9.11

Answer **A** — Answers B, C and D are incorrect as s. 47ZD allows a senior police officer (an officer of superintendent rank or above (s. 47ZB(4)(d)) to extend bail from 28 days to three months where the conditions A to D set out in s. 47ZC are met. The senior officer must arrange for the suspect or their legal representative to be invited to make representations, and must consider any that are made before making a decision. The suspect (or their representative) must be informed of the outcome. The four conditions outlined in s. 47ZC are:

Condition A—the officer has reasonable grounds for suspecting the person in question to be guilty of the relevant offence.

Condition B—the officer has reasonable grounds for believing:

(a) in a case where the person in question is or is to be released on bail under s. 37(7)(c) or 37CA(2)(b), that further time is needed for making a decision as to whether to charge the person with the relevant offence, or
(b) otherwise, that further investigation is needed of any matter in connection with the relevant offence.

Condition C—the officer has reasonable grounds for believing:

(a) in a case where the person in question is or is to be released on bail under s. 37(7)(c) or 37CA(2)(b), that the decision as to whether to charge the person with the relevant offence is being made diligently and expeditiously, or
(b) otherwise, that the investigation is being conducted diligently and expeditiously.

Condition D—the decision-maker has reasonable grounds for believing that the release on bail of the person in question is necessary and proportionate in all the circumstances (having regard, in particular, to any conditions of bail which are, or are to be, imposed).

Investigators' Manual, para. 1.10.3.2

Answer 9.12

Answer **B** — Pre-charge bail may be extended to a point six months after arrest if the conditions A to D of s. 47ZC are met where a case has been designated as 'exceptionally complex' by a senior prosecutor designated for the purpose by the Director of the SFO, the Chief Executive of the FCA or the DPP. Where so designated by the DPP, a police officer of at least the rank of assistant chief constable (Commander in the Metropolitan or City of London forces), may authorise the applicable bail period in relation to the person to be extended so that it ends at the end of the period of six months beginning with the person's bail start date (s. 47ZE).

Investigators' Manual, para. 1.10.3.2

Answer 9.13

Answer **D** — The applicable bail period may be changed by the custody officer where the person is on bail in relation to one or more offences other than the relevant offence and it is appropriate to align the person's attendance in relation to the relevant offence with the person's attendance in relation to one or more other offences (s. 47ZA(3)). This subsection applies where the custody officer believes that a decision as to whether to charge the person with the relevant offence would be made before the end of the applicable bail period in relation to the person (s. 47ZA(4)). Where subs. (3) or (4) applies, the power may be exercised so as to appoint a time on a day falling before the end of the applicable bail period in relation to the person (s. 47ZA(5)).

Investigators' Manual, para. 1.10.3.2

Answer 9.14

Answer **B** — If a person has been charged with an offence to which s. 25 of the Act applies (and rape under s. 1 of the Sexual Offences Act 2003 is such an offence), they will not be granted bail if they have a previous conviction for certain offences. CAVANAGH (with a previous conviction for attempted murder) and JONES (with a previous conviction for assault by penetration) fall into this category. Section 18 wounding is not relevant to this area of law and so DAVEY *could* be granted bail.

Investigators' Manual, para. 1.10.5

Answer 9.15

Answer **C** — The Bail Act 1976 provides that a surety may notify a constable *in writing* that the accused is unlikely to surrender to custody and for that reason he/she wishes to be relieved of his/her obligations as surety. This written notification provides a constable with the power to arrest the accused without warrant (s. 7(3)).

Investigators' Manual, para. 1.10.7.4

Answer 9.16

Answer **A** — Section 47ZD of PACE 1984 allows a senior officer (an officer of superintendent rank or above (s. 47ZB(4)(d)) to extend bail from 28 days to three months when certain conditions are met.

Investigators' Manual, para. 1.10.3.2

10 Disclosure of Evidence

QUESTIONS

Question 10.1

DC SMART is the OIC in a case involving ELDIN who has been charged with an offence of s. 18 assault. ELDIN's solicitor makes a request for advanced information to help decide whether ELDIN will plead guilty or not guilty. ELDIN's solicitor requests a summary of the prosecution case together with copies of the statements of the proposed prosecution witnesses. DC SMART considers that providing copies of the witness statements might lead to a witness being intimidated.

What course of action should DC SMART take?

A The officer should consult with the CPS as the rules allow the prosecutor to limit disclosure of some or all of the prosecution case.

B The officer must disclose all the material requested by the defence solicitor in order to comply with Article 6 of the European Convention on Human Rights and the Human Rights Act 1998.

C DC SMART need not disclose any statements to the defence at this stage, as they have no entitlement to any material.

D Unless the material undermines the prosecution case, there is no requirement for the statements of witnesses to be disclosed.

Question 10.2

LUNN is arrested and charged with an offence of rape and the case goes to trial. The OIC of the case, DC ATTWOOD, accidentally fails to comply with disclosure rules under the Criminal Procedure and Investigations Act 1996, although there is sufficient credible evidence available which would justify a safe conviction.

Which of the following statements is true with regard to the effect this non-compliance will have on the trial?

A An accidental failure to disclose will not affect the trial and the accused will still have to make defence disclosure to the prosecution.

B A failure to comply with disclosure rules in these circumstances will not automatically mean the trial will be stayed for an abuse of process.

C The prosecution will offer no evidence as otherwise the trial will be stayed on the grounds that there has been an abuse of process.

D The courts are obliged to adjourn the trial in order for the prosecution to make adequate disclosure to the defence.

Question 10.3

BARBER is charged with an offence of murder and is committed to Crown Court for trial.

When should the prosecution make primary disclosure?

A 7 days after BARBER is committed to Crown Court.

B 14 days after BARBER is committed to Crown Court.

C 21 days after BARBER is committed to Crown Court.

D As soon as practicable after the duty arises.

Question 10.4

DS CHRISTIE is overseeing the prosecution of a series of aggravated burglaries committed by KEYWOOD. The operation to arrest KEYWOOD was intelligence-led and KEYWOOD was the subject of numerous intelligence reports eventually leading to his arrest. On arrest, KEYWOOD assaulted DC POULOS, resulting in KEYWOOD being charged with a s. 47 assault against the officer. Due to the amount of material generated in the investigation, DS CHRISTIE decides to appoint a disclosure officer for the case.

Which of the following statements is true with regard to the appointment of a disclosure officer by DS CHRISTIE?

A An unsworn member of support staff would not be allowed to perform this function.

B DS CHRISTIE could appoint DC POULOS as the disclosure officer.

C Generally speaking, there is no restriction on who can perform the role of disclosure officer.

D There can only be one disclosure officer for each case.

Question 10.5

WATTIS has been arrested and charged with an offence of rape. You are the officer in charge of the case and have the assistance of PC SMEDLEY who is acting as the disclosure officer. PC SMEDLEY approaches you and asks your advice regarding the disclosure of material that may be relevant to the investigation.

Which of the comments is correct in respect of relevant material?

A A draft version of a witness statement where the content of the draft version differs from the final version of the statement would not be classed as relevant material.

B A written record of an interview with a potential witness would not be classed as relevant material.

C The identity of a potential witness to the arrest of WATTIS would not be classed as relevant material.

D The fact that house-to-house enquiries were made and that no one witnessed anything would not be classed as relevant material.

Question 10.6

DCs MIDDLEMORE and KHOJA receive information that HENLEY is dealing in drugs outside a school. The officers drive to the school in an unmarked police vehicle and park near the front gates where they can observe HENLEY. The officers witness HENLEY dealing drugs and arrest him for supplying a controlled drug. HENLEY is charged and the case goes to trial. During the trial the defence apply to cross-examine the officers on the location of their observations in order to test what they could see. This includes the colour, make and model of the vehicle the officers used.

Considering the ruling in *R* v *Johnson*, will the prosecution be able to withhold this information?

A Yes, the court will follow the ruling in *R* v *Johnson* which states that the exact location of the observations need not be revealed.

B No, the ruling in *R* v *Johnson* is based on the protection of the owner or occupier of premises and would not apply in this case.

C Yes, although the prosecution will have to supply details of the location of the vehicle.

D No, under no circumstances can the location of observation posts be withheld from the defence.

Question 10.7

HOOD is being prosecuted for an offence of s. 18 wounding (contrary to the Offences Against the Person Act 1861) (an indictable only offence). The prosecution make primary disclosure to HOOD's defence team who, in line with s. 5 of the Criminal Procedure and Investigations Act 1996, must now provide a defence statement to the court and the prosecutor.

Although the courts can extend the period, within what time period must HOOD's defence team normally provide the defence statement?

A Within 7 days of the prosecution making primary disclosure.
B Within 14 days of the prosecution making primary disclosure.
C Within 21 days of the prosecution making primary disclosure.
D Within 28 days of the prosecution making primary disclosure.

Question 10.8

LEXINGTON is convicted of an offence of theft and is sentenced to three months' imprisonment for the offence; he is released after having served one month of the sentence.

For how long should material relating to this case be retained?

A Until LEXINGTON is released from his custodial sentence.
B Three months from the date of LEXINGTON's conviction for theft.
C Six months from the date of LEXINGTON's conviction for theft.
D Twelve months from the date of LEXINGTON's conviction for theft.

Question 10.9

DC REWSON is the disclosure officer in a case of s. 20 wounding (contrary to the Offences Against the Person Act 1861) where the offender is alleged to have passed the HIV virus to a sexual partner. DC REWSON is aware that a nearby hospital and a local GP both have records regarding the medical condition of the defendant that are relevant to the prosecution case. DC REWSON reasonably considers that this material might be capable of undermining the prosecution case.

Which of the following comments is correct in respect of this material?

A DC REWSON should seek access to the material at the hospital and from the GP but if access is refused there is nothing further that can be done.
B DC REWSON will be able to access the material held by the hospital but would not be able to access material held by the GP in any circumstances.

C Should the hospital or GP refuse access to the material and DC REWSON believes it is still reasonable to seek its production then the prosecutor should apply for a witness summons causing a representative of the hospital and GP to produce the material at court.

D If information regarding the medical condition of the offender comes into the possession of the prosecution from the hospital or from the GP then whether it is disclosed is entirely a matter for the prosecutor.

ANSWERS

Answer 10.1

Answer **A** — The prosecution is required, on request, to supply the defence with a summary of the prosecution case and/or copies of the statements of the proposed witnesses, making answer C incorrect. The defence are entitled to this disclosure to consider whether the defendant will plead guilty or not guilty and this has no relevance to whether the material undermines the prosecution case, making answer D incorrect. However, if the OIC considers that such disclosure may lead to witnesses being intimidated or some other interference with justice, the prosecutor may limit some or all of the prosecution case, making answer B incorrect.

Investigators' Manual, paras 1.11.3, 1.11.3.1

Answer 10.2

Answer **B** — Any failure to comply with the rules of disclosure, by the prosecution or the defence, may affect the trial. A failure by the prosecution to comply with their obligations means the accused does not have to make defence disclosure, making answer A incorrect. The court is under no obligation to adjourn the trial, making answer D incorrect. Although a failure to comply may mean the trial is stayed for abuse of process, this is not necessarily always the case (*R* v *Feltham Magistrates' Court, ex parte Ebrahim*; *Mouat* v *DPP*; *R* v *Feltham Magistrates' Court, ex parte DPP* [2001] 1 WLR 1293). In this case it was stated that in such circumstances the trial should proceed, leaving the defendant to seek to persuade the jury or magistrates not to convict because evidence that might otherwise have been available was not before the court through no fault of the defendant, making answer C incorrect.

Investigators' Manual, para. 1.11.2

Answer 10.3

Answer **D** — The Criminal Procedure and Investigations Act 1996 in effect only applies once a defendant has been committed/transferred to the Crown Court or is proceeding to trial in the magistrates' or youth court. While there are provisions to set specific time periods by which primary disclosure must be met, none currently exists. Until such times, primary disclosure must be made as soon as practicable after the duty arises, making answers A, B and C incorrect.

Investigators' Manual, para. 1.11.10.2

Answer 10.4

Answer **C** — For investigations carried out by the police, generally speaking there is no restriction on who performs the role of the 'Disclosure Officer'. The role could be performed by unsworn support staff (Criminal Procedure and Investigations Act 1996, Codes of Practice, paras 2.1 and 3.3), making answer A incorrect. However, para. 7 of the Attorney General's Guidelines on disclosure states that an individual must not be appointed as disclosure officer if that role is likely to result in a conflict of interest, for example, if the disclosure officer is a victim of the alleged crime which is the subject of criminal proceedings. Therefore, DC POULOS should not be appointed, making answer B incorrect. There may be occasions where the police investigation has been intelligence-led and there may be an additional disclosure officer appointed to deal with the intelligence material, making answer D incorrect.

Investigators' Manual, paras 1.11.5, 1.11.6

Answer 10.5

Answer **C** — Paragraph 5.4 of the Code of Practice for the Criminal Procedure and Investigations Act 1996 gives details of material that might be considered to be relevant material. This *includes* the items listed at answers A, B and D, making those answers incorrect. In *DPP* v *Metten*, 22 January 1999, the defence claimed that officers knew the identity of potential witnesses to the arrest of the offender and that these had not been disclosed. The court stated that this was not relevant to the case as it concerned the time of the arrest and not what happened at the time the offence was committed.

Investigators' Manual, paras 1.11.5.4, 1.11.8

Answer 10.6

Answer **B** — In *R* v *Johnson* [1988] 1 WLR 1377, the judge ruled that the exact location of premises used to carry out observations need not be revealed, making answer D incorrect. The rule is based on the protection of the owner or occupier of premises and not on the identity of the observation post. So, in *R* v *Brown* (1987) 87 Cr App R

52, where a surveillance operation was conducted from an unmarked police car, information relating to the surveillance and the colour, make and model of the vehicle should not be withheld, making answers A and C incorrect.

Investigators' Manual, para. 1.11.9.5

Answer 10.7

Answer **D** — Once the prosecution provides the initial disclosure, the defence have 14 days in respect of summary proceedings, or 28 days in respect of Crown Court proceedings within which the accused in criminal proceedings must give: a compulsory defence statement under s. 5 of the Act; a voluntary defence statement under s. 6 of the Act; or a notice of his/her intention to call any person, other than him/herself, as a witness under s. 6C of the Act (alibi witness).

Investigators' Manual, para. 1.11.11.4

Answer 10.8

Answer **C** — All material which may be relevant must be retained at least until:

- the person is released from custody or discharged from hospital in cases where the court imposes a custodial sentence or hospital order;
- in all other cases, for six months from the date of conviction.

If the person is released from the custodial sentence or discharged from hospital earlier than six months from the date of conviction (LEXINGTON), the material must be retained for at least six months from the date of conviction.

Investigators' Manual, para. 1.11.8

Answer 10.9

Answer **C** — If the investigator, disclosure officer or prosecutor seeks access to material or information held by a third party (e.g. a local authority, a social services department, a hospital, a doctor, etc.) but the third party declines or refuses to allow access to it, the matter should not be left, making answer A incorrect. If, despite any reasons offered by the third party it is still believed reasonable to seek production of the material or information, and the requirements of s. 2 of the Criminal Procedure (Attendance of Witnesses) Act 1965 or as appropriate s. 97 of the Magistrates' Courts Act 1980 are satisfied, then the prosecutor or investigator should apply for a witness summons causing a representative of the third party to produce that material at court, making answer B incorrect. Answer D is incorrect as when such information comes into the possession of the prosecution, consultation with the other agency should take place before disclosure is made.

Investigators' Manual, para. 1.11.6.6

11 Regulation of Investigatory Powers Act 2000

QUESTIONS

Question 11.1

TI GRIFFIN has spoken to a number of people on the telephone in respect of crime taking place in and around her police station. She is concerned that her contacts may well fall into the definition of a CHIS (Covert Human Intelligence Source) and approaches you for some advice on the matter. She describes the conversations and activities that have taken place on the telephone.

Which of the following statements is correct?

A KELLY is a member of the public who has contacted TI GRIFFIN to supply some general information regarding crime in the locality. TI GRIFFIN should treat KELLY as a CHIS.

B MOSELEY is a member of staff at a bank who has come across information in the ordinary course of her job and suspects criminal activity. TI GRIFFIN should treat MOSELEY as a CHIS.

C PARSAD heard about a drug deal taking place in a pub. TI GRIFFIN asked PARSAD to return to the pub and find out who was involved and what future deals were planned. TI GRIFFIN should treat PARSAD as a CHIS.

D TI GRIFFIN would not need to treat any person as a CHIS if the information being passed to the officer is being communicated by telephone.

Question 11.2

DC EVAN is approached by TREDMAN (who is 13 years old). TREDMAN tells DC EVAN that he can supply a large amount of quality information about the activities of a gang of burglars operating in DC EVAN's area. DC EVAN is keen to utilise TREDMAN as a CHIS (Covert Human Intelligence Source).

Which of the following statements is correct in respect of TREDMAN?

A A juvenile cannot be utilised as a CHIS in any circumstances.

B A superintendent could authorise the use of TREDMAN as a CHIS for a maximum period of three months.

C An assistant chief constable/commander can authorise the use of TREDMAN as a CHIS for a maximum period of four months.

D A juvenile CHIS can only be authorised by an officer of the rank of chief constable or his/her nominated deputy for a maximum period of one week.

Question 11.3

DC HUNT is tasked with dealing with a number of robberies that have occurred near a cash-point in a shopping centre. Victims are being attacked near the cash-point just after they have withdrawn cash and the offender runs off and out of the shopping centre. The shopping centre has an overt high-quality CCTV system with several cameras that can cover the cash-point and nearby area. It is DC HUNT's intention to use the CCTV system to specifically focus on the area of the cash-point while other officers are stationed nearby. Should an incident take place, DC HUNT will notify his colleagues, who will move into the shopping centre and make an arrest.

With regard to directed surveillance, which of the following statements is correct?

A DC HUNT is covertly and specifically using the CCTV system in connection with a planned operation and this may amount to directed surveillance.

B The monitoring of a CCTV system could never be covered by the Regulation of Investigatory Powers Act 2000 (RIPA 2000).

C As DC HUNT is not using the CCTV system to search for an individual specifically identified for the purposes of the operation, this would not qualify as directed surveillance.

D This is not directed surveillance as the CCTV cameras in the centre are not 'covert'.

Question 11.4

DS DONNELLY wishes to carry out intrusive surveillance as part of a large ongoing drugs operation against KIRK.

Who will authorise this surveillance?

A An officer of the rank of inspector or above.

B An officer of the rank of superintendent or above.

C An officer of the rank of chief constable.

D The Home Secretary.

Question 11.5

DC FAIRWEATHER wishes to place a surveillance device inside a private vehicle owned by RODAN who is the suspected leader of a gang carrying out high-value armed robberies. The officer hopes to obtain intelligence and evidence in respect of RODAN's criminal activities by recording RODAN's conversations with other members of the gang inside the private vehicle.

With regard to the Regulation of Investigatory Powers Act 2000, which of the following statements is correct?

A This is intrusive surveillance and if authorised would last for a period of one month.

B This is directed surveillance and if authorised would last for a period of one month.

C This is intrusive surveillance and if authorised would last for a period of three months.

D This is directed surveillance and if authorised would last for a period of three months.

Question 11.6

DC KENT is approached by JAMAL who tells the officer that he can provide him with information about a paedophile ring operating in the officer's policing area. JAMAL tells the officer the ring has been discussing killing any child they abuse to avoid leaving witnesses and other evidence. JAMAL tells DC KENT the ring is meeting in 2 hours' time. DC KENT requires urgent authorisation to make JAMAL a CHIS.

Which of the following comments is correct in respect of such urgent authorisation?

A In an urgent case, a superintendent can give authorisation for JAMAL's CHIS activities. This authorisation must be written and will last for 48 hours.

B In an urgent case, an inspector can give authorisation for JAMAL's CHIS activity. The authorisation can be oral or written and will last for 48 hours.

C In an urgent case, a superintendent can give authorisation for JAMAL's CHIS activities. The authorisation must be written and will last for 72 hours.

D In an urgent case, an inspector can give authorisation for JAMAL's CHIS activities. The authorisation must be written and will last for 72 hours.

Question 11.7

The Regulation of Investigatory Powers Act 2000 governs the use of surveillance when it is directed or intrusive and it provides definitions of such activities that all police officers should be aware of so that they do not carry out unlawful activities.

In respect of those definitions, which of the following comments is correct?

A PC ILKS is in a shop situated 20 metres away from a house he is watching. The officer is using long-range audio equipment to monitor the conversations of the occupants of the house. The equipment is of such quality that it provides the same kind of results that a device actually placed in the house would. This is directed surveillance.

B A police officer who is on plain clothes patrol sees a suspicious male hanging around near a jewellers shop. The officer hides behind a bush to watch the male and see what he does. This is directed surveillance.

C DC KULLA wishes to place a recording device in a hotel room occupied by GODSEN to record conversations that take place in the room. This is intrusive surveillance.

D DC QUEEN wants to attach a 'tracker' device to a car driven by HENNIMORE to provide information about the location of the vehicle. This is intrusive surveillance.

Question 11.8

DC VEMEER wishes to obtain evidence about the people-smuggling activities of DUNN and to do so he needs to obtain an authorisation for directed surveillance to watch/record DUNN in his workplace and an intrusive surveillance authorisation to watch/record DUNN'S activities in his home. DC VEMEER considers the surveillance could last a considerable period of time.

Which of the following comments is correct in respect of those authorisations?

A An authorisation for directed surveillance will ordinarily cease to have effect after one month, beginning on the day it was granted.

B An intrusive surveillance authorisation will not take effect until a Surveillance Commissioner has approved it and given written notification to that effect to the authorising officer.

C Authorisation for both types of surveillance would last for three months and can be renewed but only after they cease to have effect.

D If the situation became urgent, an inspector could authorise intrusive surveillance for a maximum period of 72 hours.

Question 11.9

The Halton Shopping Centre is being targeted by a small gang of shoplifters during the Christmas rush and you wish to use the CCTV at the shopping centre for non-urgent directed surveillance, to gather intelligence and identify the offenders. This is both proportionate and necessary.

Which of the following is correct with regard to persons who can authorise directed surveillance and the period such surveillance would last under the Regulation of Investigatory Powers Act (RIPA) 2000?

A It must be authorised in writing by an ACC/Commander or above and will last for a period of one month.

B It must be authorised in writing by an ACC/Commander or above and will last for a period of three months.

C It must be authorised in writing by a superintendent or above and will last for a period of one month.

D It must be authorised in writing by a superintendent or above and will last for a period of three months.

Question 11.10

WALTON contacts the police to complain about what she thinks is large-scale drug dealing and drug use taking place outside the rear of a social club in a village location. WALTON is aware of the activity as her house is one of a number of houses located at the rear of the social club. WALTON speaks to DC FLETCHER about the activity and tells DC FLETCHER that he can use her house to watch what is going on. DC FLETCHER wishes to obtain evidence in relation to this activity by the use of a surveillance device (in this case a camera) and also from officers who will operate the camera and make notes of the activity. The camera and the officers will be located in WALTON's house.

Thinking about the law in relation to directed and intrusive surveillance (dealt with by the Regulation of Investigatory Powers Act 2000), which of the following comments is true?

A Such activity would be classed as directed surveillance and an authorisation for the surveillance to take place should be sought from an officer of the rank of inspector or above.

B Such activity would be classed as intrusive surveillance and an authorisation for the surveillance to take place should be sought from an officer of the rank of superintendent or above.

C Such activity would be classed as intrusive surveillance and an authorisation for the surveillance to take place should be sought from an officer of the rank of chief constable/commissioner (or his/her designated deputy).

D Such activity would be classed as directed surveillance and an authorisation for the surveillance to take place should be sought from an officer of the rank of superintendent or above.

ANSWERS

Answer 11.1

Answer **C** — A CHIS is someone who establishes or maintains a relationship with another person for the covert purpose of obtaining information or providing access to information. Clearly this can be accomplished on the telephone, making answer D incorrect. However, the definition would not cover activities of a member of the public passing general information to the police (answer A) or a person who passes information to the police that they have come across in the ordinary course of their job (answer B). If a person supplying information is asked by the police to do something further to develop or enhance it this could well make the individual a CHIS.

Investigators' Manual, para. 1.12.3

Answer 11.2

Answer **C** — A juvenile CHIS can be used for certain activities (making answer A incorrect). The use of a juvenile CHIS is authorised by an officer of the rank of assistant chief constable/commander or above for a maximum period of four months, making answers B and D incorrect.

Investigators' Manual, para. 1.12.3.2

Answer 11.3

Answer **A** — CCTV will not normally be covered by RIPA 2000 as in most cases it is not covert. However, the use of the cameras in the way the officer is considering could well make such activities 'directed surveillance'. This is because the surveillance is (i) covert, (ii) for the purposes of a specific operation, (iii) likely to result in the obtaining of private information about a person (whether or not that person has been specifically identified for the purposes of the operation) and (iv) not in immediate response to events.

Investigators' Manual, paras 1.12.4, 1.12.4.1

Answer 11.4

Answer **C** — The authorising officer for intrusive surveillance by the police is the chief constable.

Investigators' Manual, para. 1.12.4.2

Answer 11.5

Answer **C** — Answers B and D are incorrect as this is intrusive surveillance. Intrusive surveillance is surveillance that is covert, carried out in relation to anything taking place on any residential premises or in any private vehicle and involves the presence of an individual on the premises or in the vehicle, or is carried out by means of a surveillance device. Intrusive surveillance, if authorised, will be authorised for a period of three months, making answer A incorrect.

Investigators' Manual, para. 1.12.4.2

Answer 11.6

Answer **D** — Urgent authorisation for CHIS activity can be given by a superintendent or an inspector. That authorisation will last for 72 hours, making answers A and B incorrect. However, an inspector cannot give an oral authorisation (a superintendent can)—any authorisation by an inspector must be written.

Investigators' Manual, para. 1.12.3.2

Answer 11.7

Answer **C** — If a police officer is acting in immediate response to events/circumstances where it would not be reasonably practicable to seek prior authorisation for surveillance and that surveillance is not intrusive, then no authorisation for the officer's activities will be required, making answer B incorrect. Answer A is incorrect as although the officer might not be in the residential premises he is monitoring, if the device he uses produces such images/sound as to give the same result as if the device were on the premises, then this is intrusive surveillance. Placing a 'tracker' device on or even in a vehicle to provide information about its geographical location is directed surveillance, making answer D incorrect. Hotel rooms are considered to be residential premises and placing a recording device in a hotel room would be intrusive surveillance.

Investigators' Manual, paras 1.12.4 to 1.12.4.2

Answer 11.8

Answer **B** — An officer of the rank of inspector cannot authorise intrusive surveillance in any circumstances, making answer D incorrect. Surveillance can be renewed and this can take place before the operating authorisations cease to have effect as long as the criteria for authorisation are still satisfied, making answer C incorrect. Directed surveillance will last for three months from the date it is granted (72 hours if urgent), making answer A incorrect. Intrusive surveillance has to wait until the Surveillance Commissioner gives written approval (unless it is an urgent situation when the surveillance can commence when authorised by a chief constable or his/her deputy).

Investigators' Manual, paras 1.12.4 to 1.12.4.2

Answer 11.9

Answer **D** — The relevant rank for authorisation of directed surveillance is superintendent or above—in ordinary circumstances the authorisation will be for three months (making answers A, B and C incorrect).

Investigators' Manual, para. 1.12.4.2

Answer 11.10

Answer D — Intrusive surveillance is covert surveillance that is carried out in relation to anything taking place *on residential premises* or *in any private vehicle*, and that involves the presence of an individual on the premises or in the vehicle or that is carried out by means of a surveillance device. The activity that is described in this question is not taking place *on* residential premises or in a private vehicle (although the observations are taking place *from* residential premises). Therefore, this activity is not intrusive surveillance, making answers B and C incorrect. Directed surveillance is covert surveillance that is not intrusive but is carried out in relation to a specific investigation or operation in such a manner as is likely to result in the obtaining of *private information* about any person (other than by way of an immediate response to events or circumstances such that it is not reasonably practicable to seek *authorisation* under the 2000 Act). The activity described in the question is certainly directed surveillance. The Regulation of Investigatory Powers (Directed Surveillance and Covert Human Intelligence Sources) Order 2003 (SI 2003/3171), as amended, sets out the relevant roles and ranks for those who can authorise directed surveillance. In the case of the police, the relevant rank will generally be at superintendent level and above, making answer A incorrect.

Investigators' Manual, paras 1.12.4 to 1.12.4.2

PART 2

Serious Crime and Other Offences

12 Homicide

QUESTIONS

Question 12.1

FOZIA despises her husband, ALI. For years, ALI has subjected FOZIA to repeated physical and verbal abuse, making her life a misery. One night FOZIA is severely beaten by ALI. The attack proves to be 'the last straw' for FOZIA. After the attack FOZIA decides that enough is enough and plans to kill ALI. She waits for him to fall asleep and attacks him with a claw hammer. She strikes ALI five times about the head, causing serious injuries but not, as she intended, ALI's death.

Which of the following statements is correct?

A FOZIA has committed an attempted murder but because she suffered abuse over a prolonged period, she may raise the 'special defence' of loss of control.

B FOZIA has committed an attempted murder and would be able to use any of the 'special defences' provided by the Homicide Act 1957 or by the Coroners and Justice Act 2009.

C FOZIA's intention to kill ALI provides the *mens rea* needed to support a charge of attempted murder but she would not be able to use any 'special defences'.

D FOZIA has committed an attempted murder but could raise diminished responsibility as a defence if she can prove she was suffering from 'battered wives' syndrome'.

Question 12.2

PIGGOT and LAY both own burger bars. They pitch next to each other in a prime location on a bridge over a subway near a football ground on match days. The subway is a well-used route to the football ground by pedestrians; a fact that both PIGGOT and LAY are fully aware of. The pair become involved in an argument about stealing trade from each other and PIGGOT, in a fit of rage, picks up a tray of canned drinks from the counter of LAY's burger bar and throws the tray over the bridge. The tray of drinks strikes YEO, who is walking along the subway to the match, and kills him.

Does PIGGOT commit the offence of manslaughter by unlawful act?

A Yes, as long as PIGGOT foresaw the risk of somebody being harmed.

B No, as PIGGOT does not have the *mens rea* for assault.

C Yes, the risk of someone being harmed will be judged objectively.

D No, as PIGGOT's initial action was not directed or aimed at a person.

Question 12.3

CHALLINOR and BARNSLEY, both British citizens, are on holiday in Cuba (a country not forming part of the Commonwealth). The two men are having dinner when an argument takes place over who will pay for the meal. CHALLINOR loses his temper, picks up a steak knife from the table and stabs BARNSLEY in the chest. BARNSLEY immediately dies from his injuries.

Could CHALLINOR be tried in this country for the offence of murder?

A No, as the offence was committed outside the jurisdiction of the English courts CHALLINOR would have to be tried in Cuba under Cuban law.

B Yes, any British citizen who commits a murder anywhere in the world may be tried in England and Wales.

C No, the Offences Against the Person Act 1861 makes it clear that such offences may only be tried in this country if the act is committed in a country belonging to the Commonwealth.

D Yes, but this is only because both CHALLINOR and BARNSLEY are British citizens.

Question 12.4

STEWARD is seven months pregnant when MORRELL, her boyfriend, finds out that she has had an affair and the child may not be his. MORRELL attacks STEWARD intending to cause her serious harm. He stabs her in the stomach and, in the process of doing so, not only seriously injures STEWARD but also injures the unborn child. STEWARD is rushed to hospital where, as a result of the attack, she prematurely gives birth. The child is born alive but subsequently dies three days after the incident from the injuries received from being stabbed whilst in STEWARD's womb.

Considering the law regarding murder and manslaughter only, what is MORRELL's criminal liability regarding the child?

A In these circumstances, MORRELL has no criminal liability regarding the child.

B MORRELL can only face criminal charges relating to the child if he intended to kill STEWARD.

C As MORRELL intended to cause serious harm to STEWARD, he is guilty of the murder of the child.

D MORRELL's intention to cause serious injury to STEWARD may support a charge of manslaughter of the child.

Question 12.5

BUSHELL is involved in a fight with GREY. BUSHELL intends to cause grievous bodily harm to GREY and does so. BUSHELL is arrested and convicted for a s. 18 wounding (contrary to the Offences Against the Person Act 1861) and receives a 15-year jail sentence. Two years after the attack, GREY dies as a direct consequence of the injuries received during the fight with BUSHELL.

With regard to the law relating to murder, which of the following statements is correct?

A BUSHELL cannot be charged with the murder of GREY as the *mens rea* needed for a murder conviction is the intention to kill only.

B As BUSHELL has already been convicted in circumstances connected with the death of GREY, the consent of the Attorney General is needed before bringing a prosecution.

C If convicted of murder, BUSHELL must be sentenced to life imprisonment unless there are exceptional circumstances surrounding the case.

D BUSHELL cannot be charged with murder as he has already been convicted of an offence committed under the circumstances connected with the death.

Question 12.6

APPLETON is employed by Jays Heating Ltd to fit a central heating system in CURTIS's house. The company director, HUNTER, failed to check whether APPLETON had any formal qualifications to fit the system; APPLETON does not. As a consequence he fails to connect a vital part of the central heating system. The result of this failure is that CURTIS dies from leaking fumes. Sergeant JENNINGS investigates the incident.

Which of the following comments is correct?

A In these circumstances APPLETON could be guilty of manslaughter by gross negligence.

B Whether a defendant's conduct amounts to gross negligence is a question of law which falls to the trial judge to decide.

C APPLETON must have committed an unlawful act in order to be successfully prosecuted for an offence of manslaughter by gross negligence.

D Jays Heating Ltd could not be prosecuted for an offence of manslaughter by gross negligence unless the company director (HUNTER) was physically responsible for the central heating system failure.

Question 12.7

DCs MORA, PERCOX, RUSSELL and POOLE are seconded to a murder enquiry and are discussing the offence. During their discussion, several statements are made regarding the offence of murder.

Which one of their statements is correct?

A DC MORA states that if a victim of an alleged murder dies more than a year and a day after receiving their injury, then the consent of the Attorney General is required before bringing a prosecution.

B DC PERCOX states that a defendant who successfully advances the defence of 'loss of control' will be acquitted of the offence of murder and found guilty of involuntary manslaughter.

C DC RUSSELL states that in order to prove an offence of murder, the prosecution must show some degree of premeditation on the part of the defendant.

D DC POOLE states that the term 'unlawful killing' includes occasions where someone fails to act after creating a situation of danger.

Question 12.8

Section 5 of the Domestic Violence, Crime and Victims Act 2004 creates an offence of causing or allowing a child or vulnerable adult to die or suffer serious physical harm.

What does the term 'child' mean for the purposes of this offence?

A A 'child' is a person under the age of 10.

B A 'child' is a person under the age of 14.

C A 'child' is a person under the age of 16.

D A 'child' is a person under the age of 18.

Question 12.9

HANCOCK is wanted for an armed robbery where he used a revolver to threaten staff. He resides in a small block of flats and a team of armed officers go to his flat in the early hours of the morning to arrest him. The officers surround the premises but, before they go up the stairs to his flat, HANCOCK appears at the top landing and fires two shots at PC FLINT, one of the armed officers. FLINT returns fire but, a split second before he does so, HANCOCK reaches out to his girlfriend (SIMPSON) who is standing near him. He punches her in the face and pulls her in front of him to use as a shield. The officers return fire and kill SIMPSON as a result. HANCOCK then places his hands in the air in surrender and is formally arrested—he did not intend to kill or seriously injure SIMPSON as a consequence of his actions although he did intentionally injure her when he punched her in the face.

Which of the following statements is correct with regards to the criminal liability of HANCOCK?

A HANCOCK is guilty of the murder of SIMPSON.

B HANCOCK is guilty of the voluntary manslaughter of SIMPSON.

C HANCOCK is guilty of involuntary manslaughter (manslaughter by unlawful act).

D HANCOCK is not liable in these circumstances for the death of SIMPSON.

ANSWERS

Answer 12.1

Answer **C** — FOZIA's *mens rea* to kill ALI is the only state of mind that would support a charge of attempted murder. Regardless of the motives FOZIA has to commit the offence, she does not kill ALI and would, therefore, only be liable for that offence. The 'special defences' of diminished responsibility, loss of control and suicide pact are only available to a defendant who is responsible for murder, making answers A, B and D incorrect.

Investigators' Manual, paras 2.1.2, 2.1.3, 2.1.3.1, 2.1.3.2

Answer 12.2

Answer **C** — This is an offence of manslaughter by an unlawful act. To prove the offence there must be: (i) an inherently unlawful act by the defendant; (ii) evidence that the act involved the risk of somebody being harmed (a risk that will be judged objectively, making answer A incorrect); and (iii) proof that the defendant had the required *mens rea* for the unlawful act which leads to the death of the victim. The unlawful act does not have to be aimed or directed against a person; it can be aimed at property, making answer D incorrect. Answer B is incorrect for the same reason; the *mens rea* required is for the specific act carried out by the defendant, in this case, theft of the tray of drinks and not necessarily the offence of assault.

Investigators' Manual, paras 2.1.4, 2.1.4.1

Answer 12.3

Answer **B** — Under the provisions of s. 9 of the Offences Against the Person Act 1861, any British citizen who commits a murder anywhere in the world may be tried in England or Wales. Jurisdiction is not an issue, making answer A incorrect. Whether the country where the offence took place is a part of the Commonwealth or not makes no difference, so answer C is incorrect. The only issue relating to country of origin is if the defendant, not the victim, is a British citizen, making answer D incorrect.

Investigators' Manual, para. 2.1.2

Answer 12.4

Answer **D** — This is a complex area of the law touching on the doctrine of transferred mens rea. If a defendant intended to kill or cause serious injury to the mother, that intention cannot support a charge of murder in respect of the baby if it goes on to die after being born alive. It may, however, support a charge of manslaughter (*Attorney-General's Reference (No. 3 of 1994)* [1998] AC 245). It would certainly be appropriate to charge a person with the murder of the child if he/she intended the child to die after having been born alive (*Attorney General's Reference (No. 3 of 1994)* [1998] AC 245).

Investigators' Manual, para. 2.1.2

Answer 12.5

Answer **B** — Answer A is incorrect as the *mens rea* for murder is an intention to kill or an intention to cause grievous bodily harm. Answer C is incorrect as the sentence for murder is a mandatory life sentence regardless of the surrounding circumstances. If a defendant has already been convicted of an offence relating to the incident that causes the eventual death of the victim it will not prevent a charge of murder being made against the defendant. The consent of the Attorney General is required for such action (s. 2(2)(a) of the Law Reform (Year and a Day Rule) Act 1996), making answer D incorrect and answer B correct.

Investigators' Manual, paras 2.1.2, 2.1.2.1, 2.1.2.2

Answer 12.6

Answer **A** — Whether a defendant's conduct amounts to gross negligence is a question for the jury to decide, not the judge, making answer B incorrect. An unlawful act is not required for a person to be prosecuted for the offence of manslaughter by gross negligence, making answer C incorrect. Answer D is incorrect as it does not matter whether HUNTER was physically responsible for the central heating system failure; it is not possible to bring proceedings for gross negligent manslaughter against a company or other organisation to which the offence under the Corporate Manslaughter and Corporate Homicide Act 2007 applies (s. 20 of the Corporate Manslaughter and Corporate Homicide Act 2007).

Investigators' Manual, paras 2.1.4, 2.1.4.1, 2.1.4.2

Answer 12.7

Answer **D** — Statement A is incorrect as the consent of the Attorney General is only required if the victim dies more than three years after receiving their injury or if the defendant has already been convicted of an offence committed under the circumstances connected with the death. Statement B is incorrect as a successful special defence plea reduces the offence from murder to *voluntary* manslaughter. Statement C is incorrect as premeditation is not required to prove an offence of murder.

Investigators' Manual, paras 2.1.2, 2.1.3

Answer 12.8

Answer **C** — For the purposes of an offence under s. 5 of the Act, a 'child' is a person under the age of 16.

Investigators' Manual, para. 2.1.5

Answer 12.9

Answer **C** — This question links to the text of the Manual in relation to manslaughter by unlawful act and the case law of *R* v *Pagett* (1983) 76 Cr App R 279 (firing a gun at police officers then holding someone else in front of you when officers return fire). Answer A is incorrect as there is no intention to kill or cause GBH (no *mens rea* for murder). Answer B is incorrect as voluntary manslaughter is a finding by a court when one of the three 'special defences' to murder is successfully utilised and that is not the case here. All three elements required for an offence of manslaughter by unlawful act are present:

- an unlawful act;
- the unlawful act is likely to cause bodily harm (firing a gun at police officers and holding someone else in front of you when the officers return fire (*R* v *Pagett*)); and
- the defendant had the *mens rea* for the unlawful act.

This means that answer D is incorrect.

Investigators' Manual, para. 2.1.4.1

13 Misuse of Drugs

QUESTIONS

Question 13.1

TURVEY has just lost his job and is finding money hard to come by. RANDELL feels sorry for TURVEY and gives him a packet of ten cigarettes that also contains a small amount of cocaine. TURVEY knows nothing about the cocaine inside the packet of cigarettes. Several hours later, TURVEY is stopped by PC MAIR, who discovers the cocaine inside the cigarette packet.

Which of the following statements is correct with regard to TURVEY?

A Provided TURVEY has physical control of the cigarettes and knows of their presence he has 'possession' of the drug.

B The only requirement for 'possession' is that TURVEY had the drug in his physical control.

C To show that TURVEY has 'possession' of the drug you must show that he actually knew that what he possessed was cocaine.

D TURVEY cannot be in 'possession' of the cocaine because he does not know of its existence.

Question 13.2

WILLSON is the landlord of a flat rented out to BOWN. WILLSON is aware of the fact that BOWN is cultivating several cannabis plants in the flat. BOWN goes on holiday and asks MELLING to water his plants until he returns. MELLING has no idea that the 'plants' are cannabis plants and is watering them when the police execute a warrant at the premises.

Apart from BOWN, who, if either, commits the offence of cultivation of cannabis (contrary to s. 6 of the Misuse of Drugs Act 1971)?

A Only WILLSON, as the landlord, commits the offence.

B Only MELLING commits the offence.

C Both WILLSON and MELLING commit the offence.

D Neither WILLSON nor MELLING commit the offence.

Question 13.3

You are taking part in a drugs operation. The subjects of the operation are MENSAH and ROWLES, both well-known drug dealers. MENSAH arrives at the car park of a local pub and begins to deal. Shortly afterwards, ROWLES arrives driving a van. You and your colleagues carry out the operation and MENSAH and ROWLES are detained in the car park. In ROWLES's van is £20,000 worth of heroin. ROWLES states that the heroin belongs to MENSAH, that he was going to return it to him and he was only looking after it for £100 while MENSAH dealt the drug.

What offence(s) under the Misuse of Drugs Act 1971 does ROWLES commit?

A Possession of a controlled drug (contrary to s. 5(2)) only.

B Supplying a controlled drug (contrary to s. 4(3)) only.

C Possession of a controlled drug (contrary to s. 5(2)) and possession with intent to supply a controlled drug (contrary to s. 5(3)) only.

D Possession with intent to supply (contrary to s. 5(3)) and supplying a controlled drug (contrary to s. 4(3)).

Question 13.4

It is SHANAHAN's birthday and he gets drunk with some friends at a pub. On his way home McFADDEN stops him. SHANAHAN knows McFADDEN is a drug dealer. McFADDEN asks SHANAHAN to drop an envelope at an address and gives SHANAHAN £100 to deliver it. Because SHANAHAN is drunk he has no reason to suspect the envelope contains drugs and accepts the offer. SHANAHAN is approaching the delivery address when he is arrested for possessing a controlled drug (which was inside the envelope) with intent to supply.

Would SHANAHAN have any defence under s. 28(2) of the Misuse of Drugs Act 1971?

A Yes, in these circumstances SHANAHAN's 'reason to suspect' was impaired by his drunken condition and because the 'reason to suspect' is judged subjectively he will be able to use a defence.

B No, the fact that SHANAHAN was drunk is irrelevant. He knew McFADDEN was a drug dealer and should have suspected that the envelope contains drugs because of the large reward for delivering it.

C Yes, SHANAHAN could state that he neither knew nor suspected that the envelope contained a controlled drug and that he neither knew nor suspected that he was supplying it to another.

D No, this section only provides a defence to the offence of unlawful possession of a controlled drug.

Question 13.5

DC BAUGH is working undercover in an area well known for the sale and distribution of controlled drugs. She is approached by CREIGHTON, who is considering robbing DC BAUGH. To find out if DC BAUGH has any money and is worth robbing, CREIGHTON offers to supply some cocaine to her for £200. CREIGHTON does not have any cocaine and has no intention of supplying DC BAUGH with the drug.

Which of the following statements is correct?

A CREIGHTON commits an offence (under s. 4(3) of the Misuse of Drugs Act 1971) when he offers to supply a controlled drug to DC BAUGH.

B No offence is committed by CREIGHTON, as he did not possess the cocaine to make good on his offer to DC BAUGH.

C CREIGHTON is not guilty of an offence, as he had no intention of supplying the drug to DC BAUGH.

D As CREIGHTON made his offer to an undercover police officer, he can claim that the offer to supply was not a 'real' offer.

Question 13.6

MOSTAFA is convicted of an offence of supplying a controlled drug (contrary to s. 4(3) of the Misuse of Drugs Act 1971) and is sentenced to five years' imprisonment for the offence.

Considering the law with regard to travel restriction orders (under the Criminal Justice and Police Act 2001), which of the following statements is correct?

A This offence of supplying a controlled drug is not covered by the legislation in relation to travel restriction orders.

B The minimum period for such an order is four years.

C MOSTAFA must surrender his UK passport as part of the order.

D If an order was made then MOSTAFA may apply to the court that made the restriction order to have it revoked or suspended.

Question 13.7

GRAPNELL is subject to a travel restriction order under the Criminal Justice and Police Act 2001. A rival gang of drug dealers kidnaps him outside his home address in London. The gang drives GRAPNELL to Scotland and then takes him to Northern Ireland. From Northern Ireland the gang takes GRAPNELL to France.

At what stage, if at all, does GRAPNELL commit an offence of contravening the travel restriction order?

A When he enters Scotland.
B When he enters Northern Ireland.
C When he enters France.
D The offence is not committed.

Question 13.8

One of the main practical effects of being able to identify the classification of a controlled drug is to determine the mode of trial and sentencing powers of the court.

Which of the following drugs would be classified as Class B?

A Heroin.
B 'Magic mushrooms' (containing psilocin).
C Methadone.
D Codeine.

Question 13.9

CUTLER and HAVELIN are both drug addicts who use heroin on a regular basis. They obtain some heroin and HAVELIN obtains two items, a tourniquet and a hypodermic syringe, to assist in the administration of the drug. HAVELIN offers to supply both articles to CUTLER so that he can administer the drug to himself.

With which, if any, of the two items would HAVELIN commit the offence of supplying articles for administering or preparing controlled drugs (contrary to s. 9A of the Misuse of Drugs Act 1971)?

A The tourniquet only.
B The hypodermic syringe only.
C The tourniquet and the hypodermic syringe.
D Neither of the two items.

Question 13.10

MIRZA owns a cafe that is managed by NORTHALL. The cafe is regularly frequented by a group of teenagers who smoke cannabis inside the cafe. NORTHALL is fully aware that the teenagers use controlled drugs in the cafe but does not know what drug they use and as the teenagers are such good customers he decides to ignore their activities. MIRZA has no idea that the teenagers even use the cafe let alone smoke cannabis on the premises.

With regard to the offence of being the occupier or manager of premises and permitting drug use (contrary to s. 8 of the Misuse of Drugs Act 1971), which of the following statements is correct?

A Neither MIRZA nor NORTHALL would commit the offence because smoking cannabis or cannabis resin is not covered by this particular piece of legislation.

B The fact that MIRZA does not know the teenagers smoke drugs in the cafe is immaterial; this is an offence of strict liability and as the cafe owner he commits the offence.

C NORTHALL commits the offence but would only be found guilty if the prosecution could show that he knew what type of drugs were being used by the teenagers.

D MIRZA does not commit the offence because he does not know that the teenagers are smoking cannabis in his cafe.

Question 13.11

DC PHILLIPS (in plain clothes) has been taking a witness statement and is walking back to her car when she sees BOND and FARMER acting suspiciously. BOND is talking to FARMER, who is sitting in a car and smoking. DC PHILLIPS approaches the two and as she does so she smells what she thinks is cannabis being smoked. She suspects that the two men are committing offences contrary to the Misuse of Drugs Act 1971 and that she will find drugs on their persons and in the car.

With regard to the power of entry, search and seizure under s. 23 of the Misuse of Drugs Act 1971, which of the following comments is correct?

A DC PHILLIPS cannot exercise powers under s. 23 unless she is in uniform.

B DC PHILLIPS can search both BOND and FARMER and also search the car FARMER is sitting in.

C The power cannot be exercised unless DC PHILLIPS reasonably believes that offences contrary to the Act are being committed.

D DC PHILLIPS can search BOND and FARMER but not FARMER's car.

Question 13.12

The Home Secretary has the power, under the Misuse of Drugs Act 1971, to make any drug subject to temporary control. Ethylphenidate, which has been marketed as an alternative to cocaine and is often referred to as 'Gogaine' or 'Burst', has been made subject to such an order. DC GAD is on plain clothes patrol when he sees FURMAN and CLAY walking towards him. FURMAN is holding a bright red packet labelled 'Gogaine'. As the officer draws level with FURMAN, FURMAN says to CLAY, *'Here, you try some, you're going to love this high!'* and hands the packet to CLAY.

Which of the following comments is correct in relation to the law surrounding such temporary control and the powers of DC GAD?

A CLAY has committed an offence merely by being in possession of a drug that is subject to a temporary class order.

B A temporary drug class order comes into immediate effect when it is made and lasts for up to 24 months.

C DC GAD could not search FURMAN or CLAY using his powers under s. 23 of the Misuse of Drugs Act 1971.

D FURMAN has committed an offence by supplying a controlled drug to CLAY.

Question 13.13

DC LONGWELL receives information about a house owned by MALLORY being used to manufacture a variety of drugs. The officer applies for a warrant to search the premises under s. 23 of the Misuse of Drugs Act 1971 and the application is granted.

How long will such a warrant last?

A It lasts for a period of one month from the date of issue.

B It lasts for a period of two months from the date of issue.

C It lasts for a period of three months from the date of issue.

D It lasts for a period of four months from the date of issue.

Question 13.14

DC SAFFORD is in plain clothes and is standing on a street corner carrying out authorised surveillance activities in an area well known for the supply and use of drugs. EMERSON approaches the officer thinking that DC SAFFORD is a drugs dealer and asks the officer to supply him with some heroin.

Considering only the Misuse of Drugs Act 1971, what offence, if any, has EMERSON committed?

A EMERSON has not committed an offence under the Misuse of Drugs Act 1971 as asking someone to supply you with a controlled drug is not an offence known to law.

B EMERSON commits an offence under s. 4(3) of the Act as he is 'concerned' in the supply of a controlled drug.

C EMERSON has committed the offence of 'incitement' under s. 19 of the Act.

D EMERSON has not committed an offence under the Misuse of Drugs Act 1971 as DC SAFFORD is an undercover police officer and there was no possibility of the officer actually being induced to commit the offence.

Question 13.15

MYLO is in his local village pub when a stranger to the village, TIMPSON, comes into the pub, buys a beer and sits down. After a short time MYLO engages TIMPSON in conversation. MYLO says to TIMPSON, '*I have some cannabis resin in my car, would you like some?*' MYLO has no drugs, he just sees TIMPSON as an easy target, but MYLO has some cubes of old chocolate in his car which in the dark would pass as cannabis resin. TIMPSON says that he is interested and enquires into the cost. MYLO states that a small cube as it is 'good stuff' will be £20. MYLO gets up from his seat when the local PCSO comes into the pub to speak to the licensee about an unconnected matter. In view of this, MYLO says to TIMPSON that the offer is off and leaves the pub.

Considering the offence of supplying a controlled drug (contrary to s. 4 of the Misuse of Drugs Act 1971), does MYLO commit an offence?

A No, he does not commit the offence as he withdrew the offer to supply.

B Yes, he commits the offence as soon as he makes the offer to supply to TIMPSON.

C No, he does not commit the offence as he was in possession of chocolate not cannabis.

D Yes, he commits the offence when the price is agreed for the supplying of the drug.

Question 13.16

Under s. 33 of the Criminal Justice and Police Act 2001, a court is empowered to give an offender a travel restriction order for a drug trafficking offence. This is to prohibit them from leaving the United Kingdom after their release from prison. They are guilty of an offence if they do not comply and they may have to surrender their passport.

Under s. 33 of the Criminal Justice and Police Act 2001, which of the following statements is the criteria for the court issuing such an order for a drug trafficking offender?

A Must have had a sentence imposed of at least three years, and then the restriction order is for a minimum of two years.

B Must have had a sentence imposed of at least four years, and then the restriction order is for a minimum of two years.

C Must have had a sentence imposed of at least three years, and then the restriction order is for a minimum of three years.

D Must have had a sentence imposed of at least four years, and then the restriction order is for a minimum of three years.

Question 13.17

CORCORAN (who is 20 years old) is sitting outside a school in his car and decides to smoke some cannabis (a Class B drug). As it is 11.00 hours and classes are taking place at the school, a number of school pupils and several members of staff at the school see what is going on. Staff alert the police and PC WHITE is sent to the incident. Before the officer arrives, SHAW (who is 17 years old and a friend of CORCORAN's), walks past CORCORAN and the two start a conversation. After several minutes, CORCORAN finishes smoking the cannabis and just then PC WHITE arrives in a marked police vehicle. As the officer arrives, CORCORAN panics and hands SHAW a large bag of cannabis saying, *'I want to smoke this later so look after it for me and I'll pay you £20.'* SHAW knows that he is being handed cannabis and agrees and walks away and watches as PC WHITE searches CORCORAN and his car. Finding nothing, the officer leaves. SHAW walks back to CORCORAN and returns the cannabis to him. CORCORAN gives £20 to SHAW and drives off.

Considering the offence of supplying a controlled drug (contrary to s. 4(3) of the Misuse of Drugs Act 1971) and the law in relation to that offence, which of the following comments is correct?

A CORCORAN and SHAW are guilty of the offence. Because of the time and place of the offence, the court will be required to consider 'aggravating' factors (under s. 4A of the Act) in relation to CORCORAN only.

B CORCORAN and SHAW are guilty of the offence. Because of the time and place of the offence, the court will be required to consider 'aggravating' factors (under s. 4A of the Act) in relation to both men.

C Only CORCORAN is guilty of the offence. Because of the time and place of the offence, the court will be required to consider 'aggravating' factors (under s. 4A of the Act) in relation to it.

D Only SHAW is guilty of the offence. As he is under 18 years of age, the court will not consider the offence 'aggravated' (under s. 4A of the Act).

ANSWERS

Answer 13.1

Answer **A** — This question does not ask if TURVEY has committed an offence, merely if he satisfies what the law requires for 'possession' of the drug. In order to be in possession of anything, the common law requires physical control of the object plus knowledge that it contains something, making answers B and C incorrect. The fact that TURVEY does not know of the existence of the cocaine within the cigarette packet may afford him a defence to a charge of possession but he still 'possesses' the drug, making answer D incorrect.

Investigators' Manual, paras 2.2.3, 2.2.3.1 to 2.2.3.7

Answer 13.2

Answer **B** — Although WILLSON knows of the existence of the cannabis plants, this does not mean that he commits the offence. For the offence to be committed you must show some element of attention to the plant by the defendant, making answers A and C incorrect. The element of attention could be watering the plant. In proving the offence it is only necessary to show that the plant is of the genus *Cannabis* and that the defendant cultivated it; it is not necessary to show that the defendant knew it to be a cannabis plant (*R* v *Champ* (1981) 73 Cr App R 367), making answer D incorrect.

Investigators' Manual, para. 2.2.8

Answer 13.3

Answer **C** — This question is as per the circumstances in *R* v *Maginnis* [1987] AC 303. Clearly, ROWLES is in possession of a controlled drug, ruling out answers B and D. To 'supply' something, the person who you are giving the item to must obtain some benefit from it. If ROWLES had given the drugs to MENSAH, MENSAH would have benefitted as he could sell the drugs so if that transaction had taken place, ROWLES would have 'supplied' MENSAH. However, he did not so there cannot be an actual 'supply'. As ROWLES intended to give the drugs to MENSAH in these circumstances there is an offence of possession with intent to supply, meaning answer A is incorrect.

Investigators' Manual, paras 2.2.4, 2.2.5

Answer 13.4

Answer **B** — Section 28 provides a defence for several offences under the Act, one of those being possession with intent to supply, making answer D incorrect. The fact that SHANAHAN knew McFADDEN as a drugs dealer and was paid a large amount of money to deliver the envelope would negate any defence he may attempt to raise as he should have 'reason to suspect' the envelope contained drugs in these circumstances, making answer C incorrect. The 'reason to suspect' is judged objectively (*R* v *Young* [1984] 1 WLR 654) so where a 'reason to suspect' is not apparent because the defendant is too intoxicated to see it, the defence will not apply, making answer A incorrect.

Investigators' Manual, paras 2.2.9, 2.2.9.1 to 2.2.9.3

Answer 13.5

Answer **A** — The offence under s. 4(3) states that it is an offence to supply or offer to supply a controlled drug. The offence is complete when the offer is made. It is irrelevant whether or not the defendant actually has the means to meet the offer or even intends to carry it out (*R* v *Goodard* [1992] Crim LR 588), making answers B and C incorrect. If the offer was made to an undercover police officer the offence is still committed (*R* v *Kray*, 10 November 1998, unreported).

Investigators' Manual, paras 2.2.4, 2.2.4.1, 2.2.4.2

Answer 13.6

Answer **D** — The offences that are covered by travel restriction orders include the supply of controlled drugs, making answer A incorrect. Answer B is incorrect as the minimum period for such an order is two years (s. 33(3)). Answer C is incorrect as an offender *may* be required to surrender his/her UK passport as part of the order.

Investigators' Manual, para. 2.2.16

Answer 13.7

Answer **C** — The offence is committed when the person subject to the order leaves the United Kingdom. It is immaterial that GRAPNELL has been kidnapped, as the conduct of the defendant does not have to be voluntary.

Investigators' Manual, para. 2.2.16

Answer 13.8

Answer **D** — Answers A, B and C are all Class A drugs.

Investigators' Manual, para. 2.2.2

Answer 13.9

Answer **A** — Hypodermic syringes, or parts of them, are not covered by this offence (s. 9A(2)), making answers B and C incorrect. The tourniquet would be covered as this offence deals with 'articles' used in the administration or preparation of drugs to 'himself or another', making answer D incorrect.

Investigators' Manual, para. 2.2.6

Answer 13.10

Answer **D** — Cannabis and cannabis resin are covered by this offence (s. 8(d)), making answer A incorrect. This offence can only be committed if the occupier or person concerned in the management of the premises *knowingly* permits the use of drugs in the prescribed manner. This is not an offence of strict liability and so answer B is also incorrect. It is not necessary to show that the defendant knew exactly what drugs were being produced, supplied, etc.; only that they were 'controlled drugs' (*R* v *Bett* [1999] 1 All ER 600), making answer C incorrect.

Investigators' Manual, para. 2.2.11

Answer 13.11

Answer **B** — The power under s. 23 is exercisable by a constable who does not have to be in uniform and who has *reasonable grounds to suspect* that a person is in possession of a controlled drug in contravention of the Act, making answers A and C incorrect. Answer D is incorrect as the Act provides the power to search and detain persons and any vehicle or vessel in which the constable suspects that the drug may be found.

Investigators' Manual, paras 2.2.17, 2.2.17.1, 2.2.17.2

Answer 13.12

Answer **D** — The Home Secretary has the power, under the Misuse of Drugs Act 1971, to make any drug subject to temporary control. The order will come into immediate effect and will last for up to 12 months, subject to Parliament agreeing to it within 40 sitting days of the order being made, making answer B incorrect. Such a drug will be referred to as a 'temporary class drug' and will be a 'controlled drug' for the purposes of the Misuse of Drugs Act 1971, and other legislation such as the Proceeds of Crime Act 2002, unless otherwise stated. With the *exception of the possession offence*, all the offences under the Misuse of Drugs Act will apply, including possession in connection with an offence or prohibition, under ss. 3, 4 and 5(3) of the Act, i.e. possession with intent to supply. So CLAY would not commit an offence but FURMAN would (making answer A incorrect). Simple possession of a temporary class drug is not an offence under the 1971 Act; however, law enforcement officers have been given the following powers to enable them to take action to prevent possible harm to the individual:

- search and detain a person (or vehicle etc.) where there are reasonable grounds to suspect that the person is in possession of a temporary class drug;
- seize, detain and dispose of a suspected temporary class drug;
- arrest or charge a person who commits the offence of intentionally obstructing an enforcement officer in the exercise of their powers.

This makes answer C incorrect (in s. 23 note that the powers are available to a constable 'who has reasonable grounds to suspect that any person is in possession of a controlled drug in contravention of this Act or of any regulations or *orders*').

Investigators' Manual, paras 2.2.2.1, 2.2.17.1

Answer 13.13

Answer **A** — A warrant issued under s. 23 of the Act lasts for a period of *one month* from the date of issue.

Investigators' Manual, para. 2.2.17.1

Answer 13.14

Answer **C** — The Misuse of Drugs Act 1971, s. 19 states:

It is an offence for a person to incite another to commit an offence under any other provision of this Act.

So answer A is incorrect as this offence has been committed by EMERSON. Asking to be supplied with drugs is not an offence under s. 4(3) making answer B incorrect. A person inciting an undercover police officer may commit an offence under s. 19 even though there was no possibility of the officer actually being induced to commit the offence (*DPP* v *Armstrong* [2000] Crim LR 379), making answer D incorrect.

Investigators' Manual, para. 2.2.14

Answer 13.15

Answer **B** — Section 4 of the Misuse of Drugs Act 1971 states:

(a) to supply or to offer to supply a controlled drug to another in contravention of subsection (1); or
(b) to be concerned in the supplying of such a drug to another in contravention of that subsection; or
(c) to be concerned in the making to another in contravention of that subsection of an offer to supply such a drug.

An offer may be by words or conduct. If it is by words, it must be ascertained whether an offer to supply a controlled drug was made. Whether the accused had a controlled drug in his possession or had access to controlled drugs or whether the substance in his possession was a controlled drug at all is immaterial. Whether the accused intends to carry the offer into effect is irrelevant; the offence is complete upon making of an offer to supply. The offence is committed whether or not the offer is genuine and once the offer is made it cannot be withdrawn.

Investigators' Manual, para. 2.2.4.1

Answer 13.16

Answer **B** — The Criminal Justice and Police Act 2001 makes provision for courts to impose travel restrictions on offenders convicted of drug trafficking offences to prohibit the offender from leaving the United Kingdom at any time during the period beginning with his/her release from custody (other than on bail or temporary release for a fixed period) and up to the end of the order.

The minimum period for such an order is two years (s. 33(3)) where a court:

- has convicted a person of a drug trafficking offence; and
- has determined that a sentence of four years or more is appropriate.

This makes B the correct answer.

Investigators' Manual, para. 2.2.16

Answer 13.17

Answer **A** — Section 4 of the Misuse of Drugs Act 1971 states:

> (3) Subject to section 28 of this Act, it is an offence for a person—
> (a) to supply or offer to supply a controlled drug to another in contravention of subsection (1) above; or
> (b) to be concerned in the supplying of such a drug to another in contravention of that subsection; or
> (c) to be concerned in the making to another in contravention of that subsection of an offer to supply such a drug.

In *R* v *Maginnis* [1987] AC 303, the House of Lords held that 'supply' involves more than a mere transfer of physical control of the item from one person to another but includes a further concept, namely that of 'enabling the recipient to apply the thing handed over to purposes for which he desires or has a duty to apply it'. In other words, *the person to whom the drug is given must derive some benefit from being given the drug.* So the key to working out if there has been a 'supply' is to ask 'Does being given the drug benefit the person to whom the drug has been given?' If the answer is 'Yes' then the person *giving the drug* is 'supplying' it. In this question, CORCORAN offers SHAW £20 to look after the cannabis—so SHAW benefits from being given the drug and therefore CORCORAN supplies it to him. When SHAW hands the cannabis back to CORCORAN, CORCORAN benefits from it as he can smoke the cannabis—therefore SHAW supplies CORCORAN.

So at this stage CORCORAN and SHAW have committed the offence under s. 4(3) meaning that answers C and D are incorrect.

Section 4A of the Misuse of Drugs Act 1971 requires courts to treat certain conditions as 'aggravating' factors when considering the seriousness of the offence under s. 4(3) if committed by a *person aged 18 or over*. This means that s. 4A will not apply to SHAW as he is 17 years old and means that answer B is incorrect.

Investigators' Manual, paras 2.2.4.1 to 2.2.4.2

14 Firearms and Gun Crime

QUESTIONS

Question 14.1

NIELSEN is the owner of a slaughterhouse and is licensed under s. 10 of the Firearms Act 1968 to possess slaughtering instruments. One of the instruments that he keeps for this purpose is a hand-held electric 'stun gun'. The stun gun develops a fault and is beyond repair but rather than throw it away, NIELSEN takes the broken stun gun to his home address. He intends to keep it in a display cabinet to show his friends the sort of instruments he uses at work.

Considering only the offence of possessing a prohibited weapon contrary to s. 5 of the Firearms Act 1968, which of the following statements is true?

A NIELSEN commits the offence as the stun gun is a prohibited weapon and he has it in his possession away from his place of work.

B No offence is committed because NIELSEN is a licensed slaughterer and s. 10 of the Act allows him to possess the stun gun.

C As NIELSEN only intends to keep the stun gun as a display item the offence would not be committed.

D NIELSEN cannot commit this offence because an electric stun gun is only a prohibited weapon as long as it can discharge an electric current.

Question 14.2

CALVER buys an antique vase from LAVERICK for £15,000 and, although LAVERICK has asked for the money several times, CALVER has always refused to pay it. LAVERICK goes to CALVER's home address and demands payment. The two have an argument during which CALVER tells LAVERICK that he will never pay him. LAVERICK puts his hands behind his back and onto an imitation 9 mm Beretta pistol. He tells CALVER that he has a gun and that if CALVER does not pay him he will be shot and killed.

Why is no offence under s. 16 of the Firearms Act 1968 committed?

A No offence is committed because LAVERICK has not actually endangered CALVER's life.

B No offence is committed because the threat is a conditional one.

C No offence is committed because the threat is made with an imitation firearm.

D No offence is committed because the firearm was never produced or shown to CALVER.

Question 14.3

PC SHANKS carries out a s. 1 PACE search on YOUNIS, who has been found trespassing in a building. In the course of the search, PC SHANKS finds an imitation pistol in YOUNIS's back pocket. She seizes the pistol and arrests YOUNIS for an offence under s. 20(1) of the Firearms Act 1968 (trespassing with a firearm in a building). YOUNIS struggles with the officer and punches her in the face attempting to prevent PC SHANKS from making the arrest. YOUNIS manages to take hold of the imitation pistol and points it at the officer, telling her to leave him alone. YOUNIS then strikes PC SHANKS in the face with the butt of the pistol.

At what stage, if at all, does YOUNIS commit an offence under s. 17 of the Firearms Act (using a firearm to resist arrest)?

A When he initially struggles with PC SHANKS and punches her in the face.

B When he takes hold of the imitation pistol and points it at PC SHANKS.

C When he strikes PC SHANKS in the face with the butt of the pistol.

D The offence under s. 17 of the Act is not committed.

Question 14.4

WHITHAM assaults GORMLEY, breaking GORMLEY's wrist during the attack. GORMLEY reports the assault to DC BUTTERS who visits WHITHAM's home address two days after the original assault. WHITHAM invites the officer into his house and into the lounge, where DC BUTTERS arrests WHITHAM for a s. 20 grievous bodily harm (contrary to the Offences Against the Person Act 1861). As the arrest is made, DC BUTTERS sees an imitation Magnum 44 on a lounge table.

Is WHITHAM liable for an offence of possessing a firearm while being arrested for a sch. 1 offence?

A No, because a s. 20 grievous bodily harm is not a sch. 1 offence.

B Yes, but only if WHITHAM is found guilty of the s. 20 assault.

C No, as WHITHAM must actually have the weapon in his physical possession.

D Yes, it is immaterial that the weapon is an imitation firearm.

Question 14.5

You arrest CHU for an offence of robbery and he is later sentenced to a term of imprisonment for three years.

When, if ever, would CHU be able to legally possess a firearm without committing an offence under s. 21 of the Firearms Act 1968?

A CHU must not have a firearm in his possession at any time before the end of a three-year period beginning on the date of his release.

B CHU must not have a firearm in his possession at any time before the end of a five-year period beginning on the date of his release.

C CHU must not have a firearm in his possession at any time before the end of a seven-year period beginning from the date of his release.

D CHU must not, at any time, have a firearm in his possession.

Question 14.6

MILLER discovers that PALFREY has been having an affair with his wife. He finds PALFREY drinking in a pub and approaches him. MILLER is holding several fingers inside his jacket and points them at PALFREY saying, *'Stand still or I'll blow you away.'* MILLER intends PALFREY to believe he has a firearm. PALFREY believes MILLER and stands still. MILLER picks up a glass from the bar, breaks it and pushes it into PALFREY's neck intending to and actually causing grievous bodily harm to PALFREY (a s. 18 offence under the Offences Against the Person Act 1861).

Is MILLER guilty of possessing a firearm while committing a sch. 1 offence (contrary to s. 17(2) of the Firearms Act 1968)?

A No, sch. 1 does not extend to causing grievous bodily harm with intent under s. 18 of the Offences Against the Person Act 1861.

B Yes, the offence can be committed when in possession of an imitation firearm and MILLER's fingers would represent an imitation firearm.

C No, MILLER must be in possession of a firearm as opposed to an imitation firearm.

D Yes, as long as MILLER is subsequently convicted of the offence of causing grievous bodily harm with intent.

Question 14.7

KING and HUNSTONE are both released from prison on the same day. KING had been sentenced to four years' imprisonment for an offence of robbery and HUNSTONE had been sentenced to 12 months' imprisonment for an offence of burglary.

According to s. 21 of the Firearms Act 1968, when, if ever, can KING and HUNSTONE lawfully possess a firearm?

A KING and HUNSTONE can never lawfully possess a firearm.

B KING can never lawfully possess a firearm; HUNSTONE can lawfully possess a firearm five years after his release.

C KING can lawfully possess a firearm five years after his release; HUNSTONE can lawfully possess a firearm three years after his release.

D KING can lawfully possess a firearm three years after his release; HUNSTONE can lawfully possess a firearm one year after his release.

Question 14.8

The Firearms Act 1968 contains certain offences dealing with the shortening and conversion of firearms. Section 4(1) of the Act deals with the offence of shortening the barrel of a shotgun.

With regard to the offences under s. 4(1), which of the following comments is correct?

A The maximum sentence for this offence is 10 years' imprisonment on indictment.

B The offence is committed when the barrel of a shotgun is shortened to a length of less than 24 inches.

C Registered firearms dealers are not excluded from committing this offence.

D The offence is committed when the barrel of a shotgun is shortened to a length of less than 28 inches.

Question 14.9

NOCTOR is in the habit of boasting that he was a member of the IRA many years ago. This is total fabrication and when he makes the boast (yet again) at his local pub, it is one time too many for FALLIS, a regular customer at the pub, who shouts out that NOCTOR is '*the king of bullshit*' and that everyone knows he is lying. NOCTOR is fuming about this humiliation and to try and add some credibility to his tall stories he manages to purchase an empty magazine to a self-loading rifle and a telescopic sight for the same type of rifle. He takes these items to his pub and shows them to

FALLIS as proof that his story is true. SMITH is in the pub when this display takes place and is concerned about what is going on and contacts the police. NOCTOR leaves the pub and is walking along the street outside the pub when he is stopped by PC HOUGHTON who searches NOCTOR under s. 47 of the Firearms Act 1968 and finds the items concerned.

Considering only the offence of having a firearm or imitation firearm in a public place (contrary to s. 19 of the Firearms Act 1968), which of the following statements is correct.

A NOCTOR commits the offence but only in relation to the empty magazine.
B NOCTOR commits the offence but only in relation to the telescopic sight.
C NOCTOR commits the offence in relation to both items.
D NOCTOR does not commit the offence in these circumstances.

Question 14.10

DOWNEY is a fanatical 'airsoft' enthusiast ('airsoft' is a military simulation sport where players participate in mock combat with authentic military-style weapons and tactics). DOWNEY has a large arsenal of weapons to enable him to enjoy his hobby. By trade DOWNEY is an engineer and in order to obtain a tactical advantage when engaging in airsoft activities he modifies two guns. He modifies an airsoft sniper rifle (which discharges 1 shot at a time) so that the kinetic energy at the muzzle measures 3 joules; he modifies an airsoft machine gun (which discharges two and more missiles without repeated pressure on the trigger) so that the kinetic energy at the muzzle measures 1.2 joules.

Would these technical modifications mean that either airsoft gun would be classed as a 'firearm' under s. 57A(2) of the Firearms Act 1968?

A Both modifications would mean that the permitted energy at the muzzle of each weapon exceeds the permitted kinetic energy level for an airsoft weapon, consequently both airsoft guns would now be classed as firearms.
B The airsoft sniper rifle would be classed as a firearm; the airsoft machine gun would not.
C These modifications do not exceed the permitted kinetic energy level for either type of weapon—they would both continue to be classed as airsoft guns.
D The airsoft machine gun exceeds permitted energy levels and would be classed as a firearm; the sniper rifle weapon does not exceed the permitted levels and is still an airsoft weapon.

Question 14.11

PC UNIS is on plain clothes patrol when he sees OSLOW (aged 25 years) walking along the public street towards him. OSLOW is carrying a bag which PC UNIS reasonably suspects contains a firearm.

Which of the following comments is correct in respect of PC UNIS's powers under s. 47 of the Firearms Act 1968?

A PC UNIS has no powers under this legislation as the officer must be in uniform to exercise them.

B PC UNIS has no powers under the legislation unless he reasonably believes that OSLOW has a firearm in his possession.

C PC UNIS has no power to ask OSLOW to hand over the bag unless he reasonably suspects OSLOW is or is about to commit an offence with the firearm.

D PC UNIS can require OSLOW to hand over the firearm for examination.

Question 14.12

PCs FRODEN and GRAY are on uniform mobile patrol as armed response officers. They receive information from a concerned member of banking staff that he has seen three men with guns near to the bank he works in. The three men are all reported to be sitting in a Ford Mondeo registration number MV07 OHG, parked in a public street near the bank. The officers drive to the scene and as they arrive they see HUGHES and LOPEZ standing next to the open driver's door of that particular car. In the driving seat of the car is DRAY. As the officers get closer to the men, there is no sign of any firearms. However, the fact that all three men are either in or near the car causes the officers to reasonably suspect they are the persons referred to by the member of bank staff.

Could the officers search the vehicle and/or persons under the powers given by s. 47 of the Firearms Act 1968?

A Yes, but only DRAY and the Mondeo could be searched.

B No, not unless the officers suspect that the men are committing or about to commit an offence.

C Yes, all three men and the Mondeo could be searched.

D No, as s. 47 of the Firearms Act 1968 relates to searches carried out on private land and not in a public place.

Question 14.13

Sections 22 to 24 of the Firearms Act 1968 create a number of summary offences restricting the involvement of people of various ages in their dealings with certain types of firearms and ammunition.

In respect of those restrictions, which of the following comments is correct?

A A person under 21 years of age must not purchase a shotgun.

B It is an offence to sell an imitation firearm to a person under the age of 21.

C A person under 17 may not have with them an assembled shotgun unless supervised by a person aged at least 21.

D A person under 14 must not have in their possession a s. 1 firearm or ammunition.

Question 14.14

PARK is in possession of ammunition for a Magnum 44 firearm. He is also in possession of an imitation firearm. It is PARK's intention to give the ammunition and the imitation firearm to HALSTEAD so that HALSTEAD can use them to endanger the life of GUEST.

Does PARK commit an offence contrary to s. 16 of the Firearms Act 1968 (possession with intent to endanger life)?

A Yes, but only in relation to the ammunition for the Magnum 44.

B No, because it is HALSTEAD and not PARK who would endanger GUEST's life.

C Yes, in respect of both the ammunition and the imitation Magnum 44.

D No, as this offence can only be committed with a firearm (not ammunition or imitation firearms).

Question 14.15

CROW commits an offence of robbery. At the time he commits the offence he is in possession of some ammunition for a Browning 9 mm pistol. CROW nets a substantial amount of money from the robbery and immediately after the offence is committed he visits a criminal associate and buys a genuine Uzi machine gun and an imitation Colt 45 pistol—the criminal associate buys the 9 mm Browning ammunition from CROW. CROW returns to his home address but has been identified as the person responsible for the offence of robbery and shortly after he arrives home the police attend his home and he is arrested for the offence. When CROW is arrested he is in possession of the genuine Uzi machine gun and the imitation Colt 45 pistol.

Considering the offence of possession of a firearm while committing or being arrested for a sch. 1 offence (contrary to s. 17(2) of the Firearms Act 1968), which of the following comments is true?

A CROW commits the offence in respect of the ammunition for the Browning 9 mm pistol and also the Uzi machine gun and the imitation Colt 45 pistol at the time of his arrest.

B CROW has committed the offence but only in relation to the Uzi machine gun and the imitation Colt 45 pistol.

C CROW has committed the offence but only in relation to the Uzi machine gun.

D CROW has not committed the offence in these circumstances.

Question 14.16

PC KITCHENER is out on patrol when he sees RYDER in the local park with what appears to be an electric stun gun. RYDER willingly hands over the electric stun gun for examination by PC KITCHENER. RYDER states that it is broken and does not work. PC KITCHENER examines the electric stun gun and then arrests RYDER for possession of a prohibited weapon in a public place.

Does RYDER commit an offence of possessing or distributing prohibited weapons or ammunition (contrary to s. 5 of the Firearms Act 1968)?

A Yes, RYDER commits the offence even if the stun gun is not working.

B No, an electric stun gun is not a prohibited weapon under the Firearms Act 1968.

C Yes, RYDER would commit the offence if the electric stun gun was working.

D No, an electric stun gun is not a firearm, within the Firearms Act 1968.

Question 14.17

UNWIN and GAYNOR are at UNWIN's house watching a film. From the conversation between the two, GAYNOR realises that UNWIN has been having sex with her boyfriend and confronts her. UNWIN admits that they are having sex. Enraged, GAYNOR picks up a pair of scissors on the coffee table and stabs UNWIN in the arm (a s. 18 wounding, contrary to the Offences Against the Person Act 1861) and GAYNOR leaves the house. GAYNOR's description is circulated and a passing patrol sees her on the street and arrests her for the s. 18 wounding. In GAYNOR's pocket they find an imitation firearm (a small pistol). The arresting officer, PC DENTON, comes to the CID office and asks if GAYNOR has committed any firearm offences.

Considering s. 17(2) of the Firearms Act 1968 (possessing a firearm while committing a sch. 1 offence), which of the following is correct with regard to the liability of GAYNOR?

A For the offence to be committed it must be a real firearm.

B Mere possession at the time of arrest for a sch. 1 offence is sufficient.

C Section 18 wounding is not included in sch. 1.

D You would need to prove that she also had the firearm with her at the time of the s. 18 wounding even though it was not used.

ANSWERS

Answer 14.1

Answer **A** — Answer D is incorrect as an electric stun gun has been held to be a prohibited weapon as it discharges an electrical current (*Flack* v *Baldry* [1988] 1 WLR 393) and it continues to be a prohibited weapon even if it is not working (*R* v *Brown*, The Times, 27 March 1992). The test as to whether a weapon is prohibited or not is purely objective and is not affected by the intentions of the defendant (*R* v *Law* [1999] Crim LR 837), making answer C incorrect. Although s. 10 of the Act allows licensed slaughterers to possess such items, this is only applicable when the weapon is possessed in any slaughterhouse or knackers' yard in which the person is employed and if this condition is not met, then the exemption will not apply. This makes answer B incorrect.

Investigators' Manual, paras 2.3.8.1, 2.3.8.2

Answer 14.2

Answer **C** — The intention does not have to be an immediate one and it may be conditional (*R* v *Bentham* [1973] QB 357), making answer B incorrect. There is no need for the firearm to be produced or shown to another, making answer D incorrect. This is an offence of intent and it is not required that the life of another be endangered, only that the intent to do so exists, making answer A incorrect. The offence cannot be committed using an imitation firearm.

Investigators' Manual, para. 2.3.11.1

Answer 14.3

Answer **B** — It is an offence for a person *to make any use whatsoever* of a firearm or imitation firearm with intent to resist or prevent the lawful arrest or detention of himself or another.

Investigators' Manual, paras 2.3.11.2, 2.3.11.3

Answer 14.4

Answer **D** — Section 20 assaults are covered by sch. 1 to the Act, making answer A incorrect. There is no need for the defendant to be subsequently convicted of the sch. 1 offence. All that is needed is to prove that he/she had the weapon in his/her possession at the time of his/her arrest for the offence (*R* v *Nelson (Damien)* [2000]

QB 55), making answer B incorrect. With regard to possession, you need to prove that the person was in possession of the firearm but not that they actually had it with them (*R* v *North* [2001] Crim LR 746), making answer C incorrect.

Investigators' Manual, para. 2.3.11.5

Answer 14.5

Answer **D** — A person who has been sentenced to custody for life or to preventive detention, imprisonment, corrective training, youth custody or detention in a young offender institution for three years or more must not, at any time, have a firearm or ammunition in his/her possession.

Investigators' Manual, para. 2.3.14

Answer 14.6

Answer **A** — Answer B is incorrect as although the offence can be committed with an imitation firearm, 'fingers' have been held not to constitute an imitation firearm (*R* v *Bentham* [2005] 1 WLR 1057). Answer C is therefore incorrect as the offence can be committed with an imitation firearm. Answer D is incorrect as there is no need for the defendant to be subsequently convicted of the sch. 1 offence (*R* v *Nelson (Damien)* [2000] 3 WLR 300).

Investigators' Manual, paras 2.3.2.4, 2.3.10.1

Answer 14.7

Answer **B** — A person sentenced to three plus years' imprisonment can never lawfully possess a firearm; a person sentenced to three plus months' imprisonment *but less than three years*, can possess a firearm five years after the date of their release.

Investigators' Manual, para. 2.3.14

Answer 14.8

Answer **B** — The maximum sentence on indictment for this offence is five years' imprisonment, making answer A incorrect. Registered firearms dealers are exempted from this offence, making answer C incorrect. The offence is committed when the barrel of a shotgun is shortened to a length of less than 24 inches, making answer D incorrect.

Investigators' Manual, para. 2.3.5.2

Answer 14.9

Answer **D** — The offence is not committed as neither of these items would be a 'firearm'. The definition of a firearm (under s. 57 of the Firearms Act 1968) states:

(1) In this Act, the expression 'firearm' means—

(a) a lethal barrelled weapon (see subsection (1B));
(b) a prohibited weapon;
(c) a relevant component part in relation to a lethal barrelled weapon or a prohibited weapon (see subsection (1D));
(d) an accessory to a lethal barrelled weapon or a prohibited weapon where the accessory is designed or adapted to diminish the noise or flash caused by firing the weapon.

In relation to s. 57(1)(c), the Act now states what a relevant component part is. Each of the following items is a relevant component part in relation to a lethal barrelled weapon or a prohibited weapon:

- a barrel, chamber or cylinder,
- a frame, body or receiver,
- a breech block, bolt or other mechanism for containing the pressure of discharge at the rear of the chamber,

but only where the item is capable of being used as a part of a lethal barrelled weapon or a prohibited weapon (s. 57(1D)).

However, magazines, sights and furniture are not considered 'component parts' meaning that neither of the items in NOCTOR's possession are firearms so he has not committed the offence (correct answer D).

Investigators' Manual, para. 2.3.2.1

Answer 14.10

Answer **B** — An airsoft gun is not regarded as a firearm for the purposes of this Act (s. 57A).

Section 57A(2) states that an airsoft gun is a barrelled weapon of any description which:

- is designed to discharge only a small plastic missile (whether or not it is also capable of discharging any other kind of missile), and
- is not capable of discharging a missile (of any kind) with kinetic energy at the muzzle of the weapon that exceeds the permitted level.

The 'small plastic missile' is a missile made wholly or partly from plastics, is spherical and does not exceed 8 millimetres in diameter (s. 57A(3)). However, the exemption is not absolute—if the kinetic energy at the muzzle exceeds the permitted level then it will be a firearm. The permitted kinetic energy level is:

- in the case of a weapon which is capable of discharging two or more missiles successively without repeated pressure on the trigger (an automatic weapon), 1.3 joules;
- in any other case (a single shot variant), 2.5 joules.

So the machine gun would not be a firearm, making answers A and D incorrect. The sniper rifle would be a firearm, making answer C incorrect.

Investigators' Manual, para. 2.3.2.1

Answer 14.11

Answer **D** — Section 47 of the Firearms Act 1968 states:

> A constable may require any person whom he has reasonable cause to suspect—
> (a) of having a firearm, with or without ammunition, with him in a public place; or
> (b) to be committing or about to commit, elsewhere than a public place, an offence relevant for the purposes of this section,

to hand over the firearm or any ammunition for examination by the constable.

Uniform is irrelevant, making answer A incorrect. Answer B is incorrect as the power requires reasonable *suspicion* not belief and answer C is incorrect as (a) allows the officer to require the firearm etc. to be handed over.

Investigators' Manual, para. 2.3.13

Answer 14.12

Answer **C** — Section 47 of the Firearms Act 1968 states:

> A constable may require any person whom he has reasonable cause to suspect—
> (a) of having a firearm, with or without ammunition, with him in a public place; or
> (b) to be committing or about to commit, elsewhere than a public place, an offence relevant for the purposes of this section,

to hand over the firearm or any ammunition for examination by the constable.

In order to exercise the power, a police officer may search the person concerned. Further, if the officer has reasonable cause to suspect that there is a firearm in a vehicle in a public place, he/she may search the vehicle. Therefore, all three men and the vehicle can be searched (answer C).

Investigators' Manual, para. 2.3.13

Answer 14.13

Answer **D** — A person under 18 must not purchase or hire any firearm or ammunition (s. 22(1)(a))—there would be nothing illegal about a person who is 18 years old (or older) purchasing a shotgun, making answer A incorrect. It is an offence to sell an imitation firearm to a person under the age of 18 (s. 24A(2)) but there would be nothing wrong with selling an imitation firearm to a person who is 18 years old (or older), making answer B incorrect. Answer C is incorrect as a person under 15 may not have with them an assembled shotgun unless supervised by a person aged at least 21 or while the shotgun is securely covered so that it cannot be fired (s. 22(3)). Answer D is correct as a person under 14 must not have in his/her possession a s. 1 firearm or ammunition (s. 22(2)).

Investigators' Manual, para. 2.3.15

Answer 14.14

Answer **A** — The offence under s. 16 of the Act cannot be committed with an imitation firearm, making answer C incorrect. The offence is committed by being in possession of a firearm or ammunition with intent by means thereof to endanger life or to enable another person by means thereof to endanger life, whether any injury has been caused or not. The fact that HALSTEAD and not PARK will endanger life is irrelevant, making answer B incorrect. As the offence can be committed with ammunition, answer D is incorrect.

Investigators' Manual, para. 2.3.11.1

Answer 14.15

Answer **B** — Section 17(2) of the Firearms Act 1968 does not apply to ammunition, making answer A incorrect. It does apply to firearms and imitations in the possession of the defendant when an offence under sch. 1 is committed (such as robbery) or when they are arrested for such an offence (making answers C and D incorrect).

Investigators' Manual, para. 2.3.11.5

Answer 14.16

Answer **A** — Section 5 of the Firearms Act 1968 states:

> (1) A person commits an offence if, without the authority of the Secretary of State or the Scottish Ministers, he has in his possession, or purchases, or acquires, or manufactures sells or transfers [a prohibited weapon].

An electric 'stun gun' has been held to be a prohibited weapon as it discharges an electric current (*Flack* v *Baldry* [1988] 1 WLR 393) and it continues to be such even if it is not working (*Brown* v *DPP* (1992) The Times, 27 March).

This clearly makes A the correct answer.

Investigators' Manual, paras 2.3.8.1, 2.3.8.2

Answer 14.17

Answer **C** — Section 17(2) of the Firearms Act 1968 states:

> If a person, at the time of his committing or being arrested for an offence specified in schedule 1 to this Act, has in his possession a firearm or imitation firearm, he shall be guilty of an offence under this subsection unless he shows that he had it in his possession for a lawful object.

Schedule 1 lists many offences but does not include specifically s. 18 wounding, making C the correct answer.

Investigators' Manual, para. 2.3.11.5

15 Terrorism and Associated Offences

QUESTIONS

Question 15.1

Section 1 of the Terrorism Act 2000 provides a definition of the term 'terrorism'.

According to that definition, which of the following comments is correct?

A The definition limits 'terrorism' to the use or threat of action inside the United Kingdom.

B 'Terrorism' is limited to circumstances where the action of an individual or group endangers a person's life, other than that of the person committing the action.

C Actions designed to seriously interfere or disrupt an electronic system are not covered by the definition.

D 'Terrorism' incorporates the use or threat of action where the use or threat is made for the purpose of advancing a racial cause.

Question 15.2

MASON holds extreme views about the Muslim faith and strongly believes that the activities of al-Qaeda (a proscribed organisation under Part II of the Terrorism Act 2000) are fully justified. He visits a mosque to attempt to rally support for the al-Qaeda cause. MASON stands outside the Mosque and puts on an armband that has the words 'al-Qaeda member' written on it (MASON is not a member of al-Qaeda). Several people approach MASON and speak to him, during which time MASON invites them to support the activities of al-Qaeda. Six people tell MASON they are interested in what he has to say and so MASON arranges a meeting with the six people at his private house. MASON will address the meeting.

At what point, if at all, does MASON commit an offence contrary to the Terrorism Act 2000?

A When he puts on the armband stating that he is a member of al-Qaeda.
B When he invites people to support the activities of al-Qaeda.
C When he arranges the meeting at his house.
D No offence is committed by MASON.

Question 15.3

PARDEW manages investment funds for a number of organisations and individuals. One of the accounts he manages belongs to MASTERSON. While PARDEW is at work and administering the funds in MASTERSON's account, he becomes aware of certain irregularities in the way in which the money for the account is obtained. PARDEW makes several enquiries about the fund and is provided with information by CRAY which suggests that the funds in the MASTERSON account are funding terrorist activity. This causes PARDEW to suspect that the funds in the account are connected to terrorism.

According to s. 19 of the Terrorism Act 2000, what, if anything at all, must PARDEW do?

A There is no obligation on PARDEW to do anything unless he believes the money he administers is connected to terrorism.
B PARDEW must make further enquiries in relation to the funds to establish if they are legitimate before making contact with a law enforcement agency.
C PARDEW must, as soon as is reasonably practicable, disclose the suspicion and the information on which it is based to a constable.
D PARDEW must inform his company director who, in turn, must contact the police within 7 days of being notified by PARDEW about the suspicions relating to the MASTERSON account.

Question 15.4

WATTS (a British citizen who lives in Birmingham) is on holiday in Spain and on the last night of his holiday he strikes up a conversation with NUMAN (who is also a British citizen living in Birmingham) in a bar. The two men get very drunk and begin to talk about politics. NUMAN expresses extremist right-wing views about immigration and tells WATTS that he despises Muslims. He informs WATTS that he has had enough and is going to attack a mosque with a machine gun he has purchased when he returns to Birmingham the following week. WATTS believes NUMAN is serious; the fact is that NUMAN is not serious at all and is merely ranting in a drunken conversation. WATTS returns to Birmingham the following day, landing at Birmingham airport, but does not tell anyone about the conversation with NUMAN.

Considering the offence relating to information about acts of terrorism (contrary to s. 38B of the Terrorism Act 2000), which of the following comments is correct?

A When WATTS arrives in Birmingham he must disclose the information regarding NUMAN to a constable as soon as reasonably practicable.

B WATTS has not committed the offence as he came by the information when he was outside the United Kingdom.

C When WATTS arrives in Birmingham he must disclose the information regarding NUMAN to any person in authority.

D WATTS has not committed the offence as the offence relating to information about acts of terrorism can only be committed by a person coming by the information in a professional capacity.

Question 15.5

Section 41 of the Terrorism Act 2000 provides a power of arrest without warrant in relation to 'terrorism'.

Which of the following comments is correct in relation to that power?

A A constable may arrest a person without warrant for being 'a terrorist' but the officer must reasonably believe the person is a terrorist.

B If a constable reasonably suspects a person of being 'a terrorist' then the constable may arrest that person without warrant, but the person arrested must have committed a specific offence relating to terrorism.

C A constable may arrest without warrant a person whom the constable reasonably suspects to be a terrorist.

D A police constable may arrest a person without warrant for being 'a terrorist' if the constable knows that the person is a terrorist.

Question 15.6

Due to a terrorist incident taking place in Manchester, it is considered expedient to set up a cordon (as per s. 33 of the Terrorism Act 2000) in a small area of the city centre for the purposes of a terrorist investigation.

In ordinary circumstances, who would authorise such a process?

A The chief constable or his/her designated deputy.

B An officer of the rank of assistant chief constable or above.

C An officer of the rank of superintendent or above.
D An officer of the rank of inspector or above.

Question 15.7

DCs ADEMAYO and TOWELL are posted to a Counter-Terrorism Unit and are receiving training regarding the powers available to the police under the Terrorism Act 2000. One of the powers discussed by the officers relates to cordons (available under s. 33 of the Terrorism Act 2000). In particular, the officers are discussing issues relating to the timing of such cordons and the authorisation process for them.

Which one of the following comments by the officers shows a correct understanding of the law?

A DC ADEMAYO states that the period for which a cordon can be authorised can begin after the order to set up the cordon is given, i.e. the cordon can begin at some time in the future.
B DC TOWELL states that the initial period to which the cordon can extend cannot extend beyond 7 days from the time the order is made.
C DC ADEMAYO states that the overall time limit for which a cordon can exist is 28 days.
D DC TOWELL states that an authorisation for a cordon could not be given by anyone below the rank of inspector.

Question 15.8

As a consequence of a terrorist investigation, a cordon designation has been provided (under s. 33 of the Terrorism Act 2000). PC JESSOP (who is wearing police uniform) and TI PANARKAR (who is wearing plain clothes) visit the area where the cordon has been established. The officers become involved with the policing of the cordon and carry out several activities within and near to the cordoned area.

Considering the powers of police officers under s. 36 of the Terrorism Act 2000 relating to cordons, which one of the following comments is correct?

A TI PANARKAR can arrange for the removal of a vehicle from the cordoned area.
B PC JESSOP can order a person immediately to leave premises which are partly in the cordoned area.
C TI PANARKAR can order a person in charge of a vehicle in a cordoned area to move it from the area immediately.
D PC JESSOP can arrange for the movement of a vehicle adjacent to a cordoned area.

Question 15.9

INNES (a citizen of the United Kingdom) has strong family connections in the Republic of Ireland and has many relatives living in Dublin. His relatives in Dublin have suffered financially as a consequence of several budget decisions made by the Republic's government and INNES is extremely angry at their predicament. INNES travels to Dublin and hides several large fireworks inside a lectern that will be used by several politicians to make speeches regarding budget cuts. Innes plans to remotely detonate the fireworks and intends to endanger the life of one or more of the politicians. CREENEY, a politician due to make a speech, begins to make his way towards the lectern but before he reaches it, INNES nervously detonates the fireworks too soon. A large explosion occurs and the lectern and part of the stage it stands on are completely destroyed; if CREENEY had been standing at the lectern he would have been killed, but fortunately neither CREENEY nor any other person is injured.

Considering the offence of causing an explosion likely to endanger life or property (contrary to s. 2 of the Explosives Substances Act 1883), which of the following statements is correct?

A INNES has not committed the offence as the action took place in the Republic of Ireland.

B INNES has not committed the offence as fireworks are not 'explosives' for the purposes of this offence.

C INNES has not committed the offence as no life was endangered.

D INNES has committed the offence in these circumstances.

Question 15.10

DUNLOP is extremely interested in explosive devices and finds an internet site that explains how to make a pipe bomb using explosives drained from fireworks. Out of pure curiosity DUNLOP purchases a number of fireworks, drains the explosives from them and makes a pipe bomb. He tells ROPER what he has done as ROPER is also interested in explosives. ROPER asks if he can have the pipe bomb to examine it and potentially make one himself, again out of pure curiosity. DUNLOP agrees and gives the pipe bomb to ROPER who stores it in a storage facility several miles away from his home. A member of staff at the storage facility finds the pipe bomb and informs the police.

Which of the following comments is correct when considering the behaviour of DUNLOP and ROPER and the offence of making or possessing explosives under suspicious circumstances (contrary to s. 4 of the Explosive Substances Act 1883)?

A No offence has been committed by either DUNLOP or ROPER as there is an absence of criminal purpose in their activities.

B DUNLOP has committed the offence but ROPER has not as he does not have the pipe bomb in his possession.

C DUNLOP and ROPER commit the offence.

D No offence has been committed as neither DUNLOP nor ROPER intended to injure or kill any person with the explosive.

Question 15.11

Intelligence of high quality is received from a reliable source to the effect that there is going to be a terrorist attack in the city centre of Birmingham. It is decided that it is appropriate to authorise the power of stop and search under s. 47A of the Terrorism Act 2000.

In respect of such an authorisation, which of the following comments is correct?

A The authorisation allows a police officer, in or out of uniform, to stop pedestrians and/or vehicles in a certain area and search the pedestrian, vehicle and/or occupants of the vehicle.

B The authorising officer in respect of this power is a police officer for the area who is of at least the rank of assistant chief constable (or commander).

C An authorisation under s. 47A may last for a period no longer than 48 hours.

D A pedestrian, vehicle and/or occupants can only be searched by a police officer exercising the power under s. 47A if the officer reasonably believes the person is involved in terrorist activities and/or the vehicle is being used for the purposes of terrorism.

Question 15.12

BORG is arrested for being a member of a proscribed organisation (an offence under s. 11 of the Terrorism Act 2000). The investigation that follows reveals that BORG rents a storage facility near to his home address and this is subsequently searched. Inside the storage facility is a box which is found to contain several electronic timers which could be used in the manufacture of explosive devices.

Considering only the offence of making or possessing an explosive substance under suspicious circumstances (contrary to s. 4 of the Explosive Substances Act 1883), has BORG committed an offence?

A Yes, the offence has been committed by BORG as he has the electronic timers under his control.

B No, BORG has not committed the offence as an electronic timer is not classed as an 'explosive substance'.

C Yes, the offence has been committed by BORG but the consent of the Director of Public Prosecutions would be required before a prosecution can be brought.

D No, the offence has not been committed as BORG does not have the electronic timers in his possession.

Question 15.13

PC SLATER is on patrol and is dispatched to a small wooded area where a person has reported finding an insecure shed. On arrival, PC SLATER cannot find the person who called the police but identifies the shed. On entering the shed, the officer finds several guns and rifles and other paraphernalia for supporting a terrorist group. PC SLATER immediately cordons the area under his powers under s. 34 of the Terrorism Act 2000 (by reason of urgency) for an investigation.

Which of the following statements is correct with regard to further compliance under s. 34 and s. 35 of the Terrorism Act 2000?

A An officer of at least the rank of superintendent is informed and, if continued designation is confirmed, the initial designation can be only for a maximum of seven days.

B An officer of at least the rank of superintendent is informed and, if continued designation is confirmed, the initial designation can be only for a maximum of 14 days.

C An officer of at least the rank of assistant chief constable/commander is informed and, if continued designation is confirmed, the initial designation can be only for a maximum of seven days.

D An officer of at least the rank of assistant chief constable/commander is informed and, if continued designation is confirmed, the initial designation can be only for a maximum of 14 days.

ANSWERS

Answer 15.1

Answer **D** — Terrorism (under s. 1 of the Terrorism Act 2000) is defined as:

(1) the use or threat of action where—
  (a) the action falls within subsection (2),
  (b) the use or threat is designed to influence the government or an international governmental organisation, or to intimidate the public or a section of the public, and
  (c) the use or threat is made for the purpose of advancing a political, religious, racial or ideological cause.
(2) Action falls within this subsection if it—
  (a) involves serious violence against a person,
  (b) involves serious damage to property,
  (c) endangers a person's life, other than the person committing the action,
  (d) creates a serious risk to the health or safety of the public or a section of the public, or
  (e) is designed to seriously interfere with or seriously disrupt an electronic system.
(3) The use or threat of action falling within subsection (2) which involves the use of firearms or explosives is terrorism whether or not subsection (1)(b) is satisfied.

The reference to 'action' here includes action outside the United Kingdom, making answer A incorrect. Answer B is incorrect as terrorism is not limited to the endangering of life (subsection (2)(c)) alone. Subsection (2)(e) includes action against electronic systems, making answer C incorrect. The purpose of advancing a 'racial' cause (correct answer D) was inserted into the definition by s. 75 of the Counter-Terrorism Act 2008.

Investigators' Manual, para. 2.4.2

Answer 15.2

Answer **A** — It is a summary offence to wear an item of clothing, or wear or carry or display an article in such a way or in such circumstances as to arouse reasonable suspicion that the defendant is a member or supporter of a proscribed organisation (s. 13). Inviting people to support al-Qaeda and arranging a meeting are also offences (s. 12(1) and s. 12(2) respectively).

Investigators' Manual, para. 2.4.2.1

Answer 15.3

Answer **C** — Section 19 states that where a person believes or suspects that another person has committed an offence under ss. 15 to 18 of the Terrorism Act 2000 and bases that belief or suspicion on information which comes to his attention in the course of a trade, profession or business or in the course of his employment (whether or not in the course of a trade, profession or business), he must disclose to a constable as soon as is reasonably practicable that belief or suspicion, and the information on which it is based, otherwise he commits an offence punishable with five years' imprisonment.

Investigators' Manual, para. 2.4.4.1

Answer 15.4

Answer **A** — The offence is committed where a person has information which he knows or believes might be of material assistance in preventing the commission by another person of an act of terrorism or in securing the apprehension, prosecution or conviction of another person, in the United Kingdom, for an offence involving the commission, preparation or instigation of an act of terrorism. This offence relates to any person who has information which he knows or believes might help prevent an act of terrorism or help bring terrorists to justice, making answer D incorrect. Section 38B(6) of the Terrorism Act 2000 has the effect that a person resident in the United Kingdom could be charged with the offence even if he was outside the country when he became aware of the information, making answer B incorrect. Disclosure in England and Wales is made to a constable, making answer C incorrect.

Investigators' Manual, para. 2.4.4.3

Answer 15.5

Answer **C** — Section 41 of the Terrorism Act 2000 gives a constable a power to arrest without warrant a person whom the constable reasonably suspects to be 'a terrorist', making answers A and D incorrect (and answer C correct). One of the benefits of the power under s. 41 is the requirement that the officer reasonably suspects the person of being a terrorist rather than suspecting his involvement in a specific offence, making answer B incorrect.

Investigators' Manual, para. 2.4.6.1

Answer 15.6

Answer **C** — Section 34 of the Terrorism Act 2000 states that a cordon authorisation may only be made by an officer for the police area who is of at least the rank of superintendent.

Investigators' Manual, para. 2.4.7.2

Answer 15.7

Answer **C** — The period of designation for the cordon begins at the time the order is made (i.e. it cannot be made to begin at some time in the future), making answer A incorrect. Answer B is incorrect as the initial authorisation period cannot extend beyond 14 days from the time the order is made (s. 35(2)). Answer D is incorrect as an authorisation can be given by an officer below the rank of superintendent in an urgent situation (s. 34(3)).

Investigators' Manual, para. 2.4.7.2

Answer 15.8

Answer **B** — The powers under s. 36 are only available if the officer is in uniform, making answers A and C incorrect. The officer in uniform has a number of powers, one of which (under s. 36(1)(e)) is to arrange for the movement of a vehicle within a cordoned area—not adjacent, making answer D incorrect.

Investigators' Manual, para. 2.4.7.3

Answer 15.9

Answer **D** — This offence is committed when a person who in the United Kingdom or (being a citizen of the United Kingdom and Colonies) in the Republic of Ireland unlawfully and maliciously causes by any explosive substance an explosion of a nature likely to endanger life or cause serious injury to property, whether or not any injury to person or property has been actually caused. Activity by a United Kingdom citizen in the Republic of Ireland would be covered, making answer A incorrect. The definition of 'explosive' under the Explosives Act 1875 applies to this offence and therefore fireworks are covered (*R* v *Bouch* [1983] QB 246), making answer B incorrect. It does not matter whether a life is actually endangered—it is the potential of the explosion that matters, so answer C is incorrect.

Investigators' Manual, para. 2.4.8

Answer 15.10

Answer **C** — Section 4 of the Explosive Substances Act 1883 states that any person who makes (DUNLOP) or knowingly has in his possession or under his control (ROPER) any explosive substance under such circumstances as to give rise to a reasonable suspicion that he is not making it or does not have it in his possession or under his control for a lawful object, shall, unless he can show that he made it or had it in his possession or under his control for a lawful object, be guilty of an offence. In *R* v *Riding* [2009] EWCA Crim 892, the defendant alleged that he had made a pipe bomb out of mere curiosity, using explosives drained from a number of fireworks. The defence contended that a 'lawful object' meant an absence of a criminal purpose rather than a positive object that was lawful. However, the court was satisfied that it meant the latter and mere curiosity could not be a 'lawful object' in making a lethal pipe bomb, making answer A incorrect. There is no requirement for an intention to kill or injure by making, possessing or controlling the explosive, making answer D incorrect. The offence includes the word 'control', which is far wider than mere possession, so 'control' over the pipe bomb in the storage facility would be covered, making answer B incorrect.

Investigators' Manual, para. 2.4.8

Answer 15.11

Answer **B** — The power is available to officers in uniform only, making answer A incorrect. Answer C is incorrect as although no actual time limit in respect of the use of the power is stated in the legislation, it does state (at s. 47A(1)(iii)) that the duration of the authorisation should be no longer than is necessary to prevent an act of terrorism. Once the power has been authorised, a constable in uniform can stop and search pedestrians, vehicles and their occupants. There is no requirement that the searching officer 'reasonably believes' the vehicle/person(s) subject to the search are involved in terrorist activities; therefore answer D is incorrect.

Investigators' Manual, para. 2.4.6.4

Answer 15.12

Answer **A** — The offence under s. 4 of the Explosive Substances Act 1883 is committed by a person who makes or knowingly has in his possession or under his control any explosive substance under such circumstances as to give rise to reasonable suspicion that he is not making it or does not have it in his possession or control for a lawful object. 'In your possession' and 'under your control' are widely interpreted—it is not just about having the substance in your immediate possession, making answer D incorrect. Articles which have been held to amount to 'explosive substances' include electronic timers (*R* v *Berry (No. 3)* [1991] 1 WLR 7 and R v G [2009] UKHL 13), making answer B incorrect. The consent of the Attorney General (or Solicitor General) is required before a prosecution can be brought, making answer C incorrect.

Investigators' Manual, para. 2.4.8

Answer 15.13

Answer **B** — The Terrorism Act 2000, s. 34(2) states:

> (2) A constable who is not of the rank required by subsection (1) may make a designation if he considers it necessary by reason of urgency.
>
> (3) Where a constable makes a designation in reliance on subsection (2) he shall as soon as is reasonably practicable—
>
> (a) make a written record of the time at which the designation was made, and
>
> (b) ensure that a police officer of at least the rank of superintendent is informed.

The period of designation begins at the time the order is made and ends on the date specified in the order. The initial designation cannot extend beyond 14 days (s. 35(2)) clearly making B the correct answer.

Investigators' Manual, para. 2.4.7.6

16 Cybercrime

QUESTIONS

Question 16.1

The police in the United Kingdom have provided a definition as to what 'cybercrime' actually is.

What is that definition?

A Cybercrime is defined as the use of any computer network for criminal activity.

B Cybercrime is defined as the use of the internet for criminal activity.

C Cybercrime is defined as the use of any computer to assist in the commission of fiduciary crimes.

D Cybercrime is defined as the use of any computer network for any criminal activity excluding those relating to sexual offences.

Question 16.2

BRIDGE works as a cleaner in the control room of a police force. As the control room is in operation 24 hours a day, BRIDGE must access the control room when resources are being despatched to incidents and also when computers are being used for a variety of police related issues. BRIDGE is vacuuming the floor of the control room when he hears one of the operators mention the name 'John HOBB' and also mentions HOBB's home address. HOBB is BRIDGE's best friend and intending to see why his friend has come to the attention of the police, BRIDGE looks over the shoulder of the operator and examines data which is displayed on the computer screen. BRIDGE intends to tell HOBB anything that he sees on the screen that he thinks will be of assistance to HOBB.

Considering the offence of unauthorised access to computer materials (contrary to s. 1 of the Computer Misuse Act 1990), which of the following comments is correct?

A BRIDGE has not committed the offence as he has not had any physical contact with the computer hardware.

B BRIDGE has committed the offence as he has secured access to restricted data.

C BRIDGE has not committed the offence as simply looking over a computer operator's shoulder to read what is on the screen would not be covered.

D BRIDGE has committed the offence which is triable on indictment only and punishable with five years' imprisonment.

Question 16.3

TIs DRAPER and EDGE are discussing the offence under s. 1 of the Computer Misuse Act 1990 and also the definition of a number of the Act's terms. The officers make a number of statements in relation to this legislation but only one is correct.

Which one is it?

A TI DRAPER states that erasing computer data would not constitute an offence under s. 1 of the Act.

B TI EDGE states that attempting to log on to a computer, even if it were unsuccessful, would still involve getting a computer to perform a function.

C TI DRAPER states that the only way a person can secure access to any program or data for the purpose of committing an offence under s. 1 is by using or copying data.

D TI EDGE states that this offence can only be committed by accessing a computer via the internet.

Question 16.4

THOMPSON commits an offence under s. 1 of the Computer Misuse Act 1990 (unauthorised access to computer materials). The information he accesses provides bank account details of several hundred customers of the bank he works for. It is THOMPSON's intention to allow ISMAY to use the bank account details sometime in the following week in order to commit offences of fraud. What THOMPSON does not know is that he has accessed the bank account details of old customers of the bank; all of the account information he accesses is useless because the accounts no longer exist.

Considering the offence of unauthorised access with intent to commit further offences (contrary to s. 2 of the Computer Misuse Act 1990), which of the following comments is correct?

A THOMPSON has not committed the offence as he intends that the information concerned will facilitate the commission of an offence by another person.

B THOMPSON has not committed the offence because he intends the information to be used in the future and not on the same occasion as the unauthorised access offence was committed.

C THOMPSON has not committed the offence as the data he has accessed is useless and makes the commission of the future offence of fraud impossible.

D THOMPSON has committed the offence in these circumstances.

Question 16.5

MAYHEW works for NOSWORTHY who provides financial advice to thousands of her customers via the internet. After a dispute, NOSWORTHY sacks MAYHEW. MAYHEW is outraged by NOSWORTHY's behaviour and wants revenge on his ex-employer. At home, MAYHEW develops a program that he intends will cause a series of problems for the computers at NOSWORTHY's business premises and impair their use. On the pretext of collecting some personal items, MAYHEW returns to the company premises and whilst in his old office he makes an unauthorised access to NOSWORTHY's computer system and runs the program he has developed. The program causes NOSWORTHY's computer system to record that information that came from one source actually came from another entirely different source. The program then generates millions of emails and sends them to NOSWORTHY's account, clogging up and impairing the use of the computer system. All of these effects are of a temporary nature and cease to operate one week after MAYHEW's visit to the company.

In relation to the offence of unauthorised acts to impair the operation of computers (contrary to s. 3 of the Computer Misuse Act 1990), at what point is the offence first committed by MAYHEW?

A When he creates the program at his home.

B When he makes the unauthorised access to NOSWORTHY's computer and runs the program.

C When the program causes NOSWORTHY's computer to incorrectly record information.

D When the program generates millions of emails.

Question 16.6

SABLE is extremely annoyed with KELLY (a neighbour of SABLE's who lives in a house opposite to SABLE) as KELLY allows his dog to foul on the footpath outside SABLE's house. SABLE picks up some of the faeces left by KELLY's dog and puts it through KELLY's letterbox. SABLE intends that KELLY should suffer distress as a consequence.

Considering the offence of sending a malicious communication (contrary to s. 1(1) of the Malicious Communications Act 1988), which of the following comments is correct?

A The offence has not been committed by SABLE as this is not a 'communication'.

B The offence has been committed by SABLE in these circumstances.

C The offence has not been committed by SABLE as the communication was not delivered in the form of a letter or electronic communication.

D The offence has not been committed as this is not a communication involving information which is false and known or believed to be false by the sender.

Question 16.7

PRICE is a night cleaner at a bank and while working at the bank one evening she notices a laptop computer left on the desk of the bank manager. PRICE thinks that there might be some useful information stored in the computer that she can pass on to her husband to assist him to commit fraud offences and so she turns the laptop on and attempts to log on. The laptop is password-protected and will not allow PRICE access.

Considering the offence of 'hacking' (under s. 1 of the Computer Misuse Act 1990) only, which of the following comments is true?

A As PRICE did not actually gain access to the computer she has committed no offence.

B PRICE's actions must be directed at a particular program otherwise the offence is not committed.

C PRICE commits the offence, as an unsuccessful attempt to log on would involve getting the computer to perform a function.

D An appropriate charge in these circumstances would be one of attempting to commit the offence.

Question 16.8

STREET works for a sales company and is considering setting up his own rival business. In order to give his fledgling business a good start, STREET gains unauthorised access to his manager's computer (committing an offence under s. 1 of the Computer Misuse Act 1990 in the process, i.e. 'hacking') intending to write down business-related information contained on his manager's computer screen detailing a large number of influential business contacts.

Is this an offence of unauthorised access with intent to commit further offences (contrary to s. 2 of the Computer Misuse Act 1990)?

A Yes, as STREET has committed an offence of 'unauthorised access' (under s. 1 of the Act) with the relevant intent.

B No, because this offence under s. 2 relates to obtaining information for another person to use in the commission of an offence.

C Yes, but STREET must actually obtain and make use of the information before the offence is complete.

D No, as STREET's activities do not constitute an offence to which this section applies.

Question 16.9

The Data Protection Act 2018 replaces the Data Protection Act 1998 and is intended to provide a comprehensive legal framework for data protection in the UK. The General Data Protection Regulation states that some of the personal data that may be processed can be more sensitive in nature and therefore requires a higher level of protection.

Which of the following personal data would be considered a 'special category' of data requiring a higher level of protection?

A Personal data about an individual's employment history.

B Personal data about an individual's criminal convictions.

C Personal data about an individual's political opinions.

D Personal data about an individual's academic qualifications.

Question 16.10

MADEN and SMITH work in the same factory and have an argument resulting in MADEN being disciplined. To get revenge on SMITH, MADEN contacts the police stating the she is SMITH and asking the police to attend her house as she has been raped. The police call at SMITH's house in response to the false allegation. A week later, MADEN sends an anonymous letter to SMITH stating that SMITH's house will be burned to the ground and her family will die in the fire. MADEN's purpose in relation to both activities is to cause SMITH distress and anxiety.

Considering only the offence under s. 1(1) of the Malicious Communications Act 1988, which of the following comments is correct?

A MADEN commits the offence in relation to both activities (the false report to the police and the threatening letter).

B MADEN commits the offence but only in relation to the false report to the police.

C MADEN commits the offence but only in relation to the threatening letter.

D MADEN does not commit the offence in these circumstances.

Question 16.11

RUTTER is having problems with her boss PATTERSON who has put her on an action plan to improve RUTTER's professional skills. RUTTER believes this is unjustified, which it is not, and therefore decides to cause PATTERSON anxiety or distress. RUTTER sends PATTERSON a false letter from a solicitor stating that PATTERSON is being taken to court by a nearby neighbour for the noise her dog makes in the garden in the morning. RUTTER also sends a text from an unidentified mobile phone stating that PATTERSON's daughter has been involved in a minor accident at school. RUTTER then puts dog faeces through PATTERSON's letterbox.

Considering the offences under s. 1(1) of the Malicious Communications Act 1988, which, if any, offences have been committed?

A None of the acts by RUTTER are covered by this legislation.

B RUTTER only commits the offence when she sends the false letter.

C RUTTER only commits the offence when she sends the false letter and the text.

D RUTTER commits the offence on all three occasions.

ANSWERS

Answer 16.1

Answer **A** — Cybercrime is defined as the use of any computer network for criminal activity. The internet could well form a part of that network but it is not so limited, making answer B incorrect. Cybercrime is not limited to the commission of fiduciary (financial) crimes, eliminating answer C. Sexual offences are one of the main areas for concern when considering computer crime and are certainly not excluded, making answer D incorrect.

Investigators' Manual, para. 2.5.1

Answer 16.2

Answer **C** — This offence involves 'causing a computer to perform any function'. This means more than simply looking at material on a computer screen or having any physical contact with the computer hardware. The case of *R* v *Bow Street Metropolitan Stipendiary Magistrate, ex parte Government of the USA* [2000] 2 AC 216 is illustrative that the purpose of the Act is to address unauthorised access as opposed to unauthorised use of data, so behaviour such as looking over a computer operator's shoulder to read what is on the screen would not be covered, making answer B incorrect. Physical contact with the hardware is not required, making answer A incorrect. The offence is triable either way and punishable with a maximum term of imprisonment of two years, making answer D incorrect.

Investigators' Manual, para. 2.5.2.1

Answer 16.3

Answer **B** — Section 17 of the Computer Misuse Act 1990 defines a number of terms used in the Act. Section 17(2) starts that a person secures access to any program or data held in a computer if by causing a computer to perform any function he (a) alters or erases the program or data, (b) copies or moves it to any storage medium other than that in which it is held or to a different location in the storage medium in which it is held, (c) uses it or (d) has it output from the computer in which it is held (whether by having it displayed or in any other manner). This makes answers A and C incorrect. The offence does not require that the computer concerned needs to be connected to the internet, making answer D incorrect. Any attempt to log on to a computer would involve getting a computer to perform a function.

Investigators' Manual, paras 2.5.2, 2.5.2.1, 2.5.2.2

Answer 16.4

Answer **D** — A person is guilty of an offence under s. 2 of the Computer Misuse Act 1990 if he commits an offence under s. 1 of the Act (as THOMPSON has done) with (a) the intention of committing another offence or (b) facilitating the commission of another offence (whether by himself or another). This makes answer A incorrect. Section 2(3) states that it is immaterial whether the further offence is to be committed on the same occasion as the unauthorised access offence, making answer B incorrect. Answer C is incorrect as s. 2(4) states that a person may be guilty of an offence under s. 2 even though the facts are such that the commission of the further offence is impossible.

Investigators' Manual, para. 2.5.2.3

Answer 16.5

Answer **B** — The offence is committed when a person does any unauthorised act in relation to a computer intending thereby to (a) impair the operation of any computer, (b) prevent or hinder access to any program or data held on any computer or (c) to impair the operation of any such program or the reliability of any such data. Therefore, the offence is committed when the unauthorised act is carried out with the requisite intention on the part of the offender (point B).

Investigators' Manual, para. 2.5.2.4

Answer 16.6

Answer **B** — The offence is not restricted to the sending of threatening or indecent communications and, in addition to sending letters, the offence covers sending any article when the sender's purpose is to cause anxiety or distress to the recipient. This will cover occasions where the article itself is indecent or grossly offensive (such as putting dog faeces through someone's letterbox).

Investigators' Manual, para. 2.5.4

Answer 16.7

Answer **C** — Answer B is incorrect as there is no need for the person's actions to be directed at any particular program or data (s. 1(2)(a) of the Act). An attempt to 'log on' involves getting the computer to perform a function (even if the function denies access) making answers A and D incorrect and answer C correct.

Investigators' Manual, para. 2.5.2.1

Answer 16.8

Answer **D** — As this is an offence of intent, there is no need for a result to take place before the offence is complete, making answer C incorrect. Answer B is incorrect as the offence can be carried out for the benefit of anyone, including the person making the unauthorised access. The offences to which this offence applies are defined under s. 2(2) of the Act; STREET's activities *do not* constitute such an offence. This is because he intends to steal *information* and this cannot be stolen as it is not property (*Oxford* v *Moss* (1978) 68 Cr App R 183).

Investigators' Manual, para. 2.5.2.3

Answer 16.9

Answer **C** — The General Data Protection Regulation (GDPR) refers to the processing of this data as 'special categories of personal data'. This means personal data about an individual's:

- race;
- ethnic origin;
- political opinions;
- religious or philosophical beliefs;
- trade union membership;
- genetic data;
- biometric data (where this is used for identification purposes);
- health data;
- sex life; or
- sexual orientation.

It does not include data regarding employment history, criminal convictions or academic qualifications, making answers A, B and D incorrect.

Investigators' Manual, para. 2.5.3

Answer 16.10

Answer **A** — The Malicious Communications Act 1988, s. 1 states:

(1) Any person who sends to another person—
- (a) a letter, electronic communication or article of any description which conveys—
  - (i) a message which is indecent or grossly offensive;
  - (ii) a threat; or
  - (iii) information which is false and known or believed to be false by the sender; or
- (b) any article or electronic communication which is, in whole or part, of an indecent or grossly offensive nature, is guilty of an offence if his purpose, or one of his purposes, in sending it is that it should, so far as falling within paragraph (a) or (b) above, cause distress or anxiety to the recipient or to any other person to whom he intends that it or its contents or nature should be communicated.

Letters are covered by the legislation (s. 1(1)(a)) making answers B and D incorrect. Answer C is incorrect as the offence can be committed by using someone else to send, deliver or transmit a message (s. 1(3)). This would include occasions where a person falsely reports that someone has been a victim of a crime in order to cause anxiety or distress by the arrival of the police.

Investigators' Manual, para. 2.5.4

Answer 16.11

Answer **D** — The Malicious Communications Act 1988, s. 1 states:

(1) Any person who sends to another person—
- (a) a letter, electronic communication or article of any description which conveys—
  - (i) a message which is indecent or grossly offensive;
  - (ii) a threat; or
  - (iii) information that is false and known or believed to be false by the sender; or
- (b) any article or electronic communication which is, in whole or part, of an indecent or grossly offensive nature.

The letter would be covered as would the text message. 'Any article' includes dog faeces—this means that answers A, B and C are incorrect.

Investigators' Manual, para. 2.5.4

17 Racially and Religiously Aggravated Offences

QUESTIONS

Question 17.1

OLLERTON and KHAN are neighbours and are in dispute over the boundary between their respective back gardens. One evening, OLLERTON comes home to find that KHAN has erected a fence between the two gardens. OLLERTON loses her temper and begins to break the fence. As OLLERTON is breaking the fence, KHAN comes out into the back garden. Motivated by frustration over the fence and also her intense hostility to Muslims, OLLERTON says to KHAN, *'How dare you put up a fence, you Muslim pig.'* KHAN is not upset by OLLERTON's comments, as he is not a Muslim.

Would this offence of criminal damage be 'racially aggravated' under s. 28 of the Crime and Disorder Act 1998?

A Yes, as it is immaterial whether OLLERTON's hostility is also based, to any extent, on any other factor.

B No, because KHAN is not personally upset by the situation.

C Yes, but only because the words uttered were said during the commission of the offence.

D No, as 'simple' criminal damage (under s. 1(1) of the Criminal Damage Act 1971) is not capable of being 'aggravated' under the Crime and Disorder Act 1998.

Question 17.2

The Crime and Disorder Act 1998 states that in certain circumstances a number of already existing offences can become 'racially or religiously aggravated'.

Which of the following offences could be 'racially or religiously aggravated' under the Act?

A An offence of riot (contrary to s. 1 of the Public Order Act 1986).

B An offence of 'aggravated' criminal damage (contrary to s. 1(2) of the Criminal Damage Act 1971).

C An offence of violent disorder (contrary to s. 2 of the Public Order Act 1986).

D An offence of stalking (contrary to s. 2A of the Protection from Harassment Act 1997).

Question 17.3

PLATT is in a bad mood as the football team he supports have just lost in a Cup Final. He was watching the match in a pub and decides to leave and walk home. On his way home, he sees a car parked at the side of the road which has a football scarf on the rear parcel shelf demonstrating support for Tottenham Hotspur (the team that PLATT's side has just lost the Cup Final to). Sitting in the front passenger seat of the car is HATCHIN. PLATT automatically presumes HATCHIN is a supporter of Tottenham Hotspur and also that HATCHIN is Jewish. PLATT opens the door of the car and drags HATCHIN out of the car, punching him in the face several times. The injuries caused to HATCHIN amount to a s. 39 battery (contrary to the Criminal Justice Act 1988). Immediately after the battery is committed, PLATT shouts, *'You filthy Jewish bastard. I hate all Spurs fans.'*

Considering the law under the Crime and Disorder Act 1998 and a 'demonstration' of hostility in particular, which of the following comments is correct?

A The circumstances could not amount to a 'demonstration' of hostility as the words were used immediately after the offence was committed, not before or during the commission of the offence.

B This could not be a religiously aggravated offence as Jewish people are not protected by the legislation.

C The circumstances of this offence mean that it could be classed as a religiously aggravated offence.

D This could not be an 'aggravated' offence as a s. 39 battery under the Criminal Justice Act 1988 cannot be racially or religiously aggravated.

Question 17.4

CHIVERTON needs money to buy drugs and decides to target Muslim people to steal from as he hates Muslims and, as far is he is concerned, they are all rich and have money to spare. He waits outside a mosque and sees NASH leave the mosque and walk towards his car. As NASH was seen leaving the mosque, CHIVERTON automatically presumes that he is a Muslim although this is not the case; NASH is a Christian and was actually visiting the mosque to speak to a friend. CHIVERTON sneaks up behind NASH and steals his wallet. NASH feels the wallet being taken and turns around to confront CHIVERTON, demanding that he hand the wallet back. CHIVERTON runs away from NASH who chases after CHIVERTON. Several minutes later, with NASH still pursuing him, CHIVERTON stops, turns around and, in order to escape, punches NASH in the face causing bruising to NASH's left cheek. NASH falls to the floor and CHIVERTON says, *'Have some of that, you Muslim tosser!'*

Thinking about the law in relation to racially and religiously aggravated offences (as per the Crime and Disorder Act 1998), which of the following comments is correct?

A CHIVERTON could be charged with an offence of religiously aggravated theft (s. 1 of the Theft Act 1968) in these circumstances.

B CHIVERTON could be charged with an offence of religiously aggravated battery (s. 39 of the Criminal Justice Act 1988) in these circumstances.

C CHIVERTON could be charged with an offence of religiously aggravated robbery (s. 8 of the Theft Act 1968) in these circumstances.

D CHIVERTON has committed theft, battery and robbery—none of these offences are religiously aggravated.

ANSWERS

Answer 17.1

Answer **A** — Section 28(3) of the Crime and Disorder Act 1998 states that it is immaterial whether or not the offender's hostility is also based, to any extent, on any other factor (correct answer A). Answer B is incorrect as the Administrative Court has held that the victim's own perception of the words used was irrelevant, as was the fact that the victim was not personally upset by the situation (*DPP* v *Woods* [2002] EWHC Admin 85). Answer C is incorrect as a racially aggravated offence can take place *immediately before, at the time of committing an offence or after committing the offence.* Answer D is incorrect as s. 1(1) 'simple' damage is capable of being an 'aggravated' offence under the Crime and Disorder Act 1998.

Investigators' Manual, paras 2.6.1, 2.6.2

Answer 17.2

Answer **D** — Some offences under the Public Order Act 1986 are covered (ss. 4, 4A and 5) but not s. 1 or 2, making answers A and C incorrect. 'Aggravated' criminal damage is not covered by the Act (although 'simple' damage is, making answer B incorrect).

Investigators' Manual, para. 2.6.2

Answer 17.3

Answer **C** — The timing of a 'demonstration' of hostility is immediately before, during or immediately after the trigger offence is committed, making answer A incorrect. Answer B is incorrect as Jews are a religious group. Answer D is incorrect as a s. 39 battery is covered by the Crime and Disorder Act 1998.

Investigators' Manual, paras 2.6.2 to 2.6.12

Answer 17.4

Answer **B** — There are a number of offences that can be racially or religiously aggravated under the Crime and Disorder Act 1998 but theft and robbery are not included in that list of offences. This makes answers A and C incorrect. Answer C is additionally incorrect as the circumstances described would not amount to an offence of robbery under s. 8 of the Theft Act 1968 (force was used in order to escape and not in order to commit the offence of theft). A s. 39 assault/battery (under the Criminal Justice Act 1988) can be racially or religiously aggravated and although the target of the assault (NASH) is not Muslim, the aggravated version of the offence has been committed.

Section 28 of the Crime and Disorder Act 1998 states:

(1) An offence is racially or religiously aggravated for the purposes of sections 29 to 32 . . . if—
  (a) at the time of committing the offence, or immediately before or after doing so, the offender demonstrates towards the victim of the offence hostility based on the victim's membership (or presumed membership) of a racial or religious group; or
  (b) the offence is motivated (wholly or partly) by hostility towards members of a racial or religious group based on their membership of that group.

Clearly CHIVERTON's behaviour when assaulting NASH demonstrates hostility towards NASH based on his presumed membership of the Muslim faith and Muslims are a religious group. This means that answer D is incorrect.

Investigators' Manual, paras 2.6.1 to 2.6.2

18 Non-Fatal Offences Against the Person

QUESTIONS

Question 18.1

GUNNING is walking his dog in a park. Although he knows his dog is bad-tempered there is nobody else in the park and so he lets his dog off its lead and allows it to run free. Just after GUNNING lets his dog free, O'HARE walks into the park. Because GUNNING has omitted to keep his dog on the lead, the dog runs towards O'HARE. O'HARE is frightened of the dog and believes it will bite him. GUNNING runs up to his dog and puts it back on the lead. O'HARE says, *'You bloody idiot, if your dog wasn't with you I'd kick your head in!'* GUNNING is annoyed by the comment and lets his dog off the lead again saying, *'Bite him boy!'* The dog bites O'HARE.

At what point, if at all, is an assault committed?

A When, because of GUNNING's omission, his dog causes O'HARE to believe he will be bitten.

B When O'HARE threatens GUNNING.

C When GUNNING sets his dog on O'HARE.

D An assault has not taken place in these circumstances.

Question 18.2

ILLINGWORTH makes a series of telephone calls to FENNEL over a period of several days. One day, he makes 14 phone calls within a one-hour period. When FENNEL answers the phone, ILLINGWORTH remains silent, sometimes for several minutes. FENNEL suffers psychiatric harm as a result.

Which of the following comments is true?

A ILLINGWORTH could only be charged with a s. 47 assault (contrary to the Offences Against the Person Act 1861), as psychiatric injuries can never amount to a s. 20 assault (contrary to the Offences Against the Person Act 1861).

B No assault is committed because 'silence' would not constitute the *actus reus* of an assault.

C ILLINGWORTH could be charged with a s. 20 assault (contrary to the Offences Against the Person Act 1861) as serious or really serious harm includes psychiatric injury.

D In these circumstances no assault is committed as the victim and the defendant are not face to face when the threats take place.

Question 18.3

LAKER is a prostitute. She is contacted by SAINSBURY, who tells LAKER that he wishes to beat her for his sexual gratification. LAKER agrees to SAINSBURY's offer and meets him in a hotel room where, during sexual intercourse, SAINSBURY punches LAKER in the face causing her to lose consciousness for a short time. A member of staff at the hotel hears LAKER crying out in pain (prior to her loss of consciousness) and calls the police, who arrive just as SAINSBURY is paying LAKER, who has re-gained consciousness, for her services.

Considering the law under s. 71(2) of the Domestic Abuse Act 2021 and issues in relation to 'consent', which of the following statements is correct?

A LAKER has consented to the use of force so any assault committed on her person is lawful and as a consequence no offence is committed.

B The injury received by LAKER amounts to a s. 47 assault and the Domestic Abuse Act 2021 states that consent to such injury cannot amount to a defence.

C Consensual activity between LAKER and SAINSBURY would not be classed as a matter for criminal investigation.

D The courts have held that consensual sadomasochistic injuries may not justifiably be made the subject of criminal law.

Question 18.4

ELVIN is a store detective who witnesses YEUNG stealing a bottle of whisky from a supermarket. ELVIN arrests YEUNG outside the supermarket, at which point YEUNG punches ELVIN in the face and runs off. ELVIN chases after YEUNG and catches her

200 metres away where the two begin fighting. GILLIGAN sees the struggle and believes that ELVIN is trying to rob YEUNG. GILLIGAN punches ELVIN in the face and as a result YEUNG manages to escape.

Who, if anyone, has committed the offence of assault with intent to resist arrest (contrary to s. 38 of the Offences Against the Person Act 1861)?

A Only YEUNG commits the offence.

B Only GILLIGAN commits the offence as he is preventing the lawful apprehension of another.

C Both YEUNG and GILLIGAN commit the offence.

D Neither YEUNG nor GILLIGAN commits the offence because ELVIN is not a police officer.

Question 18.5

BARTLEY and FABWELL play for rival Sunday League football teams. They are drinking in the same pub on the Saturday evening before the two teams meet in a grudge match. BARTLEY shouts over to FABWELL, *'You're gonna get your legs broken tomorrow!'* FABWELL replies by shouting *'And if you weren't with all your mates you'd get your legs broken now!'* BARTLEY walks over to FABWELL and says, *'If you don't leave this pub right now, you're gonna get a kicking!'*

At what point, if at all, is an assault committed?

A When BARTLEY shouts over to FABWELL *'You're gonna get your legs broken tomorrow!'*

B When FABWELL shouts at BARTLEY *'And if you weren't with all your mates you'd get your legs broken now!'*

C When BARTLEY walks over to FABWELL and says, *'If you don't leave this pub right now, you're gonna get a kicking!'*

D No offence of assault is committed in these circumstances.

Question 18.6

GAUNT is looking after his two children (aged 12 and 14). The two children are behaving badly and while play fighting with each other they topple into a TV set, smashing it in the process. GAUNT is extremely angry and hits both children. The blows result in the 12-year-old child receiving injuries that would qualify as a s. 39 battery (contrary to s. 39 of the Criminal Justice Act 1988) and the 14-year-old child receiving injuries that would qualify as a s. 47 assault (contrary to s. 47 of the

Offences Against the Person Act 1861). The children complain to the police about the assaults.

Considering the general issue of lawful chastisement and the Children Act 2004, which of the following statements is true?

A GAUNT commits an offence in respect of both assaults but could use the defence of 'lawful chastisement' in respect of the s. 39 assault against the 12-year-old child.

B The Children Act 2004 is only relevant to the 12-year-old child. GAUNT commits an offence in respect of this child only.

C The Children Act 2004 will allow GAUNT to justify both assaults as they constitute reasonable punishment.

D GAUNT commits an offence with regard to the s. 47 assault on the 14-year-old child only.

Question 18.7

PC COPPLE is dealing with an incident where several assaults and public order offences were committed. The officer is considering the possibility of charging several of the participants in the disorder with the offence of obstruct police (contrary to s. 89 of the Police Act 1996) and approaches you for some advice on the matter. The officer tells you that during the incident HARTELL was spoken to by the police but refused to answer any questions, NORRIS stood in the doorway of a house and blocked police access to the premises for several minutes, STANSFIELD made a telephone call on his mobile phone providing a false location of the disorder to the police resulting in other officers attending the incorrect address several streets away from the incident and CARTER stood in his doorway several feet from the incident and did nothing to assist the police when the disorder began. All three were later arrested for assaults.

Which of the following comments is correct?

A Obstruct police requires some sort of physical opposition so the only person who commits the offence is NORRIS.

B NORRIS and STANSFIELD commit the offence, HARTELL does not. CARTER would only commit the offence if he were under some duty towards the police to assist them.

C All four commit the offence of obstruct police in these circumstances.

D HARTELL, NORRIS and STANSFIELD commit the offence.

Question 18.8

BALDWIN hates HIGGS as the two have had numerous fights with each other. BALDWIN is drinking in his local pub when he sees ROBERTS, a friend of HIGGS, walk into the pub. BALDWIN approaches ROBERTS and says, *'Next week I'm getting a gun and I'm gonna use it to kill HIGGS.'* BALDWIN does not intend ROBERTS to believe the threat will be carried out; he just enjoys intimidating HIGGS's friends. ROBERTS believes BALDWIN and passes the threat on to HIGGS, who does not fear the threat at all.

Why has no offence of making a threat to kill (s. 16 of the Offences Against the Person Act 1861) been committed?

A Because BALDWIN has made a threat to kill another person at some time in the future.

B Because the person to whom the threat is directed (HIGGS) does not fear that the threat would be carried out.

C Because the threat has been made to a third party (ROBERTS), rather than the person to whom the threat is directed.

D Because the person making the threat does not do so with the intention that the person receiving it (ROBERTS) would fear it would be carried out.

Question 18.9

GLANVILLE is having a bonfire party but does not invite HOCKLEY. HOCKLEY feels insulted and so, when GLANVILLE is out, he places a small gas canister at the base of the bonfire believing that when it is lit the canister will explode and put the bonfire out. HOCKLEY believes that this is perfectly safe although there is a very minor chance that the explosion may hurt someone. During the party, the bonfire is lit and five minutes later the canister explodes. The gas canister hits GLANVILLE in the temple, causing him to lose consciousness.

Which of the following statements is true regarding HOCKLEY's liability for an offence of assault?

A HOCKLEY is not liable because for an assault to be committed, force must be applied directly. The placing of the canister in the bonfire is an indirect application of force.

B HOCKLEY is liable for an offence as he foresees the possibility of someone being hurt but nevertheless goes on to take the risk.

C HOCKLEY is not liable because he must actually intend to cause harm to some person when placing the canister in the bonfire.

D HOCKLEY is liable because the risk of the canister exploding and causing harm would have been obvious to any reasonable person.

Question 18.10

CATON steals a car and is pursued by PC STONE, who is driving a police livery vehicle. CATON drives into a cul-de-sac and is followed by the officer. CATON realises that there is no way out of the cul-de-sac and that he will be arrested if he does not ram PC STONE's vehicle. Intending to escape and avoid arrest, CATON drives into the officer's car. CATON realises that this may cause some harm to PC STONE. The resulting crash causes multiple cuts to PC STONE's face, requiring 100 stitches. CATON is caught several minutes later.

With regard to assaults under the Offences Against the Person Act 1861, which of the following statements is correct?

A In these circumstances, CATON has 'inflicted' the injury and so the appropriate offence would be one of a s. 20 wounding.

B CATON commits s. 20 wounding, as there was no intent to wound the officer.

C CATON's actions were malicious and carried out in order to resist arrest. This means that he commits s. 18 wounding.

D CATON's actions would not provide the evidence required for a successful prosecution under s. 18 or 20 of the Offences Against the Person Act.

Question 18.11

BROSTER puts a letter through FELLOWS's front door intending that when FELLOWS reads the letter he will fear immediate unlawful violence. To create that fear, BROSTER has written words in the letter containing numerous threats of unlawful personal violence that will take place a minute or two after FELLOWS reads the letter. FELLOWS reads the letter and as a consequence he believes that he is going to be immediately assaulted.

Would BROSTER's activities constitute an assault?

A No, because FELLOWS cannot fear immediate personal violence.

B Yes, as long as the force or violence apprehended by FELLOWS is a certainty.

C No, words, whether said or written, can never amount to an assault.

D Yes, where the words threatening immediate unlawful force come in the form of a letter, an assault may have been committed.

Question 18.12

STANFORD and HARTELL are neighbours who have had a long-standing dispute over car parking outside their respective houses. One afternoon, STANFORD parks his car directly outside HARTELL's house. HARTELL sees this and, grabbing hold of an imitation pistol, he runs outside and confronts STANFORD. Intending to make STANFORD believe he will be subject to immediate unlawful violence, HARTELL points the imitation pistol at STANFORD and says, *'If you don't move your car, I'll shoot you!'* HARTELL believes the threat and moves his car.

Considering the offences of assault and battery only (under s. 39 of the Criminal Justice Act 1988), which of the following comments is true?

A STANFORD's actions would constitute a 'battery'.

B STANFORD does not commit an assault as this is a conditional threat.

C STANFORD has committed an offence of 'assault'.

D STANFORD does not commit an assault as he cannot physically harm HARTELL with an imitation pistol.

Question 18.13

GRANT and MUSTOW have been living together for 12 months and MUSTOW is four months pregnant. One evening, they start a row and GRANT realises from what MUSTOW says that the unborn child is not his and that MUSTOW's employer, HUDSON, is actually the father of the unborn child. Enraged by this, GRANT says *'I will kill that little bastard before it is born'*, intending that the threat will cause MUSTOW to fear he will kill the unborn child. MUSTOW, however, is not frightened by this as she believes that GRANT would never carry out the threat.

Considering the offence of making a threat to kill (contrary to s. 16 of the Offences Against the Person Act 1861), which of the following statements is correct?

A GRANT commits the offence as he had the intention that the threat to kill would be feared by MUSTOW.

B GRANT does not commit the offence as the threat was made to a pregnant woman's unborn child before its birth.

C GRANT does not commit the offence as the threat to kill was to kill in the future.

D GRANT does not commit the offence as although he intended the threat to be believed, the threat was not actually believed by MUSTOW.

Question 18.14

INGRAM and COLLIER are chatting outside INGRAM's house, discussing a three-month cruise around the world that INGRAM returned from yesterday. PC TUCKER arrives at INGRAM's house and speaks to INGRAM to establish his identity. Once the officer has established INGRAM's identity, he takes hold of him and arrests him for an offence of burglary that occurred one month ago at a shop in Bradford (a lawful arrest). INGRAM knows he is innocent as he was out of the country (in the Caribbean at that time) when the offence was committed and, intending to resist his own arrest, he kicks the officer in the leg. Believing INGRAM to be innocent, COLLIER mistakenly believes that the officer is acting unlawfully and, intending to help INGRAM resist arrest, COLLIER punches the officer in the face.

Considering only the offence of assault with intent to resist arrest (contrary to s. 38 of the Offences Against the Person Act 1861), which of the following comments is true?

A Both men would have a defence to the offence in these circumstances.

B Neither INGRAM's genuine belief in his own innocence nor COLLIER's mistaken belief that the officer was acting unlawfully will provide either of them with a defence.

C INGRAM's genuine belief in his own innocence would provide him with a defence; COLLIER's mistaken belief that the officer was acting unlawfully will not.

D INGRAM's genuine belief in his own innocence would not provide him with a defence; COLLIER does not need a defence as he has not committed the offence as it is only committed when resisting your own arrest.

Question 18.15

KNUL and BURT (two ordinary members of the public) are standing on a street corner when they are approached by PC CHETTY. PC CHETTY is making enquiries into an offence of burglary at a nearby warehouse and was told by the owner of the warehouse that KNUL and BURT are always hanging around the area and might have seen something. PC CHETTY asks KNUL if he knows anything about the burglary—at this point BURT advises KNUL not to answer any of the officer's questions as he will end up getting involved in something that is none of his business. KNUL remains silent and smirks at the officer. PC CHETTY turns to BURT and asks *'Well, you seem to know a lot. Do you know anything about this burglary, then?'* BURT replies, *'Piss off! We don't have to answer any of your questions, you fuckin' pig!'*.

At what stage, if at all, is the offence of obstruct police (contrary to s. 89(2) of the Police Act 1996) first committed?

A When BURT advises KNUL not to answer any questions put to him by PC CHETTY.

B When KNUL remains silent in response to the question posed to him by PC CHETTY.

C When BURT is abusive towards the officer and tells the officer 'We don't have to answer any of your questions'.

D The offence has not been committed by BURT or KNUL.

ANSWERS

Answer 18.1

Answer **C** — Answer A is incorrect, as an assault cannot be committed by an omission. When O'HARE threatens to assault GUNNING it is a conditional threat; the assault will not be committed because of the presence of the dog and, therefore, GUNNING cannot fear immediate application of force. An assault is committed at point C because the 'indirect' application of force (via the dog) qualifies as an assault.

Investigators' Manual, paras 2.7.2, 2.7.3, 2.7.4

Answer 18.2

Answer **C** — In *R* v *Ireland* [1998] AC 147, it was held that telephone calls to a victim, followed by silences, could amount to an assault. This makes answers B and D incorrect. The harm caused in *R* v *Ireland* was psychiatric harm and the offender was charged and convicted of a s. 47 assault. This does not mean that psychiatric harm caused to the victim will limit the charge to a s. 47 assault only; there is nothing to stop an offence of s. 20 assault being committed when the harm is of a psychiatric nature, making answer A incorrect.

Investigators' Manual, paras 2.7.2.3, 2.7.13

Answer 18.3

Answer **B** — Answers A, C and D are incorrect as s. 71(2) of the Domestic Abuse Act 2021 states that it is *not a defence* that the victim of a 'relevant offence' consented to the infliction of the serious harm for the purposes of obtaining sexual gratification. A 'relevant offence' means an offence under s. 18, 20 or 47 of the Offences Against the Person Act 1861.

'Serious harm' means:

- grievous bodily harm, within the meaning of s. 18 of the 1861 Act;
- wounding, within the meaning of that section; or
- actual bodily harm, within the meaning of s. 47 of the 1861 Act.

Investigators' Manual, para. 2.7.8

Answer 18.4

Answer **A** — This offence applies to arrests made by several groups of people including store detectives, making answer D incorrect. To commit the offence the offender must assault any person knowing that the person assaulted was trying to make or help in an arrest. This knowledge is not present in GILLIGAN's mind, making answers B and C incorrect.

Investigators' Manual, para. 2.7.16.1

Answer 18.5

Answer **C** — No offence is committed at point A because the threat does not involve immediacy, i.e. the threat is to assault the next day. Point B is a conditional threat meaning that no assault will take place because BARTLEY has his friends with him. At point C an assault is committed because this is an immediate threat conditional upon some real circumstance. If FABWELL does not leave the pub he will be assaulted. This makes answer D incorrect.

Investigators' Manual, para. 2.7.2.4

Answer 18.6

Answer **A** — The Children Act 2004 applies to persons under 18 years of age, making answer B incorrect. The Children Act 2004 states that a battery of a person under 18 cannot be justified on the ground that it constituted reasonable punishment in relation to an offence of s. 18, 20 or 47 of the Offences Against the Person Act 1861, making answer C incorrect. However, where an assault amounting to an offence of s. 39 of the Criminal Justice Act 1988 is committed, although this is still an offence (making answer D incorrect) the defence of lawful chastisement is available.

Investigators' Manual, para. 2.7.9

Answer 18.7

Answer **B** — HARTELL's refusal to answer police questions is not obstruction, making answers C and D incorrect. Although obstruct police may involve some sort of physical opposition (NORRIS), it can also be committed by making it more difficult for a constable to carry out his/her duty (STANSFIELD), making answer A incorrect.

Obstruction can be caused by omission (CARTER) but only where the defendant was already under some duty towards the police or the officer.

Investigators' Manual, para. 2.7.16.2

Answer 18.8

Answer **D** — The offence of making a threat to kill can only be committed if it can be shown that the threat was made with the *intention* that *the person receiving it* would fear it would be carried out. It is the *intention* of the person who makes the threat that is important in this offence. It is immaterial that the threat to kill is a threat to kill another in the future, making answer A incorrect. It is also immaterial that the person to whom the threat is directed does not believe the threat and that that threat has been made via a third party, making answers B and C incorrect.

Investigators' Manual, para. 2.7.17

Answer 18.9

Answer **B** — An assault can be committed by the direct or indirect application of force, making answer A incorrect. The state of mind required for the offence to be complete is that the defendant either intended to cause harm or subjective recklessness as to that consequence, making answer C incorrect. Subjective recklessness involves the belief of the person committing the offence, not the objective view of a reasonable person, making answer D incorrect.

Investigators' Manual, paras 2.7.2, 2.7.3

Answer 18.10

Answer **C** — Whilst there is no intention to wound, CATON's actions are 'malicious'. Maliciousness means that the defendant must realise that there is a risk of some harm being caused to the victim. The defendant does not need to foresee the degree of harm that is eventually caused, only that his/her behaviour may bring about some harm to the victim. When the harm is caused with *intent* to *resist or prevent lawful apprehension* (arrest), the s. 18 grievous bodily harm/wounding offence is made out. This makes answers A, B and D incorrect.

Investigators' Manual, paras 2.7.14, 2.7.15

Answer 18.11

Answer **D** — Answer A is incorrect as, in *R* v *Ireland* [1998] AC 147, the House of Lords suggested that a threat to cause violence 'in a minute or two' might be enough to qualify as an assault. The force or violence apprehended by the victim does not have to be a 'certainty'. Causing fear of some possible violence can be enough (*R* v *Ireland*), making answer B incorrect. Words can amount to an assault provided they are accompanied by the required *mens rea*, making answer C incorrect. In *R* v *Constanza* [1997] 2 Cr App R 492, it was held by the Court of Appeal that where the words threatening immediate unlawful force come in the form of letters, an assault may have been committed.

Investigators' Manual, para. 2.7.2.2

Answer 18.12

Answer **C** — A 'battery' is the actual application of force requiring some degree of contact; there has been no such contact so answer A is incorrect. Answer D is incorrect as even though the pistol is an imitation and incapable of firing it is the intention of the defendant coupled with the belief of the victim that is important. These circumstances would constitute an assault (answer C). Answer B is incorrect as this *is not* a conditional threat. A conditional threat would be something like STANFORD approaching HARTELL and pointing the pistol at him and saying, *'If you ever park your car outside my house I'll shoot you!'* The threat in the question is different as it is an immediate threat conditional upon some real circumstance—move your car or else!

Investigators' Manual, paras 2.7.2, 2.7.3

Answer 18.13

Answer **B** — Section 16 of the Offences Against the Person Act 1861 states:

> A person who without lawful excuse makes to another a threat, intending that the other would fear it would be carried out, to kill another or a third person shall be guilty of an offence.

A threat to a pregnant woman in respect of her unborn child is not sufficient if the threat is to kill it before its birth (the unborn child is not a person), making B the correct answer. This makes answer A incorrect; answer C is incorrect as the threat can be to kill in the future and answer D is incorrect as the fear of the victim or third party is irrelevant to the offence—it is the intention of the person making the threat to kill that is the necessary point to prove.

Investigators' Manual, para. 2.7.17

Answer 18.14

Answer **B** — Section 38 of the Offences Against the Person Act 1861 states that whosoever shall assault any person with intent to resist or prevent the lawful apprehension or detainer of himself or of any other person for any offence, commits an offence. The definition tells us that answer D is incorrect as the offence is committed by resisting etc. your own lawful arrest or the lawful arrest of another, so INGRAM and COLLIER both commit the offence. Once the lawfulness of the arrest is established, the state of mind necessary for the offence is that required for a common assault coupled with an intention to resist/prevent that arrest/detention. It is irrelevant whether or not the person being arrested/detained has actually committed an offence. These principles were set out by the Court of Appeal in a case where the defendant mistakenly believed that the arresting officers had no lawful power to do so. The court held that such a mistaken belief does not provide a defendant with the defence of 'mistake'. Similarly, a belief in one's own innocence, however genuine or honestly held, cannot afford a defence to a charge under s. 38. Therefore, neither man would have a defence in the circumstances described, making answers A and C incorrect and answer B the correct option.

Investigators' Manual, para. 2.7.16

Answer 18.15

Answer **D** — Section 89(2) of the Police Act 1996 states that any person who resists or wilfully obstructs a constable in the execution of his duty, or a person assisting a constable in the execution of his duty, shall be guilty of an offence. Answer A is incorrect as advising a person not to answer questions is not obstructing a police officer (*Green* v *DPP* (1991) 155 JP 816). Answers B and C are incorrect as refusing to answer an officer's questions is not obstruction (*Rice* v *Connolly* [1966] 2 QB 414). Whether that unwillingness to answer is delivered in a polite or rude way does not change anything. If the defendant was under some duty to provide information then that would change the situation but whilst ordinary members of the public have a 'civic' duty to assist the police, they do not have to do so if they do not want to do so. No offence of obstruct police is committed (correct answer D).

Investigators' Manual, para. 2.7.16.2

19 Hatred and Harassment Offences

QUESTIONS

Question 19.1

ASPINALL is unemployed and desperately needs cash. He is given £25 by POWELL to hand out leaflets to members of the public. POWELL promises ASPINALL that if he hands out all the leaflets he will receive a further £25. The leaflets contain material on white supremacy movements and are intended to stir up racial hatred against black people. ASPINALL is aware of the content of the leaflets and their purpose but only wants to distribute them to receive payment from POWELL and begins distributing the leaflets to members of the public.

With regard to s. 19 of the Public Order Act 1986 only, which of the following statements is correct?

A This offence can only be committed in a public place.

B Although ASPINALL commits the offence, he would be able to claim a defence under s. 19, as he did not intend to stir up racial hatred.

C ASPINALL does not commit the offence because he did not publish the written material.

D ASPINALL commits the offence as having regard to all the circumstances racial hatred is likely to be stirred up.

Question 19.2

HOLCROFT and STEVENSON live opposite each other in the same street. There have been a number of disagreements between the two and this has resulted in several arguments taking place. HOLCROFT decides to send a letter to STEVENSON in which she tells STEVENSON that '*You are a bastard and an inconsiderate bitch to everyone in the street and we all hope you die of cancer!'* STEVENSON is extremely upset by the contents of the letter. Several months later, HOLCROFT hears about the effect her letter has had and is delighted. In order to make STEVENSON's life even more miserable she sends an email to STEVENSON saying, *'The entire street hates you ... Please die of something horrible and die soon!'* On each occasion, HOLCROFT is well aware that her conduct would amount to harassment of STEVENSON.

In relation to the offence of harassment (under s. 1 of the Protection from Harassment Act 1997), which of the following comments is correct?

A HOLCROFT commits the offence when she sends the letter to STEVENSON.

B The offence has not been committed as the offence requires that the activity making up the 'course of conduct' be of the same nature and these two incidents are different.

C HOLCROFT commits the offence when she sends the email to STEVENSON.

D The offence has not been committed as the two instances of behaviour by HOLCROFT are several months apart.

Question 19.3

AKRAM (who is of Pakistani origin) moves into a house next door to McKENNA. McKENNA is outraged as he does not like anyone of Asian origin. As AKRAM is moving his furniture into his new house, McKENNA leans out of his front bedroom window and shouts to AKRAM, *'Sometime this week I think I'll pop round and give you a Paki bashing.'* AKRAM is frightened by the comment and fears that McKENNA may use violence against him. The next morning, AKRAM is still moving furniture into the house when McKENNA leans out of the front bedroom window again and says, *'You still here, Paki? Maybe I'll give your kids a beating instead of you.'* These words cause AKRAM to fear that violence will be used against his children.

In relation to the offence of putting people in fear of violence (under s. 4 of the Protection from Harassment Act 1997), which of the following comments is correct?

A The offence under s. 4 of the Act has not been committed by McKENNA at any time.

B The offence has been committed by McKENNA but only when he makes the second remark to AKRAM.

C The offence has been committed by McKENNA and, because of the nature of the comments by McKENNA, McKENNA should be charged with the racially aggravated version of this offence.

D The offence has not been committed as McKENNA was in a dwelling when the course of conduct took place.

Question 19.4

BUCKLEY works at a laboratory which uses animals in experiments. He has been followed from the laboratory where he works to his home address by PLATT and WALLER who are now standing outside BUCKLEY's home address holding placards with the word 'Murderer' written on them. DC MORGAN is near to BUCKLEY's house and hears the radio call dispatching officers to the scene. DC MORGAN decides to attend the scene and on arrival he identifies himself as a police officer and speaks to PLATT and WALLER, who say that they are outside BUCKLEY's house to persuade BUCKLEY to stop working at the laboratory. When the officer speaks to BUCKLEY, he tells the officer that he is extremely upset and distressed by the presence of PLATT and WALLER.

With regard to a police direction to prevent intimidation or harassment (under s. 42 of the Criminal Justice and Police Act 2001), which of the following comments is correct?

A DC MORGAN would have no power under s. 42 as he is not in uniform.

B If DC MORGAN believes, on reasonable grounds, that the presence of PLATT and WALLER is likely to cause alarm or distress to BUCKLEY, he may direct them to leave the vicinity of the premises in question.

C The power under s. 42 is only exercisable by an officer of the rank of inspector or above.

D DC MORGAN can require PLATT and WALLER to leave the vicinity of the premises in question but this requirement has to be made in writing.

ANSWERS

Answer 19.1

Answer **D** — Section 19 of the Public Order Act 1986 deals with the publishing or distribution of written material with intent to stir up racial hatred. Answer A is incorrect as this offence can be committed in public or in private. Answer B is incorrect as although there is a defence to this offence, it is only available if the person can show that they were unaware of the content of the material and did not suspect and had no reason to suspect that it was threatening, abusive or insulting. Answer C is incorrect as the offence can be committed by distribution to the public or a section of the public, as well as by publication to that group.

Investigators' Manual, paras 2.8.2.3, 2.8.2.4

Answer 19.2

Answer **C** — Section 1 of the Protection from Harassment Act 1997 states that a person must not pursue a course of conduct which amounts to harassment of another and which he/she knows or ought to know amounts to harassment of the other. Under s. 2 of the Act, such behaviour amounts to an offence. A 'course of conduct' in the case of a single person (HOLCROFT) means conduct on at least two occasions in relation to that person, meaning that answer A is incorrect. There is no specific requirement that the activity making up the course of conduct be of the same nature, making answer B incorrect. Answer D is incorrect as on occasions the courts have accepted that instances of behaviour by the defendant several months apart will suffice. Where a defendant wrote two threatening letters to a member of the Benefits Agency staff, he was convicted of harassment even though there had been a four and a half month interval between the two letters (*Baron* v *CPS*, 13 June 2000, unreported).

Investigators' Manual, paras 2.8.4 to 2.8.4.6

Answer 19.3

Answer **A** — Section 4 of the Protection from Harassment Act 1997 states that a person whose course of conduct causes another to fear, on at least two occasions, that violence will be used against him is guilty of an offence. The defendant's course of conduct must cause the victim to fear that violence will (rather than might) be used against him or her (rather than someone else). So causing a person to fear, on at least two occasions, that violence would be used against a member of their family is not enough (*Mohammed Ali Caurti* v *DPP* [2001] EWHC Admin 867). So, in these circumstances the offence has not been committed meaning that answers B and C are incorrect. There is no 'dwelling' exception to this offence (similarly, just because the conduct described takes place from a dwelling house would not provide anyone with a defence), meaning that answer D is incorrect.

Investigators' Manual, paras 2.8.5, 2.8.5.1

Answer 19.4

Answer **B** — The Criminal Justice and Police Act 2001 gives the police specific powers to prevent the intimidation or harassment of people in their own or others' homes. Situations envisaged by the legislation typically arise where protestors gather outside a house where a particular individual is believed to be. Under such circumstances s. 42 provides the *most senior ranking police officer* at the scene with discretionary powers to give directions to people in the vicinity, meaning that answer C is incorrect. The power arises where:

- the person is outside (or in the vicinity of) any premises that are used by any individual as his/her dwelling; and
- the constable believes, on reasonable grounds, that the person is there for the purpose of representing or persuading the resident (or anyone else);
- that he/she should not do something he/she is entitled or required to do; or
- that he/she should do something that he/she is under no obligation to do; and
- the constable also believes, on reasonable grounds, that the person's presence amounts to, or is likely to result in, the harassment of the resident or is likely to cause alarm or distress to the resident.

A direction given under s. 42 requires the person(s) to do all such things as the officer specifies as being *necessary* to prevent the harassment, alarm or distress of the resident, including:

- a requirement to leave the vicinity of the premises in question; and
- a requirement to leave that vicinity and not to return to it within such period as the constable may specify, not being longer than three months;

and (in either case) the requirement to leave the vicinity may be to do so immediately or after a specified period of time (s. 42(4)).

The direction may be given orally and, where appropriate, may be given to a group of people together (s. 42(3)), meaning that answer D is incorrect. There is no requirement that the officer giving the direction be in uniform, meaning that answer A is incorrect.

Investigators' Manual, para. 2.8.7

20 Child Protection

QUESTIONS

Question 20.1

HILL has separated from his common-law wife, YEO. There is a 15-year-old child by this relationship and the two have an informal understanding that HILL will have the child at weekends and YEO will have the child during the week. On Tuesday afternoon, YEO comes to your police station to report an offence of child abduction. She tells you that she has received a telephone call from HILL telling her that he has taken the child to Germany and will not be back for two more weeks. HILL stated that he had attempted to contact YEO but had been unable to communicate with her. YEO wants HILL arrested and charged with the offence of child abduction (contrary to s. 1 of the Child Abduction Act 1984).

What will you tell her?

A HILL has not committed an offence under this legislation as it only applies to a child under the age of 14.

B HILL has committed the offence but he may be able to avail himself of a defence to the charge in these circumstances.

C HILL has not committed the offence as the child has been taken out of the United Kingdom for less than one month.

D HILL has committed the offence but the consent of the Attorney General is required before a charge of child abduction is brought.

Question 20.2

HAYMAN (aged 16 years) and NICHOLL (aged 13 years) are in a park when they are approached by EAMES (aged 30 years). EAMES tells them that he has just had his bike stolen and asks them if they will help him to look for it. This is not true as EAMES's real motive is to attack the boys and sexually assault them at the first opportunity. Both boys willingly agree to EAMES's request and walk towards some nearby bushes where EAMES claims that he left the bike. After walking some 30 metres with EAMES, the boys have second thoughts and run off.

Has EAMES committed an offence of child abduction (contrary to s. 2 of the Child Abduction Act 1984)?

A Yes, but only in relation to NICHOLL.

B No, because both HAYMAN and NICHOLL consented to go with EAMES.

C Yes, both HAYMAN and NICHOLL are covered by the legislation.

D No, neither of the boys has been removed from the lawful control of any person.

Question 20.3

POTTS and OLDFIELD lived together as common-law husband and wife but the relationship has ended. There were two children by this relationship, ANN (aged 12 years) and MARTIN (aged 16 years). Both children now live with their mother (OLDFIELD), who has lawful custody of the children. One evening, POTTS visits his children. While OLDFIELD goes out shopping, POTTS persuades the two children to go on holiday with him to Spain for two weeks. The children agree and all three leave for Spain without the consent of OLDFIELD.

Would this constitute an offence of child abduction (contrary to s. 1 of the Child Abduction Act 1984)?

A No, as POTTS has taken the children outside the United Kingdom for less than one month.

B Yes, but only in relation to ANN.

C No, because POTTS is the father of both children.

D Yes, in relation to ANN and MARTIN.

Question 20.4

DC WELL receives information that PORT has physically abused her children and visits PORT, who lets the officer into her house. DC WELL speaks to JANE PORT (aged 16 years) and ALEX PORT (aged 12 years). JANE PORT has several cuts and bruises to her face; ALEX PORT shows no signs of being physically abused. JANE PORT tells the officer that her mother is responsible for her injuries and that this is not the first time she has been assaulted by her. ALEX PORT tells the officer that he has heard his mother beating his sister and it frightens him and he cannot eat as a result. Because of what he has seen and heard, DC WELL is considering taking both children into 'Police Protection' (under s. 46 of the Children Act 1989).

Which of the following statements is correct?

A DC WELL can take ALEX PORT into 'Police Protection' but cannot take JANE PORT into 'Police Protection' because she is not a 'child' for the purposes of the Act.

B DC WELL can take JANE PORT into 'Police Protection' if he has reasonable cause to believe that she will suffer significant harm and ALEX PORT because of any impairment he may suffer from hearing his sister being ill-treated.

C DC WELL can take JANE PORT into 'Police Protection' but cannot take ALEX PORT into 'Police Protection' because he has not suffered any physical abuse.

D DC WELL cannot take either of the children into police protection in these circumstances.

Question 20.5

DC HAMBLING has taken JEPHCOTT into 'Police Protection' (under s. 46 of the Children Act 1989).

What is the maximum period that JEPHCOTT can spend in 'Police Protection'?

A 24 hours.

B 48 hours.

C 72 hours.

D 96 hours.

Question 20.6

MILBURN (aged 13 years) is subject to an emergency protection order and is in the care of his social worker, PRINCE. MILBURN's stepfather, HOLT, rings MILBURN on his mobile phone and tells him that life would be far better for him if he ran away from PRINCE's care and came back to his family. HOLT tells MILBURN that if he does run away from PRINCE he will take him to Disneyland in Florida.

Has HOLT committed an offence of acting in contravention of a protection order (contrary to s. 49 of the Children Act 1989)?

A Yes, he has induced and incited MILBURN to run away from a responsible person.

B No, this offence can only be committed by taking MILBURN away from the responsible person.

C Yes, but only if MILBURN actually runs away from the responsible person.

D No, this offence relates to children who are in care or in police protection and not to those subject to an emergency protection order.

Question 20.7

JUDSON leaves FOXLEY, her common-law husband, after their relationship breaks down and takes their three-year-old child with her. FOXLEY contacts DC BANHAM and reports the child's absence. DC BANHAM later locates JUDSON, who is staying in a women's refuge with her three-year-old child. At the request of JUDSON, DC BANHAM tells FOXLEY that the child is safe but refuses to tell him where the child is. FOXLEY hires a solicitor and *ex parte* (i.e. without telling the police) applies for an order from the County Court under s. 33 of the Family Law Act 1986, requiring the police to disclose the information.

Considering the law with regard to the disclosure of a child's whereabouts, which of the following statements is correct?

A If FOXLEY obtains such an order then DC BANHAM will have to provide him with details of the child's whereabouts.

B An order under s. 33 in respect of the police will be made without their presence (*ex parte*) in all cases.

C If FOXLEY's application is successful then DC BANHAM will have to tell FOXLEY's solicitor of the child's whereabouts.

D It has been held that only in exceptional circumstances will the police be asked to divulge the whereabouts of a child under a s. 33 order.

Question 20.8

Section 1 of the Child Abduction Act 1984 provides a defence whereby a person does not commit an offence under this section by taking or sending a child out of the United Kingdom without the appropriate consent if that person either has a child arrangement order in force in respect of the child or is a special guardian of the child. This defence under s. 1 of not requiring the appropriate consent has time limits for the sending or taking of the child out of the United Kingdom.

In relation to those time limits, which of the statements below is correct?

A Both persons with a child arrangement order and special guardians can take or send a child out of the United Kingdom without the appropriate consent for a period of less than one month.

B Both persons with a child arrangement order and special guardians can take or send a child out of the United Kingdom without the appropriate consent for a period of less than three months.

C Persons with a child arrangement order can take or send a child out of the United Kingdom without the appropriate consent for less than one month and special guardians for less than three months.

D Persons with a child arrangement order can take or send a child out of the United Kingdom without the appropriate consent for less than three months and special guardians for less than one month.

ANSWERS

Answer 20.1

Answer **B** — This legislation applies to children under the age of 16, making answer A incorrect. A person would not commit an offence if they took a child out of the United Kingdom for less than a month *and* they are a person in whose favour there is a residence order in force with respect to the child. In this case there is an informal arrangement, making answer C incorrect. Although HILL commits the offence, it is the consent of the Director of Public Prosecutions that is required before bringing a charge under this legislation. HILL may be able to avail himself of the defence under s. 1(5)(b) of the Act, i.e. that he has taken all reasonable steps to communicate with YEO but has been unable to communicate with her.

Investigators' Manual, paras 2.9.2.1, 2.9.2.2

Answer 20.2

Answer **A** — The legislation covers children under the age of 16 years, making answer C incorrect. The fact that the boys consented to go with EAMES is irrelevant, making answer B incorrect. The Act talks about the taking or detaining of a child and this includes keeping a child where they are found or inducing the child to remain with the defendant or another person. Effectively, this taking or keeping is complete when the defendant substitutes his/her authority or will for that of the person in lawful control of the child and in this example the substitution takes place when EAMES walks with the boys towards the bushes (*R* v *Leather* (1993) 98 Cr App R 179). Therefore, answer D is incorrect.

Investigators' Manual, para. 2.9.2.3

Answer 20.3

Answer **B** — This offence can be committed by any person listed under s. 1(2) of the Act who is connected to the child/children. The Act states that a person is connected with a child (at s. 1(2)(b)) in the case of a child whose parents were not married to each other at the time of his/her birth, if there are reasonable grounds for believing that he is the father of the child, i.e. POTTS. However, just because POTTS is the father of the children does not afford him immunity from this offence, making answer C incorrect. The offence can only be committed in relation to a child under the age of 16 so it cannot be committed in relation to MARTIN, making answer D incorrect. The fact that POTTS has taken the children outside the United Kingdom for less than one month is immaterial. The time factor is only relevant if there is a residence order in existence in favour of POTTS (and there is not); what is relevant is that POTTS has taken ANN outside the United Kingdom without the consent of OLDFIELD, making answer A incorrect.

Investigators' Manual, para. 2.9.2.1

Answer 20.4

Answer **B** — Section 46 of the Act states that where a constable has reasonable cause to believe that a child would otherwise be likely to suffer significant harm, he may remove the child to suitable accommodation. Answer A is incorrect as a 'child' is someone who is under 18 years old (s. 105). Answer C is incorrect as the definition of 'harm' is very broad and includes forms of ill-treatment that are not 'physical'. It also covers the impairment of health (physical or mental) and also physical, intellectual, emotional, social or behavioural development. The definition also extends to impairment suffered from seeing or hearing the ill-treatment of *any other person*. Answer D is incorrect for these reasons.

Investigators' Manual, para. 2.9.4

Answer 20.5

Answer **C** — The longest period that a child can spend in 'Police Protection' is 72 hours (s. 46(6)).

Investigators' Manual, para. 2.9.4

Answer 20.6

Answer **A** — Answer D is incorrect as s. 49(2) states that this offence applies to a child who is in care, subject of an emergency protection order or in police protection (s. 46). A 'responsible person' is any person who at the time has care of the child by virtue of a care order, an emergency protection order or by s. 46 of the Act, i.e. PRINCE. The offence can be committed by (a) taking a child to whom this section applies away from a responsible person, or (b) keeping such a child away from a responsible person or (c) inducing, assisting or inciting such a child to run away from or stay away from the responsible person. Therefore, answers B and C are incorrect.

Investigators' Manual, para. 2.9.4.2

Answer 20.7

Answer **D** — This question relates to the circumstances in *S* v *S (Chief Constable of West Yorkshire Intervening)* [1998] 1 WLR 1716. In this case, Butler-Sloss LJ stated that an order under s. 33 provides for the information to be disclosed to the court and not to any other party or his/her solicitor, making answers A and C incorrect. She also stated that an order made under s. 33 should not normally be made in respect of the police without their being present, making answer B incorrect.

Investigators' Manual, para. 2.9.4.3

Answer 20.8

Answer **C** — The Child Abduction Act 1984, s. 1 states:

(4) A person does not commit an offence under this section by taking or sending a child out of the United Kingdom without the appropriate consent if—
- (a) he is a person named in a child arrangements order as a person with whom the child is to live, and he takes or sends the child out of the United Kingdom for a period of less than one month; or
- (b) he is a special guardian of the child and he takes or sends the child out of the United Kingdom for a period of less than 3 months.

Therefore C is the correct answer.

Investigators' Manual, para. 2.9.2.2

21 Offences Involving the Deprivation of Liberty

QUESTIONS

Question 21.1

SMITH is selling her house to GLYNN and the two have verbally agreed a price. Before any contracts are signed, SMITH has her house revalued and discovers that she can obtain another £20,000 should she put it back up for sale. In view of this, SMITH contacts GLYNN to ask for more money. GLYNN is outraged and goes to SMITH's house. SMITH lets GLYNN into her house but when he becomes abusive she demands he leave; he refuses. SMITH then tries to leave the house but GLYNN stops her by telling her that she is not leaving until she signs a contract agreeing to sell at the lower price. SMITH begins to cry and several minutes later GLYNN decides to leave.

Considering the offence of false imprisonment only, which of the following statements is correct?

A The offence is not committed because SMITH has not been physically detained.

B The offence will only be committed if GLYNN intends to restrain SMITH's movements.

C Keeping SMITH in her home for however short a time may amount to false imprisonment.

D Common law states that false imprisonment cannot be committed in the home of the complainant.

Question 21.2

MARSTON is part of a religious commune. UNWIN believes that MARSTON is in danger as the commune will ask MARSTON to turn all her property over to them. UNWIN decides that she will return MARSTON to her parents' home by whatever means are necessary. UNWIN visits the commune and finds MARSTON. She asks MARSTON to walk with her while they discuss her situation and MARSTON agrees. MARSTON refuses to return with UNWIN, who then lies to MARSTON stating that MARSTON's mother is seriously ill and that she must come with her. MARSTON agrees and begins walking with UNWIN. Several minutes later, MARSTON asks for proof of her mother's illness from UNWIN who, at this point, physically drags MARSTON along for several metres before she lets her go.

At what point, if at all, does UNWIN first commit the offence of kidnap?

A When UNWIN initially begins walking with MARSTON intending to return her by whatever means necessary.

B When she lies to MARSTON about her mother and MARSTON walks with her for several minutes.

C When UNWIN uses physical force to drag MARSTON for several metres.

D UNWIN does not commit the offence because she has a lawful excuse to carry away MARSTON.

Question 21.3

RICKWOOD works in a high security building where all the doors to the section where he works are controlled electronically. BRADISH approaches the control panel for the door locks and turns it off. This causes all of the doors in RICKWOOD's section of the building to lock shut. BRADISH believes that someone may have been locked in the building as a consequence of his actions but is not sure. As a result, RICKWOOD is locked in his section for 20 minutes until the door locks are released.

Which of the following statements is correct with regard to the offence of false imprisonment?

A RICKWOOD would have to be detained for several hours before a charge of false imprisonment would be appropriate.

B The offence is not committed because BRADISH did not actually intend anyone's freedom to be restrained.

C The fact that BRADISH was reckless as to whether anyone would be locked in means the offence is committed.

D BRADISH will only be found guilty of the offence if a jury consider his actions were reckless.

Question 21.4

DUNBAR (a UK national) visits Cairo (in Egypt) with a view to recruiting a number of adults to come to England and beg on the streets of London. DUNBAR intends to exploit any adults he recruits and to use or threaten force against them to make them carry out begging activities once they are in London and he intends to keep any money they make. In Egypt, DUNBAR speaks to AHMED (an adult) and tells him that he can provide him with transport to England and get him a job in London. AHMED is delighted and voluntarily agrees to travel with DUNBAR from Cairo to Alexandria (also in Egypt) where he will be transported by boat to mainland Europe and onwards to the United Kingdom. DUNBAR and AHMED travel to Alexandria together but, in Alexandria, AHMED changes his mind about going to England and returns to Cairo.

Considering only the offence of human trafficking (contrary to s. 2 of the Modern Slavery Act 2015), which of the following comments is correct?

A DUNBAR does not commit the offence as he did not intend to sexually exploit AHMED.

B The offence has not been committed because the travel that took place only took place within Egypt.

C As no actual exploitation of AHMED occurred, the offence has not been committed.

D DUNBAR has committed the offence in these circumstances.

Question 21.5

KING is convicted of an offence under s. 2 of the Modern Slavery Act 2015 (human trafficking). The court makes a slavery and trafficking prevention order in relation to KING.

How long may such an order last?

A For a fixed period of at least two years or until further order.

B For a fixed period of at least three years or until further order.

C For a fixed period of at least four years or until further order.

D For a fixed period of at least five years or until further order.

Question 21.6

GRANT works in the local travel agents in a large shopping centre and her manager is AZIZ. AZIZ fancies GRANT but he knows this is not reciprocated. AZIZ decides that he is going to kidnap GRANT; he knows from working with GRANT that she loves fast, flashy cars. He texts her from the underground car park of the shopping centre and lies to her that he has come to work in his brother's Ferrari and would she like to go for a ride. GRANT cannot resist the temptation and goes to the underground car park. On arrival there, there is no Ferrari but a large van. AZIZ jumps out of the van, takes hold of GRANT and throws her into the back of the van, binds her with rope and then drives off.

Considering the offence at common law, at what point does AZIZ first commit the offence of kidnap?

A AZIZ first commits kidnap when he sends the text to GRANT.

B AZIZ first commits kidnap when GRANT walks from her desk to the car park.

C AZIZ first commits kidnap when he throws GRANT into the back of the van.

D AZIZ first commits kidnap when he drives off with GRANT in the vehicle.

Question 21.7

BUCHANAN is a British citizen who owns several holiday homes in Italy. He is visiting Naples when he sees ALI, a refugee from Libya, begging on a street. BUCHANAN approaches ALI and asks her if she is interested in working for him as a maid in one of his holiday homes a short distance away on the Amalfi coast of Italy. He tells her the job comes with food and lodging. ALI is delighted at the prospect and replies that she is interested. BUCHANAN tells her that she will need to meet him in a side street around the corner from their current location in one hour and he will drive her to the holiday home. BUCHANAN actually intends to take ALI to the house to exploit her by forcing her into prostitution. One hour later, BUCHANAN meets ALI and drives her to the holiday home. During the journey, ALI becomes suspicious of BUCHANAN and manages to escape when he stops for fuel.

Has BUCHANAN committed an offence of human trafficking (contrary to s. 2 of the Modern Slavery Act 2015)?

A No, as the activity (arranging ALI's travel) takes place in Naples this would not constitute an offence under s. 2 of the Act.

B Yes, but only when BUCHANAN actually picks ALI up and drives her to his holiday home with a view to exploiting her.

C Yes, the offence has been committed by BUCHANAN as soon as he arranged the travel of ALI with a view to her being exploited.

D No, as BUCHANAN intended to exploit ALI outside the United Kingdom (he intended to exploit her in Naples).

Question 21.8

MALPASS and FROBISHER are friends and have a bet with each other. MALPASS bets £500 that FROBISHER would not have the nerve to pick up a prostitute and have sex with her. FROBISHER takes the bet and the two men drive to an area that is well known to be frequented by prostitutes. FROBISHER drops MALPASS off on a street corner so that he can witness what happens. FROBISHER then drives to the other side of the road and winds his car window down to speak to WARNER who is standing on the street corner dressed provocatively. FROBISHER asks WARNER to get into his car to 'discuss terms' and WARNER complies. Once inside the car, WARNER tells FROBISHER that sexual intercourse is £100. FROBISHER tells her that is too much and at this point locks the doors of the car and tells WARNER to drop her price or he will not let her go. WARNER panics and tells FROBISHER to let her out. FROBISHER repeats his demand that she drop her price so WARNER says she will drop it to £50; FROBISHER tells her it is still too much. At this point, WARNER starts to scream so FROBISHER unlocks the doors and tells WARNER to get out. She does so and FROBISHER drives away.

Does FROBISHER commit the offence of false imprisonment (contrary to common law)?

A Yes, FROBISHER commits the offence when he locks the doors of his car and restrains WARNER's freedom of movement.

B No, FROBISHER does not commit the offence as he has not touched WARNER and has therefore not physically restrained her freedom of movement.

C Yes, FROBISHER commits the offence but the prosecution would have to prove that he intended to restrain WARNER's freedom of movement, as recklessness in respect of this element of the offence is not enough.

D No, FROBISHER does not commit the offence as WARNER's freedom of movement was only restrained for a very short period of time.

ANSWERS

Answer 21.1

Answer **C** — There is no requirement for the detaining of a person to be carried out by a physical action, just that their movement be restrained; this may be achieved by words alone, making answer A incorrect. The mental element required to commit this offence was stated in *R* v *Rahman* (1985) 81 Cr App R 349 as being 'the unlawful and intentional or reckless restraint of a victim's movement from a particular place' so the offence can be committed recklessly, making answer B incorrect. The 'particular place' can be absolutely anywhere and this includes a victim's own house, making answer D incorrect.

Investigators' Manual, para. 2.10.1

Answer 21.2

Answer **B** — The offence of kidnap is the unlawful taking or carrying away of one person by another by force or fraud (*R* v *D* [1984] AC 778). At point A UNWIN's intentions are to remove MARSTON by any means; however, MARSTON has voluntarily consented to walk with UNWIN and no fraud or force is used. At point B the offence is committed as UNWIN has used a fraud to move MARSTON from one point to another; distance is no object. Although a 'lawful excuse' would provide UNWIN with a defence to the charge, a concern for finances or a moral or spiritual concern would not suffice; there must be a necessity recognised as law (*R* v *Henman* [1987] Crim LR 333, CA), making answer D incorrect.

Investigators' Manual, para. 2.10.2

Answer 21.3

Answer **C** — Detention for however short a period may amount to false imprisonment, making answer A incorrect. The state of mind required for this offence is 'subjective recklessness' making answers B and D incorrect.

Investigators' Manual, para. 2.10.1

Answer 21.4

Answer **D** — Section 2 of the Modern Slavery Act 2015 states that a person commits an offence if the person arranges or facilitates the travel of another person ('V') with a view to V being exploited. Exploitation takes many forms and covers sexual and non-sexual exploitation, making answer A incorrect. Section 2(5) states that 'travel' means:

(a) arriving in, or entering, any country,
(b) departing from any country,
(c) *travelling within any country.*

Section 2(6) states that a person who is a UK national commits an offence under this section regardless of where the arranging or facilitating takes place *or where the travel takes place*, so the journey from Cairo to Alexandria would be covered, making answer B incorrect. The fact that AHMED changed his mind and that no actual exploitation took place is immaterial, making answer C incorrect.

Investigators' Manual, para. 2.10.5

Answer 21.5

Answer **D** — Section 17(4) of the Modern Slavery Act 2015 states that a slavery and trafficking prevention order may last for a fixed period of at least five years or until further order.

Investigators' Manual, para. 2.10.7.3

Answer 21.6

Answer **C** — It is an offence at common law to take or carry away another person without the consent of that person and without lawful excuse.

C is the correct answer owing to the ruling in *R* v *Hendy-Freegard* [2007] EWCA Crim 1236. When a person moves from place to place 'when unaccompanied by the defendant' cannot constitute either taking or carrying away or deprivation of liberty, which are necessary elements of the offence. The carrying or taking away takes place when AZIZ throws GRANT into the back of the van.

Investigators' Manual, para. 2.10.2

Answer 21.7

Answer **C** — Section 2(6) of the Modern Slavery Act 2015 states that a person who is a UK national (that includes a British citizen) commits an offence under this section regardless of where the arranging or facilitating takes place, meaning that answer A is incorrect. Answer D is incorrect as the exploitation can take place in any part of the world. The offence under s. 2 of the Modern Slavery Act is committed by arranging or facilitating the travel of another person ('V') with a view to V being exploited. BUCHANAN therefore commits the offence when the arrangements are made (correct answer C), meaning that answer B is incorrect.

Investigators' Manual, para. 2.10.5

Answer 21.8

Answer **A** — It is an offence at common law to falsely imprison another person. The elements required for this offence are the unlawful and intentional/reckless restraint of a person's freedom of movement, making answer C incorrect. Locking someone in a vehicle or keeping him/her in a particular place for however short a time may amount to false imprisonment if done unlawfully, so answer D is incorrect. Physical contact is not required between offender and victim, meaning that answer B is incorrect.

Investigators' Manual, para. 2.10.1

PART 3

Property Offences

22 Theft

QUESTIONS

Question 22.1

BOYLAN and HAMILL are employed in a small shop and regularly chat to each other. During one such conversation, BOYLAN asks if HAMILL will help her with a problem. She tells HAMILL that over 12 months ago she lent £2,000 to IRONS, another shop employee, and that since then IRONS has flatly refused to pay any part of the money back. BOYLAN offers HAMILL £200 to act on her behalf and recover the loan from IRONS. HAMILL tells BOYLAN not to worry and that he will somehow resolve the situation. After work, HAMILL goes to IRONS's home and breaks into and takes IRONS's car, which HAMILL thinks is worth around £2,000, from the drive. He takes the car to BOYLAN's house and presents it to BOYLAN as payment of the loan.

With regard to s. 2 of the Theft Act 1968, which of the following statements is correct?

A HAMILL's actions will not be dishonest if he honestly believes that he has a right in law to deprive IRONS of the car on behalf of BOYLAN.

B HAMILL must have a reasonable belief that he has a right in law to act as he did. If this is not the case then he has acted dishonestly.

C Section 2 of the Theft Act 1968 only allows an individual to appropriate property on behalf of himself and not, as in this case, on behalf of a third person.

D HAMILL's behaviour is dishonest as it falls below the standards of reasonable and honest people.

Question 22.2

CANHAM is a committed anti-vivisectionist and is a long-standing member of the Animal Liberation Front. He breaks into a laboratory and releases a variety of animals used for testing medicines. CANHAM personally believes that freeing the animals from captivity is not dishonest but an ethically and morally correct and proper decision. He does realise that, according to the ordinary standards of reasonable and honest people, what he has done would be considered dishonest. As he leaves the laboratory he is caught and arrested. At his trial, CANHAM maintains that his behaviour was not 'dishonest'.

Considering case law decisions regarding 'dishonesty', which of the following statements is correct?

A A jury must take into account the fact that CANHAM's behaviour has not been dishonest according to his own moral values and in such a situation he should be acquitted of the charge.

B The prosecutor will place before the court the facts of what CANHAM did and thought and then invite the court to hold that he was dishonest according to the standards of ordinary decent people.

C In such a situation, if s. 2 of the Theft Act 1968 is not applicable or helpful, the decision regarding whether CANHAM was dishonest is a matter for the judge to decide.

D CANHAM's actions can still be dishonest as what he did will be tested against the ordinary standards of reasonable and honest people along with the fact that he knew his actions were dishonest by those standards.

Question 22.3

MILSOM is shopping in his local supermarket when he notices that a member of staff has left a price-labelling machine on a display stand. He thinks it will be funny to create new price labels for goods in the store and cause chaos as a result. MILSOM walks around the store placing new and cheaper price labels on a wide variety of goods. MILSOM's only intention is to create confusion, not to benefit himself or any other customers in the supermarket.

Considering s. 3 of the Theft Act 1968 (appropriation) only, which of the following statements is correct?

A Although MILSOM swaps price labels, he is not appropriating the property. To do this effectively, he must pay for the goods.

B MILSOM's actions fall short of a full appropriation. This can only be accomplished by a combination of label swapping and the removal of an item from the shelf.

C It does not matter that MILSOM's further intention is to cause chaos and confusion; his conduct would constitute an appropriation.

D In order for MILSOM to appropriate property, he must have a dishonest intention. As this is not present, he does not appropriate.

Question 22.4

PC TROTMAN starts an attachment to the CID. He is told to take over the workload of a colleague who has retired. A few days later, PC TROTMAN approaches you with numerous reports that have been recorded as thefts. He believes that several of these reports do not represent offences of theft as there are some elements of the offence missing.

In which one of the following reports will you tell the officer that there has been an offence of theft?

A JOBLING was stopped in a stolen Mercedes. He had bought the car in good faith, paying a reasonable price for it but refused to hand it back to the original owner when he found out it was stolen.

B YU speaks little English. He shows ADEY, a taxi driver, a written address and gives him £10. The fare should be £9.50. ADEY indicates that this is not enough and takes a £50 note from YU's wallet. YU permits him to do so.

C PIT was arrested for stealing a caravan. The caravan was never recovered by the police and was left in a lay-by while PIT was interviewed. When he was released and before the true owner recovered the caravan, PIT took the caravan again.

D RODWELL was stop searched and found in possession of a £1,000 gold ring stolen in a theft. RODWELL states that when he innocently found the ring he believed he would never find the true owner.

Question 22.5

EALES rents a house under a tenancy agreement from his local council. EALES is short of money and decides to sell off several items from the house to help him through his cash crisis.

At what stage, if at all, does EALES first commit an offence of theft?

A When he picks flowers from the front garden of the house to sell commercially at a car-boot sale.

B When he severs a large amount of topsoil to sell to his neighbour.

C When he removes a fireplace to sell at a nearby second-hand shop.

D As EALES is in possession of the land under a tenancy agreement, he cannot steal land, things forming part of the land or severed from it or fixtures or structures let which are to be used with the land.

Question 22.6

LONGWORTH is a medical student with a keen interest in human anatomy. To satisfy her desire for experimentation she enters a university laboratory and takes a whole human body and several amputated and preserved body parts.

Which of the following statements is correct?

A LONGWORTH would be guilty of the theft of the human body and of the preserved body parts.

B LONGWORTH would only be guilty of the theft of the human body.

C LONGWORTH would be guilty of the theft of the preserved body parts.

D LONGWORTH would not be guilty of theft as human bodies and preserved body parts are not property for the purposes of s. 4 of the Theft Act 1968.

Question 22.7

GRATTON is a registered charity collector and is collecting in a shopping precinct. WHITBREAD approaches GRATTON and places a £20 note into his collecting tin. Moments later, WHITBREAD realises that he will not have enough cash to buy a computer game and returns to speak with GRATTON. He asks GRATTON for the money back but GRATTON refuses. WHITBREAD grabs hold of the collecting tin, removes the £20 and gives the tin back to GRATTON.

For the purposes of s. 5 of the Theft Act 1968, has WHITBREAD taken property 'belonging to another'?

A No, for although the money is no longer in WHITBREAD's direct control, he still retains a proprietary right or interest in the property.

B Yes, where money is given to charity collectors it becomes the property of the charitable trustees at the moment it goes into the collecting tin.

C No, as GRATTON is only the representative of the charity, 'ownership' of the money would remain with WHITBREAD until it is officially handed to the relevant charitable trustees.

D Yes, because you can steal property belonging to yourself. The money may be WHITBREAD's but it 'belongs' to GRATTON.

Question 22.8

DENYER opens a garden centre specialising in water features. One large fountain has a sign next to it that says '*Make a wish, all donations go to local charity.*' After a couple of months the garden centre is having financial problems. DENYER decides to collect the coins in the fountain and place the cash into the company bank account instead of giving it to charity. DENYER intends to replace the charity funds if her business survives the difficult period.

Has DENYER committed the offence of theft?

A Yes, DENYER has received and retained money to use in a specific way. She has contravened this obligation and is guilty of theft.

B No, as DENYER intends to replace the money she cannot commit the offence of theft.

C Yes, but only if she is unable to repay the money to the nominated charity.

D No, ownership of the money has been transferred to DENYER who has a moral and not a legal obligation to pass the money on to a local charity.

Question 22.9

While visiting a council art gallery, POINTON removes a painting worth £30,000 from the premises. When he takes the painting, his intention is to return it provided the council make a £3,000 donation to a local charity. The incident receives a large amount of press coverage, which causes POINTON to panic. He returns the picture to the gallery the next day.

Considering the offence of theft only, which of the following statements is correct?

A Although POINTON does not intend the gallery to permanently lose the painting, he treats the painting as if it were his own and therefore commits theft.

B This is not theft as there is no intention to permanently deprive the gallery of the painting at the time of the appropriation.

C POINTON commits theft as he may not be able to return the painting in the circumstances he imagines and this amounts to treating the painting as his own.

D Theft cannot be committed in these circumstances as at no stage does POINTON intend to permanently deprive the gallery of the picture.

Question 22.10

QUILTEY is walking his dog in a park when he finds £300 in £10 notes on the footpath. QUILTEY honestly believes that the person to whom the money belongs cannot be discovered by taking reasonable steps and decides to keep the money. The money was lost by GILL 20 minutes before QUILTEY found it. GILL reported the loss at a police station near to the park where the money was lost.

Is s. 2 of the Theft Act 1968 applicable in these circumstances?

A Yes, because QUILTEY has not taken reasonable steps to discover the person to whom the property belongs.

B No, and as s. 2 is not applicable, the issue of whether QUILTEY was dishonest or not will have to be decided by reference to the ruling in *Barlow Clowes International (in liq)* v *Eurotrust International Ltd* [2006] 1 All ER 333.

C Yes, as it is QUILTEY's honest belief that is important, not the fact that he did or did not go on to take reasonable steps to find the owner of the property.

D No, as QUILTEY does not appropriate the property in the belief that he has a right in law to deprive a person of it.

Question 22.11

BEST becomes friendly with BROOK. BROOK is in her 70s and of limited intelligence. Over a period of time, BEST worms his way into BROOK's affections and persuades BROOK to provide him with cash from her bank account and after some six months, BROOK has given BEST £30,000. This is done with the consent of BROOK who has made an absolute gift of the money to BEST. BROOK's son finds out about BEST's activities and reports the matter to the police.

Considering the law with regard to 'appropriation', which of the following statements is correct?

A In a prosecution for theft it will be necessary to prove that the taking of the property was done without the owner's consent.

B BEST cannot appropriate property belonging to another because BROOK has made an absolute gift of the money to BEST.

C In these circumstances, it is immaterial whether the act of appropriation was done with BROOK's consent or authority.

D As BROOK consented to the appropriation, BEST does not commit the offence of theft.

Question 22.12

The term 'property' is defined under s. 4 of the Theft Act 1968.

Which of the following comments is correct with regard to that term?

A A person cannot steal land, or things forming part of land in any circumstances.

B A person's characteristics and their administrative data (such as a national insurance number) would constitute property.

C A trademark is 'property' and is capable of being stolen.

D Confidential information can be classed as property.

Question 22.13

The term 'belonging to another' is defined by s. 5 of the Theft Act 1968.

Which of the following statements is correct with regard to that term?

A Unless property is stolen from an individual who has possession or control over it, there can be no theft.

B In determining whether a person has 'possession' of property, the period of possession can be finite (i.e. for a given number of hours, days, etc.) or infinite.

C In a prosecution for theft it is necessary to show who owns the property.

D In proving theft, you do not need to show that the property belonged to another at the time of the appropriation.

Question 22.14

Section 176 of the Anti-social Behaviour, Crime and Policing Act 2014 inserted s. 22A into the Magistrates' Courts Act 1980, which provides that low-value shoplifting is to be a summary offence. However, if the value of the goods exceeds a certain amount this will not be the case.

What is that amount?

A £100.

B £150.

C £200.

D £250.

Question 22.15

BLEAZE and ROMFORD are out shopping in a town centre and are examining goods in a large but expensive department store. BLEAZE is interested in a T-shirt priced at £180 and tells ROMFORD he is going to steal it. ROMFORD tells BLEAZE that he will help him by acting as a look-out while the theft takes place. BLEAZE takes the T-shirt and the two leave the department store. Outside the store, they are detained by a store detective and the police are called to the scene. PC FORD arrests BLEAZE and ROMFORD on suspicion of theft and takes them to a designated police station.

Considering the law of theft, in particular that relating to low-value shoplifting (dealt with by s. 22A of the Magistrates' Courts Act 1980), which of the following comments is correct?

A ROMFORD has not committed an offence as you cannot aid the commission of a summary-only offence (such as low-value shoplifting).

B BLEAZE and ROMFORD could be dealt with by way of a fixed penalty for committing this theft offence.

C As low-value shoplifting is a summary-only offence, PC FORD could not use powers under s. 18 of the Police and Criminal Evidence Act 1984 to search the homes of BLEAZE and ROMFORD.

D If BLEAZE and ROMFORD plead guilty to this offence, they could not be sent to the Crown Court for trial or committed there for sentence.

Question 22.16

ATKINS is director of Guy Wilkes Ltd, a manufacturing company. Wilkes Ltd owns 20 acres of land a short distance from the factory which over the years has been used for testing off-road vehicles. The land is no longer of use to the company, but has a value for agricultural purposes of about £12,000 per acre. ATKINS is tasked by the company to sell the land on behalf of the company with a view to the company making a profit from the sale of the land. ATKINS sells the land to himself at £5,000 per acre thinking that once he owns the land he can sell it for the correct market value and make a large amount of money.

Considering the law with regard to the offence of theft (under s. 1 of the Theft Act 1968) and specifically the law under s. 4(2) of the Theft Act 1968, does ATKINS commit theft?

A Yes, because any person can steal land.

B No, as land can never be classed as property (and therefore stolen) for the purposes of theft.

C Yes, he commits the offence in these circumstances.

D No, because you can only steal items severed from the land.

Question 22.17

FORD is staying at and looking after MORRIS's house whilst MORRIS is on holiday. FORD is a drug addict and he receives a phone call from his drug dealer saying that he wants £500 that FORD owes him. FORD does not have the money but, in order to immediately pay off his drug dealer, he takes MORRIS's computer to a pawn shop and pawns it, raising the £500 needed to pay off his drug dealer. FORD intends to loan the £500 needed to get the computer back from his mother in a few days and replace it before MORRIS returns from holiday.

Considering the offence of theft (under s. 1 of the Theft Act 1968) and the law relating to s. 6 of the Theft Act 1968 (intention to permanently deprive), is FORD liable for theft?

A No, FORD is not liable because he had legal access to the property from MORRIS.

B Yes, FORD is liable if you can prove that he would never have the resources to recover the computer from the pawn shop.

C No, FORD is not liable because he had no intention to permanently deprive when he exchanged the computer for cash.

D Yes, FORD is liable as this behaviour amounts to treating the property as his own (an intention to permanently deprive).

ANSWERS

Answer 22.1

Answer **A** — Section 2 of the Theft Act 1968 provides three instances where appropriation of property will not be regarded as dishonest. This question centres on s. 2(1)(a), which states appropriation will not be dishonest 'if he appropriates the property in the belief that he has in law the right to deprive the other of it, on behalf of himself or of a third person'. The belief of the defendant need only be honest and not reasonable, therefore answer B is incorrect. The appropriation can take place on behalf of a third person, making answer C incorrect. Answer D is incorrect as it relates to the ruling in *Barlow Clowes International (in liq)* v *Eurotrust International Ltd* [2006] 1 All ER 333 and *Royal Brunei Airlines Sdn Bhd* v *Tan* [1995] 3 All ER 97 and although relevant to the issue of dishonesty, it does not form any part of s. 2 of the Act.

Investigators' Manual, paras 3.1.3, 3.1.4

Answer 22.2

Answer **B** — Plainly, A is incorrect; to attribute dishonesty purely on the basis of the individual moral beliefs of the defendant would be unsound. Answer C is incorrect as whether someone has been dishonest or not is a question of fact for the jury (or the magistrates as the case may be) to decide.

What CANHAM thinks about his behaviour (whether he thinks his actions are dishonest by the standards of ordinary decent people) is irrelevant (making answer D incorrect).

The test for dishonesty in criminal cases is the same as it is for civil cases. This test was set out in *Barlow Clowes International (in liq) v Eurotrust International Ltd* [2006] 1 All ER 333 and *Royal Brunei Airlines Sdn Bhd v Tan* [1995] 3 All ER 97.

When dishonesty is in question, the magistrates/jury will first have to ascertain the actual state of the individual's knowledge or belief as to the facts (this does not have to be a reasonable belief—the question is whether the belief is genuinely held). Once his/her actual state of mind as to knowledge or belief is established, the question of whether his/her conduct had been honest or dishonest was to be determined by the magistrates/jury by applying the (objective) standards of ordinary decent people. There is no requirement that the defendant had to appreciate that what he/she had done was, by those standards, dishonest.

The test retains a role for the state of mind of the defendant (in relation to the facts) but it removes the requirement for him/her to appreciate the dishonesty of his/her actions.

Taking this approach means that to prove dishonesty a prosecutor need only place before a court facts of what the defendant did and thought and then invite the court to hold that he was dishonest according to the standards of ordinary decent people (correct answer B).

Investigators' Manual, para. 3.1.4

Answer 22.3

Answer **C** — Appropriation under s. 3 of the Theft Act 1968 is an assumption by a person of the rights of an owner and there is no requirement for a dishonest intention, making answer D incorrect. There have been a number of cases involving the swapping of price labels but after *R* v *Gomez* [1993] AC 442, the House of Lords concluded that the mere swapping of the price labels on goods amounted to an 'appropriation'; this eliminates answers A and B. This was the case regardless of any further intentions of the defendant.

Investigators' Manual, para. 3.1.5

Answer 22.4

Answer **B** — Answer A is incorrect because although the buyer of the car 'appropriates' property, this has been done in good faith and for value and, as per s. 3(2) of the Theft Act 1968, this will not amount to theft. Answer D is incorrect as although an appropriation has taken place it is not accompanied by circumstances of dishonesty as per s. 2(1)(c) of the Theft Act 1968. Answer C is incorrect as although stolen property can be 'appropriated', the same property cannot be stolen again by the same thief (*R* v *Gomez* [1993] AC 442). The same stated case dealt with answer B. It is immaterial that the owner of the property permits or consents to an appropriation; it is still theft.

Investigators' Manual, para. 3.1.5

Answer 22.5

Answer **C** — Under s. 4(2)(c) of the Theft Act 1968, a tenant can appropriate fixtures or structures let to be used with the land, i.e. the fireplace. This makes answer D incorrect. Answers A and B are incorrect as a tenant cannot steal things forming part of the land (the flowers) or the land itself (the topsoil) when he/she is in possession of the land.

Investigators' Manual, para. 3.1.6

Answer 22.6

Answer **C** — A person cannot steal a human body. Human bodies are not classed as property under the Theft Act 1968 (*Doodeward* v *Spence* (1908) 6 CLR 406) unless some work has been carried out on the body for preservation or for a scientific purpose. This makes answers A and B incorrect. This conclusion was reached in *R* v *Kelly* [1999] QB 621, where body parts taken from the Royal College of Surgeons were classed as stolen. This makes answer D incorrect.

Investigators' Manual, para. 3.1.7

Answer 22.7

Answer **B** — In *R* v *Dyke* [2002] Crim LR 153, it was stated that the moment money given by members of the public to charity collectors goes into the collecting tin, it becomes the property of the relevant charitable trustees. So once the money is in the tin, it no longer 'belongs' to WHITBREAD, making options A and C incorrect. Option D is also incorrect because, whilst you cannot steal your own property, the money does not belong to WHITBREAD.

Investigators' Manual, para. 3.1.8

Answer 22.8

Answer **A** — Section 5(3) of the Theft Act 1968 states that when a person receives property from another and is under an obligation to deal with that property in a particular way, the property shall be regarded (as against him) as belonging to the other. An 'obligation' is a legal one not a moral one. This makes answer D incorrect. Section 6(2) of the Theft Act makes it clear that regardless of an intention to repay, a person parting with property under a condition as to its return that may not be possible commits theft, making answers B and C incorrect.

Investigators' Manual, para. 3.1.9

Answer 22.9

Answer **A** — If there is an intention to permanently deprive at the time of the appropriation then an offence of theft will be committed. The intention to permanently deprive is defined in s. 6(1) of the Theft Act 1968 and states that a person who appropriates property without meaning the other to permanently lose it has this intention if their intent is to treat the thing as their own regardless of the other's rights. POINTON's intention to 'ransom' the painting (regardless of his motives) would be caught by this section, making answers B and D incorrect. Answer C is incorrect as it relates to s. 6(2) of the Theft Act 1968, where someone parts with property belonging to another under a condition as to its return which he may not be able to perform, and does not relate to this scenario.

Investigators' Manual, para. 3.1.11

Answer 22.10

Answer **C** — Section 2 of the Theft Act relates to dishonesty, in particular what is *not* dishonest rather than what is. There are several circumstances where a defendant will not be dishonest and one of those (s. 2(1)(a)) is where the person appropriates property in the honest belief that he has a right in law to deprive the other of it. There are three other circumstances including (s. 2(1)(c)) if the person appropriates the property in the honest belief that the person to whom the property belongs cannot be discovered by taking reasonable steps. This makes answer D incorrect as a belief in the right in law is not the only time a person will/will not be dishonest. It also makes answer B incorrect as the ruling in *Barlow Clowes International (in liq)* v *Eurotrust International Ltd* [2006] 1 All ER 333 would only need to be considered when s. 2 is not applicable or helpful and s. 2(1)(c) clearly relates to the circumstances of this question. Answer A is incorrect as it is the defendant's *belief* at the time of the appropriation that is important, not that the defendant went on to take reasonable steps to discover the person to whom the property belonged.

Investigators' Manual, paras 3.1.3, 3.1.4

Answer 22.11

Answer **C** — In a prosecution for theft it is unnecessary to prove that the taking was without the owner's consent (*Lawrence* v *Metropolitan Police Commissioner* [1972] AC 626), making answer A incorrect. It is immaterial whether the act of appropriation was done with the owner's consent or authority (*R* v *Gomez* [1993] AC 442), making answer D incorrect. In *R* v *Hinks* [2001] 2 AC 24, the court held that even though the complainant had made an absolute gift of property, retaining no proprietary interest in the property or any right to resume or recover it, an appropriation can still take place. This makes answer B incorrect.

Investigators' Manual, para. 3.1.5

Answer 22.12

Answer **C** — Answer A is incorrect as although a person cannot steal land *in general*, there are several circumstances under s. 4(2) of the Act that are exceptions to this rule. Answers B and D are incorrect as a person's characteristics and administrative data and confidential information (*Oxford* v *Moss* (1978) 68 Cr App R 183) are not intangible property for the purposes of the Theft Act 1968.

Investigators' Manual, paras 3.1.6, 3.1.7

Answer 22.13

Answer **B** — Answer A is incorrect as property can be stolen from a person who has a right or interest in that property. Answer C is incorrect as in a prosecution for theft it is not necessary to show who owns the property, only that it belongs to someone else other than the defendant. Answer D is incorrect as you *must show* that the property belonged to another at the time of the appropriation.

Investigators' Manual, para. 3.1.8

Answer 22.14

Answer **C** — Shoplifting is not a specific offence as such but constitutes theft under s. 1 of the Theft Act 1968; accordingly, s. 22A(3) of the Magistrates' Courts Act 1980 defines shoplifting for the purposes of this provision, which applies if the value of the stolen goods does not exceed £200. This makes answers A, B and D incorrect.

Investigators' Manual, para. 3.1.2

Answer 22.15

Answer **D** — An offence of low-value shoplifting includes secondary offences such as aiding and abetting, meaning that answer A is incorrect. Answer B is incorrect as to be dealt with by way of a fixed penalty for theft, the value of the goods cannot exceed £100. Section 22A(6) provides that certain powers conferred by the Police and Criminal Evidence Act 1984 on the police and others in respect of indictable offences remain available in respect of low-value shoplifting, notwithstanding that it is reclassified as summary only. The powers concerned include a power of arrest exercisable by a person other than a constable (e.g. a store detective), powers enabling police officers to enter and search premises and vehicles in various circumstances for the purposes of searching for evidence in connection with an investigation or arresting individuals suspected of committing offences, and powers enabling a magistrate to authorise such entry and search. This means that answer C is incorrect. The effect of s. 22A is that offences of low-value shoplifting cannot be sent to the Crown Court for trial or committed there for sentence; they will attract a maximum penalty of six months' custody; and they will be brought within the procedure in s. 12 of the Magistrates' Courts Act 1980 that enables defendants in summary cases to be given the opportunity to plead guilty by post (correct answer D).

Investigators' Manual, para. 3.1.2

Answer 22.16

Answer **C** — Under s. 4(2) of the Theft Act 1968 you cannot generally steal land (answer A is incorrect) but there are three exceptions.

(1) Trustees or personal representatives or someone in a position of trust to dispose of land belonging to another, can be guilty of stealing it if in such circumstances, they dishonestly dispose of it.

You do not have to 'sever' the land to steal it in such circumstances (answer D is incorrect). In these circumstances, ATKINS is a 'trustee' (he is a director of the company concerned) and has committed the offence, making C the correct answer.

The other exceptions are persons not in possession of the land and actions in certain circumstances of tenants (in these exceptions land can be stolen so answer B is incorrect).

Investigators' Manual, para. 3.1.6

Answer 22.17

Answer **D** — The Theft Act 1968, s. 6(2) states:

> where a person, having possession or control (lawfully or not) of property belonging to another, parts with the property under a condition as to its return which he may not

> be able to perform, this (if done for the purposes of his own and without the other's authority) amounts to treating the property as his own . . . regardless of the other's rights.

Section 6(2) deals with occasions such as pawning another's property. In pawning the property, the defendant parts with the property (in this case a computer belonging to MORRIS) on the basis that he might be able to recover it (there could never be any certainty of recovery). Such behaviour will amount to an offence of theft (correct answer D).

Investigators' Manual, para. 3.1.11

23 Robbery

QUESTIONS

Question 23.1

CREW, MUSGROVE and BYER play cards together on a regular basis. As a result, BYER falls into debt, owing CREW and MUSGROVE £500 each. One evening, BYER is drinking in a bar when CREW and MUSGROVE approach him. CREW places the tip of a knife against BYER's face and MUSGROVE says, '*Give us all you have or your face might not have a future*.' BYER hands over his wallet and all his gold jewellery. CREW and MUSGROVE honestly believe they are legally entitled to the property but realise they are not entitled to use force to get it.

Which of the following statements is correct with regard to the offence of robbery (contrary to s. 8 of the Theft Act 1968)?

A CREW and MUSGROVE commit robbery. It does not matter that they believe in a right to take the property; they have used force in order to obtain it.

B The beliefs of CREW and MUSGROVE are immaterial as such a gambling debt amounts to a moral obligation to repay the money. This is a robbery.

C There is no dishonesty by CREW or MUSGROVE and as a robbery involves theft and therefore no dishonesty is present, the offence of robbery is incomplete.

D Only CREW is guilty of robbery as he is the only person actually using force against BYER.

Question 23.2

ASGHAR and CULLEM are pickpockets. On a train station platform ASGHAR nudges into GLENN, knocking him off-balance and into CULLEM, who steals a wallet from inside GLENN's jacket. GLENN realises the wallet has been stolen and tells ASGHAR and CULLEM he is going to inform the police. CULLEM produces a flick-knife and threatens GLENN with it, telling him to keep quiet or he will be stabbed.

At what point, if at all, has the full offence of robbery been committed?

A When ASGHAR nudges into GLENN knocking him off-balance.

B When CULLEM steals the wallet from inside GLENN's jacket.

C When CULLEM threatens GLENN with the flick-knife.

D At no time has an offence of robbery been committed.

Question 23.3

DEIGHTON is part of a football crowd who become involved in a street brawl with a group of rival supporters. During the course of the fight, DEIGHTON punches and kicks WATTON to the floor, knocking WATTON unconscious. Even though WATTON is unconscious and can offer DEIGHTON no resistance, DEIGHTON continues to punch WATTON about the head and face with his right fist for pure sadistic pleasure. At the same time he removes WATTON's wallet with his left hand.

Has DEIGHTON committed robbery?

A Yes, as DEIGHTON has used force on WATTON immediately before a theft was committed.

B No, WATTON was unconscious during the theft so DEIGHTON cannot put or seek to put him in fear of being then and there subjected to force.

C Yes, at the time the theft takes place, DEIGHTON has used force against WATTON.

D No, DEIGHTON's use of force against WATTON was not in order to commit theft.

Question 23.4

The police receive information that ROCK is planning to steal the takings from a shop owned by MAN. MAN wishes to help and volunteers to run the shop on his own at the time of the offence as part of a trap laid by the police. Three police officers are waiting in a small room behind the till when ROCK enters the shop. ROCK produces a toy pistol and points it at MAN, demanding the takings. Although MAN hands over some cash from the till, he does not believe he will be subjected to force because there are police officers nearby and he realises the gun is a fake.

Which of the following statements is correct with regard to these circumstances?

A The force used during a robbery should at least amount to an assault. As MAN does not apprehend the immediate infliction of force there can be no robbery.

B This is not a robbery as the police were nearby and MAN realised the gun was a fake. Therefore, MAN cannot fear that ROCK would be able to use force on him or even threaten to do so.

C ROCK's state of mind is irrelevant to the offence of robbery. Whether ROCK intended to put MAN in fear of force being used or not is an objective decision to be made by a jury.

D The fact that MAN could have successfully resisted if he wished is immaterial. The offence of robbery is committed because ROCK seeks to put MAN in fear of being subjected to force.

Question 23.5

HONEYBOURNE owns and operates a hot dog stand and has had a particularly good day's business at a music festival. As he is counting his takings, he is approached by ORDISH who produces an imitation firearm and says, *'Hand over the money!'* ORDISH intends HONEYBOURNE to believe the gun is real and that he will be shot if he does not do as ORDISH demands. HONEYBOURNE does not believe he will be subjected to force as he used to be in the army and realises that the gun is not real. He laughs at ORDISH and tells him if he wants to rob people he should get a real gun. ORDISH flees empty-handed.

Which of the following statements is correct?

A This is not an offence of robbery because ORDISH did not actually use force against HONEYBOURNE.

B An offence of robbery has not been committed because ORDISH has not actually stolen the takings.

C As HONEYBOURNE realised the gun was a fake and did not fear that he would be subjected to force, an offence of robbery is not committed.

D Robbery has not been committed because ORDISH did not verbally threaten HONEYBOURNE with violence.

Question 23.6

TI FRAY has several reports on her desk. All the reports have been recorded as offences of robbery (contrary to s. 8 of the Theft Act 1968). However, only one of the reports is actually an offence of robbery.

Which one of the following is actually an offence of robbery?

A ROSE was leaving work when an offender demanded her watch or he would beat her up when she left work the next day. ROSE handed over her watch.

B DREW was detained for robbery after he punched his employer and took £100 from his employer's pocket. DREW states that he honestly believed he was legally entitled to the money as his employer had not paid him for a month.

C WARD intended to put GREY in fear of being then and there subjected to force and demanded GREY hand over her purse. GREY was not frightened but felt sorry for WARD and handed him her purse.

D PHIN (a pickpocket) was in the process of stealing a wallet from MONK while on a train when the train jolted and PHIN accidentally collided with MONK. In the process of the collision between the two, PHIN stole MONK's wallet.

Question 23.7

CARMEN approaches GREEN who is sitting in the cab of his HGV. The HGV load is several hundred thousand pounds of cigarettes. CARMEN opens the passenger door and gets into the vehicle. He tells GREEN to hand over the keys to the vehicle or *'the next time I see you I will shoot you'*. GREEN refuses to do so. CARMEN then produces a photograph of GREEN's wife and tells GREEN that unless he hands the keys to the HGV over to him, GREEN's wife will be beaten up. GREEN does not believe CARMEN and refuses. CARMEN produces a mobile phone which shows live pictures of GREEN's living room (a hundred miles away from GREEN's present location). GREEN can see that his wife is in the process of being assaulted by CARMEN's associate. CARMEN once again demands the keys and tells GREEN the assault will continue if he does not give in. At this point GREEN hands over the keys and gets out of the cab of the HGV. CARMEN drives off with the load of cigarettes.

At what point, if at all, is an offence in respect of robbery (contrary to s. 8 of the Theft Act 1968) actually committed?

A When CARMEN threatens to shoot GREEN the next time he sees him.

B When CARMEN threatens GREEN's wife.

C When CARMEN shows GREEN pictures of his wife being assaulted.

D When CARMEN drives off with the load of cigarettes.

Question 23.8

Late one evening whilst going home, JOHNSON is walking down the road when he sees NICKLIN walking towards him. JOHNSON decides that he is going to rape NICKLIN and approaches her and punches her in the face. The force of the blow knocks her to the ground and as she hits the pavement her purse falls out of her bag. Instead of raping NICKLIN, he takes the purse. JOHNSON runs off and continues his journey home. As he crosses a car park he sees MURRAY who he knows used to work in a garage. JOHNSON approaches MURRAY and pulls a knife on him and says *'When I come into the garage where you work tomorrow I want a full tank of petrol for free in my car understood?'* When JOHNSON goes to the garage the next day MURRAY is not working so he has to pay for his petrol.

Which of the following statements is correct with regard to offences committed by JOHNSON?

A The offences against NICKLIN are theft and assault; the offence against MURRAY is blackmail.

B The offence against NICKLIN is robbery and the offence against MURRAY is blackmail.

C The offences against NICKLIN are theft and assault; the offence against MURRAY is attempted robbery.

D The offence against NICKLIN is robbery; the offence against MURRAY is attempted blackmail.

Question 23.9

WILLIS is walking along a railway platform carrying a metal briefcase; the briefcase contains documents and his laptop. WILLIS is unaware that he is being followed by LAMBERT. WILLIS cuts through a car park followed closely by LAMBERT. LAMBERT removes a lump hammer from his coat and, from behind, strikes the metal briefcase with the hammer violently intending to steal the briefcase. The handle of the briefcase remains in WILLIS's hand but the briefcase falls to the ground; this is what LAMBERT intended. LAMBERT picks up the briefcase and makes good his escape.

Does LAMBERT commit the offence of robbery (contrary to s. 8 of the Theft Act 1968)?

A No, because WILLIS was not put in fear of the use of force, prior to the theft.

B Yes, force can be used against a person's property for an offence of robbery.

C No, because the force was not directly used on WILLIS.

D Yes, but you would need to prove some physical injury to WILLIS from the actions of LAMBERT.

Question 23.10

MILES is considering paying to have sexual intercourse with a prostitute and is walking in an area known for prostitution activities. On one of the street corners he sees CALDERSHAW and presumes she is a prostitute. As he walks towards her, he realises that he has come out of his house with no cash so he decides to rape CALDERSHAW instead. MILES approaches CALDERSHAW and punches her in the face and she falls to the ground. MILES is about to rape her but notices that a large amount of cash has fallen out of CALDERSHAW's jacket pocket as she fell to the ground. MILES changes his mind, picks up the cash and runs off. A short time later, he sees NOWAKOWSKI looking into a shop window and he can see her purse sticking out of her handbag so he decides to steal it. MILES places his hand on the purse and picks it out of her handbag (NOWAKOWSKI is totally unaware of this activity). At that moment, a person behind MILES accidentally bumps into him and in turn he accidentally pushes NOWAKOWSKI into the shop window causing a deep wound to her face. MILES makes good his escape.

Considering only the offence of robbery (contrary to s. 8 of the Theft Act 1968), which of the following statements is correct?

A MILES commits robbery only with regard to CALDERSHAW.

B MILES commits robbery only with regard to NOWAKOWSKI.

C MILES commits robbery against both CALDERSHAW and NOWAKOWSKI.

D MILES does not commit a robbery offence in these circumstances.

ANSWERS

Answer 23.1

Answer **C** — One of the essential elements of an offence of robbery is that there must be a theft. Theft in robbery is the same as s. 1 of the Theft Act 1968 and the elements of dishonesty under s. 2 will therefore apply. The honest belief of CREW and MUSGROVE means that they are not dishonest. This principle stems from *R* v *Robinson* [1977] Crim LR 173, CA, where it was held that all the defendant had to show was an honest belief in the entitlement to the property and not an honest belief in an entitlement to take it in the way he did. The fact that the requirement to repay the gambling debt is a moral obligation does not affect the situation.

Investigators' Manual, para. 3.2.1

Answer 23.2

Answer **B** — A theft has taken place and, immediately before the theft, force has been used, making answer D incorrect. When CULLEM threatens GLENN with a flick-knife it is not in order to steal but to deter him from reporting the matter, making answer C incorrect. When force is used, no theft has taken place and so the full offence is incomplete, making answer A incorrect, although this may be an attempted robbery. Although the use of force in nudging into GLENN may appear minimal it is nevertheless a use of force (*R* v *Dawson and James* (1976) 64 Cr App R 170).

Investigators' Manual, para. 3.2.1

Answer 23.3

Answer **D** — An offence of robbery is committed when the offender not only uses force against the victim immediately before or at the time of stealing but also *in order to do so*. Therefore, if the violence has no connection with the offence of theft and is effectively an unnecessary and sadistic activity, it is not a robbery. Answer A is incorrect as the force used is because of a fight and not in order to commit theft. Answer C is incorrect for the same reason. Answer B is incorrect as the definition also includes the direct application of force as a means of committing the offence as well as the threat of its use.

Investigators' Manual, para. 3.2.1

Answer 23.4

Answer **D** — There is no requirement that the force used during a robbery should amount to an assault, making answer A incorrect. The fact that the victim does not resist or is unafraid because of the surrounding circumstances is of no consequence; the offence is still committed, so answer B is incorrect. It is enough that the offender puts or seeks to put the victim in fear of force being used at that time and so the state of mind of the offender is significant. It is not an objective decision made by the jury and so answer C is incorrect.

Investigators' Manual, para. 3.2.1

Answer 23.5

Answer **B** — Although many robbery offences will involve the use of force, the offence can just as easily be committed without it by the use of a threat, i.e. the defendant puts or seeks to put any person in fear of being then and there subjected to force, therefore answer A is incorrect. Putting a person in such fear does not require a verbal threat of violence as actions (pointing an imitation firearm at the intended victim) can satisfy this part of the offence, making answer D incorrect. The fact that the victim is not in fear of the threat is immaterial as it is the intention of the defendant that is important, making answer C incorrect. There is no offence of robbery in these circumstances as there was no actual theft; this is an *attempted* robbery.

Investigators' Manual, para. 3.2.1

Answer 23.6

Answer **C** — Answer A is incorrect as the force must be used or threatened 'immediately before or at the time' of the theft. Here force is threatened to be used the next day. Answer B is incorrect as to have a robbery there must be a theft. If one of the theft elements is missing (here there is no dishonesty), then there is no theft and therefore no robbery. Answer D is incorrect as the accidental application of force is not willed by the offender, i.e. there is no voluntary conduct and therefore no *actus reus*. The fact that GREY (in answer C) is not actually in fear does not matter—it is the intent of the offender that is all important.

Investigators' Manual, para. 3.2.1

Answer 23.7

Answer **D** — A robbery is committed *when a person steals* and immediately before or at the time of doing so, and in order to do so, uses force on any person or puts or seeks to put any person in fear of being then and there subjected to force. For the full offence to be committed there must be a theft and until that takes place there is no robbery.

Investigators' Manual, para. 3.2.1

Answer 23.8

Answer **A** — The force used against NICKLIN was not used in order to facilitate an offence of theft so NICKLIN is not the victim of a robbery, ruling out answers B and D. The threat to use force against MURRAY is not one that is 'there and then' so this is not robbery either, although it is an offence of blackmail as once the unwarranted demand is made, the offence is complete, making answer C incorrect.

Investigators' Manual, para. 3.2.1

Answer 23.9

Answer **B** — Robbery can be committed in a variety of ways, not just by the fear of force (answer A is incorrect) as the Theft Act 1968, s. 8 states:

> (1) A person is guilty of robbery if he steals, and immediately before or at the time of doing so, and in order to do so, he uses force on any person or puts or seeks to put any person in fear of being then and there subjected to force.

There is no requirement to prove physical injury (answer D is incorrect). Force does not actually have to be used 'on' *the person*, i.e. on the actual body of the victim (answer C is incorrect). It may be used indirectly, for example on something the victim is carrying (such as a metal briefcase) and thereby transferring the force to the person: *R* v *Clouden* [1987] Crim LR 56 (correct answer B).

Investigators' Manual, para. 3.2.1

Answer 23.10

Answer **D** — Robbery—s. 8 of the Theft Act 1968 states:

> A person is guilty of robbery if he steals and immediately before or at the time of doing so, and in order to do so, he uses force on any person or puts or seeks to put any person in fear of being there and then subjected to force.

No robbery offences are committed in the circumstances. In relation to CALDERSHAW, the force was not used in order to steal (answers A and C are therefore incorrect). In relation to NOWAKOWSKI, force was applied accidentally (there is no voluntary application of force) meaning that answer B is incorrect).

Investigators' Manual, para. 3.2.1

24 Blackmail

QUESTIONS

Question 24.1

LONGSTAFF needs money to fund his drug habit. He waits in the car park of a supermarket and watches McCOY park her car and enter the supermarket with her three-month-old daughter. LONGSTAFF follows McCOY into the store. While McCOY is shopping, LONGSTAFF approaches her and tells her that it is dangerous to park where she has. He demands that she hand over her purse or he will wait by her car and stab her and her daughter when they return to the car. McCOY hands over her purse and LONGSTAFF runs away.

At what stage, if at all, is the offence of blackmail committed?

A When LONGSTAFF tells McCOY that it is dangerous to park where she has.

B When LONGSTAFF makes the demand for the purse.

C When McCOY hands over her purse to LONGSTAFF.

D No offence of blackmail is committed; this is a robbery.

Question 24.2

GARWOOD has placed a large bet on the outcome of a local Sunday league football match. Two days before the match is due to take place he finds out that the team he has backed have lost four of their star players after they were involved in a car accident. Worried that he will lose his money, GARWOOD approaches the referee of the match. GARWOOD tells the referee, *'If you don't call off the game my friends will rape your wife.'* The referee takes no notice of GARWOOD and two days later the game goes ahead. GARWOOD loses his bet.

Considering the offence of blackmail (contrary to s. 21 of the Theft Act 1968) only, which of the following statements is true?

A GARWOOD does not commit the offence because he did not 'gain' any money.

B GARWOOD does not commit the offence because the threat is that his friends rather than GARWOOD would rape the referee's wife.

C As the game went ahead, GARWOOD commits an offence of attempted blackmail.

D In these circumstances GARWOOD commits the offence as he intended to keep what he already had (his original bet).

Question 24.3

GILCHRIST has just started a new job at a bank when she is approached by BAXTER, who tells her that he knows she used to be a prostitute and that if she does not have sexual intercourse with his friend, HUMPHRIES, he will inform the bank manager and she will probably be sacked. GILCHRIST reluctantly agrees to BAXTER's demand and has sexual intercourse with HUMPHRIES.

Is this an offence of blackmail (contrary to s. 21 of the Theft Act 1968)?

A Yes, because BAXTER makes the unwarranted demand with a view to gaining a benefit for another.

B No, because 'gain' is to be construed as extending only to a gain in money or other property.

C Yes, as a 'gain' refers to anything at all and not necessarily something with a monetary value.

D No, because BAXTER did not make the demand with a view to gain for himself.

Question 24.4

BRIDALE, FORD and HILL all work at the same office. BRIDALE and FORD are having an affair and need somewhere that they can meet and have sex. BRIDALE approaches HILL and tells him that unless he hands over the keys to his flat and leaves the flat for one night a week, he (BRIDALE) will inform the management that HILL has been stealing from the tills. HILL believes that BRIDALE will carry out his threat and does as BRIDALE demands.

Would this constitute an offence of blackmail (contrary to s. 21 of the Theft Act 1968)?

A Yes, as the gain and loss of property can be temporary.

B No, because BRIDALE did not threaten HILL with any form of violence.

C Yes, but only because HILL actually believes BRIDALE will carry out his threat.

D No, as the gain and loss must both be of a permanent nature.

Question 24.5

GILPIN is a keen golfer and has entered a competition he believes he can win if he uses a high quality set of golf clubs. EGAN (GILPIN's friend) believes the same and approaches CORK (who works as a shop assistant in a golf shop) and asks if he can hire a set of clubs from the shop for GILPIN to use. CORK refuses. EGAN then tells CORK that he will tell CORK's employers that he has been stealing from the till if he does not allow him to use the clubs for free. CORK gives EGAN the clubs and after GILPIN wins the competition, EGAN returns them to CORK.

With regard to the offence of blackmail, which of the following statements is correct?

A EGAN does not commit the offence because 'gain' and 'loss' in blackmail only relate to money.

B The offence has not been committed because EGAN has made the demand with a view to gain for GILPIN.

C EGAN does not commit the offence because the 'gain' he has made is not permanent.

D In these circumstances, EGAN has committed the offence.

Question 24.6

SCHULTEN approaches WARNER in the street. SCHULTEN tells WARNER that he has been watching him and knows that WARNER has a nine-year-old son. Intending to make money from WARNER, SCHULTEN tells WARNER that unless WARNER pays him £20,000 the following day, he will kidnap WARNER's son and subject the boy to a serious sexual assault. WARNER does not believe SCHULTEN and tells him to go away and that the money will never be paid to him.

Considering the offence of blackmail (contrary to s. 21 of the Theft Act 1968), which of the following statements is correct?

A Blackmail has not been committed because there has been no offence of theft.

B An offence of blackmail has been committed by SCHULTEN the moment he makes the demand of WARNER.

C Blackmail has not been committed because WARNER did not believe SCHULTEN.

D These circumstances would constitute an offence of attempted blackmail.

Question 24.7

MIFFLIN is a hypochondriac and believes that she has a serious condition which is causing her a great deal of pain (this is not true). She visits her local surgery and speaks with her general practitioner, Dr PATTEN, and asks for a pain-killing injection to ease her suffering. Dr PATTEN refuses the injection as he is aware of MIFFLIN's hypochondria and knows that she is not in any pain. MIFFLIN tells Dr PATTEN that if he does not provide her with the pain-killing injection, she will leave the surgery and slash all the tyres on his expensive sports car which is parked directly outside the surgery. Dr PATTEN believes MIFFLIN and provides her with the pain-killing injection.

Which of the following is true?

A This is not a case of blackmail as there has been no 'gain' or 'loss' in property.

B The offence of blackmail is committed at the moment MIFFLIN makes the demand for the pain-killing injection accompanied by the threats to damage Dr PATTEN's car.

C This is not a case of blackmail as the menaces were not threatened 'then and there'; the damage was going to take place at another time and in another place.

D The offence of blackmail is committed at the moment Dr PATTEN provides the pain-killing injection to MIFFLIN.

ANSWERS

Answer 24.1

Answer **B** — The offence of blackmail is committed when the demand with menaces is made as the offence of blackmail is aimed at the making of the demands rather than the consequences of them. Answers A and C are incorrect because at point A no demand has been made, although this would form part of the menace. At point C the offence has already been committed. Answer D is incorrect, as although blackmail and robbery are closely linked, a robbery cannot occur where the threat to use force is not immediately before or at the time of the theft.

Investigators' Manual, paras 3.3.1 to 3.3.4

Answer 24.2

Answer **D** — There is no such offence as 'attempted blackmail', making answer C incorrect. It is immaterial whether the menaces relate to action to be taken by the person making the demand, making answer B incorrect. 'Gain' for the purposes of blackmail includes a gain by keeping what one has, making answer A incorrect.

Investigators' Manual, paras 3.3.1 to 3.3.4

Answer 24.3

Answer **B** — The demand can be made with a view to gain for another, making answer D incorrect. The 'gain' must be in money or other property, making answers A and C incorrect.

Investigators' Manual, paras 3.3.1 to 3.3.4

Answer 24.4

Answer **A** — Answer B is incorrect as there is no requirement for violence to form any part of the demand with menaces. Answer C is incorrect as there is no need for the victim of the offence to actually believe the threat by the offender (even if the victim did not believe the threat, the offence would be committed). The gain or loss in blackmail can be in money or in other property (the flat) and this gain and loss can be either permanent or temporary. HILL has lost his flat for one evening a week—the temporary loss of property, making answer D incorrect and answer A correct in the process.

Investigators' Manual, paras 3.3.1 to 3.3.4

Answer 24.5

Answer **D** — A 'gain' and 'loss' relate to money and other property, making answer A incorrect. Answer B is incorrect because the demand can be made with a view to gain for 'himself or another'. Answer C is incorrect as the gain need not be permanent.

Investigators' Manual, paras 3.3.1 to 3.3.4

Answer 24.6

Answer **B** — An offence of blackmail is committed the moment a person makes the demand with menaces. This makes it almost impossible to have an offence of attempted blackmail, making answer D incorrect. Answer A is incorrect as there is no requirement for a theft to take place for the offence of blackmail to be complete. Whether the person to whom the demand with menaces is made actually believes the demand and/or reacts to it is surplus to requirements for the offence to be committed, therefore answer C is incorrect.

Investigators' Manual, paras 3.3.1 to 3.3.4

Answer 24.7

Answer **B** — Answer A is incorrect as the pain-killing drug is a form of property (*R* v *Bevans* (1987) 87 Cr App R 64). Blackmail is, essentially, an unwarranted demand with menaces, so answer C is incorrect as it does not matter that the menaces of criminal damage were not going to take place 'there and then' (words relevant to robbery and not blackmail). The offence of blackmail is complete at the moment the unwarranted demand with menaces is made and a transfer of property does not need to take place for the offence to be complete, meaning that answer D is incorrect.

Investigators' Manual, paras 3.3.1 to 3.3.4

25 Burglary

QUESTIONS

Question 25.1

WILKIN is a tramp with a long record for burglary offences. He breaks into a garden shed but is arrested as he is leaving the shed with a mower in his hands. He tells the arresting officer that he was going to sell the mower to buy drink. In interview WILKIN states that initially, he never intended to take anything from the shed; stealing the mower was just an idea he had once he was inside. The reason he entered the shed was that he was looking for shelter.

What offence is WILKIN guilty of?

A As WILKIN was only looking for shelter, he commits theft (contrary to s. 1 of the Theft Act 1968) when he steals the mower.

B WILKIN commits burglary (contrary to s. 9(1)(a) of the Theft Act 1968) as soon as he enters the shed.

C WILKIN commits burglary (contrary to s. 9(1)(b) of the Theft Act 1968) when he steals the mower.

D WILKIN commits burglary (contrary to s. 9(1)(a) of the Theft Act 1968) when he steals the mower.

Question 25.2

CATER asks her neighbour, TEW, to look after her house while she is away on holiday. CATER gives TEW a key to her house and tells him he is welcome to go into the house and watch the satellite TV system, situated in the lounge, any time he likes while she is away. TEW decides to steal from the house and at 02.00 hrs one morning, while CATER is on holiday, he uses the key to get into CATER's house. He goes into the main bedroom and steals all of CATER's jewellery. TEW is aware that CATER would never have consented to this activity.

Which of the following statements Is correct with regard to TEW?

A As CATER has given TEW permission to enter the premises, he is not a trespasser and in these circumstances would be guilty of theft rather than burglary.

B TEW is guilty of burglary but if the jewellery were in the same room as the satellite TV, then TEW would be guilty of theft alone.

C As TEW is the temporary owner of the property, he has a 'charge' on it and its contents and cannot be guilty of any offence in these circumstances.

D As TEW has gone beyond a condition of entry, he is a trespasser and would be guilty of burglary.

Question 25.3

HILLEN is the 'nominated driver' on a stag night. While he drinks orange juice all evening, his four friends get extremely drunk in a pub. All five decide to go to a nightclub and are all walking along a street when the four drunken men decide to drag HILLEN into a house for a joke. The four men kick open the door of a house and throw HILLEN into the hallway against his will. HILLEN gets up and decides that while he is in the house he may as well make it worth his while, intending to steal something from the house. He spots £50 on a table in the hallway, takes the money and leaves.

What offence does HILLEN commit?

A HILLEN commits burglary (contrary to s. 9(1)(a) of the Theft Act 1968) when he forms the intent to steal from the house.

B HILLEN commits theft (contrary to s. 1 of the Theft Act 1968) when he steals the money from the hallway.

C HILLEN commits burglary (contrary to s. 9(1)(b) of the Theft Act 1968) when he steals the money from the hallway.

D HILLEN commits burglary (contrary to s. 9(1)(b) of the Theft Act 1968) but would have a defence in these circumstances.

Question 25.4

HAYDEN goes into his local store to do some shopping. While he is walking around the shopping area he notices that the door to the staff room is ajar and that there is an open safe containing several bundles of cash inside it. HAYDEN decides to steal the cash and hides behind a large cardboard display in the corner of the shopping area, intending to come out when the shop is closed. The shop closes and HAYDEN comes out from behind the display. He walks across the shopping area to the staff room door and enters the staff room. Once inside the staff room he approaches the open safe and steals the cash contents. To get out, HAYDEN has to force a fire exit at the rear of the staff room.

At what stage does HAYDEN commit an offence of burglary?

A When he decides to steal the cash and hides behind the cardboard display.

B When he comes out from behind the display after the shop has closed.

C When he enters the staff room and approaches the safe.

D When he forces the fire exit to get out of the store.

Question 25.5

KYRIACOU has made a grappling hook that, if pushed through a letterbox, will enable her to take hold of letters from the floors of houses. She intends to take any money or valuable goods from the letters she manages to seize. She goes to a house and puts the grappling hook through the letterbox of a porch at the front of the house. Unfortunately for KYRIACOU the grappling hook is not long enough to reach some of the letters on the floor and she has to put her hand through the letterbox to enable the hook to reach the letters. She manages to hook the letters and pulls them through the letterbox.

Which of the following statements is correct?

A The front porch of a house would not be classed as a building for the purposes of burglary; KYRIACOU commits theft.

B When KYRIACOU uses the grappling hook she does not commit burglary. It is only when her hand goes through the letterbox that this offence is committed.

C These circumstances would not qualify as an 'effective and substantial' entry for the purposes of burglary; KYRIACOU has committed theft.

D Using the grappling hook as an extension of her body means that KYRIACOU has 'entered' premises and would be guilty of an offence of burglary.

Question 25.6

KEYS owns a builders' merchants and is owed £5,000 by BEATON. KEYS phones BEATON and demands the money; BEATON tells KEYS he will not pay a penny and that KEYS will have to take it from him. KEYS goes to BEATON's home and breaks in, intending to find some or all of the £5,000. KEYS's honest belief is that he is legally entitled to act in this way because of BEATON's debt. There is no money in the house and so he goes to the building site where BEATON is working. He enters an unfinished house and demands the money from BEATON. When BEATON refuses, KEYS assaults him, breaking BEATON's arm.

Which of the following statements is correct?

A KEYS only commits burglary when he breaks into BEATON's house with intent to steal.

B KEYS only commits burglary when he inflicts grievous bodily harm on BEATON.

C KEYS commits burglary when he breaks into BEATON's house and also when he inflicts grievous bodily harm on BEATON.

D At no stage does KEYS commit the offence of burglary.

Question 25.7

The GARTONs go on holiday for a week in a houseboat and constantly move around the country's canal system, never staying in one location for more than a day. They moor the boat and go to 'The Hen' pub for lunch. When they return to the boat some three hours later, they find that it has been broken into and a camera has been stolen.

Would the houseboat be classed as a 'building' for a burglary offence?

A Yes, the term 'building' would apply to an inhabited vessel and it would also apply when the person living in or on the vessel is not there as well as times when he/she is.

B No, the term 'building' should be given its everyday meaning as a structure of some permanence. As the houseboat is continually moored in different places it is not permanent and cannot be a 'building' for the purposes of burglary.

C No, a vehicle or vessel can only be a building if a person has a habitation in it. In these circumstances, the houseboat was empty when the offence took place and therefore it is not a 'building'.

D Yes, but the houseboat would be classed as an 'other building' rather than a 'dwelling' and as such the maximum sentence for this offence would be 10 years' imprisonment.

Question 25.8

BUCKNALL visits GRETTON's house to install a new television. BUCKNALL arrives at GRETTON's house and is shown into the downstairs lounge where GRETTON wants the television fixed to the wall. GRETTON tells BUCKNALL that she is going out to visit a friend and that he should make his own way out when the television is fixed to the wall. While GRETTON is out, BUCKNALL decides to steal from GRETTON's house. He searches the downstairs lounge and finds £500 in a moneybox, which he takes. He decides to look around the rest of the house to see if there is anything else worth stealing and leaves the lounge and goes into the hallway. He enters a study situated off the hallway and once inside the study, steals a computer before leaving the house.

At what stage, if at all, does BUCKNALL commit burglary?

A When he takes £500 in cash from a money box in the lounge.

B When he goes into the hallway from the lounge.

C When he enters GRETTON's study and steals her computer.

D BUCKNALL does not commit burglary, as he is never a trespasser.

Question 25.9

LLOYD visits DERMOT's house to pick up a drill. DERMOT invites LLOYD into his house and asks him to wait in the hall while he fetches the drill. While waiting, LLOYD spots an envelope on the hall window ledge; he can see it contains cash.

LLOYD quickly picks up the envelope and puts it in his pocket. DERMOT returns with the drill, hands it to LLOYD and LLOYD leaves. The envelope contains £2,000. A few minutes later, DERMOT discovers the envelope has gone. He chases after LLOYD and accuses him of taking the envelope. LLOYD pushes DERMOT over and runs away.

With regard to the Theft Act 1968 only, what offence does LLOYD commit?

A LLOYD commits theft (contrary to s. 1 of the Theft Act 1968).

B LLOYD commits burglary (contrary to s. 9(1)(b) of the Theft Act 1968).

C LLOYD commits burglary (contrary to s. 9(1)(a) of the Theft Act 1968).

D LLOYD commits robbery (contrary to s. 8 of the Theft Act 1968).

Question 25.10

The offence of burglary (contrary to s. 9(1)(a) of the Theft Act 1968) can be committed in a variety of ways.

In which of the following situations has such an offence been committed?

A HEDGELAND breaks into a house intending to cause actual bodily harm against MOORE. MOORE is not in the house so HEDGELAND does not carry out the offence.

B PANG breaks into a garage intending to commit an offence of taking a conveyance (contrary to s. 12 of the Theft Act 1968).
C TAMM breaks into a warehouse intending to steal but finds nothing worth taking. Out of spite, TAMM turns on all the warehouse lights, committing an offence of abstracting electricity (contrary to s. 13 of the Theft Act 1968).
D YOUNGER breaks into a garden shed looking for shelter. Once inside he commits criminal damage (contrary to s. 1(1) of the Criminal Damage Act 1971) to several gardening tools stored inside the shed.

Question 25.11

MORROW owns a Bentley Continental GT car and keeps it locked in a large garage which is separated from his house by several metres. KOLB is a friend of MORROW's and has asked MORROW on several occasions if he can take the Bentley for a drive—MORROW has always refused as he thinks KOLB is a poor driver. MORROW goes on holiday and whilst he is away, KOLB breaks into the garage intending to take the Bentley out for a drive and then return it to the garage. Once inside the garage, KOLB realises he will not be able to get into the Bentley and in a fit of rage he scratches the side of the Bentley causing thousands of pounds of damage to the vehicle. He is about to leave when he sees an expensive toolkit in the garage and decides to make his venture worthwhile and steals the toolkit.

In relation to the offence of burglary under s. 9(1)(a) of the Theft Act 1968, which of the following statements is correct?

A KOLB commits the offence when he breaks into the garage intending to take the Bentley for a drive.
B KOLB commits the offence when he damages the Bentley.
C KOLB commits the offence when he steals the toolkit.
D KOLB does not commit the offence of s. 9(1)(a) burglary.

Question 25.12

MILWARD is owed £500 by HARPER who has refused to pay MILWARD after repeated requests. MILWARD has run out of patience and decides he will get his money back by any means. HARPER lives in a motor home behind a farm so MILWARD visits the motor home and breaks open the door. He enters the motor home intending to 'rough up' HARPER (causing him relatively minor injury). He searches the motor home but HARPER is not there. MILWARD lashes out at a TV set in the motor home and smashes it in the process. He leaves the motor home and is walking away when he decides he will damage more of HARPER's property. He returns to the motor home, goes inside and smashes every electrical item inside.

At what stage, if at all, does MILWARD commit a burglary contrary to s. 9(1)(a) of the Theft Act 1968?

A When he enters the motor home intending to cause minor injury to HARPER.

B When he smashes the TV set in the motor home.

C When he enters the motor home intending to damage HARPER's property.

D The offence has not been committed as the activity took place inside a motor home and that is not a 'building'.

Question 25.13

PC HEWITT is on uniform patrol and is carrying a baton and handcuffs. The officer is sent to a report of persons acting suspiciously at the rear of a house. On arrival, PC HEWITT goes to the rear of the house where, through a kitchen window, he can see a large amount of cash on the kitchen table. PC HEWITT finds that the rear of the property is secure and he returns to the front of the house. He tries the front door and it is insecure and it opens. He enters the hallway of the house and announces himself to see if anybody is in the house and to ensure everything is alright. There is no reply and it becomes obvious that nobody is in. PC HEWITT has a large debt from gambling and he decides that he is going to steal the cash from the kitchen table. He then enters the kitchen from the hallway and puts the cash inside his clothing and leaves the premises.

Considering offences under the Theft Act 1968, which of the following statements is correct?

A PC HEWITT commits burglary contrary to s. 9(1)(a) of the Theft Act 1968 when he decides to steal the money from the kitchen.

B PC HEWITT commits burglary contrary to s. 9(1)(a) of the Theft Act 1968 when he enters the kitchen from the hallway and steals the cash.

C PC HEWITT commits aggravated burglary contrary to s. 10 of the Theft Act 1968 when he enters the kitchen from the hallway and steals the cash.

D PC HEWITT would be guilty of theft contrary to s. 1 of the Theft Act 1968.

ANSWERS

Answer 25.1

Answer **C** — Breaking into the garden shed clearly makes WILKIN a trespasser for the purposes of the offence of burglary. However, his lack of intent to commit any of the ulterior offences of theft, grievous bodily harm or criminal damage when he entered the shed means that he cannot be guilty of an offence under s. 9(1)(a) of the Theft Act 1968, making B and D incorrect. Although WILKIN does commit theft, he has entered as a trespasser and stolen, falling into the category of a burglary under s. 9(1)(b) of the Theft Act 1968 and making answer C correct. Answer A is incorrect because committing a theft after entering as a trespasser makes WILKIN a burglar.

Investigators' Manual, paras 3.4.1 to 3.4.5

Answer 25.2

Answer **D** — Answer C is incorrect as looking after property in such a manner would not prohibit the person in 'charge' of the property being guilty of theft should they treat it as TEW has done. CATER's permission for TEW to enter was granted 'conditionally'; that is, to watch the satellite TV. This conditional permission has been violated and that violation turns TEW into a trespasser (*R* v *Jones and Smith* [1976] 3 All ER 54), making answer B incorrect. TEW's intention to steal from the premises from the outset and his entry as a trespasser makes him guilty of burglary under s. 9(1)(a) of the Theft Act 1968. Even if the jewellery were in the same room as the satellite TV, TEW is a trespasser with intent to steal the moment he enters the house; this makes answer A incorrect.

Investigators' Manual, para. 3.4.1

Answer 25.3

Answer **B** — Answers A, C and D are incorrect because HILLEN is never a trespasser for the purposes of burglary. A crime is committed when there is a meeting of *mens rea* with *actus reus* but that *actus reus* must be voluntary. HILLEN's entry to the house must be deliberate or reckless and so, as he was not responsible for being thrown into the house by his drunken friends, the *actus reus* of burglary must be eliminated. Once inside the house he decides to steal, therefore, HILLEN is now guilty of theft.

Investigators' Manual, para. 3.4.1

Answer 25.4

Answer **C** — Initially, HAYDEN is not a trespasser as he enters the shop as a genuine and honest customer and with the implied permission of the shop owner. Even when he decides to hide and steal, he remains in the part of the shop he has legitimate access to and is not a trespasser at this stage, making answer A incorrect. When the shop closes, he *does* become a trespasser. This is because, at that time, he had no right to be in the store. But although he is a trespasser, you must remember that in order for a burglary to be committed the person must *enter as a trespasser*—not become one by exceeding a condition of entry (and this is what has happened at this stage), making answer B incorrect. The offence of burglary would be committed when he moves into the staff room as at this point he *enters part of a building as a trespasser* with intent to steal, making answer D incorrect as a result.

Investigators' Manual, para. 3.4.3

Answer 25.5

Answer **D** — Answer A is incorrect, as the front porch of a house would be classed as a building or part of a building. Although *R* v *Collins* [1973] QB 100 stated that entry must be 'effective and substantial', this ruling was altered by *R* v *Brown* [1985] Crim LR 212, CA, where it was stated that entry had only to be 'effective'. This does not mean that the defendant needs to get the whole of their body into premises and any part of the body would be sufficient, making answer C incorrect. A person may use an object as an extension of himself or herself to enter, which makes B incorrect.

Investigators' Manual, para. 3.4.1

Answer 25.6

Answer **B** — If KEYS honestly believes that he has a right in law to deprive a person of property then he is not dishonest and cannot commit theft. Therefore, if there is no theft, KEYS does not commit burglary at BEATON's house, making answers A and C incorrect. An unfinished house is a building for the purposes of burglary and KEYS has entered as a trespasser and committed grievous bodily harm, satisfying the requirements for an offence under s. 9(1)(b) of the Theft Act 1968, making answer D incorrect.

Investigators' Manual, paras 3.4.1 to 3.4.5

Answer 25.7

Answer **A** — Section 9 of the Theft Act 1968 defines a building and states that the word 'building' applies to inhabited vehicles or vessels (the houseboat) and applies to those vehicles or vessels at times when they are unoccupied (when the GARTONs go for a meal).

Investigators' Manual, para. 3.4.2

Answer 25.8

Answer **B** — To work out when BUCKNALL commits burglary you must decide when he enters a building or part of a building as a trespasser. At point A, GRETTON has invited BUCKNALL into her lounge to install a TV. BUCKNALL has no intent to commit one of the trigger offences for burglary under s. 9(1)(a) (DIT—Damage, Inflicting GBH, Theft) so is not a trespasser for burglary under s. 9(1)(a) at this point. When GRETTON leaves, BUCKNALL decides to steal from the lounge and takes £500 from a moneybox. You could never say that GRETTON would be happy with such behaviour (she did not invite BUCKNALL into her house to steal)—BUCKNALL has gone beyond a condition of entry and would become a trespasser when he steals. However, this does not make him a burglar as he did not enter the lounge as a trespasser. When you are thinking about burglary, it is essential that the person concerned enters as a trespasser or the offence cannot be completed. At point A BUCKNALL is a thief, not a burglar. At point B BUCKNALL has moved from one part of a building to another (from the lounge into the hallway) with the intention to steal (s. 9(1)(a) burglary). He has gone beyond the conditional entry permission given by GRETTON and as a consequence he enters a part of a building as a trespasser. The fact that he enters with the intention of stealing is all that is required and it is immaterial whether he enters with the idea to steal if there is 'anything worth stealing' (*R* v *Walkington* [1979] 1 WLR 1169). As a consequence, answers C and D are incorrect.

Investigators' Manual, paras 3.4.1 to 3.4.5

Answer 25.9

Answer **A** — LLOYD cannot commit burglary because he never entered a building or part of a building as a trespasser. DERMOT invited him into his house and, when he entered, LLOYD had no criminal intentions, making answers B and C incorrect. No robbery has been committed because the force has been used after the property has been appropriated, making answer D incorrect.

Investigators' Manual, paras 3.4.1 to 3.4.5

Answer 25.10

Answer **C** — Answer A is incorrect as actual bodily harm is not a trigger offence for the purposes of s. 9(1)(a). Answer B is incorrect as an intent to steal will not include an intention to commit an offence of taking a conveyance (as there is no intent to permanently deprive). Answer D is incorrect as an offence of criminal damage is only relevant to an offence under s. 9(1)(a) of the Theft Act 1968. As YOUNGER did not *enter* with such an intent, there is no burglary. Answer C is a burglary as the offender breaks in with the intention of stealing. The fact that the offender goes on to commit an offence of abstracting electricity out of spite is immaterial.

Investigators' Manual, paras 3.4.1 to 3.4.5

Answer 25.11

Answer **D** — A burglary under s. 9(1)(a) of the Theft Act 1968 is committed when a person enters a building or part of a building with the intention of stealing anything in the building or part of the building in question, of inflicting on any person therein any grievous bodily harm or of doing unlawful damage to the building or anything therein. When KOLB enters the garage he does not intend to steal the Bentley (he intends to commit an offence of taking a conveyance which does not include the element of permanent deprivation required for theft), making answer A incorrect. The only time a s. 9(1)(a) burglary can be committed is at the point of entry into the building or part of a building and so once KOLB is in the garage the time frame in which the offence can be committed has come and gone, meaning that answers B and C are incorrect. When KOLB damages the Bentley he commits criminal damage—when he steals the toolkit he commits a burglary under s. 9(1)(b) of the Act.

Investigators' Manual, paras 3.4.1 to 3.4.5

Answer 25.12

Answer **C** — A burglary under s. 9(1)(a) of the Theft Act 1968 is committed when a person enters a building or part of a building with the intention of stealing anything in the building or part of the building in question, of inflicting on any person therein any grievous bodily harm or of doing unlawful damage to the building or anything therein. An inhabited motor home would be classed as a 'building', making answer D incorrect. Answer A is incorrect as when MILWARD first enters the motor home he does not have one of the states of mind required to commit an offence under s. 9(1)(a). The s. 9(1)(a) offence is committed on *entry only* so when damage is caused *after* entry it would not amount to a burglary, making answer B incorrect. When MILWARD leaves then re-enters the motor home intending to commit criminal damage, the offence is committed (answer C).

Investigators' Manual, paras 3.4.1 to 3.4.3

Answer 25.13

Answer **C** — The Theft Act 1968, s. 10 states:

> A person is guilty of aggravated burglary if he commits any burglary and at the time has with him any firearm or imitation firearm, any weapon of offence, or any explosive.

Answer A is incorrect as although PC HEWITT has formed the intention to steal, this is after he entered the hallway of the house and he did not enter as a trespasser. Once he moves into the kitchen (another part of the building) with the intention of stealing, he does enter the kitchen as a trespasser—the intention to steal turns him into one. At this stage we have a s. 9(1)(a) burglary. The defences of lawful authority or reasonable excuse in relation to the possession of an offensive weapon do not apply to the offence of aggravated burglary. Therefore, when he enters the kitchen from the hallway he clearly at this point is a trespasser with intent to steal; the items 'with him' (baton and handcuffs) make it an aggravated burglary making answer C the correct answer.

Investigators' Manual, paras 3.5.1, 3.5.2

26 Aggravated Burglary

QUESTIONS

Question 26.1

SOUTHALL decides to burgle a stately home. He visits the home during the day to look at the security arrangements and sees that apart from some security cameras there is a warning sign telling people to 'Beware of the Dog!' He returns later the same night to burgle the stately home. In his possession he has a piece of meat containing a large quantity of Valium (used to incapacitate any guard dog inside the home) and a screwdriver he intends to use to force a window and gain entry. SOUTHALL uses the screwdriver to force a window and enters the stately home with both the screwdriver and the meat in his possession.

Does SOUTHALL commit an aggravated burglary?

A No, in these circumstances neither of the articles in his possession relate to an aggravated burglary offence.

B Yes, but only in respect of the drugged meat. This would be classed as a 'weapon of offence' as it is designed to incapacitate.

C Yes, both items are classed as 'weapons of offence' in these circumstances. The drugged meat is designed to incapacitate and the screwdriver could be adapted to cause injury.

D No, although both items are 'weapons of offence', SOUTHALL would actually have to use one or both of them to cause injury or incapacitate before the full offence is committed.

Question 26.2

CRADDOCK intends to break into and steal from ELVIN's house. CRADDOCK knows that ELVIN is 80 years old but does not wish to take any chances and so before he goes to the house he decides to take a piece of cord with him to tie up ELVIN, should

ELVIN be in. He breaks into the house through a ground floor window and enters the lounge of the house with the cord ready in his hands. He searches the lounge but finds nothing worth taking so he goes through the lounge door into the dining room. In the dining room is ELVIN who has come from his bedroom after hearing the noise of the break-in. CRADDOCK decides to steal from the dining room and ties ELVIN's hands with the cord before committing theft.

At what stage does CRADDOCK first commit the offence of aggravated burglary?

A When, before he goes to the house, he decides to take the piece of cord with him to tie up any occupants.

B When he enters the house after forcing the ground floor lounge window.

C When he enters the dining room (another part of the building).

D When he uses the cord to tie the hands of the occupant and commits theft.

Question 26.3

LAMONT and HEWITSON break into a house intending to steal from it. They are stealing from the premises when the police arrive and both men are arrested. When LAMONT is searched he is found to have a cutlery knife in his coat pocket. The arresting officer asks LAMONT why he has the knife and LAMONT replies, '*For self-defence because it's a dodgy area out there*.' HEWITSON had no idea that LAMONT had a knife in his possession.

Has an offence of aggravated burglary been committed?

A Yes, LAMONT commits the offence. HEWITSON does not as he would have to know of the existence of the cutlery knife and its purpose to be guilty of aggravated burglary.

B No, neither man commits the offence. LAMONT does not intend to use the cutlery knife in the course of the burglary and HEWITSON has no knowledge of its existence.

C Yes, both men commit the offence. The mere fact that LAMONT has a weapon of offence with him (the cutlery knife) is all the evidence that is required.

D No, the cutlery knife is not a weapon of offence because it is not an article made or adapted for use of causing injury or incapacitating a person.

Question 26.4

HULBERT breaks into a house using a screwdriver to force a downstairs window. He walks into the lounge and starts searching for items to steal. As he searches, the owner of the house, WEEDON, confronts him. HULBERT threatens WEEDON with the screwdriver, telling her to leave him alone or he will stab her with the screwdriver. WEEDON backs away from HULBERT into a hallway. HULBERT decides to rape WEEDON and follows her into the hallway, threatening her with the screwdriver as he does so. He rapes WEEDON in the hallway, then, worried about leaving a witness, he stabs WEEDON in the throat with the screwdriver causing her grievous bodily harm in the process. He returns to the lounge, steals some cash and leaves.

At what point does HULBERT first commit an aggravated burglary?

A When he threatens WEEDON with the screwdriver in the lounge.

B When he decides to rape WEEDON and follows her into the hallway.

C When he stabs WEEDON in the throat with the screwdriver.

D When he returns to the lounge and steals the cash.

Question 26.5

RULE and HOQUE intend to steal from O'HALLORAN's house. The two men go to the back garden of the house where RULE smashes a window to the kitchen. He makes so much noise that O'HALLORAN comes outside and challenges the two men. HOQUE instantly picks up a piece of wood from the back garden and starts to hit O'HALLORAN on the head with it, intending to cause grievous bodily harm to him. O'HALLORAN runs away from the house, followed by HOQUE who is still hitting him with the piece of wood. RULE climbs into the kitchen and steals cash from the house.

Have RULE and HOQUE committed an offence of aggravated burglary?

A Yes, both men commit the offence as a piece of wood can be a weapon of offence and its use in these circumstances has enabled entry to the premises.

B No, the piece of wood can never be an offensive weapon for the purposes of aggravated burglary.

C Yes, but only HOQUE commits the offence as he intends to cause O'HALLORAN grievous bodily harm.

D No, when the burglary is committed nobody actually enters the premises with a weapon of offence.

Question 26.6

DARE decides to steal from the offices of a printing firm owned by SHEA. Thinking there might be a security guard on the premises he takes a pair of handcuffs with him in case he needs to incapacitate the guard. At 05.00 hrs when DARE gets to the offices and is standing outside the premises, it becomes obvious that there is no security guard on duty so he throws the handcuffs away. He breaks into the offices and begins searching. Minutes later DARE is confronted by SHEA who has come to work early. In order to escape, DARE picks up a pair of scissors (not intending to steal them) and threatens SHEA to stay back or he will be stabbed. SHEA backs away from DARE. Still holding the scissors, DARE picks up a cash-box and makes off.

Which of the following statements is correct?

A As the handcuffs are designed to incapacitate, DARE would commit an offence of aggravated burglary when he goes to the offices intending to steal.

B DARE is guilty of burglary but not aggravated burglary. The handcuffs were disposed of prior to entry and the scissors are used only to assist in his escape.

C When DARE steals the cash-box he commits an offence of aggravated burglary.

D When DARE picks up the scissors and threatens SHEA he commits an offence of aggravated burglary.

Question 26.7

LEAVY intends to break into a house to steal property. In his pocket he is carrying a screwdriver which he intends to use to cause injury against anyone who tries to prevent him from escaping. LEAVY forces a downstairs lounge window and enters the house. Once inside the lounge he steals several ornaments before being disturbed by the householder. LEAVY pulls out the screwdriver and threatens the householder, who is not afraid and approaches LEAVY. LEAVY stabs the householder causing him grievous bodily harm.

At what point, if at all, does LEAVY first commit an offence of aggravated burglary (contrary to s. 10 of the Theft Act 1968)?

A When he initially breaks into the house.

B When he actually steals the ornaments.

C When he stabs the householder, causing him grievous bodily harm.

D The offence of aggravated burglary is not committed in these circumstances.

Question 26.8

CALTHORPE is a homeless military veteran looking for somewhere to shelter for the night because he is cold. To protect himself from the elements, he breaks into a house owned by TAYLOR. Once inside the lounge of the house he turns on an electric fire to warm himself up. Several minutes later he hears a noise in the house and, thinking that someone is in the house, he picks up a hammer which is on a table in the lounge to protect himself by hitting anyone who confronts him (he does not intend to keep the hammer). He hears another noise and panics—he smashes a window in the lounge to escape, drops the hammer and runs away.

Considering the law in relation to burglary, which of the following comments is correct?

A CALTHORPE commits a burglary (under s. 9(1)(b) of the Theft Act 1968) when he turns the electric fire on.

B CALTHORPE commits an aggravated burglary (under s. 10 of the Theft Act 1968) when he picks up the hammer.

C CALTHORPE commits an aggravated burglary (under s. 10 of the Theft Act 1968) when he smashes the window.

D CALTHORPE does not commit a burglary offence in the circumstances described.

Question 26.9

GATE breaks into a warehouse intending to steal from the premises. As soon as he is inside the warehouse he sees an office which is actually within the warehouse itself. He thinks there will be property worth stealing in the office and breaks down the door to see what is inside. Whilst he is inside the office and searching for something to steal, he hears the sound of footsteps approaching him and he picks up a large carving knife from a shelf in the office. GATE does not want to keep the carving knife but thinks it will certainly deter anyone who challenges him whilst he is on the premises and if threatening someone with the carving knife is not enough, he decides he will use it on anyone who tries to stop him. A security guard enters the office and GATE points the carving knife at the security guard shouting *'Stay back or I'll stab you!'* The security guard takes no notice and approaches GATE. A struggle between GATE and the security guard takes place during which GATE stabs the security guard causing the security guard serious injury. GATE grabs hold of a laptop from the office, drops the carving knife and runs away.

At what point is the offence of aggravated burglary (contrary to s. 10 of the Theft Act 1968) first committed?

A When GATE picks up the carving knife.

B When GATE threatens the security guard.

C When GATE injures the security guard.

D When GATE steals the laptop.

Question 26.10

STANLEY has had a number of arguments with his neighbour DREW about the noise her dog makes at all times of the day. One afternoon DREW's dog is barking loudly and STANLEY decides he has had enough. He goes round to DREW's house and breaks in by smashing the back door off its hinges intending to threaten DREW with violence if she does not sort her dog out. DREW is not inside the house but STANLEY can hear her dog barking in the kitchen. He returns to his own house, grabs hold of some masking tape and returns to DREW's house intending to wrap the masking tape around the mouth of the dog to shut it up. He enters the kitchen but the dog is so aggressive that he cannot get close to it. He picks up a large knife from the kitchen and stabs the dog, seriously injuring it in the process.

Which of the following comments is correct in respect of STANLEY's activity and the offence of burglary under the Theft Act 1968?

A STANLEY commits a s. 9(1)(a) burglary when he enters DREW's house intending to threaten her with violence.

B STANLEY commits a s. 10 aggravated burglary when he enters DREW's house with the masking tape.

C STANLEY commits a s. 10 aggravated burglary when he picks up the knife and seriously injures the dog.

D STANLEY has not committed an offence of burglary in these circumstances.

ANSWERS

Answer 26.1

Answer **A** — One way an aggravated burglary can be committed is when a person enters premises in possession of a weapon of offence. A screwdriver is not a weapon of offence 'per se' and SOUTHALL would have to intend for the screwdriver to be used as such for this item to fall into the category of offensive weapon. This makes answer C incorrect. Drugged meat to incapacitate a dog is not an offensive weapon as the weapon must be to incapacitate a person, making answer B incorrect. Answer D is incorrect as neither of the items is a weapon of offence.

Investigators' Manual, para. 3.5.1

Answer 26.2

Answer **B** — There are two questions to ask to obtain the correct answer to this question: (i) Is the cord a weapon of offence? (ii) What type of burglary is this? The piece of cord intended to tie up any occupants is a weapon of offence as it is intended to incapacitate a person. This is a burglary under s. 9(1)(a) of the Theft Act 1968 as CRADDOCK intends to break in and steal from the house and burglary is committed when he enters with that intent. Where these two points meet is where the aggravated burglary is first committed.

Investigators' Manual, para. 3.5.1

Answer 26.3

Answer **A** — Answer D is incorrect as the definition of a weapon of offence is incomplete; you should add 'or intended by the person having it with him for such use'. On this basis, the knife will become a weapon of offence. The fact that LAMONT had the weapon of offence in his possession for some other purpose than to use during the course of the burglary is irrelevant. The harm this section aims to protect the public from is that a burglar may be tempted to use such a weapon to injure someone during a burglary, making answer B incorrect. Finally, answer C is incorrect as HEWITSON must know of the existence of the knife and, because it is not an offensive weapon per se, its purpose.

Investigators' Manual, para. 3.5.1

Answer 26.4

Answer **C** — The screwdriver is not a weapon of offence until HULBERT intends to use it to cause injury and this intention is accompanied by an offence under s. 9(1)(a) or (b) of the Theft Act 1968. When HULBERT threatens WEEDON with the screwdriver, it instantaneously changes from a screwdriver to a weapon of offence (think about the concept of 'instant arming') but while he remains in the lounge an aggravated burglary can only be committed if he commits or attempts to commit one of the offences under s. 9(1)(b) of the Theft Act 1968, i.e. theft or grievous bodily harm. It cannot be under s. 9(1)(a) at this moment as he has already entered the premises when the intention regarding the use of the screwdriver is formed. When HULBERT decides to rape WEEDON and moves from the lounge to the hall, he does not commit burglary as his intention is to commit an offence of rape—this is not a 'trigger' offence for the purposes of the s. 9(1)(a) offence. The offence of aggravated burglary is *first committed* when HULBERT stabs WEEDON, as at this point he has entered the hall as a trespasser and committed GBH.

Investigators' Manual, para. 3.5.1

Answer 26.5

Answer **D** — The inclusion of an article intended by a person to cause injury or incapacitate within the definition of a weapon of offence means that absolutely anything can instantaneously become a weapon of offence in the hands of the burglar, making answer B incorrect. This is a burglary under s. 9(1)(a) of the Theft Act 1968 and so to become an aggravated burglary the weapon of offence must be with the offender at the time of entry. This is not the case. The fact that entry has been gained because of the use of the piece of wood against O'HALLORAN is irrelevant; RULE is the only person entering the premises and he does not have any weapon at the time of entry, making answer A incorrect. HOQUE does not commit the offence as he never enters the premises, therefore answer C is incorrect.

Investigators' Manual, para. 3.5.1

Answer 26.6

Answer **C** — Although handcuffs are a weapon of offence, DARE disposes of them prior to entry and so cannot commit aggravated burglary because he does not have the weapon in his possession at the time of entry, making answer A incorrect. At this stage, DARE is guilty of burglary alone. When he picks up the scissors they become a weapon of offence, but a mere threat to use them does not make his burglary aggravated so answer D is incorrect. As DARE then commits a theft by stealing the cash-box he commits a burglary under s. 9(1)(b) and is in possession of an offensive weapon when he does so. This makes him guilty of aggravated burglary so answer B is incorrect.

Investigators' Manual, para. 3.5.1

Answer 26.7

Answer **A** — At point A LEAVY has committed a burglary contrary to s. 9(1)(a) of the Theft Act 1968 and has with him a weapon of offence (his intent to use it to cause injury makes it a weapon of offence), making this an aggravated burglary. It does not matter that he only intended to use it to assist in his escape.

Investigators' Manual, paras 3.5.1, 3.5.2

Answer 26.8

Answer **D** — CALTHORPE enters the house as a trespasser but not for any purposes under s. 9(1)(a) of the Theft Act 1968. Once inside the lounge he could commit a burglary (under s. 9(1)(b) of the Act) if he stole or attempted to steal, committed or attempted to commit grievous bodily harm—he turns on an electric fire to warm himself up but this is not theft as electricity is not property so he does not commit a burglary under s. 9(1)(b) of the Act, making answer A incorrect. He hears a noise and picks up a hammer; however, he does not intend to steal it. This is not a burglary so he cannot commit an aggravated burglary at this stage, making answer B incorrect. When CALTHORPE smashes the window he commits criminal damage but this is not an offence of burglary under s. 9(1)(b) so, again, he does not commit aggravated burglary, making answer C incorrect. No burglary offence is committed by CALTHORPE (answer D is correct).

Investigators' Manual, paras 3.5.1, 3.5.2

Answer 26.9

Answer **C** — An aggravated burglary occurs when a burglary (under s. 9(1)(a) or 9(1)(b)) is committed and at the time of that offence the offender has with them a weapon of offence, firearm, imitation firearm or explosive. A weapon of offence can be made, adapted or intended to cause injury and the carving knife would fall into the 'intended' category. But when GATE picks up the carving knife no burglary occurs as whilst he has a weapon of offence with him, he does not intend to keep it, making answer A incorrect. When GATE threatens the security guard, no burglary occurs (GATE could only commit a s. 9(1)(b) burglary in the office and he has not stolen/attempted to steal or inflicted/attempted to inflict grievous bodily harm upon a person), making answer B incorrect. When he injures the security guard he commits a s. 9(1)(b) burglary and at the time has a weapon of offence with him, meaning he commits aggravated burglary at this point. He also commits an aggravated burglary when he steals the laptop but he *first* committed the offence at point C, therefore making answer D incorrect.

Investigators' Manual, paras 3.5.1, 3.5.2

Answer 26.10

Answer **D** — A burglary under s. 9(1)(a) of the Theft Act 1968 is committed when a person enters a building or part of a building with the intention of stealing anything in the building or part of the building in question, of inflicting on any person therein any grievous bodily harm or of doing unlawful damage to the building or anything therein. When STANLEY enters the house he has none of these intentions, making answer A incorrect. He does not have any of these intentions when he returns to the house with the masking tape, making answer B incorrect. Inside the kitchen he can only commit a s. 9(1)(b) burglary if he stole or attempted to steal, committed or attempted to commit grievous bodily harm—he does not do so when he seriously injures the dog, meaning that answer C is incorrect. No burglary is committed by STANLEY (answer D is correct).

Investigators' Manual, paras 3.5.1, 3.5.2

27 Taking a Conveyance Without Consent

QUESTIONS

Question 27.1

GLEASE finds a paper driving licence in the street (it is in the name of JOHN BRADY). GLEASE thinks this will be useful and decides to hire a car using the licence (GLEASE does not possess a driving licence of any description). He visits a car hire business and when asked if he has a full driving licence he states that he has and hands over the licence in the name of JOHN BRADY to the shop assistant. He pays the hire fee to use the car for the week and the assistant in the shop hands the keys to the vehicle to GLEASE. GLEASE has no intention of keeping the vehicle forever, he just wants to use it to drive to Skegness for a holiday.

In relation to the offence of taking a conveyance without consent (contrary to s. 12 of the Theft Act 1968) only, which of the following comments is correct?

A GLEASE has committed the offence as he has obtained the use of the car by fraud (presenting the driving licence) so this would not amount to 'true' consent.

B GLEASE has not committed the offence as he has 'lawful authority' to use the car as he has paid a fee to use it in this way.

C GLEASE has committed the offence which, in addition to any imprisonment the court thinks appropriate, also carries a mandatory disqualification period of six months.

D GLEASE has not committed the offence because he has the consent of the assistant at the shop to take the vehicle.

Question 27.2

JEFFERSON is driving around late at night and sees a rubber dinghy on the driveway of a house. JEFFERSON decides to take the rubber dinghy as his friend HINES could use it at weekends on his fishing trips. JEFFERSON places the dinghy on the roof rack of his car and drives off. JEFFERSON is later stopped by police and arrested.

Considering the offence of taking a conveyance without the owner's consent, contrary to s. 12(1) of the Theft Act 1968, which of the following statements is correct?

A JEFFERSON has committed the offence in these circumstances.
B JEFFERSON has attempted the offence.
C JEFFERSON has not committed the offence as the rubber dinghy is not a mechanically propelled vehicle.
D JEFFERSON has not committed the offence as he is not the person who is going to use the dinghy.

Question 27.3

WIRE and DEMER visit an agricultural show where they get drunk and begin to behave in an anti-social manner. WIRE climbs up into the cab of a tractor and releases the handbrake of the vehicle; fortunately his behaviour is seen by SMITH who gets into the cab of the tractor before it can move and reapplies the handbrake. While this is taking place, DEMER climbs onto a horse and, sitting in the saddle, he kicks the horse which moves forward several feet. Staff at the show drag DEMER off the horse and both men are ejected from the showground.

Who, if anyone at all, commits the offence of taking a conveyance without consent (contrary to s. 12 of the Theft Act 1968)?

A The offence has not been committed by either person.
B Only WIRE commits the offence.
C Only DEMER commits the offence.
D WIRE and DEMER commit the offence.

Question 27.4

BARRY takes a Nissan 370Z vehicle from a car park; he does not intend to steal it, just to enjoy driving it for a while before he abandons it somewhere. As he is driving around, he sees FOX and pulls over at the side of the road and opens the passenger door. BARRY tells FOX how he came by the Nissan 370Z and FOX thinks this is funny. FOX gets in to the passenger seat for a few minutes while BARRY tells him what he has done with the vehicle (at no time whilst FOX is in the vehicle does it move). FOX gets out of the vehicle and BARRY decides to accompany him and abandons the vehicle. The vehicle is actually blocking the driveway of a house belonging to TESTO, who, believing he has a right in law to do so, gets in to the driver's seat of the Nissan 370Z, releases the handbrake and moves the vehicle 20 feet along the road.

In relation to the offence of taking a conveyance without consent (contrary to s. 12 of the Theft Act 1968), which of the comments below is correct?

A FOX committed the offence when he got in to the vehicle knowing it had been taken without the consent of the owner or other lawful authority.

B TESTO committed the offence when he sat in the vehicle and released the handbrake but he could potentially avail himself of a defence to the offence under s. 12(6) of the Act.

C FOX has committed the offence but TESTO has not.

D TESTO has committed the offence; he would not be able to use the fact that he thought he had a lawful right to move the vehicle as a defence.

Question 27.5

LISTON commits an offence of taking a conveyance without consent (contrary to s. 12(1) of the Theft Act 1968) in relation to a Mercedes CLA (a mechanically propelled vehicle). He drives the vehicle on to some private land and begins to carry out driving behaviour that is incredibly dangerous. Due to the way the vehicle is being driven, LISTON loses control of the vehicle which skids violently and crashes into a ditch on the private land, causing serious damage to the rear of the vehicle.

Has LISTON committed the offence of aggravated vehicle taking (contrary to s. 12A of the Theft Act 1968)?

A No, as no person was injured due to the way the vehicle was driven.

B Yes, the offence is complete when LISTON drives the vehicle dangerously on the private land.

C No, as the activity took place on private land and not a road or public place.

D Yes, but the offence is committed only when the vehicle is damaged.

Question 27.6

SUTTER is walking home one night because he has missed the last bus. SUTTER is frustrated by this and walks up the road looking for cars he could take and use to drive for his journey home (he does not intend to steal a car). SUTTER approaches a Vauxhall Astra and he can see the car keys on the driver's seat but the vehicle is locked. SUTTER smashes the driver's window, gets into the car and starts the engine and drives off. It is a frosty evening and when he drives around a tight right-hand bend of a road he takes it too quickly and the vehicle slides on the ice and smashes into the front garden wall of a house. Police attend the scene and arrest SUTTER.

Considering an offence of aggravated vehicle-taking (contrary to s. 12A of the Theft Act 1968), which of the following statements is correct?

A SUTTER does not commit this offence.

B SUTTER commits this offence when he damages the vehicle for the original taking but not the damage caused to the vehicle in the accident because there must be evidence of dangerous driving.

C SUTTER commits this offence when he damages the vehicle for the original taking and the damage caused to the vehicle during the accident.

D SUTTER does not commit this offence when he damages the vehicle for the original taking but does with regards to the damage caused to the vehicle during the accident.

Question 27.7

BANSKI is part of a coach tour visiting 'Needley Hall County House'. The house and grounds are all on private land. A large farm show is taking place on the land with lots of different commercial stands set up as part of the show. One of the stands is run by CHALMER who is a luxury car dealer who owns several expensive cars on display including an Audi Q7 motor vehicle. BANSKI examines the Q7 and although he does not have a driving licence, BANSKI asks CHALMER if he can drive it around the showground rather than arrange a test drive. CHALMER refuses the request. BANSKI sees the keys to the Q7 on a table near to the vehicle and takes them. He gets into the Q7 and starts the engine. He sits in the vehicle for 30 seconds with the engine running and then drives the vehicle out of the display area and slowly drives it around the area of the farm show. Even though he is being extremely careful, BANSKI causes a slight scratch to the driver's door of the Q7 as he drives it through a narrow gateway. He returns it to the display area where he is confronted by CHALMER. As he parks the Q7, he accidentally runs over CHALMER's foot causing severe bruising to CHALMER's foot.

At what stage does BANSKI first commit the offence of aggravated vehicle taking (contrary to s. 12A of the Theft Act 1968)?

A When he starts the engine of the vehicle.

B When he drives the vehicle out of the display area.

C When he causes damage to the vehicle.

D When he causes injury to CHALMER.

ANSWERS

Answer 27.1

Answer **D** — This question follows the circumstances and the decision made in *Whittaker* v *Campbell* [1984] QB 318. Consent, even if obtained by a deception, is still a valid consent. *This will be the case unless the deception is one where identity is an issue*. In the example in the 'Keynotes' of your *Investigators' Manual* you are presented with a scenario that states the following:

> John Smith (who does not possess a driving licence) is walking along the street when he finds a driving licence in the name of Paul Grey. Smith takes the driving licence and visits a car hire company and asks to hire a car for a day. The assistant at the reception of the car hire company asks Smith for a driving licence and Smith produces the licence he found in the street (in the name of Paul Grey). The assistant photocopies the licence and asks for the fee of £100 which Smith pays. The assistant hands over a set of car keys and Smith drives away in the car (intending to return it later that day).

This is effectively the question you are dealing with. The *Investigators' Manual* rightly states that the above scenario *would not* represent an offence of TWOC; this is because the assistant has handed over a set of keys to Smith and consented to Smith taking the car. The relevant deception here relates to the possession of the driving licence, *not to the name on the driving licence*. The assistant would have handed over the keys to the car if the name on the driving licence was 'Bugs Bunny'; identity is not an issue. So the offence has not been committed, making answers A and C incorrect. Answer B is incorrect as this is nothing to do with 'lawful authority' having paid a fee to use the vehicle.

Investigators' Manual, paras 3.6.1, 3.6.2

Answer 27.2

Answer **A** — Section 12(1) of the Theft Act 1968 states:

> A person shall be guilty of an offence if, without having the consent of the owner or other lawful authority, he takes a conveyance for his own or another's use or knowing that any conveyance has been taken without such authority, drives it or allows himself to be carried in or on it.

A conveyance is taken even if it is put onto another vehicle to do so (*R* v *Pearce* [1973] Crim LR 321, where a rubber dinghy was put on the roof rack of a car and taken away); the dinghy was ultimately going to be used as a conveyance by someone in the future, making A the correct answer.

Investigators' Manual, paras 3.6.2, 3.6.4

Answer 27.3

Answer **A** — To commit this offence you need to *take* a *conveyance*. Section 12(7)(a) of the Theft Act 1968 states that a 'conveyance' means any conveyance *constructed or adapted* for the carriage of a person or persons whether by land, water or air, except that it does not include a conveyance constructed or adapted for use only under the control of a person not carried in or on it, and 'drive' shall be construed accordingly. A horse is not a conveyance because it has not been '*constructed or adapted*' to carry people, meaning that answers C and D are incorrect. Answer B is incorrect as to 'take' a conveyance means that the conveyance must move—even if only by a small amount. This does not happen when the handbrake of the tractor is released.

Investigators' Manual, paras 3.6.4, 3.6.5

Answer 27.4

Answer **B** — A person shall be guilty of an offence if, without having the consent of the owner or other lawful authority, he takes any conveyance for his own or another's use or, knowing that any conveyance has been taken without such authority, drives it or allows himself to be carried in or on it. But, to commit the 'allow to be carried' element of this offence, you need to be 'carried', i.e. the conveyance must move. This has not happened with FOX, so he would not commit the offence, meaning that answers A and C are incorrect. TESTO has committed the offence but s. 12(6) provides a defence to the offence as it states that a person does not commit an offence under this section by anything done in the belief that he has lawful authority to do it or that he would have had the owner's consent if the owner knew of his doing it and the circumstances of it. TESTO believes that he has a lawful right to move the vehicle so he would be able to use the defence, making answer D incorrect.

Investigators' Manual, paras 3.6.7, 3.6.8

Answer 27.5

Answer **D** — Section 12A of the Theft Act 1968 states:

(1) Subject to subsection (3) below, a person is guilty of aggravated taking of a vehicle if—
   (a) he commits an offence under section 12(1) above (in this section referred to as a 'basic offence') in relation to a mechanically propelled vehicle; and
   (b) it is proved that, at any time after the vehicle was unlawfully taken (whether by him or another) and before it was recovered, the vehicle was driven, or injury or damage was caused, in one or more of the circumstances set out in paragraphs (a) to (d) of subsection (2) below.

(2) The circumstances referred to in subsection (1)(b) above are—
   (a) that the vehicle was driven dangerously on a road or other public place;
   (b) that, owing to the driving of the vehicle, an accident occurred by which injury was caused to any person;
   (c) that, owing to the driving of the vehicle, an accident occurred by which damage was caused to any property, other than the vehicle;
   (d) that damage was caused to the vehicle.

Dangerous driving must take place on a road or public place meaning that LISTON would not commit the offence when he drives the vehicle in that manner, making answer B incorrect. But the offence has been committed (making answers A and C incorrect) as damage has been caused to the vehicle and this can take place anywhere (including private land).

Investigators' Manual, para. 3.6.9

Answer 27.6

Answer **D** — The circumstances in which this is committed under s. 12A(2) of the Theft Act 1968 are:

(a) he commits an offence under section 12(1) above (in this section referred to as a 'basic offence') in relation to a mechanically propelled vehicle; and
(b) that, owing to the driving of the vehicle, an accident occurred by which injury was caused to any person;
(c) that, owing to the driving of the vehicle, an accident occurred by which damage was caused to any property, other than the vehicle;
(d) that damage was caused to the vehicle.

Damage caused for the original taking of the vehicle is not covered (as at that stage the vehicle concerned *has not moved* and you do not have the elements of the 'basic' s. 12(1) offence), so therefore the breaking of the window is not included for the offence under s. 12A and answers B and C are incorrect. In *R* v *Hughes* [2013] 2 All ER 613, the Supreme Court held that in cases of causing death by driving when uninsured (s. 3ZB of the Road Traffic Act 1988) the defendant must be proved to have done something more than merely drive his/her vehicle on the road so that it was there to be involved in a fatal accident. It must be proved that the defendant did or omitted to do something else that contributed in a more than minimal way to the death. There must, in other words, be something more than mere 'but for' causation. The same approach has now been adopted in respect of aggravated vehicle taking. So in order for a defendant to be guilty of an offence committed under s. 12A, it must be proved that the defendant did or omitted to do something that contributed in a more than minimal way to the outcome—*the defendant must 'cause' the outcome in some way*. In *R* v *Taylor* [2016] 1 WLR 500, the defendant was charged with taking a truck without consent, and that 'owing to the driving of the vehicle, an accident occurred by which [death] was caused'. But although the truck was involved in a fatal collision with a scooter while the defendant was driving it, the fault was *entirely that of the scooter rider*, so the defendant could not be said to have 'caused' the latter's death. There must be a direct causal connection between the driving and the death, injury and/or damage. That is present in this question meaning that the offence is committed and answer A is incorrect—therefore D is the correct answer.

Investigators' Manual, para. 3.6.9

Answer 27.7

Answer **C** — Section 12A of the Theft Act 1968 states:

(1) Subject to subsection (3) below, a person is guilty of aggravated taking of a vehicle if—
   (a) he commits an offence under section 12(1) above (in this section referred to as a 'basic offence') in relation to a mechanically propelled vehicle; and
   (b) it is proved that, at any time after the vehicle was unlawfully taken (whether by him or another) and before it was recovered, the vehicle was driven, or injury or damage was caused, in one or more of the circumstances set out in paragraphs (a) to (d) of subsection (2) below.

(2) The circumstances referred to in subsection (1)(b) above are—
   (a) that the vehicle was driven dangerously on a road or other public place;
   (b) that, owing to the driving of the vehicle, an accident occurred by which injury was caused to any person;
   (c) that, owing to the driving of the vehicle, an accident occurred by which damage was caused to any property, other than the vehicle;
   (d) that damage was caused to the vehicle.

The first thing that is required for the offence under s. 12A to be committed is that the 'basic' offence (under s. 12 of the Theft Act 1968) must be committed. The offence under s. 12 (taking a conveyance without consent) requires the conveyance to move—starting the ignition does not accomplish that so the 'basic' offence is not committed at answer A. Additionally, none of the circumstances listed at s. 12A(2)(a) to (d) have occurred at this stage. The fact that BANSKI does not have a driving licence has no bearing on the commission of an offence under s. 12A. Driving the vehicle out of the display area would result in the commission of the s. 12 offence (TWOC) but there is still no 'aggravated' activity, meaning answer B is incorrect. The offence is *first* committed at answer C as at that time damage is caused to the vehicle (an aggravating factor under s. 12A(2)(d)). The offence is also committed at answer D but the question specifically asks when it is *first* committed.

Investigators' Manual, para. 3.6.9

28 Handling Stolen Goods

QUESTIONS

Question 28.1

FENSHAW is a collector of rare records. He visits a car-boot sale to see if there are any bargains available. While browsing at a stall run by REAY, he spots a record that he knows would cost over £1,000 from his normal reputable source. He asks REAY how much the record costs and REAY tells him he can buy the record for £30. FENSHAW remarks that this is a bargain, to which REAY replies '*Easy come and easy go.*' FENSHAW buys the record.

If FENSHAW were later arrested for handling stolen goods, what state of mind would be required for a prosecution to succeed?

A FENSHAW would have to know or believe the record to be stolen goods.
B FENSHAW would have to presume that the record was stolen goods.
C FENSHAW would have to think it probable that the record was stolen goods.
D FENSHAW would have to suspect that the record was stolen goods.

Question 28.2

GOODCHILD steals a car from TURVEY and sells it to CLIFF for £2,000. This is a cheap price for the car and although CLIFF is suspicious of GOODCHILD, she buys the car nevertheless. CLIFF drives the car for several days and eventually finds papers in the car belonging to TURVEY. CLIFF telephones TURVEY, who tells her that the car is stolen. CLIFF quickly hangs up and retains the car for two days while she decides what she will do. Realising that she may lose the car if she returns it to TURVEY, CLIFF sells the car to MARTINEZ for £500.

At what stage, if at all, does CLIFF commit the offence of handling stolen goods (contrary to s. 22 of the Theft Act 1968)?

A When CLIFF buys the car for £2,000 from GOODCHILD.

B When CLIFF retains the car knowing it is stolen.
C When CLIFF sells the car to MARTINEZ.
D CLIFF does not commit the offence in these circumstances.

Question 28.3

VENN breaks into a house and steals a quantity of jewellery. He takes the jewellery to AUSTEN and tells him about the burglary. AUSTEN gives VENN £100 for the jewellery. VENN uses the money to buy a games console. AUSTEN exchanges the jewellery for two tickets to a football match. He keeps one ticket for his own use and gives the other to PEERS as a birthday present. PEERS knows nothing about the origin of the ticket.

Which of the following statements correctly identifies 'stolen goods' from this scenario for the purposes of the offence of handling stolen goods?

A Only the £100 given to VENN and the games console he buys with the money would be 'stolen goods'.
B Only the jewellery (in the hands of AUSTEN alone) would be 'stolen goods'.
C All of the property except for the ticket in the hands of PEERS would be 'stolen goods'.
D Only the jewellery and both tickets in the hands of AUSTEN would be 'stolen goods'.

Question 28.4

GREEN orders a computer from a company owned by FORD. FORD dispatches the computer using a postal firm but the computer is stolen in transit. Two months later, SMITH is arrested in possession of the computer and is charged with an offence of handling stolen goods. The prosecution wish to serve a statutory declaration on SMITH under s. 27 of the Theft Act 1968 as proof that the computer was stolen.

Which of the following statements is correct?

A Only GREEN can make the declaration and a copy of it must be given to SMITH at least three days before the trial.
B Either GREEN or FORD can make the declaration and a copy of it must be given to SMITH at least seven days before the trial.
C Only FORD can make the declaration and this must be given to SMITH at least 14 days before the trial.
D Only GREEN can make the declaration, a copy of which must be given to SMITH at least 21 days before the trial.

Question 28.5

POPPITT contacts HUNN and tells him that he plans to steal a lorry full of designer clothes. HUNN tells POPPITT that he will store the goods after the theft and then sell them on for a share of the proceeds that will go to POPPITT.

Which of the following statements is correct with regard to the offence of handling stolen goods?

A Even though HUNN's actions are merely preparatory to the receiving of stolen goods, he commits the offence as he has arranged to receive them.

B HUNN commits an offence of handling stolen goods as the act of receiving does not require the physical reception of the goods.

C HUNN does not commit an offence of handling stolen goods in these circumstances.

D HUNN commits the offence of handling stolen goods as he has arranged to act for the benefit of another.

Question 28.6

DEAKIN has been charged with offences of handling stolen goods and theft. DEAKIN has a previous conviction for handing stolen goods that is six years old and a previous conviction for theft that is four years old.

Would the prosecution be able to use s. 27 of the Theft Act 1968 to prove that DEAKIN knew or believed the goods to be stolen goods?

A No, as both convictions are over 12 months old.

B Yes, but only in relation to the conviction for theft.

C No, as DEAKIN has been charged with theft as well as handling stolen goods.

D Yes, both previous convictions could be used.

Question 28.7

STEWARD has been charged with an offence of handling stolen goods. The prosecution wish to use s. 27(3) of the Theft Act 1968 to show STEWARD's previous misconduct. STEWARD has a previous conviction for handling stolen goods that is eight years old and a previous conviction for theft that is four years old.

Which of the following statements is true?

A Provided that seven days' notice in writing has been given to STEWARD of the intention to prove the convictions, both convictions would be admissible.

B Provided that three days' notice in writing has been given to STEWARD of the intention to prove the conviction, the handling stolen goods conviction would be admissible.

C Provided that seven days' notice in writing has been given to STEWARD of the intention to prove the conviction, the theft conviction would be admissible.

D Provided that three days' notice in writing has been given to STEWARD of the intention to prove the convictions, both convictions would be admissible.

Question 28.8

CLAY knows that BANNER is having an affair and blackmails him, stating that if he does not give him some money and goods he will tell BANNER's wife of his affair. In response to the demand, BANNER gives CLAY £100 and a small gold necklace. CLAY keeps the money for himself and gives the necklace to his girlfriend, TRENT, as a gift. TRENT thinks this is suspicious but keeps the necklace. A few days later, TRENT overhears CLAY bragging to his friends of his blackmail of BANNER and TRENT now knows that the necklace is stolen, but she likes it so much that she decides to keep it.

Which of the following is correct with regard to any criminal responsibility of TRENT?

A TRENT commits the offence of theft when she realises the necklace is stolen and decides to keep it.

B TRENT commits the offence of handling stolen goods when she first accepts the necklace as a gift.

C TRENT commits the offence of handling stolen goods when she overhears that the necklace is stolen and decides to keep it.

D TRENT does not commit theft and does not commit handling stolen goods as goods obtained by blackmail are not property for the purpose of handling.

ANSWERS

Answer 28.1

Answer **A** — Section 22 of the Theft Act 1968 states that a person can only handle stolen goods if he/she *'knows or believes'* the goods to be stolen. Any other state of mind, including suspicion, will not suffice, making answers B, C and D incorrect.

Investigators' Manual, para. 3.7.1

Answer 28.2

Answer D — CLIFF must know or believe the goods to be stolen and mere suspicion will not suffice, making answer A incorrect. To commit an offence of handling stolen goods, the retention, removal, disposal or realisation must be by or for the benefit of *another*. If the only person 'benefiting' from the defendant's actions is the defendant, this element of the offence will not be made out (*R* v *Bloxham* [1983] 1 AC 109). In *Bloxham*, the appellant bought and part-paid for a car which he subsequently discovered to be stolen. He then sold the car at a slight loss and was convicted of handling in respect of this sale, the allegation being that he 'realised' the car for the benefit of the buyer. The House of Lords reversed this decision holding that the mischief at which the Act was aimed was the actions of those who knowingly received from the thief or facilitated the disposal of stolen goods. A purchaser of goods purchased in good faith who sells the goods after discovering they have been stolen *does not come within the ambit of the section*, even if the transaction could be described as a disposal or realisation for the benefit of the person to whom they sell it. The phrase 'by or for the benefit of another' limits the reach of the law to the situation where the handler acts *on another's behalf* in removing, disposing, realising or retaining goods (the possession of the stolen property would now be caught by s. 329 of the Proceeds of Crime Act 2002 and the sale of the vehicle by fraud by false representation (s. 2 of the Fraud Act 2006)). Retaining the car and then disposing of it is only done for the benefit of CLIFF so the offence is not made out, making answers B and C incorrect.

Investigators' Manual, paras 3.7.1 to 3.7.3

Answer 28.3

Answer **C** — 'Stolen goods' under s. 24 of the Theft Act 1968 are those that directly or indirectly represent the stolen goods in the hands of the thief or the handler, or the original stolen goods themselves. The jewellery in the hands of VENN would be considered as stolen goods as he is the original thief. The £100 given to VENN and the games console he buys with the money indirectly represent the stolen goods in the hands of the thief. The jewellery in the hands of AUSTEN is the original stolen goods in the hands of the handler. The tickets exchanged for the jewellery indirectly represent the stolen goods in the hands of the handler. The ticket passed on to PEERS ceases to be 'stolen goods' as PEERS is in innocent possession of the ticket and has no idea as to its origin. Therefore, answers A, B and D are incorrect.

Investigators' Manual, para. 3.7.2

Answer 28.4

Answer **B** — Section 27 of the Theft Act 1968 allows a declaration of proof that goods were stolen to be made in proceedings for any theft or handling stolen goods from that theft. The declaration can be made by the person who dispatched the goods (FORD) or the person who failed to receive the goods (GREEN) and is admissible if a copy of the statement is given to the person charged (SMITH) at least seven days before the hearing or trial. This makes answers A, C and D incorrect.

Investigators' Manual, para. 3.7.6

Answer 28.5

Answer **C** — Although the conduct mentioned in answers A, B and D would qualify as activities associated with the offence of handling stolen goods, the offence will only be committed if the goods are stolen. If the goods have yet to be stolen, as in this case, then the offence is not committed.

Investigators' Manual, para. 3.7.1

Answer 28.6

Answer **C** — Section 27 of the Act can be used to prove that the defendant knew or believed the goods to be stolen goods if he: (i) had in his possession, or has undertaken or assisted in the retention, removal, disposal or realisation of, stolen goods from any theft taking place not earlier than 12 months before the offence charged; and (ii) evidence that he has within five years preceding the date of the offence charged been convicted of theft or of handling stolen goods. Therefore the conviction for handling stolen goods cannot be used, making answer D incorrect. Answer A is incorrect in relation to the time limits regarding the previous convictions. The prosecution may only use s. 27 if the defendant is being proceeded against in relation to a charge of handling stolen goods *alone* and not any other offence. As DEAKIN has been charged with theft in addition to handling stolen goods, the power under s. 27 cannot be used, making answer B incorrect.

Investigators' Manual, para. 3.7.5

Answer 28.7

Answer **C** — Seven days' notice in writing must be given to the defendant that the prosecution intend to prove previous convictions, making answers B and D incorrect. The defendant's previous convictions can be for theft or handling stolen goods; however, the conviction for the offence must be in the five years preceding the date of the offence charged. Therefore the handling conviction would not be admissible, making answer A incorrect.

Investigators' Manual, para. 3.7.5

Answer 28.8

Answer **A** — Answer B is incorrect as when TRENT first receives the necklace she only has suspicions about the necklace, and does not know or believe it to be stolen. Answer C is incorrect as when TRENT overhears that the necklace is stolen she is 'retaining' the necklace and this activity must be done 'by or for the benefit of another'—here TRENT is retaining the necklace for her own benefit so she does not 'handle' the necklace. When TRENT decides to keep the necklace having found out that it is stolen, TRENT commits theft; making A the correct answer. Here TRENT appropriated the necklace when it was given as a gift and later dishonestly kept the property (see s. 3 of the Theft Act 1968). Answer D is incorrect as she has committed theft, and goods obtained by blackmail are property for the purposes of handling.

Investigators' Manual, paras 3.7.1, 3.1.1 to 3.1.5

29 Fraud

QUESTIONS

Question 29.1

Section 1 of the Fraud Act 2006 creates three different ways in which an offence of fraud can be committed.

Which of the following conditions is one of those fraud offences?

A Fraud by impersonation of an individual.
B Fraud by failing to disclose information.
C Fraud by data theft.
D Fraud by communication deception.

Question 29.2

THORP steals BING's wallet, which contains a store card for 'Callows Auto Parts' store in BING's name. THORP decides to use the store card to obtain a large quantity of car tools from the store for his own use. THORP goes into the store and puts £800 worth of car tools into his shopping trolley and takes them to the till. Intending to fool the cashier into thinking the card is his, THORP hands over BING's card in payment but does not say anything to the cashier. The cashier is not fooled by THORP and realises that the card does not belong to THORP as he has seen the real owner, BING, in the store on several previous occasions. However, the cashier is not at all concerned by THORP's behaviour and asks him to sign for the card payment which THORP does. THORP leaves the store with the power tools.

Considering the offence of fraud by false representation (contrary to s. 2 of the Fraud Act 2006), which of the following statements is correct?

A THORP has not committed the offence in these circumstances because he did not use any words to represent that the credit card belonged to him.

B The offence has not been committed because the cashier was not fooled into thinking that THORP was in fact BING.

C The offence has been committed. By handing the card to the cashier THORP represents that he has authority to use it for that transaction. It does not matter that the cashier is not deceived or that words were not used.

D The offence has not been committed as fraud by false representation relates to a 'gain' for another and in these circumstances the gain is directly for the benefit of THORP.

Question 29.3

TIs VENABLES and YOUNG are taking the National Investigators' Examination and are testing each other on the law contained in the Fraud Act 2006. The officers make several remarks relating to the Fraud Act, in particular about the offence of fraud by false representation (s. 2 of the Act). However, only one of those remarks is correct.

Which remark is correct?

A TI VENABLES states that the 'dishonesty' referred to in the offence of fraud by false representation is the same as the 'dishonesty' referred to in s. 2 of the Theft Act 1968.

B TI YOUNG states that the 'gain and loss' referred to in the offence of fraud by false representation must actually take place for the offence to be complete.

C TI VENABLES states that a false representation carried out by post would only be complete when the letter was received by the intended victim.

D TI YOUNG states that if a person makes an untrue statement in the honest belief that it is in fact true, they could not commit the offence.

Question 29.4

VANDER sends out a large number of emails purporting to represent a well-known bank in the hope that people receiving the email will send him their bank account details. VANDER intends to use any details he receives to remove money from his victims' bank accounts and place it into his own account. IBBET is deceived by the email and sends VANDER a return email containing all of his bank account details. VANDER telephones an automated banking facility at IBBET's bank and transfers the entire contents of IBBET's account into his own.

At what stage, if any, does VANDER first commit the offence of fraud by false representation (contrary to s. 2 of the Fraud Act 2006)?

A When he sends out the bulk emails purporting to represent a well-known bank.

B When he receives the return email from IBBET, providing him with his bank account details.
C When he telephones the automated banking facility and removes money from IBBET's account.
D The offence is not committed in these circumstances.

Question 29.5

PURDY is a solicitor who has a written contract with SORRELL to look after her property portfolio and the money that is earned from it, as SORRELL owns 30 houses and does not have the time to administer them herself. PURDY and SORRELL have an argument during which SORRELL insults PURDY. PURDY is extremely offended by SORRELL and to get revenge he does not tell SORRELL when several of her tenants fail to pay their rent. As a consequence of PURDY's inaction, SORRELL loses several thousand pounds in rent.

Would this constitute an offence under s. 3 of the Fraud Act 2006?

A Yes, as PURDY would be under a legal duty to disclose the information to SORRELL.
B No, because the relationship between PURDY and SORRELL is not a fiduciary one.
C Yes, but only because the contract between PURDY and SORRELL was written.
D No, because PURDY acted in order to cause a loss to SORRELL rather than make a gain for himself.

Question 29.6

NEWBURY works for a printing company and is responsible for marketing the company and securing new contracts. NEWBURY is working on obtaining a major contract that will provide the company with £10 million worth of business when he is approached by the owner of a rival firm. The owner of the rival firm tells NEWBURY that if he allows his company to win the battle for the printing contract then he will hire NEWBURY as the General Manager and give him a pay rise worth £50K a year. NEWBURY agrees and as a result he fails to take up the chance of the contract, allowing the rival company to take it up at the expense of his current employer.

Considering offences under the Fraud Act 2006 only, what offence, if any, does NEWBURY commit?

A Fraud by false representation (contrary to s. 2 of the Fraud Act 2006).
B Fraud by failing to disclose information (contrary to s. 3 of the Fraud Act 2006).
C Fraud by abuse of position (contrary to s. 4 of the Fraud Act 2006).
D NEWBURY does not commit any offence in these circumstances.

Question 29.7

COXSEY is a career criminal who specialises in offences of fraud. He has a large amount of material at his disposal in order to commit these offences, which he keeps at various locations. The police raid COXSEY's home address and arrest him for fraud-related offences. In the searches that follow his arrest the police find a 'phishing' kit in a bedroom at his home address (which COXSEY used last week to carry out an offence of fraud by false representation (contrary to s. 2 of the Fraud Act 2006)). In COXSEY's car, which was parked on the front drive of his home address, they find several blank credit cards (which COXSEY later states he was going to use to commit offences of fraud by false representation (contrary to s. 2 of the Fraud Act 2006)) and in a store room rented by COXSEY but several miles away from his home address, they find several hundred blank bank statements (which COXSEY states he was looking after for a friend who was going to use them to commit fraud-related offences).

In relation to which items does COXSEY commit the offence of possession or control of articles for use in frauds (contrary to s. 6 of the Fraud Act 2006)?

A The 'phishing' kit and the blank credit cards only.

B The blank credit cards only.

C The blank bank statements only.

D The blank credit cards and the blank bank statements only.

Question 29.8

ASTBURY works for a credit card company. He is short of money and decides to supplement his income by selling a list of other people's credit card details that he has downloaded from the company computer onto a USB stick. He takes the USB stick to FOXLEY whom he knows commits offences of fraud and sells the USB stick to him. During the sale of the USB stick, ASTBURY offers to supply and sell FOXLEY 1,000 blank credit cards (even though he does not actually have possession of the cards). FOXLEY agrees to buy the cards and gives ASTBURY £500 for the USB stick and £500 for the blank credit cards.

With regard to the offence of making or supplying articles for use in frauds (contrary to s. 7 of the Fraud Act 2006), which of the following comments is true?

A ASTBURY commits the offence but only in respect of the USB stick containing lists of other people's credit card details.

B ASTBURY does not commit the offence as a USB stick containing other people's credit card details is not an 'article' and making an offer to supply requires the offender to be in possession of the article concerned.

C ASTBURY commits the offence but only in respect of the offer to supply the 1,000 credit cards to FOXLEY.

D ASTBURY commits the offence in respect of the USB stick and the offer to supply the 1,000 credit cards to FOXLEY.

Question 29.9

HANCOCK is a volunteer worker. He visits the homes of senior citizens and carries out a variety of maintenance work on their houses; he does not charge anyone for the work he carries out. MORGAN, a 35-year-old, is not very good at 'Do-it-Yourself' and so contacts HANCOCK. MORGAN lies to HANCOCK and tells him that her 85-year-old grandmother requires some repair work to be carried out on her roof and gives HANCOCK her own home address as the location for the work. MORGAN lives alone and would not be entitled to HANCOCK's help unless she was over 65 years of age. HANCOCK believes MORGAN and agrees to complete the work. He visits MORGAN's house and carries out the roof repair at no cost to MORGAN.

Has MORGAN committed the offence of obtaining services dishonestly (contrary to s. 11 of the Fraud Act 2006)?

A Yes, as the fraud used by MORGAN has caused HANCOCK to provide services that MORGAN would not normally be entitled to.

B No, obtaining services dishonestly can only be committed where the service should be paid for. As HANCOCK provided the services for free the offence is not committed.

C Yes, as soon as HANCOCK agrees to carry out the work the offence is committed.

D No, providing maintenance work for free would not fall within the definition of a 'service' for the purposes of this offence.

Question 29.10

MALIN is interested in buying TBT Ltd (a company producing and distributing soft furnishings around the United Kingdom). He makes his interest known to FLYNN who is the owner of the company. The company is not performing too well at the moment and has just made a loss because a major customer owing thousands of pounds to TBT Ltd went bust. FLYNN decides that he will not enter this loss in the company account books to make TBT Ltd a more attractive proposition to purchase. He also rips out several pages from the account books and destroys them with the idea of, once again, making the company look financially sound. MALIN examines the company accounts but decides not to buy TBT Ltd after all (the company accounts have no bearing on this decision).

Considering the offence of false accounting only (contrary to s. 17 of the Theft Act 1968), which of the following comments is correct?

A The offence is first committed when FLYNN omits to include details in the accounts about his loss.

B The offence is first committed when FLYNN rips out and destroys several pages from the account books.

C The offence is first committed when MALIN examines the accounts.

D The offence has not been committed in these circumstances.

Question 29.11

HAINES arrives at a driving test centre for a practical driving test for a car. HAINES shows driving documents to the tester covering the photograph on the driving licence with his thumb; however, the documents shown to the tester are that of his cousin KEEN. HAINES intends to take the test for KEEN because KEEN has failed on his last two attempts. This ruse does not work and the police attend.

Relating to an offence of fraud contrary to s. 2 of the Fraud Act 2006 (fraud by false representation) which of the following statements is correct?

A Neither HAINES nor KEEN are guilty of the offence as a driving licence pass certificate is not property under the Fraud Act 2006.

B Both HAINES and KEEN are guilty of the offence; even though it was HAINES who made the false representation, it can be inferred that KEEN was complicit in the false representation.

C Because there was no pass certificate issued, both HAINES and KEEN would be guilty of attempting to commit the offence.

D Only HAINES is guilty of the offence as he was the person who made the false representation, it cannot be inferred that KEEN was complicit.

Question 29.12

MAY is short of money and wants to go to his friend's house for a couple of days. MAY's friend lives in York so MAY goes to the local transport cafe—where haulage lorries park up while their drivers have refreshments—and sneaks into the rear of one of the lorries destined to deliver goods to York. When the lorry stops on the outskirts of York, MAY gets out of the lorry and walks towards his friend's house. Whilst walking through a 'red light' area he is approached by LOMAS, a street prostitute, who offers to masturbate him for £10. Being too good an opportunity to miss, and having no intention of paying LOMAS, he allows LOMAS to masturbate him. Once LOMAS has finished, he runs off and later arrives at his friend's house.

Which of the following statements is correct with regards to the criminal responsibility of MAY under s. 11 of the Fraud Act 2006 (obtaining services dishonestly)?

A MAY commits two offences: when he gets a free ride to York and in non-payment to the prostitute.

B MAY only commits the offence when he does not pay the prostitute.

C MAY only commits the offence when he gets a free ride to York.

D MAY does not commit any offence in these circumstances as neither the free ride nor the masturbation by the prostitute are classed as a service.

Question 29.13

KNOWLE and COLLIER are drinking in a pub and discussing their sex lives. KNOWLE tells COLLIER that he has not had sex for six months. COLLIER feels sorry for KNOWLE and tells him that he knows a prostitute (ORCHARD) who will have sex with KNOWLE for £100. KNOWLE tells COLLIER that he does not have the money so COLLIER tells KNOWLE he will '*treat him*'. They visit ORCHARD's home address and on arrival COLLIER asks to speak to ORCHARD in private. COLLIER lies to ORCHARD telling her that he has paid her 'pimp' the £100 for her to have sex with KNOWLE so there will be no need for cash to be exchanged. ORCHARD believes COLLIER and, on the basis that the sex has been paid for, she has sexual intercourse with KNOWLE. KNOWLE has no idea about what COLLIER has done.

Has an offence of obtaining services dishonestly (contrary to s. 11 of the Fraud Act 2006) been committed by COLLIER in these circumstances?

A No, as the 'service' that has been obtained related to prostitution and prostitution is contrary to law, therefore the offence has not been committed.

B Yes, the offence is committed at the point when COLLIER lies to ORCHARD about the money being paid to her 'pimp'.

C No, the offence has not been committed by COLLIER as the service he obtained was not for himself.

D Yes, the offence is committed when ORCHARD has sexual intercourse with KNOWLE.

ANSWERS

Answer 29.1

Answer **B** — Fraud by failing to disclose information is an offence created by virtue of s. 1(2)(b) of the Fraud Act 2006. Answers A, C and D are all fabricated.

Investigators' Manual, para. 3.8.2

Answer 29.2

Answer **C** — The fact that THORP has not actually said anything in order to accomplish the offence makes no difference. The offence can be committed by a representation that is express or *implied* and is communicated by words or *conduct*. THORP's conduct would suffice, making answer A incorrect. Answer B is incorrect as whether the cashier was fooled by THORP is immaterial. What matters is that THORP makes a representation knowing that it is false, or might be. Answer D is incorrect as the 'gain' for this offence can be for the individual or another.

Investigators' Manual, para. 3.8.3

Answer 29.3

Answer **D** — The 'dishonesty' referred to in the offence of fraud by false representation is as per the test in *Barlow Clowes International (in liq)* v *Eurotrust International Ltd* [2006] 1 All ER 333, making answer A incorrect. Answer B is incorrect as the 'gain and loss' does not actually have to take place. Answer C is incorrect as a false representation carried out by post would be complete when the letter is posted.

Investigators' Manual, para. 3.8.3

Answer 29.4

Answer **A** — The practice of 'phishing' is covered by the Fraud Act 2006. The offence would be committed when VANDER initially sends out the email falsely representing that he is from a well-known bank.

Investigators' Manual, para. 3.8.4

Answer 29.5

Answer **A** — A fiduciary relationship is one relating to the responsibility of looking after someone else's money in a correct way. Looking after SORRELL's property portfolio would be such a relationship, making answer B incorrect. The offence under s. 3 (fraud by failing to disclose information) is committed when a person has a legal duty to disclose information. Such a duty can arise from oral or written contracts, making answer C incorrect. Answer D is incorrect as the harm caused by failing to disclose such information is either to make a gain or cause a loss to another (see s. 3(b) of the Act).

Investigators' Manual, para. 3.8.5

Answer 29.6

Answer **C** — This is one of the examples provided in your Manual as to how an offence under s. 4 of the Fraud Act 2006 (fraud by abuse of position) may be committed. The crux of the offence is the abuse of a position of trust and while this may relate to the positive action of the defendant, it can also relate to omission.

Investigators' Manual, para. 3.8.6

Answer 29.7

Answer **D** — The offence of possession of articles for use in frauds relates to items that will be used in the *future* to commit such offences. This removes the 'phishing' kit from the equation as it was used last week to commit an offence and therefore answer A is incorrect. The offence is committed by having possession or *control* over items (covering both the blank credit cards and blank bank statements) not only for the defendant's own use but also for use by another to commit offences of fraud, which means that both the blank credit cards and blank bank statements would be covered, making answers B and C incorrect.

Investigators' Manual, para. 3.8.7

Answer 29.8

Answer **D** — Section 8 of the Fraud Act 2006 deals with the term 'article' and this will encompass programs or data held in electronic form (such as a USB stick containing other people's credit card details). Making and selling such an item would be caught by the offence, making answers B and C incorrect in the process. Making an offer to supply an article for use in frauds is similar to the concept of making an offer to supply a drug, i.e. it does not matter whether you actually have the goods; what matters is you made the offer. This makes answer A incorrect.

Investigators' Manual, paras 3.8.7, 3.8.8

Answer 29.9

Answer **B** — Answer A is incorrect as unless the services are provided on the basis that they are chargeable then, regardless of the behaviour of the defendant, the offence cannot be committed. Services provided for free are not covered by the Act. Answer C is further incorrect as the offence of obtaining services dishonestly is a result crime and requires the actual obtaining of the service before it is complete. Answer D is incorrect as the term 'service' has not been defined by the Act.

Investigators' Manual, para. 3.8.9

Answer 29.10

Answer **A** — The offence can be committed in a variety of ways such as destroying, defacing, concealing or falsifying records or documents required for an accounting purpose. It can be committed by omission so in failing to enter the loss the *actus reus* of the offence is complete. The mental element includes 'with a view to gain for himself or another' and will not require the gain to be made, just that the person does something with that possibility in their mind. When FLYNN omits to put that loss in the account book, this state of mind exists and he commits the offence at point A.

Investigators' Manual, para. 3.8.10

Answer 29.11

Answer **B** — Section 2 of the Fraud Act 2006 states:

(1) A person is in breach of this section if he—
  (a) dishonestly makes a false representation, and
  (b) intends by making the representation—
    (i) to make a gain for himself or another, or
    (ii) to cause loss to another or to expose another to a risk of loss.

(2) A representation is false if—
  (a) it is untrue or misleading, and
  (b) the person making it knows that it is, or might be, untrue or misleading.

(3) 'Representation' means any representation as to fact or law, including a representation as to the state of mind of—
 (a) the person making the representation, or
 (b) any other person.

Owing to the fact that this offence is in the *conduct and ulterior intent* of the defendant, the offence is complete when the false representation is made, so is therefore not covered by the Criminal Attempts Act 1981 making C incorrect. Answer A is incorrect as a driving pass certificate is 'other property' and answer D is incorrect as in the case of *Idrees* v *DPP* [2011] EWHC 624 (Admin). When an unidentified imposter presented himself to take a driving test in D's name, it could be inferred that D was complicit in any false representation made by that person with a view to gaining a pass certificate in his name.

Investigators' Manual, para. 3.8.4

Answer 29.12

Answer **B** — Section 11 of the Fraud Act 2006 states:

(1) A person is guilty of an offence under this section if he obtains services for himself or another—
 (a) by a dishonest act, and
 (b) in breach of subsection (2).
(2) A person obtains services in breach of this subsection if—
 (a) they are made available on the basis that that payment has been, is being or will be made for or in respect of them,
 (b) he obtains them without any payment having been made for or in respect of them or without payment having been made in full, and
 (c) when he obtains them, he knows—
  (i) that they are being made available on the basis described in paragraph (a), or
  (ii) that they might be,
 but intends that payment will not be made, or will not be made in full.

When MAY sneaks into the haulage lorry he does not commit the offence under s. 11 because the haulage company does not provide transport for people—it is transport for goods. Therefore no 'service' has been obtained by obtaining the free ride to York. However, he does commit the offence when he obtains the 'service' of a prostitute intending and not paying for the service, making B the correct answer.

Investigators' Manual, para. 3.8.9

Answer 29.13

Answer **D** — Section 11 of the Fraud Act 2006 states:

(1) A person is guilty of an offence under this section if he obtains services for himself or another—

  (a) by a dishonest act, and

  (b) in breach of subsection (2).

(2) A person obtains services in breach of this subsection if—

  (a) they are made available on the basis that payment has been, is being or will be made for or in respect of them,

  (b) he obtains them without any payment having been made for or in respect of them or without payment having been made in full, and

  (c) when he obtains them, he knows—

    (i) that they are being made available on the basis described in paragraph (a), or

    (ii) that they might be,

  but intends that payment will not be made, or will not be made in full.

The offence is committed if a person dishonestly obtains a service for another (in this case COLLIER obtains the 'service' for KNOWLE), making answer C incorrect. The term 'service' is not defined by the Act. The fact that 'service' is not defined means that in the situation where a person obtains the 'services' of a prostitute without intending to pay him/her, that person can commit an offence under s. 11 of the Fraud Act 2006, making answer A incorrect. Unlike the other Fraud Act 2006 offences, the offence under s. 11 is not a conduct crime; it is a result crime and requires the actual obtaining of the service to be complete. The offence would not be complete at point B when COLLIER lies to ORCHARD about the payment having been made—no service had been provided at that stage.

Investigators' Manual, para. 3.8.9

30 Proceeds of Crime

QUESTIONS

Question 30.1

BARSTOW is a well-known handler of stolen goods. The police carry out a raid on his home address and find a large amount of property that they believe is associated with BARSTOW's criminal activity. Included in this property is a £30,000 sports car that BARSTOW bought with the proceeds of his handling enterprises, a painting by a local artist valued at £1,000 (BARSTOW actually bought the painting for cash, half of which was from a legitimate source, the other half from his handling offences) and a Rolex watch which BARSTOW had been given by a criminal associate. BARSTOW suspects that the watch is stolen but does not know for sure.

Which of these items, if any, would be covered by the term 'criminal property' under the Proceeds of Crime Act 2002?

A The £30,000 sports car only.

B The £30,000 sports car and the painting only.

C The £30,000 sports car, the painting and the Rolex watch.

D None of the items mentioned would be covered as the Proceeds of Crime Act relates to money only.

Question 30.2

MUTCH is a thief and steals several widescreen TV sets from a retail outlet. MUTCH alters the serial numbers and several other identification marks on the televisions to disguise them and make them look legitimate when he comes to sell them. Before he can actually sell them, MUTCH is arrested for the theft and the property is recovered from his home address.

Has MUTCH committed the offence of concealing criminal property (contrary to s. 327 of the Proceeds of Crime Act 2002)?

A No, because MUTCH is the original thief and cannot commit this offence as a consequence.

B Yes, as he has disguised criminal property.

C No, because he has not actually sold the property or exchanged it for other goods.

D Yes, as long as it can be shown that he intended to sell the goods outside the United Kingdom.

Question 30.3

ASTON is a career criminal involved in serious and high-value robbery offences. He carries out a robbery on a van carrying gold bullion and manages to get away with the contents of the van. To ship the gold abroad, he takes the gold to PULCHER and instructs PULCHER to melt the gold, turn it into Eiffel Tower-shaped paperweights and ship it abroad to France—PULCHER is well aware of where the gold has come from. ASTON promises to pay PULCHER a hefty fee from the sale of the gold as and when he finally disposes of it abroad. PULCHER does as ASTON asks and six months later he receives a bank transfer from ASTON for £50,000.

Considering only the offence of acquisition, use and possession of criminal property (contrary to s. 329 of the Proceeds of Crime Act 2002), when does PULCHER first commit the offence?

A When he takes possession of the gold bullion from ASTON.

B When he melts the gold bullion down.

C When he ships the gold abroad.

D When he receives the £50,000 from ASTON.

Question 30.4

KELLY works as an accountant and is struggling with significant debts. He tells his supervisor, BROWN, about his debt situation and BROWN tells KELLY that he can help him. KELLY handles accounts for THOMAS who BROWN knows is a drug dealer looking to launder money through his accounts. BROWN speaks to THOMAS who agrees to pay off KELLY's debts if KELLY helps him to launder some of his drug money. BROWN approaches KELLY and puts the deal to him. KELLY is not certain but suspects where the money originates from but is desperate and agrees to do as requested. Before any transfer of funds takes place, THOMAS is arrested in connection with supplying controlled drugs.

Considering only the offence of arrangements in relation to criminal property (contrary to s. 328 of the Proceeds of Crime Act 2002), which of the following comments is correct?

A The offence has not been committed by KELLY as no transfer of funds ever took place.

B The offence has been committed but only by KELLY.

C The offence has not been committed by KELLY as he only suspects that the money is drug-related funds.

D The offence has been committed by KELLY and by BROWN.

Question 30.5

DOBBS is a well-known drug dealer and also owns a night club. He is notorious in the area for his criminal behaviour, but all prosecutions have been unsuccessful. DOBBS asks READ, a local builder, to quote him for a new roof for his garage block. READ's quote is for £4,500—a realistic price for the work—and DOBBS tells READ that he will pay in cash. READ is aware of DOBBS's drug-dealing activities but accepts the job as his business is struggling. READ completes the work and is paid in cash and declares the full amount of this as income on his accounts. DOBBS is arrested 18 months later and a successful prosecution brought against him for drug dealing.

Does READ commit an offence contrary to s. 329 of the Proceeds of Crime Act 2002 (acquisition, use and possession of criminal property)?

A No, as DOBBS was arrested more than 12 months after the money was paid to READ.

B Yes, READ is guilty of the offence as he knows about DOBBS's drug-dealing activities.

C No, as READ received the money as adequate consideration for the work he completed.

D Yes, because he accepted cash being aware of DOBBS's criminal activities and this assisted in its disposal.

ANSWERS

Answer 30.1

Answer **C** — The term 'criminal property' relates to property that:

(a) constitutes a person's benefit from criminal conduct or represents such a benefit (in whole or in part and whether directly or indirectly); and
(b) the alleged offender knows or suspects that it constitutes or represents such a benefit.

It is not limited to money only, making answer D incorrect. The 'benefit' of BARSTOW's criminal activity is the sports car, the painting (even though half of the painting's purchase price came from a legitimate source) and the Rolex watch. In respect of the watch, the defendant need only suspect that the property constitutes or represents such a benefit.

Investigators' Manual, para. 3.9.3

Answer 30.2

Answer **B** — Answer A is incorrect as whereas handling only occurs 'otherwise than in the course of stealing' and 'by or for the benefit of another', the offence under s. 327 can potentially be committed *during the commission of an offence* and *for the benefit of the thief.* On a literal reading of s. 327, a thief who conceals, disguises or sells property that he has just stolen may thereby commit offences under that section because the definition of criminal property applies to the laundering of an offender's own proceeds of crime as well as those of someone else. The property need not be moved outside the United Kingdom, making answer D incorrect. The offence is committed if a person:

(a) conceals criminal property;
(b) disguises criminal property;
(c) converts criminal property;
(d) transfers criminal property;
(e) removes criminal property from England and Wales and Scotland or from Northern Ireland.

MUTCH therefore commits the offence when he disguises the TV sets.

Investigators' Manual, para. 3.9.4

Answer 30.3

Answer **A** — The offence under s. 329 is committed when a person acquires, uses or has possession of 'criminal property'. The gold bullion is most certainly criminal property so as soon as PULCHER takes possession of the gold bullion the offence is committed.

Investigators' Manual, paras 3.9.2, 3.9.3, 3.9.6

Answer 30.4

Answer **D** — A person commits an offence under s. 328 of the Proceeds of Crime Act 2002 if he/she enters into or becomes concerned in an arrangement which he/she knows or suspects facilitates (by whatever means) the acquisition, retention, use or control of criminal property by or on behalf of another person. The fact that no transfer of funds ever took place is immaterial, making answer A incorrect. Answer C is incorrect as *suspicion* as to the nature of the criminal property will be enough. Answer B is incorrect as KELLY has entered into an arrangement and BROWN is concerned in the arrangement.

Investigators' Manual, para. 3.9.5

Answer 30.5

Answer **C** — The Proceeds of Crime Act 2002, s. 329 states:

> A person commits an offence if he—
> (a) acquires criminal property;
> (b) uses criminal property;
> (c) has possession of criminal property.

An additional defence exists (as well as those that are mentioned in the offences under ss. 327 and 328 of the Act) under s. 329(2)(c), which states that a person will not commit the offence if he acquired or used or had possession of the property for adequate consideration. The effect of the defence is that persons, such as trades people, who are paid for ordinary consumable goods and services in money that comes from crime, are not under any obligation to question the source of the money, making C the correct answer.

Investigators' Manual, para. 3.9.6

31 Criminal Damage

QUESTIONS

Question 31.1

HARDCASTLE assists his wife in her job as a warden of a block of flats for pensioners. HARDCASTLE's wife constantly complains about the poor condition of the fire alarm and worries that if it is not changed the pensioners' lives will be in danger and there might be a large amount of damage caused to the flats if there is a fire. To demonstrate to the owner of the flats that the fire alarm is defective and needs changing, HARDCASTLE sets fire to some bedding in one of the flats. Eventually, the fire alarm activates and the fire is put out. HARDCASTLE is arrested for arson.

Would HARDCASTLE be able to claim that he had a lawful excuse to commit criminal damage?

A Yes, because the damage was caused in order to protect the property.

B No, because what has been done by HARDCASTLE is not done in order to protect property.

C Yes, because the damage was caused in order to protect the lives of the pensioners.

D No, because the element of 'lawful excuse' does not apply to offences of arson.

Question 31.2

WATE is a vicar who wishes to protest against British armed forces involvement in several recent military operations in the Middle East. He visits the Houses of Parliament and, as a sign of his disapproval of the military activities, he writes a quotation from the Bible in ink on a pillar outside the main door to the building. He honestly believes what he has done is morally right.

Considering the offence of criminal damage (contrary to s. 1(1) of the Criminal Damage Act 1971), which of the following statements is correct?

A WATE would have a defence if he claims he had damaged the property as a reasonable means of protecting other property located in the Middle East from being damaged by warfare.

B WATE would have a defence if he claimed that he was carrying out God's instructions and therefore had a lawful excuse based on his belief that God was entitled to consent to such damage.

C WATE has not committed criminal damage. It is immaterial whether his beliefs for causing criminal damage were justified; what matters is that the beliefs were honestly held.

D WATE is guilty of criminal damage because it has been held that a belief in The Almighty's consent is not a lawful excuse and that such conduct would be too remote from any need to protect property in the Middle East.

Question 31.3

DYKE has a long-standing disagreement with MONK over who owns a section of land that lies between their respective houses. One evening, after DYKE has been drinking at his local pub, he decides to get revenge on MONK and walks up the drive of MONK's house intent on damaging MONK's property.

At what point does DYKE first commit an offence of criminal damage?

A As DYKE enters the driveway he stamps on and destroys some flowers that are growing wild at the entrance to the drive.

B DYKE passes a garden shed owned by MONK and, although he knows it will easily be washed off, he smears the word 'Wanker' in mud across the shed.

C DYKE picks up a large container of black paint and pours this over MONK's front lawn.

D DYKE approaches a chicken coop and reaches inside. He picks up a chicken and breaks its legs.

Question 31.4

FALLON is homeless and searching for somewhere to sleep for the night. He breaks into an abandoned detached house and, using some old furniture for fuel, sets a fire that quickly burns out of control, destroying part of the house. FALLON only escapes with his life because of the rapid attendance of the fire brigade. Because of the gap between the neighbouring houses there is no likelihood that the fire will spread to any other buildings.

Would FALLON be liable for an offence under s. 1(2) of the Criminal Damage Act 1971?

A Yes, because of FALLON's actions he recklessly endangered his own life.

B No, because FALLON did not intend to endanger his own or any other person's life.

C Yes, what matters is the potential for damage and danger created by FALLON's conduct.

D No, because the fire brigade attended and because of the gap between the houses, there was no actual danger to life.

Question 31.5

MAYHEW breaks off his engagement to CUTHBERT, who takes the news badly. CUTHBERT is desperate to rekindle the relationship and phones MAYHEW telling him that unless the two of them get back together, she will steal his car, set it alight and burn herself alive in it. CUTHBERT does not intend to carry out her threat but does intend for MAYHEW to believe her. Unknown to CUTHBERT, MAYHEW has sold his car and so does not actually fear that the threat will be carried out.

Which of the following statements is correct with regard to a threat to destroy or damage property under s. 2 of the Criminal Damage Act 1971?

A CUTHBERT is not guilty of the offence because MAYHEW has sold his car and therefore knows that the threat is incapable of being carried out.

B The offence is not committed because CUTHBERT has not threatened to destroy or damage her own property.

C The offence is not committed because CUTHBERT never intended to carry out her threat.

D CUTHBERT has committed the offence because her intention was to make MAYHEW fear that the threat would be carried out.

Question 31.6

FISHER argues with NEGUS and decides that he will take revenge on him by pouring a container of paint stripper over NEGUS's car. FISHER does not have any paint stripper and so visits a garage owned by SMITH and asks if he will provide him with the paint stripper. When SMITH asks why FISHER wants it, FISHER tells him of his plan. SMITH tells FISHER that the paint stripper is at the back of his garage and advises FISHER to wait for a week before he actually commits the criminal damage so that NEGUS will not suspect that FISHER is responsible. FISHER collects the paint stripper and tells SMITH that he will take his advice.

Considering the offence of having articles with intent to destroy or damage property (s. 3 of the Criminal Damage Act 1971) only, which of the following statements is correct?

A In these circumstances, both SMITH and FISHER would commit the offence.

B Only SMITH commits this offence as FISHER is not the owner of the paint stripper and therefore cannot have custody or control over it.

C Only FISHER commits the offence as he is the only person who actually has physical possession of the paint stripper.

D Neither SMITH nor FISHER commits the offence as the criminal damage will take place at some time in the future.

Question 31.7

HATTON has been arrested for a motoring offence; his detention has been authorised and he has been placed in a cell while the officers make further enquiries. HATTON is disgusted by his arrest and therefore to cause trouble and reckless as to the consequences, he places the blanket provided in his cell down the toilet in the cell. HATTON then continually flushes the toilet. When the custody sergeant makes his first check on HATTON, the concrete floor of the cell is flooded and the blanket is soaking wet.

Considering the offence of criminal damage (contrary to s. 1(1) of the Criminal Damage Act 1971), does HATTON commit the offence?

A No, HATTON would not commit criminal damage in these circumstances as both the floor and the blanket could be dried out without any resulting damage to either.

B Yes, HATTON would commit criminal damage to the blanket, but not the floor as it could be dried out undamaged.

C No, HATTON would not commit criminal damage in these circumstances as there was no intention to damage property; it was just frustration at his circumstances.

D Yes, HATTON would be guilty of criminal damage to both the blanket and the floor.

ANSWERS

Answer 31.1

Answer **B** — Answer D is incorrect as the element of lawful excuse is contained within the s. 1(2) offence. Section 5(2) of the Criminal Damage Act 1971 gives the circumstances when a person may have a lawful excuse to damage or destroy property. This must involve an *immediate* need for the action taken in order to protect the property and also that the means adopted were reasonable having regard to the circumstances. In this question, HARDCASTLE's activities would not fall into either of the last two categories and the element of 'lawful excuse' would not be satisfied, making answers A and C incorrect (action taken in order to draw attention to a defective fire alarm and not done in order to protect property would not be a 'lawful excuse').

Investigators' Manual, para. 3.10.2.6

Answer 31.2

Answer **D** — This question is based on the case of *Blake* v *DPP* [1993] Crim LR 586. Although the two defences under s. 5(2)(a) and (b) both involve the honestly held belief of the defendant, it does not mean that *any* honestly held belief will suffice, making answer C incorrect. *Blake* protested against military activities relating to the Gulf War and damaged a pillar outside the Houses of Parliament. His defence was as per answers A and B and the Divisional Court's response was as per answer D.

Investigators' Manual, para. 3.10.2.6

Answer 31.3

Answer **B** — Under s. 10 of the Criminal Damage Act 1971, flowers growing wild on any land would not be classed as property making answer A incorrect. The items referred to in options B, C and D would all be classed as property; land can be subject to criminal damage along with wild creatures that are ordinarily kept in captivity or have been reduced into possession (the chickens). There is no requirement that criminal damage be associated with an economic loss. It has been held by the Divisional Court that graffiti smeared in mud, even though it is easily washed off, can amount to criminal damage (*Roe* v *Kingerlee* [1986] Crim LR 735). Therefore, the offence is first committed at point B.

Investigators' Manual, para. 3.10.2.2

Answer 31.4

Answer **C** — The aggravated form of criminal damage can only be committed if the life endangered is someone else's other than the defendant's, making answers A and B incorrect. Answer B is further incorrect as the offence can be committed recklessly. Answer D is incorrect, as it does not matter that there was no *actual* danger to life. What is relevant is the *potential danger* to life.

Investigators' Manual, para. 3.10.3

Answer 31.5

Answer **D** — The central element for the commission of this offence is that the defendant *intended* the complainant to fear that the threat would be carried out. That threat can be to destroy or damage property belonging to that or another person or to destroy or damage his/her own property in a way that will endanger the life of that other or a third person, making answer B incorrect. The fact that CUTHBERT never intended to carry out her threat or that the threat is incapable of being carried out makes no difference, making answers A and C incorrect.

Investigators' Manual, para. 3.10.5

Answer 31.6

Answer **A** — The offence under s. 3 of the Act is committed when an individual has anything in his *custody or control* intending without lawful excuse to *use it* or *cause or permit another to use it* to destroy or damage property belonging to another or to destroy or damage his own or another's property in such a way that he knows is likely to endanger the life of some other person. It is not necessary to be the owner of the item in order to commit this offence, making answer B incorrect. Neither is it necessary to actually have physical possession of the item, making answer C incorrect. The fact that the damage is planned for a week's time is immaterial as it is the intention of the parties that is relevant for this offence, making answer D incorrect.

Investigators' Manual, para. 3.10.6

Answer 31.7

Answer **D** — A person commits an offence if they, without lawful excuse, destroy or damage any property belonging to another intending to destroy or damage any such property or being reckless as to whether any such property will be destroyed or damaged. The case of *R* v *Fiak* [2005] EWCA Crim 2381 has the same circumstances as this question. The reality was that the blanket could not be used until it had been dried and the flooded cell was out of action until the water had been cleared. Therefore, both had sustained damage for the purposes of the Act. Making D the correct answer.

Investigators' Manual, para. 3.10.2.1

PART 4

Sexual Offences

32 Sexual Offences, Rape and Sexual Assault

QUESTIONS

Question 32.1

LAMBERT (aged 19 years) alleges that she is the victim of an offence of sexual assault by penetration (contrary to s. 2 of the Sexual Offences Act 2003). She speaks to DC SALK (the officer in the case), as she is concerned that her identity will be disclosed during the forthcoming investigation.

What advice should DC SALK offer?

A LAMBERT is entitled to anonymity throughout her lifetime.

B Only rape victims are entitled to anonymity.

C LAMBERT's identity will only be protected if a person is arrested and the case goes to trial—in that case, LAMBERT will be a 'complainant' and entitled to anonymity.

D Anonymity is only provided to a victim or complainant where violence has formed part of the offence.

Question 32.2

WRIGHT works with LAKER and during an office party he suggests to LAKER that they have sex together; LAKER refuses. This annoys WRIGHT and later on he follows LAKER into the female toilets. WRIGHT demands that LAKER talk with him in one of the toilet cubicles and, once inside, WRIGHT locks the door. WRIGHT demands to know why LAKER refused to have sex with him and when LAKER begins to cry, WRIGHT tells her he would be happy if she took part in oral sex with him. LAKER asks to be let out of the cubicle but WRIGHT refuses. LAKER realises that WRIGHT will not let her out, so agrees to have oral sex with him and allows WRIGHT to put his penis in her mouth.

Considering the offence of rape only (contrary to s. 1 of the Sexual Offences Act 2003), which of the following statements is correct?

A No offence of rape has been committed because LAKER consented to the act of oral sex.

B Rape can only be committed if WRIGHT penetrates the vagina or anus of LAKER.

C WRIGHT commits rape, as LAKER was unlawfully detained at the time of the relevant act.

D WRIGHT has not committed rape because he has not used violence or caused LAKER to believe immediate violence would be used against her.

Question 32.3

DUPONT approaches THOMPSON in the street. He shows her a photograph of her three-year-old son and says, *'Me and my mate have been watching you and your boy, my mate's watching him now. Unless you do as I say, my mate will hurt your kid.'* THOMPSON believes that her son is in immediate danger and that DUPONT's associate will harm him. DUPONT demands that THOMPSON follow him into a nearby alleyway where he puts his fingers into DUPONT's vagina. DUPONT does not have a friend watching THOMPSON's child, who is in no actual danger at the time of the act.

Has DUPONT committed an offence of rape?

A Yes, because at the time of the relevant act he has caused THOMPSON to believe that immediate violence would be used against another person.

B No, because he did not use violence against THOMPSON or cause her to believe that immediate violence would be used against her.

C Yes, because he has intentionally deceived THOMPSON into taking part in the relevant act.

D No, because intentionally penetrating THOMPSON's vagina with his fingers is not the *actus reus* of rape.

Question 32.4

SALHAN goes to a house party but because she is taking medication she only drinks orange juice. Her friend, CROSS, thinks it will be funny to spike SALHAN's drinks and without SALHAN's knowledge adds several vodkas to SALHAN's orange juice, causing SALHAN to become disorientated and drowsy. SALHAN goes to a bedroom in the house and lies down to get some rest. ALLEN walks into the room and seeing SALHAN on the bed he suggests that they have sexual intercourse. ALLEN has no idea that SALHAN is suffering from the combined effects of the medication and the vodka. SALHAN agrees and the two have sexual intercourse. The next day, SALHAN realises what has happened and accuses ALLEN of rape.

Which of the following statements is true?

A ALLEN is not guilty of rape, as he did not know that SALHAN had had her drinks spiked.

B The offence could only be committed if ALLEN was the person who had spiked SALHAN's drinks.

C ALLEN is guilty of rape, as at the time the sexual intercourse took place, a substance had been administered to SALHAN that was capable of causing her to be stupefied.

D Administering a substance capable of causing the complainant to be stupefied or overpowered would not constitute an offence of rape.

Question 32.5

ALLDAY and MASSEY (both males) have consensual anal intercourse. Immediately after the act, ALLDAY feels extremely guilty and begs MASSEY not to tell either of their wives what they have done. MASSEY punches ALLDAY in the face and tells him he will do what he likes. MASSEY then demands that ALLDAY place his penis in MASSEY's mouth or he will beat ALLDAY up. Compelled under the threat of violence, ALLDAY does so. Several minutes later, MASSEY demands anal intercourse. ALLDAY refuses but MASSEY tells him that he will tell their wives of their activities and as a result (in fear of MASSEY exposing what has taken place between the two men), ALLDAY allows MASSEY to have anal sexual intercourse with him.

At what stage, if at all, is the offence of rape committed?

A When MASSEY punches ALLDAY in the face immediately after the act of anal sexual intercourse.

B When ALLDAY is compelled to put his penis into MASSEY's mouth.

C When ALLDAY, out of fear, allows MASSEY to have anal sexual intercourse for a second time.

D The offence of rape is not committed.

Question 32.6

HARRISON has recently had gender reassignment surgery where the penis was removed and replaced with a surgically constructed vagina. HARRISON attends a party and flirts with DARVEL, suggesting that the two of them should have sexual intercourse, to which DARVEL agrees. The two go to a bedroom and begin to have sexual intercourse (penis to surgically constructed vagina). Several minutes into the act, HARRISON feels sick and asks DARVEL to stop. DARVEL takes no notice of HARRISON and continues to have sexual intercourse with HARRISON for several minutes despite HARRISON's protests. DARVEL then penetrates HARRISON's anus with his penis against HARRISON's wishes.

Which of the following statements is correct?

A A surgically constructed vagina would not be classed as part of the body for the purposes of rape.

B DARVEL commits rape when, after HARRISON asks him to stop, he continues to penetrate HARRISON's surgically constructed vagina.

C No offence of rape is committed because HARRISON initially consented to sexual intercourse with DARVEL.

D DARVEL only commits rape when he penetrates HARRISON's anus.

Question 32.7

ABLITT is in a nightclub where he begins talking to RICHARDS, who is an actress. ABLITT tells RICHARDS that he is only in the country for a week, after which he will fly out to America where he will be directing a film starring a major Hollywood actor; this is a lie as ABLITT is in fact a plumber. ABLITT tells RICHARDS that he can get her a part in the film but he will only do so if she has sexual intercourse with him. To further her acting career, RICHARDS goes to ABLITT's house, where she has sexual intercourse with him.

What effect will s. 76 of the Sexual Offences Act 2003 have on ABLITT's actions?

A As ABLITT has deceived RICHARDS regarding the nature of the act, RICHARDS will be presumed not to consent to it.

B RICHARDS will be presumed not to have consented to the act as ABLITT has intentionally deceived her by impersonating a film director.

C It will have no effect as ABLITT has not impersonated a person known personally to RICHARDS.

D It will have no effect as this section relates to the use of violence to obtain consent from the victim.

Question 32.8

CHANNON (aged 35 years) kidnaps ILIFF (aged 12 years) and forces ILIFF to have sexual intercourse with him (penis to vagina). CHANNON is later arrested for an offence of rape (s. 1 of the Sexual Offences Act 2003).

Which of the following statements is correct?

A The prosecution will have to prove intentional penetration alone.

B The prosecution will have to prove the child's age alone.

C The prosecution will have to prove intentional penetration and the child's age.

D The prosecution will have to prove intentional penetration, the child's age and the fact that ILIFF did not consent to the act.

Question 32.9

SHARPE kidnaps YOUNG and locks her in the basement of his house for several days. During this time SHARPE compels YOUNG to put a vibrator into her mouth. SHARPE tells his friend, HEMMING, about YOUNG and invites HEMMING to watch him abuse her. HEMMING enters the basement and watches YOUNG being abused. HEMMING asks YOUNG if she will have sexual intercourse with him. YOUNG does not reply so HEMMING has sexual intercourse with her (penis to vagina).

Which of the following statements is correct with regard to the Sexual Offences Act 2003?

A HEMMING commits the offence of rape (contrary to s. 1 of the Sexual Offences Act 2003).

B Both SHARPE and HEMMING commit the offence of rape (contrary to s. 1 of the Sexual Offences Act 2003).

C SHARPE commits the offence of assault by penetration (contrary to s. 2 of the Sexual Offences Act 2003).

D Both SHARPE and HEMMING commit the offence of assault by penetration (contrary to s. 2 of the Sexual Offences Act 2003).

Question 32.10

STARREN meets PORTER in a pub and the two get on very well with each other. STARREN invites PORTER back to her house for a drink. At STARREN's house the couple begin to kiss and touch each other and PORTER asks STARREN if she will have sexual intercourse with him. STARREN replies that she will but because this is a 'one-night-stand' she will only do so if PORTER wears a condom on his penis while they are having sexual intercourse; PORTER agrees to do so. While PORTER is trying to place the condom on his penis he accidentally rips it so that it is useless. He wants to have sexual intercourse with STARREN so he tells her that he has put a condom on and as a consequence she allows him to have sexual intercourse (penis to vagina) with her.

Considering the issues surrounding the offence of rape (contrary to s. 1 of the Sexual Offences Act 2003), which of the following statements is correct?

A This is not an offence of rape as STARREN has not been deceived as to the nature of the act.

B This is an offence of rape and the evidential presumptions in respect of consent under s. 75 of the Sexual Offences Act 2003 would be applicable in these circumstances.

C This is not an offence of rape as STARREN has consented to sexual intercourse with PORTER.

D This is an offence of rape as STARREN would only consent to sexual intercourse if PORTER was wearing a condom at the time and he was not.

Question 32.11

CLAY goes to a party held at PIKE's house. During the evening of the party he goes into the bathroom where he sees WEBSTER lying on the floor having passed out from drinking too much. CLAY locks the bathroom door and removes all of WEBSTER's clothes. CLAY lies next to WEBSTER and kisses her, putting his tongue into WEBSTER's mouth in the process. Several minutes later he places his tongue into WEBSTER's vagina. CLAY then puts his penis inside WEBSTER's mouth before he puts a finger into WEBSTER's vagina.

At what point does CLAY commit an offence of assault by penetration (contrary to s. 2 of the Sexual Offences Act 2003)?

A When he puts his tongue into WEBSTER's mouth.

B When he puts his tongue into WEBSTER's vagina.

C When he puts his penis into WEBSTER's mouth.

D When he puts his finger into WEBSTER's vagina.

Question 32.12

HUNN and her common-law husband, DARROW, kidnap POOLE in a bid to extort a cash ransom from POOLE's husband. The two blindfold and handcuff POOLE and keep her in a basement flat for several days before the ransom is paid. During this time POOLE is subject to abuse by HUNN and DARROW. HUNN forces a candle into POOLE's vagina and while HUNN carries out this act, DARROW pushes a candle into POOLE's anus.

Considering the offence of assault by penetration (s. 2 of the Sexual Offences Act 2003) only, which of the following statements is correct?

A Only DARROW is guilty of this offence as it can only be committed by a male.

B Only DARROW commits the offence as assault by penetration only relates to the penetration of the vagina.

C Both HUNN and DARROW commit the offence.

D Neither HUNN nor DARROW commit the offence because POOLE was not penetrated with a part of the body.

Question 32.13

BEDDOW is at a nightclub and approaches GRAINGER and tries to talk to her as he finds her sexually attractive. GRAINGER is not interested in BEDDOW and tells him to go away. Later in the evening, GRAINGER is standing at the bar waiting to be served when BEDDOW approaches her from behind. To obtain sexual gratification, he takes out his penis and lightly touches GRAINGER's buttocks (through her clothing) with the tip of his penis. BEDDOW is aroused by this contact and ejaculates onto GRAINGER's skirt while he is touching her. GRAINGER is completely unaware that BEDDOW has behaved in this way.

Considering the offence of sexual assault (contrary to s. 3 of the Sexual Offences Act 2003), which of the following comments is correct?

A The offence has not been committed as no violence was used by BEDDOW.

B The offence has not been committed as BEDDOW has not touched GRAINGER's sexual organs.

C The offence has not been committed as GRAINGER is unaware that she has been touched.

D BEDDOW commits the offence in these circumstances.

Question 32.14

LAND is arrested on suspicion of a triple murder. She tells DC MOULT, the female arresting officer, that she has hidden a knife inside her vagina and the police will never get hold of it. She tells DC MOULT that at the first opportunity she will use the knife to kill a police officer in the custody area. As a result, inspector FOWLER authorises an intimate search of LAND to recover the knife. Because of the urgency of the situation, the intimate search takes place at the police station. LAND does not consent to the search and, against LAND's wishes, DC MOULT inserts her finger into LAND's vagina and recovers the knife.

Which of the following statements is correct?

A DC MOULT commits an offence of rape (contrary to s. 1 of the Sexual Offences Act 2003).

B DC MOULT commits an offence of assault by penetration (contrary to s. 2 of the Sexual Offences Act 2003).

C DC MOULT commits an offence of sexual assault (contrary to s. 3 of the Sexual Offences Act 2003).

D DC MOULT commits no offence in these circumstances.

Question 32.15

SPENCER is standing at a bus stop directly behind TUCKETT, who is holding an umbrella in his hand. TUCKETT is aware that SPENCER is relatively close to him and deliberately moves his umbrella so that the tip moves between SPENCER's legs and touches her vagina through her trousers. TUCKETT obtains sexual gratification from the act.

Considering only s. 3 of the Sexual Offences Act 2003, which of the following statements is correct?

A TUCKETT commits the offence because 'touching' includes touching with anything, in this case the umbrella.

B The offence has not been committed because TUCKETT must touch SPENCER with a part of his body.

C For the offence to be committed, the touching must amount to penetration.

D As the touching was carried out through SPENCER's trousers, the offence is incomplete.

Question 32.16

YARDLEY, MAJOR and LOCKHART (all females) are drinking together at LOCKHART's house. YARDLEY and LOCKHART take off all their clothes and begin to kiss and touch each other while MAJOR watches. LOCKHART asks MAJOR to kiss YARDLEY's breasts, to which MAJOR refuses. LOCKHART tells MAJOR that unless she does as she demands she will be assaulted. Because of the threat and against her will, MAJOR does as LOCKHART demands. YARDLEY consents to the act.

What is LOCKHART's liability in relation to the offence of causing a person to engage in sexual activity without consent (s. 4 of the Sexual Offences Act 2003)?

A LOCKHART does not commit the offence, as it must involve penetration.

B Because YARDLEY consented to the act, LOCKHART does not commit the offence.

C LOCKHART has committed the offence in these circumstances.

D As LOCKHART is a female, she cannot commit this offence.

Question 32.17

DEAR breaks into a house owned by HESSION. DEAR enters HESSION's bedroom and wakes her up by placing his hand over her mouth. HESSION can see that DEAR is holding a gun to her head and is terrified. DEAR tells HESSION to be quiet and do what he tells her to do or he will kill her; he then removes his hand. He tells HESSION he wants her to '*talk dirty to him*' and tell him how she would have sexual intercourse with him. As HESSION is graphically describing what she would do, DEAR takes out his penis and begins to masturbate. DEAR then tells HESSION that if she masturbates herself he will go away. HESSION does as DEAR demands and shortly afterwards DEAR ejaculates and then leaves.

At what point, if at all, does DEAR first commit an offence contrary to s. 4 of the Sexual Offences Act 2003 (causing sexual activity without consent)?

A When he forces HESSION to engage in a conversation of a sexual nature.

B When he masturbates himself.

C When he forces HESSION to masturbate herself.

D DEAR does not commit the offence in this situation.

Question 32.18

BARCLAY, an adult male, meets FORD, an adult female, in a bar and after a couple of drinks they go back to his flat. After a drink and some kissing, BARCLAY becomes aggressive towards FORD and proceeds to commit sexual acts with FORD without her consent. He first forces her to the ground and inserts a rubber dildo into her mouth, then BARCLAY inserts his fingers into her anus followed by the rubber dildo into her vagina.

Considering the offences of assault by penetration (contrary to s. 2 of the Sexual Offences Act 2003) only, which of the following statements is correct as to BARCLAY'S liability?

A BARCLAY does not commit this particular sexual offence.

B BARCLAY commits this offence when he inserts the dildo into FORD's mouth.

C BARCLAY commits this offence but only when he inserts his fingers into FORD's anus.

D BARCLAY commits this offence when he inserts his fingers into FORD's anus and also when he inserts the dildo into her vagina.

Question 32.19

JAGGARD and BLOUNT have lived together for many years. JAGGARD is the dominant party in the relationship and has been aggressive and sexually abusive towards BLOUNT on several occasions, so much so that BLOUNT leaves JAGGARD. The two meet up at a restaurant to try and resolve their differences and are getting on very well. They go back to a hotel and become passionate with each other. JAGGARD asks BLOUNT to have sexual intercourse with him and BLOUNT agrees but on the strict understanding that JAGGARD will not ejaculate inside her. JAGGARD tells BLOUNT he will not and states he will withdraw his penis before ejaculation. As a result, the two have sexual intercourse. During intercourse, JAGGARD deliberately, against BLOUNT's wishes, ejaculates inside her.

Considering the law in relation to rape and consent under the Sexual Offences Act 2003 and the presumptions under ss. 75 and 76 of the Act, which of the following comments is correct?

A This is not an offence of rape as BLOUNT agreed to have sexual intercourse with JAGGARD.

B This is an offence of rape by JAGGARD as he has deprived BLOUNT of freedom of choice by ejaculating inside her (a crucial feature on which her original consent was based).

C This is an offence of rape; the presumption under s. 75 will apply.

D This is an offence of rape; the presumption under s. 76 will apply.

Question 32.20

FOSTER has just been out for her morning run. On her arrival home, her friend CLAY has come round to have a coffee with her. FOSTER complains of an aching back and legs from her run and asks CLAY to massage her. CLAY agrees and gets a small rolling pin from a kitchen drawer to massage FOSTER. FOSTER lies face down on a settee and

CLAY proceeds to roll the rolling pin up and down FOSTER's back. CLAY then uses the rolling pin to massage FOSTER's inner thigh and runs the rolling pin several times over FOSTER's buttocks. CLAY then asks FOSTER to remove her vest top and bra and massages her naked back with the rolling pin. CLAY requests FOSTER to turn over, which exposes her breasts and CLAY, using her hands, then fondles FOSTER's breasts.

At what point does 'touching' (under s. 79(8) of the Sexual Offences Act 2003) first take place?

A When CLAY first massages FOSTER's back with the rolling pin.
B When CLAY massages FOSTER by using the rolling pin on her inner thigh and buttocks.
C When CLAY massages FOSTER by using the rolling pin on her naked back.
D When CLAY fondles FOSTER's breasts.

Question 32.21

WEBSTER is obsessed with SMALL and thinks that she is the most beautiful woman he has ever seen. He has made sexual advances to her on numerous occasions but she has rejected him, telling him in no uncertain terms that she would never want to have anything to do with him. This has made WEBSTER extremely angry and he decides that he will kidnap SMALL and humiliate her. He waits outside her house one evening and as she arrives home from work WEBSTER grabs her and bundles her into a van. In the van, he ties SMALL up, rips off her clothing and subjects her to a sexual attack. He forces a dildo into SMALL's mouth causing her to violently gag on it. He then pushes the dildo into her anus causing her to scream in pain. Finally, he pushes open her legs and forces the dildo into her vagina.

At what stage, if at all, is the offence of assault by penetration (contrary to s. 2 of the Sexual Offences Act 2003) first committed?

A When WEBSTER forces the dildo into SMALL's mouth.
B When WEBSTER forces the dildo into SMALL's anus.
C When WEBSTER forces the dildo into SMALL's vagina.
D The offence has not been committed as WEBSTER did not use a part of his body to carry out any of the penetrative acts.

Question 32.22

PARSON (aged 19 years) shares a two-bedroom flat with CLARK (aged 17 years). PARSON pays 70 per cent of the rent and other expenses because he earns more than CLARK (they are just flatmates). PARSON, however, believes this to be unjust and persuades CLARK that he needs some form of reward for paying the majority of the bills. PARSON persuades CLARK to masturbate him once a week as compensation; CLARK does not want to do this but complies. The owner of the flat puts up the rent and PARSON now decides that CLARK need not masturbate him anymore but will have to prostitute herself as she cannot pay any more towards the bills; she has no option but to agree to PARSON's requests. A couple of times a week, CLARK performs sexual acts with other men for money.

Considering s. 4 of the Sexual Offences Act 2003 (causing a person to engage in sexual activity without consent), which of the statements below is correct?

A PARSON only commits this offence when he forces CLARK to masturbate him.

B PARSON does not commit any offences under s. 4 because CLARK is over the age of 16.

C PARSON commits this offence when he forces her to masturbate him and when he forces her to prostitute herself.

D PARSON only commits this offence when he forces her to prostitute herself.

Question 32.23

BANKS is an adult male and he falsely imprisons both WEST, an adult male, and CARTER, an adult female. BANKS has lured them to his house on the pretext that he is thinking of selling the property knowing that they are both interested in buying his house with their respective partners. BANKS locks all the doors to the property and produces a large sword. Both WEST and CARTER are very scared and, when he demands that they both remove their clothes, they do so. BANKS then tells WEST to put his penis into CARTER's mouth and insert his fingers in her vagina. Initially, WEST refuses but after threats with the sword both WEST and CARTER submit to BANKS's requests.

Considering only offences contrary to the Sexual Offences Act 2003, which of the statements below is correct with regards to the criminal responsibility of BANKS and WEST?

A BANKS commits an offence of causing sexual activity without consent and WEST commits two offences of rape.

B BANKS would be guilty of causing sexual activity without consent if it could be shown that it was for sexual gratification.

C BANKS commits the offence of causing sexual activity without consent.

D BANKS commits causing sexual activity without consent and WEST commits rape and assault by penetration.

ANSWERS

Answer 32.1

Answer **A** — The Sexual Offences (Amendment) Act 1992, s. 1 states:

(1) Where an allegation has been made that an offence to which this Act applies has been committed against a person, no matter relating to that person shall during that person's lifetime be included in any publication, if it is likely to lead members of the public to identify that person as the person against whom the offence is alleged to have been committed.

(2) Where a person is accused of an offence to which this Act applies, no matter likely to lead members of the public to identify a person as the person against whom the offence is alleged to have been committed ('the complainant') shall, during the complainant's lifetime, be included in any publication.

(3) . . .

(3A) The matters relating to a person in relation to which the restrictions imposed by subsection (1) or (2) apply (if their inclusion in any publication is likely to have the result mentioned in that subsection) include in particular—

- (a) the person's name,
- (b) the person's address,
- (c) the identity of any school or other educational establishment attended by the person,
- (d) the identity of any place of work, and
- (e) any still or moving picture of the person.

Whether the person is a 'victim' or a 'complainant' does not change the entitlement to anonymity (making answer C incorrect). Under the Sexual Offences (Amendment) Acts 1976 and 1992, victims/complainants of most sexual offences, including rape, assault by penetration and sexual assault by touching are entitled to anonymity throughout their lifetime, making answer B incorrect. It is immaterial to anonymity whether or not violence forms part of the circumstances of the offence (making answer D incorrect).

Investigators' Manual, para. 4.1.2

Answer 32.2

Answer **C** — Rape can be committed if a male penetrates the vagina, anus or mouth of his victim, making answer B incorrect. Although the use of or threat to use violence would negate consent (s. 72(2)(a) and (b)), this is not the only way that a complainant can be deemed to have refused consent to the relevant act, making answer D incorrect. Consent will only be true consent if the person agrees by choice and has the freedom and capacity to make that choice. Under s. 75(2)(c) of the Act, the complainant is taken not to have consented to the relevant act if the complainant was, and the defendant was not, unlawfully detained at the time of the relevant act, making answer A incorrect.

Investigators' Manual, paras 4.2.1 to 4.2.7

Answer 32.3

Answer **D** — Although answer A is correct insofar as the consent obtained from THOMPSON is not true consent as it is obtained by threatening immediate violence against another person, the *actus reus* of rape is the penetration of the vagina, anus or mouth of another person with the penis, making this answer incorrect. Answer B is incorrect as had DUPONT used violence, this would still not be rape. The deception in rape must be as to the nature or purpose of the relevant act, not the circumstances leading up to the act, making answer C incorrect.

Investigators' Manual, paras 4.2.1 to 4.2.7

Answer 32.4

Answer **A** — Answer D is incorrect as these circumstances are catered for in s. 75(2)(f) of the Act. *Any person* can administer or cause the substance to be taken, making answer B incorrect. Under s. 75 (evidential presumptions about consent), it must be proved that the defendant (i) did the relevant act, (ii) that any of the circumstances specified in subsection (2) existed and (iii) that the defendant *knew* that those circumstances existed. In these circumstances, ALLEN does not know that SALHAN has had her drinks spiked and therefore is not guilty of the offence of rape, making answer C incorrect.

Investigators' Manual, paras 4.2.1 to 4.2.7

Answer 32.5

Answer **C** — Rape is committed when a person (A) intentionally penetrates the vagina, anus or mouth of another person (B) with his penis and that other person (B) does not consent to the penetration and A does not reasonably believe that B consents. The first act of anal sexual intercourse was consensual and although violence was used by MASSEY after this act, that will not alter the true consent given to anal intercourse on the first occasion, making answer A incorrect. Answer B is incorrect as rape is committed when the defendant intentionally penetrates the vagina, anus or mouth of the complainant with his penis—it is not committed when the defendant (A) forces the complainant (B) to penetrate A's mouth with B's penis. The offence is committed at point C as at this point although ALLDAY allows the penetration to take place, it is only allowed because of ALLDAY's fear that his activities will be exposed to his wife. As a result, this is not 'true' consent. 'True' consent is given by a person who agrees by choice and has the freedom and capacity to make that choice. Therefore, if a person does not have any choice in the matter, or their choice is not a genuine exercise of their free will (and ALLDAY's choice is not), they will not have consented, making answer D incorrect in the process.

Investigators' Manual, paras 4.2.1 to 4.2.7

Answer 32.6

Answer **B** — Answer A is incorrect as s. 79(3) of the Act states that references to the body include references to a part surgically constructed (in particular, through gender reassignment surgery). Answer C is incorrect because although HARRISON initially agreed to sexual intercourse with DARVEL, s. 79(2) of the Act states that penetration is a continuing act from entry to withdrawal so that where a person consents at the time of entry to penetration, but then withdraws consent and the penetration continues, the person penetrating is guilty of rape. This section makes answer D incorrect, as the offence of rape is complete when HARRISON continues penetration of DARVEL's vagina.

Investigators' Manual, paras 4.2.1 to 4.2.7

Answer 32.7

Answer **C** — This section of the Act relates to the use of some form of deception in order to obtain consent from the victim and not the use of violence to obtain consent (covered by s. 75 of the Act), making answer D incorrect. Answer A is incorrect as RICHARDS has not been deceived into the act by a misrepresentation as to the nature of the act; RICHARDS knew that what she was doing was sexual intercourse. Answer B is incorrect as the person impersonated must be known *personally* to the victim.

Investigators' Manual, paras 4.2.5, 4.2.7

Answer 32.8

Answer **C** — If the victim of the offence is under the age of 13, the prosecution simply have to prove intentional penetration and the child's age. No issue of 'consent' arises.

Investigators' Manual, para. 4.2.1

Answer 32.9

Answer **A** — Rape can only be committed by a male intentionally penetrating the vagina, anus or mouth of the victim with his penis. This makes answer B incorrect. Assault by penetration does not include penetration of the victim's mouth, making answers C and D incorrect. Where the complainant was, and the defendant was not, unlawfully detained at the time of the relevant act and the defendant knew that fact existed, it will be presumed that the victim did not consent.

Investigators' Manual, paras 4.2.1 to 4.2.6

Answer 32.10

Answer **D** — Answer B is incorrect as the presumptions under s. 75 would not be applicable to a case of this nature. Answer A is incorrect as although STARREN knows that she is having sexual intercourse, misrepresentation in relation to the nature of the act is not the only way that rape can be committed (deception in relation to the nature of the act is important when considering the presumptions under s. 76 of the Act). Answer C is incorrect as although STARREN has consented to sexual intercourse with PORTER this is conditional on the fact that he wears a condom; he is not doing so. In *Assange* v *Swedish Prosecution Authority* [2011] EWHC 2489 (Admin), the Divisional Court held that it would be open to a jury to hold that, if a complainant had made it clear that she would consent to sexual intercourse only if the appellant used a condom, then there would be no consent if, without her consent, he did not use a condom, or removed or tore the condom without her consent.

Investigators' Manual, paras 4.2.1 to 4.2.4

Answer 32.11

Answer **B** — The offence under s. 2 of the Act is committed when a person intentionally penetrates the vagina or anus of another person with a part of his body or anything else. The offence is not committed by penetration of the mouth of the victim, making answers A and C incorrect. The offence is committed at point B as at this point, CLAY penetrates WEBSTER's vagina with his tongue (a part of his body), making answer D incorrect.

Investigators' Manual, para. 4.3.1

Answer 32.12

Answer **C** — This offence can be committed by a male or female against a male or female, making answer A incorrect. The offence is committed when the vagina or anus of the victim is penetrated by the offender, making answer B incorrect. The penetration can be with a part of his/her body or anything else, making answer D incorrect.

Investigators' Manual, para. 4.3.1

Answer 32.13

Answer **D** — There is no requirement for force or violence for the offence to be committed, making answer A incorrect. Answer B is incorrect as the part of the body touched does not have to be a sexual organ. Answer C is incorrect as the victim need not be aware of being touched, so the offence was committed when the accused secretly took his penis out of his trousers and ejaculated onto a woman's clothing when pressed up against her dancing at a nightclub (*R* v *Bounekhla* [2006] EWCA Crim 1217).

Investigators' Manual, paras 4.3.3, 4.3.4

Answer 32.14

Answer **D** — Rape can only be committed by a male, making answer A incorrect. An intimate search carried out in these circumstances is legal and so the central issue in relation to these circumstances is whether the activity is 'sexual'. Section 78 of the Act defines the word 'sexual' so that it excludes medical procedures and intimate searches where (in this case) LAND does not consent to the penetration and DC MOULT does not reasonably believe that LAND consents. As the activity would not be considered 'sexual', answers B and C are incorrect.

Investigators' Manual, paras 4.3.1, 4.3.4

Answer 32.15

Answer **A** — A sexual assault under s. 3 of the Act is committed when a person intentionally touches another person, the touching is sexual and the victim does not consent to the touching and the offender does not reasonably believe that the victim consents. Section 79(8) defines 'touching' for the purposes of the Act as including touching with (a) any part of the body, (b) with anything else or (c) through anything and in particular includes touching amounting to penetration. The definition of 'touching' therefore includes the use of the umbrella to commit the offence as it falls under s. 79(8)(b) of the Act, making answers B, C and D incorrect.

Investigators' Manual, paras 4.3.3, 4.3.4

Answer 32.16

Answer **C** — Answer A is incorrect as the offence involves any activity that is 'sexual' as opposed to acts involving penetration only. The fact that YARDLEY consented to the act is immaterial as MAJOR (the victim) did not consent, making answer B incorrect. Answer D is incorrect as this offence can be committed by a male or female.

Investigators' Manual, para. 4.3.5

Answer 32.17

Answer **A** — This offence can involve a number of permutations, for example a woman making a man penetrate her, a man forcing someone else to masturbate him, or a woman making another woman masturbate a third person or even an animal. The term 'activity' is not defined and can include engaging someone in a conversation of a sexual nature (*R* v *Grout* [2011] EWCA Crim 299), meaning that the offence is committed at point A.

Investigators' Manual, para. 4.3.5

Answer 32.18

Answer **D** — For the offence of assault by penetration, s. 2 of the Sexual Offences Act 2003 states:

(1) A person (A) commits an offence if—
  (a) he intentionally penetrates the vagina or anus of another person (B) with a part of his body or anything else,

(b) the penetration is sexual,
(c) B does not consent to the penetration, and
(d) A does not reasonably believe that B consents.

The definition does not include mouth, making answer B incorrect. The offence is committed when he inserts his fingers into FORD's anus and the dildo into her vagina, making answers A and C incorrect.

Investigators' Manual, para. 4.3.1

Answer 32.19

Answer **B** — In *R (F)* v *DPP* [2013] EWHC 945 (Admin), the High Court examined an application for judicial review of the refusal of the DPP to initiate a prosecution for rape and/or sexual assault on B by A (her former partner). 'Choice' and the 'freedom' to make any particular choice must, the court said, be approached in 'a broad commonsense way'. Against what the court described as the 'essential background' of A's 'sexual dominance' of B and B's 'unenthusiastic acquiescence to his demands', the court considered a specific incident when B consented to sexual intercourse only on the clear understanding that A *would not* ejaculate inside her vagina. B believed that A intended and agreed to withdraw before ejaculation, and A knew and understood that this was the *only basis* on which B was prepared to have sexual intercourse with him. When he deliberately ejaculated inside B, the result, the court said, was B being deprived of choice relating to the crucial feature on which her original consent to sexual intercourse was based and accordingly her consent was negated. Contrary to B's wishes, and knowing that she would not have consented, and did not consent to penetration or the continuation of penetration, if B had had an inkling of A's intention, A deliberately ejaculated within her vagina. This combination of circumstances falls within the statutory definition of rape, making answer A incorrect. There would be no need to consider the presumptions under s. 75 or 76 of the Sexual Offences Act 2003—the specific situations these sections envisage are not represented in this scenario—the only issue of consent to consider is that under s. 74 and it is not present in this situation, making answers C and D incorrect.

Investigators' Manual, paras 4.2.1 to 4.2.4

Answer 32.20

Answer **A** — Section 79(8) of the Sexual Offences Act 2003 states that touching includes touching:

- with any part of the body,
- with anything else,
- through anything,

and in particular, touching amounting to penetration (this could include kissing).

The rolling pin constitutes anything and through anything includes massaging FOSTER's back in the first instance. This is not a question about committing an offence—this is just asking about the activity of 'touching'.

Investigators' Manual, para. 4.3.4

Answer 32.21

Answer **B** — An offence under s. 2 of the Sexual Offences Act 2003 is committed when a person (A)—

(a) intentionally penetrates the vagina or anus of another person (B) with a part of his body or anything else,
(b) the penetration is sexual,
(c) B does not consent to the penetration, and
(d) A does not reasonably believe that B consents.

It does not matter that the penetration in this case was using a dildo—the penetration can be with a part of the body or anything else. However, the penetration must be of the vagina or anus, not the mouth, so answer A is incorrect. The offence is first committed when WEBSTER forces the dildo into SMALL's anus (correct answer B), meaning that answers C and D are incorrect.

Investigators' Manual, para. 4.3.1

Answer 32.22

Answer **C** — The Sexual Offences Act 2003, s. 4 states:

(1) A person (A) commits an offence if—
 (a) he intentionally causes another person (B) to engage in an activity;
 (b) the activity is sexual;
 (c) B does not consent to the activity; and
 (d) A does not reasonably believe B consents.

A s. 4 offence is committed when PARSON forces CLARK to masturbate him and forces her to prostitute herself. These are examples from the Keynote area of the Manual and show how important it is to familiarise yourself with the Keynote areas in your preparation for the exam.

Investigators' Manual, para. 4.3.5

Answer 32.23

Answer **C** — Section 4 of the Sexual Offences Act 2003 (causing sexual activity without consent) states:

(1) A person (A) commits an offence if—
  (a) he intentionally causes another (B) to engage in an activity,
  (b) the activity is sexual,
  (c) B does not consent to engaging in the activity, and
  (d) A does not reasonably believe that B consents.

There is no need to prove sexual gratification so answer B is incorrect. Answers A and D are incorrect because WEST did not carry out the activities voluntarily (an essential element of attributing responsibility for criminal activity is that the *actus reus* of an offence was carried out voluntarily—it was not in these circumstances). Therefore C is the correct answer.

Investigators' Manual, para. 4.3.5

33 Sexual Offences Against Children

QUESTIONS

Question 33.1

STEADMAN (aged 17 years) is approached by KEANE (aged 14 years). KEANE has a 'crush' on STEADMAN and she asks STEADMAN if he will have sexual intercourse with her. STEADMAN refuses but states that he will take part in oral sex with KEANE. The two meet a few hours later, when STEADMAN places his penis into KEANE's mouth.

In relation to s. 9 of the Sexual Offences Act 2003 (sexual activity with a child), which of the following statements is correct?

A No offence under s. 9 is committed by STEADMAN as he is under 18 years of age.

B No offence under s. 9 is committed by STEADMAN as KEANE has consented to the act.

C No offence under s. 9 is committed by STEADMAN as KEANE is over 13 years of age.

D No offence under s. 9 is committed by STEADMAN as the sexual activity does not involve penetration of the vagina or the anus.

Question 33.2

CASE and her boyfriend PRIZEMAN (both aged 25 years) are babysitting SHIPMAN (aged 12 years). CASE and PRIZEMAN are watching television in the downstairs lounge when PRIZEMAN sees SHIPMAN looking through an open doorway into the lounge and watching the television. CASE is unaware of the presence of SHIPMAN. PRIZEMAN undresses CASE and begins to have sexual intercourse with her. He intends that SHIPMAN should see the act and wishes to obtain sexual gratification from that fact. Unknown to PRIZEMAN, who believes SHIPMAN is watching, SHIPMAN has in fact returned to her bedroom on the first floor and does not see PRIZEMAN undress CASE and have sexual intercourse with her.

Is PRIZEMAN guilty of an offence of engaging in sexual activity in the presence of a child (contrary to s. 11 of the Sexual Offences Act 2003)?

A Yes, even though SHIPMAN is not present PRIZEMAN intended the act to be viewed by her.

B No, because SHIPMAN is not present or in a place where she can observe the act.

C Yes, because PRIZEMAN believes that SHIPMAN is watching the sexual activity.

D No, because CASE was never aware of SHIPMAN's presence.

Question 33.3

An offence under s. 11 of the Sexual Offences Act 2003 is committed when a person engages in sexual activity in the presence of a child.

Which of the following statements is correct with regard to this offence?

A The person committing this offence must be at least 16 years old.

B The activity need not be carried out in order to obtain sexual gratification.

C There must be a person under 16 years old present or in a place from which the defendant can be observed.

D It is necessary to show that the child was aware of the activity.

Question 33.4

LANDEN (aged 20 years) approaches EIFION (aged 12 years) in a park. LANDEN persuades EIFION to accompany him back to his house, where LANDEN plays a DVD to EIFION that contains animated cartoon images of sexual activity. LANDEN obtains sexual gratification from this activity.

Has LANDEN committed an offence under s. 12 of the Sexual Offences Act 2003 (causing a child to watch a sexual act)?

A Yes, the images that EIFION sees can be images of imaginary persons so an animated cartoon image would be covered by the offence.

B No, the sexual act must be performed by LANDEN.

C Yes, but only because EIFION is under 13 years of age; if he were over 13, then the offence would not be committed.

D No, the image must be that of a 'person' engaged in sexual activity and not of a cartoon.

Question 33.5

HUGHES (aged 45 years) holds a barbeque at his house and invites a large number of guests and their children. Several hours after the barbeque has started, HUGHES goes into his house and into his study where he turns on his computer and goes on to the internet. While he is on the internet he visits several pornographic sites that show pictures of adults taking part in explicit sexual activity. HUGHES has left the door to his study open because he believes all of his guests are outside and nobody will see what he is doing. HUGHES's purpose when he is looking at the pictures is to obtain sexual gratification. Unknown to HUGHES, FORREST (aged 15 years) is looking at the same pictures because HUGHES has left the door to his study open.

Considering the offence of causing a child to watch a sexual act (contrary to s. 12 of the Sexual Offences Act 2003), which of the following statements is correct?

A As there are children at the party HUGHES would know of the likelihood of a child seeing the images and therefore commits an offence.

B As HUGHES has acted for the purposes of sexual gratification, the offence is complete.

C HUGHES does not commit the offence as still images are not included in this section of the legislation.

D HUGHES does not commit an offence under this section as he must intentionally cause another person to watch the activity.

Question 33.6

DEVILLE has been on holiday to Thailand on several occasions. During his holidays he took part in sexual activity with girls under 15 years old. He tells his friend, HALLBROOK, about his holiday experiences. HALLBROOK asks DEVILLE if he will arrange flights, hotel accommodation and personal contacts for him so that he can visit Thailand for the same reason. HALLBROOK tells DEVILLE that he has never done anything like this before and so when he goes to Thailand he may or may not actually have sexual contact with girls under the age of 15. DEVILLE makes the necessary arrangements for HALLBROOK in the belief that HALLBROOK will take part in sexual activity with girls under the age of 15 once he arrives in Thailand.

With regard to s. 14 of the Sexual Offences Act 2003 (arranging or facilitating the commission of a child sex offence), which of the following statements is true?

A DEVILLE does not commit the offence as he has arranged for the activities to take place outside the United Kingdom.

B DEVILLE commits the offence as he believes that HALLBROOK will carry out sexual activity with girls under 15 years of age.

C DEVILLE will commit the offence if HALLBROOK actually carries out sexual activity with girls under the age of 15; if he does not then DEVILLE does not commit the offence.

D DEVILLE does not commit the offence as he only believes rather than intends that HALLBROOK will carry out sexual activity with girls under the age of 15.

Question 33.7

EVERLY is a predatory paedophile and wishes to rape a girl under the age of 13 (contrary to s. 5 of the Sexual Offences Act 2003). He befriends CLAMP (a girl aged nine years) using an internet 'chat room' and arranges to meet her outside her school the next day in order to commit the offence. Unknown to EVERLY, CLAMP is not a nine-year-old child but is in fact a police officer using the internet to track and arrest paedophiles.

Why is no offence of arranging or facilitating the commission of a child sex offence (contrary to s. 14 of the Sexual Offences Act 2003) committed by EVERLY?

A Because this offence is only committed when a person arranges or facilitates something that he intends another person to do or believes that another person will do.

B Because rape of a child under 13 (contrary to s. 5 of the Sexual Offences Act 2003) is not an offence that is covered by this section.

C Because the offence could never be committed. The person that EVERLY had arranged to meet is a police officer and not a nine-year-old child.

D Because the arrangements were made using the internet and not face to face.

Question 33.8

BALLARD (aged 20 years) attends his cousin's 18th birthday party. During the evening of the party he speaks to GALBRAITH, who tells BALLARD that she is only 14 years old. GALBRAITH tells BALLARD that she would like to see a tennis match at Wimbledon but cannot afford a ticket. BALLARD asks GALBRAITH to meet him in a week's time as he has a contact at Wimbledon and can obtain free tickets; GALBRAITH agrees. One week later, BALLARD travels to meet GALBRAITH as he has obtained a ticket for Wimbledon for her. However, on the journey to meet her, BALLARD decides to sexually assault GALBRAITH after their meeting and travels to meet her with that intent.

With regard to the offence of meeting a child following sexual grooming (s. 15 of the Sexual Offences Act 2003), which of the following statements is correct?

A The offence is not committed as BALLARD did not intend to sexually assault GALBRAITH when they first met.

B BALLARD commits the offence as he is travelling to meet GALBRAITH with the intention to commit a relevant offence.

C BALLARD will only commit the offence when he actually meets with GALBRAITH.

D BALLARD does not commit the offence as he has not met or communicated with GALBRAITH on at least two earlier occasions.

Question 33.9

HARVEY (aged 45 years) is on holiday in Cyprus. He goes to an internet cafe where he communicates with PREECE in an internet 'chat room'. PREECE tells HARVEY that she is 15 years old and lives in the United States. During the course of his holiday, HARVEY communicates with PREECE on another five occasions, during which the two exchange home addresses. In their last communication, PREECE tells HARVEY that she would like to have sexual intercourse when she visits the United Kingdom in a week's time, an offer that HARVEY accepts (intending to have sexual intercourse with PREECE). HARVEY returns home to the United Kingdom and, one week after his return, PREECE visits HARVEY's home address. PREECE tells HARVEY that she would like to make good on her promise and have sexual intercourse with him.

Has HARVEY committed an offence contrary to s. 15 of the Sexual Offences Act 2003 (meeting a child following sexual grooming)?

A No, because the original communications took place in Cyprus and not in the United Kingdom.

B Yes, the offence is complete when PREECE travels to meet HARVEY.

C No, because the previous meeting between the two was via an internet 'chat room' rather than a face-to-face meeting.

D Yes, the offence is complete but only when PREECE arrives at HARVEY's home address.

Question 33.10

POWELL (aged 26 years) drives to a family wedding reception where he speaks to his first cousin, IMBER (aged 17 years). IMBER has lived in Australia all her life and this is the first time the two have ever met so they are totally unaware that they are cousins. The two talk to each other all night and as the evening draws to a close, IMBER tells POWELL that she wants to have sexual intercourse with him. They go outside the wedding venue, get into POWELL's car and have sexual intercourse (penis to vagina).

Considering ss. 25 and 27 of the Sexual Offences Act 2003, has POWELL committed an offence?

A No, he has never lived in the same household as IMBER or been regularly involved in caring for, training or supervising or been in sole charge of IMBER.

B Yes, because IMBER is under 18 years of age.

C No, because IMBER is over 16 years of age.

D Yes, sexual intercourse with a first cousin would constitute an offence in these circumstances.

Question 33.11

Under s. 25 of the Sexual Offences Act 2003 (sexual activity with a child family member), the prosecution will have to prove that the defendant 'touched' the victim and that the touching was 'sexual'. However, other evidence must be proved in order for a defendant to be found guilty of such an offence.

Which of the following is correct with regard to the other evidence?

A The age of the victim must be proved and the defendant will have an evidential burden to discharge in that regard.

B The existence of the relevant family relationship between the defendant and the victim and the age of the victim must be proved and the defendant will have an evidential burden to discharge in that regard.

C The existence of the relevant family relationship between the defendant and the victim must be proved and the prosecution will have an evidential burden to discharge in that regard.

D The age of the victim must be proved and the prosecution will have an evidential burden to discharge in that regard.

Question 33.12

JARVIS (aged 15 years) is the half-brother of LYONS (aged 15 years). The two attend the same school and go on a school trip to Wales, where they share a tent. One evening, LYONS takes off all of his clothes and approaches JARVIS, suggesting that they should have anal sexual intercourse together. JARVIS is offended and flatly refuses.

With regard to ss. 25, 26 and 27 of the Sexual Offences Act 2003, which of the following statements is correct?

A LYONS does not commit an offence under either section as a half-brother is not a relevant family relationship (s. 27 of the Act).

B LYONS is guilty of an offence of sexual activity with a child member (s. 25 of the Act).

C LYONS does not commit an offence under either section as he is under 18 years of age.

D LYONS is guilty of an offence of inciting sexual activity with a child member (s. 26 of the Act).

Question 33.13

RENTON (aged 25 years) visits his old foster parent, STRAKER. While visiting STRAKER, RENTON is introduced to THAWLEY (aged 16 years), who has been living with STRAKER for the past two years. Prior to this meeting, RENTON and THAWLEY have never met each other. RENTON and THAWLEY get on extremely well and begin to see each other on a regular basis as boyfriend and girlfriend. One month after their initial meeting, RENTON and THAWLEY have consensual sexual intercourse.

Has RENTON committed an offence contrary to s. 25 of the Sexual Offences Act 2003?

A Yes, as RENTON and THAWLEY have the same foster parent.

B No, because sexual intercourse between the two is consensual.

C Yes, because THAWLEY is under 18 years of age.

D No, because RENTON and THAWLEY have never lived in the same household.

Question 33.14

WOOD (aged 17 years) and PERCIVAL (aged 17 years) have been going out together for six months and have had sexual intercourse on a number of occasions. Their respective parents have met each other several times and they begin a relationship together that leads to their marriage. This results in both parents, WOOD and PERCIVAL moving into the same house.

If WOOD and PERCIVAL now have sexual intercourse, which of the following will be true with regard to s. 25 of the Sexual Offences Act 2003 (sexual activity with a child family member)?

A WOOD and PERCIVAL are now stepsister and stepbrother and they cannot have sexual intercourse without committing an offence.

B The only way that WOOD and PERCIVAL would not commit an offence would be if they were lawfully married at the time.

C WOOD and PERCIVAL will not commit an offence as their sexual relationship pre-dates the newly created family relationship.

D WOOD and PERCIVAL are both under the age of 18 and cannot commit the offence.

Question 33.15

GATRELL (aged 21 years) is living with his partner HADLOW (aged 17 years) in an enduring family relationship. GATRELL takes a dozen photographs of HADLOW taking part in simulated sex acts with INGLEY (aged 25 years). HADLOW and INGLEY are both naked in the photographs and both consent to the photographs being taken by GATRELL. GATRELL wishes to keep the photographs for his own pleasure and does not intend to distribute them in any way.

With regard to the taking of indecent photographs (contrary to s. 1 of the Protection of Children Act 1978 (as amended by s. 45 of the Sexual Offences Act 2003)), has GATRELL committed an offence?

A Yes, as the photographs show a person other than GATRELL and HADLOW.

B No, because GATRELL and HADLOW were living together in an enduring family relationship.

C Yes, because indecent photographs of a child under 18 years of age cannot be taken in any circumstances.

D No, because HADLOW consented to the photographs being taken and she is over 16 years of age.

Question 33.16

JOHNSON (aged 20 years) takes indecent photographs of LAWFORD (aged 16 years). At the time the photographs are taken by JOHNSON, all the requirements of s. 45 of the Sexual Offences Act 2003 (providing a defence to the taking of indecent photographs) are satisfied so that the actual taking of the photographs is not in itself illegal.

Considering only s. 1 of the Protection of Children Act 1978 (indecent photographs of children), at what stage, if at all, would JOHNSON first commit an offence?

A When he has the indecent photographs in his possession to view them for his own personal pleasure.

B When he has the indecent photographs in his possession with a view to showing them to his friend, MANNING (aged 23 years).
C When he has the indecent photographs in his possession and shows them to his friend, NEWPORT (aged 23 years).
D JOHNSON does not commit an offence in these circumstances.

Question 33.17

ROLFE is a local councillor who is running an anti-child pornography campaign. Because of ROLFE's campaign, PARNELL (a paedophile) decides to send ROLFE a large number of indecent photographs of children in order to offend him. PARNELL contacts OXLEY, a delivery van driver, to deliver a parcel containing hundreds of indecent photographs of children under the age of ten to ROLFE's home address. OXLEY (unaware of the contents) collects the parcel from PARNELL and places it on the front seat of his van and sets off. Several miles later, OXLEY has to brake sharply to avoid an accident and the parcel slips off the front seat and hits the dashboard of his van. In the process, the packaging is damaged and OXLEY sees the contents. OXLEY needs the money for delivering the parcel and so continues to his destination, where he delivers the parcel to ROLFE. The photographs outrage ROLFE and, believing he has a legitimate reason to show the photographs, he shows them to a local newspaper editor as evidence to highlight his anti-child pornography campaign.

Who has committed an offence contrary to s. 1 of the Protection of Children Act 1978?

A PARNELL only.
B PARNELL and OXLEY.
C PARNELL and ROLFE.
D PARNELL, OXLEY and ROLFE (although ROLFE would have a defence if charged with the offence).

Question 33.18

Section 1 of the Protection of Children Act 1978 and s. 160 of the Criminal Justice Act 1988 both deal with indecent photographs and 'pseudo-photographs' of children. These images can be obtained, in many cases, via the use of the internet. There has been a significant amount of authoritative case law in this area that investigators ought to be aware of when gathering evidence of these offences.

With regard to the authoritative case law, which of the following statements is correct?

A 'Making' a pseudo-photograph does not include voluntarily browsing through indecent images of children on and from the internet.

B Evidence showing how a computer had been used to access paedophile news groups, chat-lines and websites would not be relevant to a case relating to the creation of an indecent image of a child.

C An image consisting of two parts of two different photographs taped together (the naked body of a woman taped to the head of a child) would not be a 'pseudo-photograph'.

D Downloading images from the internet will not amount to 'making' a photograph.

Question 33.19

SANDBROOK (aged 25 years) has several indecent photographs of TAFANO (aged 14 years) posted through his front door. SANDBROOK had not made any prior request for these photographs to be delivered. SANDBROOK opens the envelope containing the photographs and, having examined them, he leaves them on a shelf in his flat. Six months later, SANDBROOK's flat is raided by the police and the photographs of TAFANO are discovered. SANDBROOK states that he has not shown or distributed the photographs of TAFANO to anyone else, nor did he intend to do so.

With regard to s. 160 of the Criminal Justice Act 1988, which of the following statements is correct?

A SANDBROOK does not commit the offence as the photographs are of a child aged over 13 years of age.

B SANDBROOK has committed the offence but would have a defence because the photographs were sent to him without any prior request.

C As SANDBROOK has not shown or distributed the photographs to anyone else, he has not committed an offence under this Act.

D SANDBROOK has committed the offence, which is punishable with up to five years' imprisonment.

Question 33.20

The police carry out a raid on a house belonging to CHAPMAN in connection with sexual offences against children. During the course of the search of the premises, a number of images are recovered. One set of images are in the form of a short video clip recovered from a mobile phone. They illustrate HARPER (a 17-year-old female) standing next to CHAPMAN who is naked and masturbating. In a video clip recovered from CHAPMAN's computer, CHAPMAN can be seen placing his penis in the anus of a cartoon (imaginary) child.

Considering the offence of possession of prohibited images of children (contrary to s. 62 of the Coroners and Justice Act 2009), which of the following statements is correct?

A The image of HARPER and the imaginary child are prohibited images.
B Only the image of HARPER is a prohibited image.
C Only the image of the imaginary child is a prohibited image.
D These images are not prohibited images under s. 62 of the Act.

Question 33.21

SMART (aged 28 years) obtains sexual gratification in a variety of different situations involving children. He establishes a relationship with CRAWLEY (aged 14 years) via an internet chat room and sends a number of emails to CRAWLEY fully aware that CRAWLEY is 14 years old when he does so. He sends an email to CRAWLEY asking, *'Do you ever have a wank?'* (obtaining immediate sexual gratification as a consequence of sending the message). CRAWLEY sees the email and sends a reply to SMART telling SMART *'Don't contact me again, you fuckin' loser!'* CRAWLEY is not upset or offended by the email from SMART and there is never any further contact between the pair. SMART never has any intention of meeting with CRAWLEY, he just enjoys communicating in a sexual manner with children via the internet.

Would the activity by SMART constitute an offence under s. 15A of the Sexual Offences Act 2003 (sexual communication with a child)?

A No, as SMART never intended to meet CRAWLEY.
B Yes, but if the sexual gratification were to be obtained at a later time, the offence would not be committed.
C No, as CRAWLEY did not respond in a 'sexual' manner.
D Yes, and this would be the case regardless of when the sexual gratification were to be taken.

Question 33.22

JULIE MULLEN is a single-parent mother and has a son, JAMES MULLEN, aged 16; his girlfriend is DIANE KINSELLA, aged 15. JULIE is aware that JAMES and DIANE are having sex, albeit she does not allow them to have sex in her house. In view of this, JAMES and DIANE visit his father, ADRIAN MULLEN, at weekends and he allows them to share a bedroom knowing that they have sex. JULIE, her son JAMES and DIANE are going on holiday to Spain and when JULIE books the holiday, JAMES and DIANE persuade JULIE to allow them to share a bedroom. JULIE does so knowing that JAMES and DIANE will have sex with each other whilst on holiday in Spain.

In relation to s. 14 of the Sexual Offences Act 2003 (arranging or facilitating the commission of child sex offences), do either JULIE MULLEN or ADRIAN MULLEN commit an offence?

A ADRIAN is guilty of facilitating and JULIE is guilty of arranging sex for another (JAMES).

B Neither is guilty of this offence as the arranging or facilitating sex for themselves or others is for persons aged 18 or over committing child sex offences.

C ADRIAN is guilty of the offence of facilitating but JULIE is not guilty of arranging because the sexual activity will not take place in this country.

D ADRIAN is guilty of the offence of facilitating because the sex has taken place; however, JULIE will not be guilty until they take the holiday.

Question 33.23

BORMAN (who is 19 years old) is standing outside a newsagents which is near to a school and is regularly frequented by school pupils on their way to the school. He engages in conversation with MOORE (who is 14 years old and dressed in school uniform) and during the conversation MOORE invites BORMAN to touch her breasts. BORMAN realises that MOORE is under 16 but this does not stop him fondling MOORE's breasts. This activity is witnessed by TANSILL who is working in the newsagents. TANSILL contacts the police and PC MILNER attends the scene.

Does BORMAN commit the offence of sexual activity with a child (contrary to s. 9 of the Sexual Offences Act 2003)?

A No, as MOORE is over 13 years old.

B Yes, and as MOORE is under 16 there is no requirement for the prosecution to prove anything regarding BORMAN's belief about MOORE's age.

C No, as MOORE consented to the activity.

D Yes, but the prosecution must show that MOORE was under 16 and that BORMAN did not reasonably believe she was 16 or over.

ANSWERS

Answer 33.1

Answer **A** — The offence under s. 9 of the Act can only be committed where the defendant is aged 18 years or over. Answer B is incorrect as whether KEANE consented to the act or not is irrelevant. Answer C is incorrect as this offence applies to a person aged under 16 years of age. Answer D is incorrect as this section covers the sexual activity that takes place between the two.

Investigators' Manual, para. 4.4.2

Answer 33.2

Answer **B** — This offence is committed if a person aged 18 or over (A) engages in sexual activity, for the purpose of obtaining sexual gratification and the activity is engaged in *when another person is present or is in a place from which (A) can be observed.* The fact that PRIZEMAN intended SHIPMAN to view the act (answer A) or the fact that he believed her to be watching the activity (answer C) are both immaterial if SHIPMAN is not present or in a place from which PRIZEMAN can be observed. Answer D is incorrect, as the fact that CASE was unaware of SHIPMAN's presence would not preclude PRIZEMAN committing the offence if SHIPMAN was present when the activity took place.

Investigators' Manual, para. 4.4.4

Answer 33.3

Answer **C** — Answer A is incorrect as the person committing this offence must be at least 18 years old. Answer B is incorrect as not only must the activity carried out be 'sexual', but also it must be carried out in order to obtain sexual gratification. Answer D is incorrect as it is not necessary to show that the child was in fact aware of the activity in every case.

Investigators' Manual, para. 4.4.4

Answer 33.4

Answer **A** — This offence relates to causing a child to watch a third person engage in sexual activity or to look at an image of any person engaging in an activity. Answer

B is incorrect on that basis. Answer C is incorrect because the offence can be committed against a child aged under 16 years of age. Answer D is incorrect as s. 79(5) of the Act states that an 'image' includes images of an imaginary person and, as such, animated cartoon images would be covered by the legislation.

Investigators' Manual, para. 4.4.5

Answer 33.5

Answer **D** — The offence of causing a child to watch a sexual act under s. 12 of the Act must be committed *intentionally*. Answer A is incorrect as although there might be a chance that children would see the images, unless HUGHES has carried out the activity with the intention that a child will obscrvc it then the offence is not committed. Answer B is incorrect as although HUGHES has carried out the act for the purposes of sexual gratification, the sexual gratification aspect of the offence is incomplete. Sexual gratification for the purposes of this section must be gained by watching the child watching the activity of a third person or an image and not by watching an image for oneself. Answer C is incorrect as the term 'image' includes a moving or a still image.

Investigators' Manual, para. 4.4.5

Answer 33.6

Answer **B** — The offence of arranging or facilitating the commission of a child sex offence can be committed if the arranging or facilitating is for an offence to be committed in any part of the world, making answer A incorrect. Answer C is incorrect as the offence is complete whether or not the sexual activity takes place. Answer D is incorrect as the offence is complete if the defendant arranges or facilitates something that he intends to do, intends another person to do, *or believes that another person will do.*

Investigators' Manual, para. 4.4.7

Answer 33.7

Answer **B** — A person can only commit an offence under s. 14 of the Act if he arranges or facilitates an offence that would be an offence under ss. 9 to 13 of the Act. The offence under s. 14 of the Act can be committed if the defendant arranges or facilitates something *that he intends to do*, as well as arranging or facilitating the acts of others, making answer A incorrect. Answer C is incorrect as this offence is complete whether sexual activity takes place or not. Whether the person contacted is a police officer makes no difference as it is the arranging or facilitating that is the crux of the offence. Answer D is incorrect as there are no limitations as to the nature or type of contact. The arrangements or facilitation can be made by any means whatsoever, the internet being a prime example.

Investigators' Manual, para. 4.4.7

Answer 33.8

Answer **B** — Answer A is incorrect as the intentions of the defendant at the time of the first meeting with a potential victim are immaterial; it is the defendant's intentions at the time of either meeting with or travelling to meet the victim after one or more previous communications or meetings that is relevant. Answer C is incorrect as the offence can be committed when travelling to meet the victim with the requisite intent. Section 36 of the Criminal Justice and Courts Act 2015 (in force from 13 April 2015) makes a small but significant change to the offence of 'grooming', changing the 'two occasions' required to one occasion and making answer D incorrect.

Investigators' Manual, para. 4.4.8

Answer 33.9

Answer **B** — The offence is committed in several different ways. One of those is when a person who is 18 or over (HARVEY) has met or communicated with another person (in this case PREECE) on one or more occasions and, subsequently (under s. 15(1)(a)(iii)), PREECE travels with the intention of meeting HARVEY anywhere in the world and HARVEY intends to do anything to PREECE that would amount to a relevant offence (relevant offences being offences under ss. 9 to 13 of the Sexual Offences Act 2003). This means that an offence has been committed by HARVEY at point B (meaning that answer D is incorrect). The meetings or communication, for the purposes of this section, can have taken place in any part of the world (s. 15(2)), making answer A incorrect. Answer C is incorrect as the communication can include text messaging or interactions via internet 'chat rooms'.

Investigators' Manual, para. 4.4.8

Answer 33.10

Answer **A** — The offence can be committed between cousins where the defendant and the victim live or have lived in the same household, or the defendant is or has been regularly involved in caring for, training, supervising or been in sole charge of the victim but that is clearly not the case in this question. If these circumstances existed, the fact that IMBER was over 16 years of age would be immaterial and the offence would be committed, making answer C incorrect. As POWELL and IMBER have never met each other this activity would not amount to an offence under s. 25, making answers B and D incorrect.

Investigators' Manual, para. 4.4.11

Answer 33.11

Answer **B** — Apart from 'touching' and 'sexual', there are two further elements that must be proved in relation to s. 25 of the Act. The first is the existence of the relevant family relationship and the second is the age of the victim (making answers A, C and D incorrect). In addition, answers C and D are incorrect in respect of both the relationship and the age of the victim; the *defendant* will have an evidential burden to discharge in that regard (s. 25(2) and (3)).

Investigators' Manual, para. 4.4.11

Answer 33.12

Answer **D** — Answer A is incorrect as the relationship of half-brother is covered by s. 27 of the Act. Answer B is incorrect as LYONS has not actually touched JARVIS and so the offence under s. 25 is incomplete. Answer C is incorrect as a person under 18 years of age can commit this offence but the maximum penalty is less in such circumstances.

Investigators' Manual, para. 4.4.11

Answer 33.13

Answer **D** — This question revolves around the issue of whether there is a relevant family relationship between RENTON and THAWLEY. Section 27 of the Act defines core family relationships and also provides additional categories where a relationship will be deemed to exist. One of those categories is when the defendant and the victim *live or have lived* in the same household and they have the same parent or foster parent. Although RENTON and THAWLEY have the same foster parent (STRAKER) they do not live and never have lived in the same household. In other words, there is no family relationship between the two. This fact makes answers A and C incorrect. Answer B is incorrect as whether the sexual intercourse was consensual or not is immaterial for the purposes of an offence under s. 25 of the Act.

Investigators' Manual, para. 4.4.11

Answer 33.14

Answer **C** — Section 29 of the Act caters for sexual relationships which pre-date family relationships. A person is not liable for a familial child sex offence under s. 25 where a lawful sexual relationship existed between the parties immediately before the onset of the circumstances giving rise to the familial relationship. Although WOOD and PERCIVAL are now stepsister and stepbrother they do not commit the offence because of s. 29, making answer A incorrect. A further exception (under s. 28 of the Act) relates to marriage exceptions; however, this is not the only exception and therefore answer B is incorrect. Answer D is incorrect as persons under the age of 18 can commit this offence.

Investigators' Manual, para. 4.4.11

Answer 33.15

Answer **A** — Section 1(1)(a) of the Protection of Children Act 1978 makes it an offence for a person to take, or permit to be taken or to make, any indecent photograph or pseudo-photograph of a child. Section 45 of the Sexual Offences Act 2003 amends the Protection of Children Act so that where photographs are concerned a person will be considered a 'child' if they are 16 or 17 years of age. However, photographs taken and used within an established relationship will not be criminalised if: (i) the defendant proves that the photograph in question was of a child aged 16 or over and at the time of the taking or making, he and the child were married or living together as partners in an enduring family relationship; (ii) the child consented to the photograph being taken or the defendant reasonably believed that the child consented; and (iii) the photograph must not be one that shows a person other than the child and the defendant. If *any* of these conditions is not satisfied then the prosecution need only prove the offence as set out in s. 1(1)(a) of the 1978 Act. Answers B and D are incorrect as they only form part of the potential defence available to

GATRELL. In addition, answer D is incorrect as it asserts that taking photographs of a child over the age of 16 is permissible with the consent of the child. Answer C is incorrect as this defence exists if all three elements are present.

Investigators' Manual, para. 4.4.12

Answer 33.16

Answer **B** — If all the requirements of s. 45 of the Sexual Offences Act 2003 are met this will mean that at the time the photographs were taken (i) LAWFORD was at least 16 years of age and JOHNSON and LAWFORD were either married or living together in an enduring family relationship; (ii) there is enough evidence to show that LAWFORD consented to the photograph being taken; and (iii) the photograph does not show any person other than the child and the defendant. This will provide an exception to offences under s. 1(1)(a), (b) and (c) of the Protection of Children Act 1978. However, just because the photographs are 'legitimate' the showing or distribution offence under s. 1(1)(b) *will be committed* if that showing or distribution is to a person other than the child, so the offence would be complete at B when JOHNSON possesses the photographs with a view to show them to MANNING.

Investigators' Manual, para. 4.4.12

Answer 33.17

Answer **D** — Under s. 1(1)(b) of the Act it is an offence to distribute or show indecent photographs or pseudo-photographs. PARNELL is guilty of this offence by sending the package containing the indecent photographs, via OXLEY, to ROLFE. OXLEY is also guilty of this offence. It would be a defence for a person charged with such an offence under s. 1(4)(b) of the Act to prove that he had not himself seen the photographs or pseudo-photographs and did not know, nor had any cause to suspect, them to be indecent. OXLEY would have been able to avail himself of this defence up until the point when he realised what the contents of the package were, meaning that answers A and C are incorrect. Answer B is incorrect as ROLFE has committed the offence. He does have a defence in this situation under s. 1(4)(b) of the Act, which states that he will have a defence if he had a legitimate reason for distributing or showing the photographs or pseudo-photographs.

Investigators' Manual, para. 4.4.12

Answer 33.18

Answer **C** — Answer A is incorrect as 'making' a pseudo-photograph *does* include voluntarily browsing through indecent images of children on and from the internet (*R* v *Smith and Jayson* [2002] EWCA Crim 683). Answer B is incorrect as evidence showing how a computer had been used to access paedophile news groups, chatlines and websites *would* be relevant to a case relating to the creation of an indecent image of a child (*R* v *Mould* (2001) 2 Cr App R(S) 8). Answer D is incorrect as downloading images from the internet *will* amount to 'making' a photograph (*R* v *Bowden* [2000] 2 WLR 1083). An image consisting of two parts of two different photographs taped together (the naked body of a woman taped to the head of a child) is not a pseudo-photograph. If such an image were copied, it could be (*R* v *Dooley* [2005] EWCA Crim 3093).

Investigators' Manual, para. 4.4.12

Answer 33.19

Answer **D** — Answer A is incorrect as a 'child' is a person under the age of 18 years of age at the material time. Answer B is incorrect as although the photographs were sent to SANDBROOK without any prior request being made by him for such material (the first part of the defence under s. 160(2)(c)), he has kept them for an unreasonable time, thereby defeating the defence. Answer C is incorrect as showing or distributing the indecent photographs relates to an offence under s. 1 of the Protection of Children Act 1978 and not to the offence of possessing indecent photographs under this Act.

Investigators' Manual, para. 4.4.12

Answer 33.20

Answer **A** — The Coroners and Justice Act 2009, s. 62 states:

(1) It is an offence for a person to be in possession of a prohibited image of a child.

(2) A prohibited image is an image which—

 (a) is pornographic,

 (b) falls within subsection (6), and

 (c) is grossly offensive, disgusting or otherwise of an obscene character.

An image falls within subs. (6) if it is an image which focuses solely or principally on a child's genitals or anal region, or portrays any of the acts mentioned below. Amongst other acts they include:

- the performance by a person of an act of intercourse or oral sex with or in the presence of a child;
- an act of masturbation by, of, involving or in the presence of a child.

Section 65 states that an 'image' includes a moving or still image (produced by any means) such as a photograph or film, or data (stored by any means) which is capable of conversion into a movable or still image such as data stored electronically (as on a computer disk), which is capable of conversion into an image. This covers material available on computers, mobile phones or any other electronic device. A 'child' means a person under the age of 18 (s. 65(5)). References to an image of a person include references to an image of an imaginary person. References to an image of a child include references to an image of an imaginary child. So the behaviour in both images is captured, making answers B, C and D incorrect.

Investigators' Manual, para. 4.4.12

Answer 33.21

Answer **D** — The Sexual Offences Act 2003, s. 15A states:

> (1) A person aged 18 or over (A) commits an offence if—
> (a) for the purpose of obtaining sexual gratification, A intentionally communicates with another person (B),
> (b) the communication is sexual or is intended to encourage B to make (whether to A or another) a communication that is sexual, and,
> (c) B is under 16, and A does not reasonably believe that B is 16 or over.

The fact that SMART never intended to meet CRAWLEY or that CRAWLEY does not respond in a 'sexual' manner would not have any impact on this offence being committed, making answers A and C incorrect.The offence criminalises conduct where an adult intentionally communicates (e.g. by email, text message, written note or orally) with a child under 16 (whom the adult does not reasonably believe to be aged 16 or over) for the purpose of obtaining sexual gratification if the communication is sexual or intended to encourage the child to make a communication that is sexual. The offence may be committed, for example, by talking sexually to a child via an internet chat room or sending sexually explicit text messages to a child as well as inviting a child to communicate sexually (irrespective of whether the invitation is itself sexual). Answer B is incorrect as the interpretation of the term 'sexual gratification' is the same taken in ss. 11 and 12 of the Act so it would not matter if the defendant made a relevant communication in order to obtain immediate sexual gratification or the obtaining of such gratification was part of a longer term plan or both.

Investigators' Manual, para. 4.4.9

Answer 33.22

Answer **A** — Section 14 of the Sexual Offences Act 2003 states:

(1) A person commits an offence if—
  (a) he intentionally arranges or facilitates something that he intends to do, intends another to do, or believes another person will do, in any part of the world; and
  (b) doing it will involve the commission of an offence under any of sections 9 to 13.

Sections 9 to 12 cover offences against children when the offender is over 18. These offences are touching, causing or inciting sexual activity in the presence of a child, and causing a child to watch a sexual act. Section 13 is a caveat to cover all ss. 9 to 12 offences when the offender is under 18 years of age. ADRIAN commits the offence when he facilitates (allows) JAMES and DIANE to use a bedroom together knowing that they are having sex. JULIE arranges when she books the holiday; sex does not have to have taken place and can be committed in any part of the world. Clearly this makes answer A correct and answers B, C and D incorrect. Section 14 was designed to prevent the sex tourism trade; however, the definition goes beyond that.

Investigators' Manual, para. 4.4.7

Answer 33.23

Answer **D** — Section 9 of the Sexual Offences Act 2003 states:

(1) A person aged 18 or over (A) commits an offence if—
  (a) he intentionally touches another person (B),
  (b) the touching is sexual, and
  (c) either—
    (i) B is under 16 and A does not reasonably believe that B is 16 or over, or
    (ii) B is under 13.

So BORMAN has committed the offence, eliminating answers A and C. The prosecution must show that the defendant intentionally touched the victim sexually and that either the victim was under 13 (in which case the offence is complete) or that the victim was under 16 and that the defendant did not reasonably believe that he/she was 16 or over, meaning that answer B is incorrect. In either case consent is irrelevant.

Investigators' Manual, para. 4.4.2

34 Sexual Offences Against People with a Mental Disorder

QUESTIONS

Question 34.1

ULLESTHORPE sneaks into a care home which specifically caters for people with mental illnesses who are unable to look after themselves. ORTON is a patient at the home and is in a constant vegetative state, unable to speak or move. ULLESTHORPE is fully aware of the nature of the home and the condition of the people who are in it and creeps into ORTON's room where he fondles ORTON's breasts to obtain sexual gratification. ULLESTHORPE becomes sexually aroused and places his erect penis in ORTON's hand. He then uses ORTON's hand to masturbate himself.

At what point, if at all, does ULLESTHORPE first commit an offence of sexual activity with a person with a mental disorder (contrary to s. 30 of the Sexual Offences Act 2003)?

A When he fondles ORTON's breasts.
B When he places his erect penis in ORTON's hand.
C When he uses ORTON's hand to masturbate himself.
D The offence has not been committed by ORTON.

Question 34.2

CORRIN is 27 years old and suffers from cerebral palsy meaning that she has an IQ of 50. CORRIN is able to speak but because of her condition, she is unable to communicate her choice in a way that other women, not suffering from such disabilities, would be able to. A further effect of the condition is that she cannot walk and is in a wheelchair. CORRIN's friend, MUXLOE, often takes her to a nearby park where GRAY (a 73-year-old man who is aware of CORRIN's condition) has befriended CORRIN and speaks to her. One afternoon MUXLOE leaves CORRIN and GRAY in the park while she visits a newsagents. GRAY moves CORRIN behind a shed and asks CORRIN if he can kiss her breasts; CORRIN says 'Yes'. GRAY kisses her breasts and then asks if he can digitally penetrate her vagina and again CORRIN says 'Yes' and GRAY penetrates CORRIN's vagina with one of his fingers.

Considering the offence under s. 30 of the Sexual Offences Act 2003 (sexual activity with a person with a mental disorder) only, which of the following comments is correct?

A The offence has not been committed as CORRIN is able to refuse to be touched by GRAY.

B The offence has been committed but only when GRAY kisses CORRIN's breasts.

C The offence has been committed but only when GRAY digitally penetrates CORRIN's vagina.

D The offence has been committed by GRAY and this will encompass him kissing CORRIN's breasts and digitally penetrating her vagina.

Question 34.3

SHAMBER is a sexual predator and has been watching the front entrance of a mental health care home for several days, waiting for an opportunity to sexually assault one or more of the residents of the care home. He watches as two female residents of the home, EDGEWARE (aged 14) and BOSS (aged 18) are escorted into a waiting minibus by JAKEMAN who sits inside the bus with them; the bus is driven by FROST. Just as the engine starts, SHAMBER runs over to the side of the minibus and jumps inside. He produces a gun and points it at FROST and tells him to drive away from the home. Due to their mental disability, EDGEWARE and BOSS are oblivious to the threat that SHAMBER poses. Two miles along the road, SHAMBER orders FROST to stop the minibus. He tells JAKEMAN and FROST to get out of the minibus and then sexually assaults EDGEWARE and BOSS by squeezing their breasts.

Has an offence under s. 30 of the Sexual Offences Act 2003 (sexual activity with a person with a mental disorder) been committed in these circumstances?

A No, as the activity did not take place in a care home for persons suffering from a mental disorder.

B Yes, but only in relation to EDGEWARE.

C No, as the activity did not involve penetration.

D Yes, the offence has been committed against EDGEWARE and BOSS.

Question 34.4

VENNING is suffering from a schizo-affective disorder and has a low IQ and a history of alcohol abuse. She is sitting in a pub and engages in conversation with GARDNER who has no idea of VENNING's mental disorder. GARDNER buys VENNING a number of drinks and then asks VENNING if she wants to have sexual intercourse with him; VENNING replies that she does. The only reason VENNING consents is because of her schizo-affective disorder causing her to become panicked and afraid of GARDNER, thereby unable to refuse GARDNER's request. The two leave the pub and go to GARDNER's house where they have oral sex (GARDNER's penis to VENNING's mouth).

Has GARDNER committed an offence of sexual activity with a person with a mental disorder (contrary to s. 30 of the Sexual Offences Act 2003)?

A No, GARDNER did not know about VENNING's mental disorder.

B Yes, and because VENNING was given alcohol by GARDNER, the presumptions under s. 75 of the Act will be applicable.

C No, as the sexual act did not involve penetration of VENNING's vagina or anus.

D Yes, but permission to prosecute the offence will be required from the Director of Public Prosecutions.

Question 34.5

McAVOY regularly visits a bingo hall with her mother. During the course of the visits McAVOY has become very friendly with TURVEY who works at the bingo hall. McAVOY's mother has told TURVEY that her daughter has a mental disorder which makes her very vulnerable to suggestion and unable to refuse anything. During one visit to the bingo hall, TURVEY tells McAVOY that he wants to have sexual intercourse with her. McAVOY replies that she has heard that people need to be married before they can have sexual intercourse and asks if TURVEY will marry her. To get McAVOY's agreement to have sexual intercourse with him, TURVEY tells McAVOY that they will get married. The two have sexual intercourse in a broom cupboard at the bingo hall but after the sexual intercourse has taken place, TURVEY tells McAVOY that he will never marry her and only said he would to make sure that she had sex with him.

Has TURVEY committed an offence under s. 34 of the Sexual Offences Act 2003 (procuring sexual activity with a person with a mental disorder)?

A No, as the nature of the act was sexual intercourse and that has not been misrepresented in any way by TURVEY.

B Yes, as TURVEY has obtained McAVOY's agreement to sexual intercourse by an inducement (the promise to marry her).

C No, as McAVOY's agreement to sexual intercourse was not obtained by a threat.

D Yes, but the prosecution must prove that the victim of the offence was unable to refuse as a consequence of her mental disorder.

Question 34.6

CLEMENT (aged 17 years) is accompanying his parents on a visit to see his grandmother who is 72 years old and suffering from advanced senile dementia, leaving her bedridden as a resident in a mental care home. CLEMENT's parents leave the room his grandmother is in leaving CLEMENT and his grandmother alone. CLEMENT deeply resents spending time visiting his grandmother and out of spite and maliciousness he takes out his penis and waves it in front of his grandmother's face and then begins to masturbate in front of her saying, *'You can't do anything like this anymore, can you old bag!'* CLEMENT is fully aware of his grandmother's condition and of the fact that she can do nothing about his behaviour.

CLEMENT has not committed the offence under s. 32 of the Sexual Offences Act 2003 (sexual activity in the presence of a mentally disordered person) but why not?

A CLEMENT has not committed this offence as he did not engage in sexual activity with another person in the presence of his grandmother.

B CLEMENT has not committed the offence because he is under 18 years of age.

C CLEMENT has not committed the offence because no inducement was offered to his grandmother to watch the sexual act.

D CLEMENT has not committed the offence because he did not act for the purpose of obtaining sexual gratification.

Question 34.7

TENANT, an adult male, is working in York for a week as a representative of a chemical company. In the bar of his hotel, he engages in conversation with HANNAH, an adult female. TENANT buys HANNAH several drinks and they start becoming very tactile with each other. Unbeknown to TENANT, HANNAH is a paranoid schizophrenic (a mental condition), so when TENANT suggests they go to his room for sex, HANNAH agrees solely because of her condition, believing that it is right to do so. In TENANT's bedroom, they have oral sex.

Does TENANT commit an offence of sexual activity with a mentally disordered person contrary to s. 30 of the Sexual Offences Act 2003?

A No, TENANT has to be aware that HANNAH was suffering from a mental disorder.

B Yes, the offence includes oral sex and there does not have to be full intercourse.

C No, as TENANT has to have sexual intercourse with HANNAH for the offence to be complete.

D Yes, but as TENANT was not aware of HANNAH's mental disorder it is therefore a summary only offence.

ANSWERS

Answer 34.1

Answer **A** — A person commits an offence under s. 30(1) if:

(a) he intentionally touches another person (B),
(b) the touching is sexual,
(c) B is unable to refuse because of or for a reason related to a mental disorder, and
(d) A knows or could reasonably be expected to know that B has a mental disorder and that because of it or for a reason related to it B is unlikely to refuse.

ULLESTHORPE clearly commits the offence when he fondles ORTON's breasts, making answers B, C and D incorrect.

Investigators' Manual, para. 4.5.3

Answer 34.2

Answer **D** — A person commits an offence under s. 30(1) if:

(a) he intentionally touches another person (B),
(b) the touching is sexual,
(c) B is unable to refuse because of or for a reason related to a mental disorder, and
(d) A knows or could reasonably be expected to know that B has a mental disorder and that because of it or for a reason related to it B is unlikely to refuse.

Answer A is incorrect as CORRIN is unable to refuse to be touched by GRAY. In *Hulme* v *DPP* [2006] EWHC 1347 (Admin), the Divisional Court examined a decision reached by a magistrates' court in relation to a complainant who was a cerebral palsy sufferer with a low IQ (aged 27). The magistrates' court had decided that the complainant was unable to refuse to be sexually touched; the Divisional Court agreed and the conviction against the defendant (who was 73) was upheld. The touching can involve penetration meaning answer B is incorrect and answer C is incorrect as the kissing of CORRIN's breasts is certainly sexual.

Investigators' Manual, para. 4.5.3

Answer 34.3

Answer **D** — A person commits an offence under s. 30(1) if:

(a) he intentionally touches another person (B),
(b) the touching is sexual,

(c) B is unable to refuse because of or for a reason related to a mental disorder, and
(d) A knows or could reasonably be expected to know that B has a mental disorder and that because of it or for a reason related to it B is unlikely to refuse.

The offence could be carried out at any location, making answer A incorrect. It can involve sexual touching and/or penetration, making answer C incorrect. There are no age restrictions in respect of the offence under s. 30, so the offence is committed against both females, making B incorrect.

Investigators' Manual, para. 4.5.3

Answer 34.4

Answer **A** — The offence under s. 30(1) can be committed by penetration or by sexual touching, making answer C incorrect. Answers B and D are incorrect as the offence has not been committed. Section 30(1)(d) states that the defendant must know or could reasonably be expected to know that the victim has a mental disorder and that because of it or for a reason related to it the victim is likely to be unable to refuse. B is further incorrect as the presumptions under ss. 74 to 76 do not apply to this offence; that is the purpose of s. 30(1)(c) and (d), and D is further incorrect as no special permission is required to prosecute the offence.

Investigators' Manual, para. 4.5.3

Answer 34.5

Answer **B** — If the defendant obtains the victim's agreement to sexual touching/activity by means of any inducement (offered or given), or a threat or deception *for that purpose*, the defendant commits a specific offence under s. 34 of the Sexual Offences Act 2003 (punishable in the same way as an offence under s. 30). An example of such an offence would be where the defendant (TURVEY) promises to give the victim (McAVOY) some reward in exchange for allowing sexual touching/activity (the promise of marriage for sex). No 'threat' is required, making answer C incorrect. In specific cases of inducements, threats or deception, there is still a need to prove that the defendant knew (or could reasonably have been expected to know) of the victim's mental disorder *but no need to prove that the victim was unable to refuse*, making answer D incorrect.

Investigators' Manual, para. 4.5.3

Answer 34.6

Answer **D** — The sexual activity carried out must be for the purpose of obtaining sexual gratification—if it is for *any other reason* no offence under s. 32 is committed.

Investigators' Manual, para. 4.5.5

Answer 34.7

Answer **A** — The Sexual Offences Act 2003, s. 30 states:

(1) A person (A) commits an offence if—
- (a) he intentionally touches another person,
- (b) the touching is sexual,
- (c) B is unable to refuse because of or for a reason related to a mental disorder, and
- (d) A knows or could reasonably be expected to know that B has a mental disorder and that because of it or for a reason related to it B is likely to be unable to refuse.

In these circumstances, as TENANT was not aware of HANNAH's condition, answer A is the correct answer.

Investigators' Manual, para. 4.5.3

35 Offences Relating to Prostitution

QUESTIONS

Question 35.1

The Sexual Offences Act 2003 provides a definition of the term 'prostitution' which is important when considering offences under the Act that deal with such behaviour and associated behaviour.

In respect of that definition, which of the following comments is true?

A The definition applies to women only.

B The definition would not apply to a person who has been compelled to offer or provide sexual services to another person.

C To be classed as a 'prostitute' a person must, on at least two occasions, offer sexual services to another person.

D The offer or provision of sexual services to another person could be made in return for a promise of payment to a third person.

Question 35.2

PARSON is a cocaine addict and is finding it hard to maintain his lifestyle as he is spending all of his income on the drug. PARSON's partner, MACE, is speaking to KELLY about the problem and KELLY offers MACE a solution. KELLY tells MACE that he will supply PARSON with all the cocaine he wants if MACE is willing to have sex with other men at a holiday cottage in France on weekends. KELLY states that he will organise the trips so MACE will have nothing to worry about. MACE agrees and travels to France where he has sexual intercourse with several men and PARSON is supplied with a large amount of cocaine as a reward. KELLY does not gain anything for himself from this arrangement, he is just trying to help MACE in his relationship with PARSON.

Thinking about the offence of causing, inciting or controlling prostitution (under s. 52 of the Sexual Offences Act 2003), which of the following statements is correct?

A KELLY has not committed the offence because MACE provides the sexual services outside the United Kingdom (in France).

B KELLY commits the offence when he suggests that MACE becomes a prostitute.

C KELLY has not committed the offence because he does not gain anything for himself as a result of this arrangement.

D KELLY commits the offence but only when MACE has sex and PARSON is rewarded with cocaine.

Question 35.3

Section 53A of the Sexual Offences Act 2003 creates an offence which is committed if someone pays or promises payment for the sexual services of a prostitute who has been subject to exploitative conduct of a kind likely to induce or encourage the provision of a sexual service.

In relation to that offence, which of the following statements is true?

A 'Exploitative conduct' only relates to the use of violence or the threat to use violence.

B It does not matter where in the world the sexual services are provided.

C To be guilty of the offence the defendant must know or ought to have known that the prostitute has been subject to 'exploitative conduct'.

D There is a defence to the offence if the defendant can prove that he/she was unaware that the prostitute providing the sexual services had been subjected to 'exploitative conduct'.

Question 35.4

HAYE owns and runs a massage parlour where ILLTEN and STONELEIGH (both female) provide massage for customers. HAYE knows that ILLTEN and STONELEIGH regularly provide 'extras' for their male customers; this takes the form of oral sex with the customers. ILLTEN and STONELEIGH charge £50 for the 'extra' service but HAYE does not take a cut of the money as he is just happy that people are using the massage parlour.

Considering the offence of keeping a brothel used for prostitution (contrary to s. 33A of the Sexual Offences Act 1956) only, which of the following comments is true?

A No offence has been committed by HAYE as he does not take any payment for the sexual services offered by ILLTEN and STONELEIGH.

B For HAYE to be convicted of the offence, the prosecution would need to prove that persons resorted to the 'brothel' on more than one occasion.

C No offence has been committed as a 'brothel' is a place to which people resort for the purposes of unlawful sexual intercourse and in this situation full sexual intercourse does not take place.

D HAYE has committed the offence in this situation.

Question 35.5

MILL has an argument with his neighbour (NEWBOLD) who strongly disapproves of MILL as he knows that MILL is a prostitute. MILL wants to upset NEWBOLD so he persuades DEESLEY (one of MILL's regular customers) to come to his house and have sexual intercourse with him in the front room of his house in front of the window so that NEWBOLD can see what they are doing when he is tending his garden. MILL tells DEESLEY that for the favour he will only charge 50 per cent of his usual fee and DEESLEY agrees. When NEWBOLD is tending his garden, MILL begins to have sexual intercourse with DEESLEY and MILL bangs on the front window to attract NEWBOLD's attention. NEWBOLD sees what the pair are doing and is outraged by their conduct and calls the police.

With regard to the common law offence of keeping a disorderly house, which of the following is correct?

A The offence requires a degree of persistence so a single instance (such as an indecent performance) would not amount to an offence.

B The offence has been committed and is punishable (on indictment only) by a term of imprisonment of 10 years.

C The offence has been committed by MILL as the house is 'open' (i.e. to a customer or customers).

D The offence has not been committed as this behaviour takes place in a dwelling house.

Question 35.6

KORIE (who is 19 years old) is a prostitute and works from her home where she has sexual intercourse with customers she picks up outside a local pub. She injures her knee meaning that she has trouble walking so she stands in the doorway of her house (which abuts the street she lives on) and offers her services to men who walk past the front door of her house.

If KORIE is to commit an offence of soliciting (under s. 1 of the Street Offences Act 1959), which of the following requirements must be met?

A Her conduct must take place on three or more occasions in any period of one month.

B Her conduct must take place on two or more occasions in any period of three months.

C Her conduct must take place on three or more occasions in any period of six months.

D Her conduct must take place on two occasions or more in any period of 12 months.

Question 35.7

MONTIGUE is searching for a prostitute to have sexual intercourse with. He is driving his vehicle along a street when he slows down and stops next to BRYSON who is standing on the street corner waiting to be picked up by her boyfriend. MONTIGUE winds the window of his car down and shouts out to BRYSON, *'You look like you need a fuck—how much for a quickie?'* BRYSON ignores MONTIGUE who then shouts out *'C'mon, don't be shy. I'll pay you good money for a shag'*. BRYSON continues to ignore MONTIGUE who steps out of his car onto the street and approaches BRYSON saying, *'Playing hard to get, eh? OK, then, I'll give you £100 for a hand-job'*. BRYSON slaps MONTIGUE in the face and walks away from him.

At what point, if at all, does MONTIGUE first commit an offence contrary to s. 51A of the Sexual Offences Act 2003 (soliciting by 'kerb-crawling')?

A When he winds the window of his car down and first speaks to BRYSON saying, *'You look like you need a fuck—how much for a quickie?'*

B *On the second occasion he speaks to BRYSON and says, 'C'mon, don't be shy. I'll pay you good money for a shag'.*

C When he is on the street and speaks to BRYSON on the third occasion saying, *'Playing hard to get, eh? OK, then, I'll give you £100 for a hand-job'.*

D MONTIGUE does not commit the offence in these circumstances.

Question 35.8

It is an offence under s. 33A of the Sexual Offences Act 1956 to keep a brothel, manage such premises or to act or assist in the management of a brothel.

Which of the following statements is correct with regards to the number/s of prostitute/s on the premises being managed for the offence to be committed?

A Only one prostitute is required.

B More than one prostitute.

C More than two prostitutes.

D More than three prostitutes.

ANSWERS

Answer 35.1

Answer **D** — A prostitute is a person (A) who:

- on at least one occasion (making answer C incorrect); and
- whether or not compelled to do so (making answer B incorrect);
- offers or provides sexual services to another person;
- in return for payment or a promise of payment to A or a third person (answer D).

Section 51(2) of the Sexual Offences Act 2003 states that the definition applies to both men and women (making answer A incorrect).

Investigators' Manual, para. 4.6.2

Answer 35.2

Answer **B** — Section 52(1) of the Sexual Offences Act 2003 states that a person commits an offence if:

(a) he intentionally causes or incites another person to become a prostitute in any part of the world, and
(b) he does so for or in the expectation of gain for himself or a third person.

Gain means any financial advantage, including the discharge of an obligation to pay or the provision of goods or services (including sexual services) gratuitously or at a discount or the goodwill of any person which is or appears likely, in time, to bring financial advantage (s. 54). So the 'gain' here is for PARSON (a third person), making C incorrect. It does not matter that the behaviour takes place in France, making answer A incorrect. The offence is committed when KELLY 'incites' MACE to become a prostitute (remembering that incitement is a form of encouragement to do something).

Investigators' Manual, para. 4.6.3

Answer 35.3

Answer **B** — Section 53A(3) states that a person engages in exploitative conduct if he/she uses force, threats (whether or not relating to violence) or any other form of coercion or practises any form of deception, making answer A incorrect. An offence is committed regardless of whether the person paying or promising payment for sexual services knows or ought to know or be aware that the prostitute has been subject to exploitative conduct, making answer C incorrect. This means that this offence is one of strict liability and no mental element is required in respect of the offender's knowledge that the prostitute was forced, threatened, coerced or deceived. There is no defence of the type mentioned in answer D.

Investigators' Manual, para. 4.6.4

Answer 35.4

Answer **D** — A brothel is a place to which people resort for the purposes of unlawful sexual intercourse with more than one prostitute. However, it is not necessary that full sexual intercourse takes place or is even offered—a massage parlour where other acts of lewdness or indecency for sexual gratification are offered may be a brothel, making answer C incorrect. Section 33A(1) states that it is an offence for a person to keep, or to manage, or act or assist in the management of, a brothel to which people resort for practices involving prostitution (whether or not also for other practices). Prostitution means offering or providing sexual services, whether under compulsion or not, to another in return for payment or a promise of payment to the prostitute or a third person, so it does not matter that HAYE does not receive a 'cut' of the money ILLTEN and STONELEIGH make, making answer A incorrect. There is no requirement for the prosecution to prove that the premises were resorted to on more than one occasion, making answer B incorrect.

Investigators' Manual, para. 4.6.5

Answer 35.5

Answer **A** — The offence is punishable with an unlimited sentence, making answer B incorrect. It makes no difference whatsoever whether the premises concerned are a dwelling house, making answer D incorrect. The house may be classed as 'open' to customers but the offence requires a degree of persistence so a single incident such as an indecent performance would not satisfy the requirements of the offence, making C incorrect.

Investigators' Manual, para. 4.6.5

Answer 35.6

Answer **B** — Conduct is 'persistent' for the purposes of this offence if it takes place on two or more occasions in any period of three months (s. 1(4)(a)), making answers A, C and D incorrect.

Investigators' Manual, para. 4.6.6

Answer 35.7

Answer **A** — Section 51A(1) of the Sexual Offences Act 2003 states that it is an offence for a person in a street or public place to solicit another (B) for the purpose of obtaining B's sexual services as a prostitute. Section 51A(2) states that the reference to a person in a street or public place includes a person in a vehicle in a street or public place. The offence is punishable on the first occasion the activity takes place, meaning the offence takes place at point A and that answers B, C and D are therefore incorrect.

Investigators' Manual, para. 4.6.6

Answer 35.8

Answer **B** — It is an offence under s. 33A of the Sexual Offences Act 1956 to keep a brothel, or to manage, or to act or assist in the management of, a brothel to which people resort for the practices of prostitution. For this offence, there must be more than one prostitute (male or female); it is not necessary that full sexual intercourse takes place or even be offered, making B the correct answer.

Investigators' Manual, para. 4.6.5

36 Preparatory Offences and Other Sexual Offences

QUESTIONS

Question 36.1

FEARING applies for a job as a lifeguard at his local swimming pool. Part of his prospective duties will include giving swimming lessons to children between the ages of five and 12 years old. FEARING's ulterior motive is to gain employment at the swimming pool and then take indecent photographs of the children (contrary to s. 1 of the Protection of Children Act 1978). To help him get the job, he forges several certificates that state he has passed examinations as a lifeguard. As a result, FEARING is given the job as a lifeguard.

Considering the offence of committing a criminal offence with intent to commit a sexual offence (s. 62 of the Sexual Offences Act 2003), which of the following statements is right?

A FEARING does not commit the offence as taking indecent photographs of children under s. 1 of the Protection of Children Act 1978 is not a 'relevant sexual offence'.

B This offence can only be committed if the criminal offence is one of kidnapping or false imprisonment, therefore FEARING has not committed the offence.

C Until FEARING commits a sexual assault on one of the children he cannot be arrested for committing this offence.

D FEARING has initially committed an offence of obtaining a pecuniary advantage by deception (s. 16 of the Theft Act 1968) and therefore commits this offence.

Question 36.2

HALLAM's car breaks down in a country lane late one night. Rather than risk getting lost, she decides to sleep in her car and seek assistance in the morning. Several hours later, MILLENSTED walks past HALLAM's car and sees her sleeping inside. He decides to sexually touch HALLAM (an activity that would constitute an offence under s. 3 of the Sexual Offences Act 2003). MILLENSTED smashes the front window of the car and crawls inside. HALLAM, who is woken by the noise, manages to open one of the car doors and gets away from MILLENSTED.

With regard to the offence of trespass with intent to commit a sexual offence (s. 63 of the Sexual Offences Act 2003), which of the following statements is correct?

A The only intention that would make MILLENSTED guilty of this offence would be an intention to rape HALLAM.

B MILLENSTED has not committed the offence as a car would not be classed as a structure or part of a structure for the purposes of this offence.

C MILLENSTED has committed the offence as the term 'premises' for the purpose of s. 62 will include a vehicle.

D As HALLAM escaped before MILLENSTED committed the relevant sexual offence, he does not commit the offence.

Question 36.3

DIX decides that he is going to break into a house owned by AVERLEY. His intention is to commit an offence of rape (contrary to s. 1 of the Sexual Offences Act 2003) against AVERLEY and so he equips himself with a rope to tie her up with, condoms to minimise any DNA evidence he may leave and a bayonet to threaten her with. When DIX arrives at AVERLEY's house he sees her next-door neighbour, LAMBURN, leaving for an evening out. DIX decides that he will break into LAMBURN's house first and steal anything of value before he breaks into AVERLEY's house to rape her. He breaks into LAMBURN's house and steals property before breaking into AVERLEY's house.

At what point, if at all, does DIX commit an offence of trespass with intent to commit a sexual offence (contrary to s. 63 of the Sexual Offences Act 2003)?

A When he decides to break into AVERLEY's house and equips himself with the rope, condoms and bayonet.

B When he breaks into LAMBURN's house.

C When he breaks into AVERLEY's house.

D DIX does not commit the offence.

Question 36.4

PEACH is drinking in a bar with McMANUS and WRIGHT. PEACH decides that he wants to have sexual intercourse with WRIGHT but knows that she is married and will never consent. He mentions this to McMANUS and gives McMANUS some Rohypnol (a 'date-rape' drug) to place in WRIGHT's drink. When WRIGHT is not looking, McMANUS puts the drug into WRIGHT's lager, intending to stupefy WRIGHT so as to enable PEACH to have sexual intercourse with her. WRIGHT drinks her drugged lager and quickly becomes ill. Before anything else happens, one of WRIGHT's friends appears and takes her home.

Which of the following statements is correct with regard to the offence of administering a substance with intent (contrary to s. 61 of the Sexual Offences Act 2003)?

A McMANUS has not committed the offence because he did not administer the drug with the intention of engaging in sexual activity with WRIGHT.

B No offence has been committed in these circumstances because no sexual activity took place.

C Only McMANUS has committed the offence in these circumstances.

D PEACH and McMANUS commit the offence in these circumstances.

Question 36.5

CHRISTON is in a nightclub and starts to chat to TRUELOCK. The two are getting on well and CHRISTON decides that he wants to have a sexual encounter with TRUELOCK. TRUELOCK is drinking triple vodka drinks and CHRISTON buys her a number of these, encouraging her to get drunk; TRUELOCK is aware that she is drinking alcohol. CHRISTON thinks that if TRUELOCK becomes drunk she will agree to masturbate him in the toilets of the nightclub.

Thinking about the offence under s. 61 of the Sexual Offences Act 2003 (administering a substance with intent) only, which of the following comments is correct?

A CHRISTON has not committed the offence because he did not intend to commit a sexual offence involving penetration.

B CHRISTON has committed the offence as he intends to stupefy TRUELOCK.

C CHRISTON has not committed the offence because TRUELOCK knew she was consuming alcohol.

D CHRISTON has committed the offence but the prosecution would have to show that a sexual act took place to prove the offence.

Question 36.6

SAMSON is a burglar and intends to steal property from a house belonging to DACE. He is watching the rear of DACE's house when he sees DACE putting some clothes on a line and decides that she is sexually attractive and that when he commits the burglary he will also rape her. A few minutes later, he enters the garden of the house by climbing over a back garden fence and then breaks into the house via the kitchen door and enters the kitchen. He hears some noise from upstairs and runs up the stairs and into a bedroom where he sees DACE trying to hide from him. He grabs her and tries to rape her but she fights him off and manages to escape by running into the street.

At what stage does SAMSON first commit the offence of trespass with intent to commit a sexual offence?

A When he enters the back garden of the house.
B When he breaks into the kitchen.
C When he runs into the upstairs bedroom.
D When he tries to rape DACE.

Question 36.7

ARCHER (aged 25 years) meets BARNARD (aged 23 years) in a bar. The two go on to a nightclub together and then go back to ARCHER's home address. ARCHER masturbates BARNARD's penis before putting her forefinger into BARNARD's anus. The two then have consensual sexual intercourse (penis to vagina). Unknown to either ARCHER or BARNARD, they are in fact brother and sister.

At what point, if at all, does the offence of sex with an adult relative (s. 64 of the Sexual Offences Act 2003) take place?

A When ARCHER masturbates BARNARD.
B When ARCHER puts her forefinger into BARNARD's anus.
C When ARCHER and BARNARD have consensual sexual intercourse.
D The offence under s. 64 is not committed in these circumstances.

Question 36.8

LAWSON is the owner of 'Swingaz' sex shop which has a bar and lounge attached to it where people who use the shop can meet and drink together. LAWSON becomes very friendly with ANDERSON (who visits the bar on a regular basis) and they discover they have similar sexual tastes, particularly in relation to sado-masochistic activity. One evening, LAWSON asks ANDERSON if he is interested in looking at some *'really hardcore'* pictures; ANDERSON replies that he is. LAWSON produces his mobile phone and shows ANDERSON several still pictures of a sexual assault on a woman where a knife is inserted in her vagina and a short film where the same woman is being forced, at gunpoint, to have sexual intercourse with several men. LAWSON tells ANDERSON that the images are genuine and that the images originate from Brazil where the woman has been kidnapped and abused. He then shows ANDERSON a cartoon image based on the abuse where the same woman is having her breasts mutilated.

In relation to the offence of possession of an extreme pornographic image (contrary to s. 63 of the Criminal Justice and Immigration Act 2008), which of the following statements is correct?

A The still images of the knife being inserted into the woman's vagina are the only images covered by the legislation.

B None of the images are covered by the legislation as they do not portray, in an explicit and realistic way, acts of sexual interference with a corpse (necrophilia) or a person performing an act of intercourse or oral sex with an animal (whether dead or alive) (bestiality).

C The still images and the short film would be covered by the legislation; the animated images would not.

D All of the images (still, film and cartoon) would be covered by the legislation.

ANSWERS

Answer 36.1

Answer **A** — Section 62 of the Sexual Offences Act 2003 states that a person commits an offence under this section if he commits any offence with the intention of committing a relevant sexual offence. There are no restrictions on the nature or type of offence committed as long as it can be shown that there was an intention, when committing the original offence, to commit a relevant sexual offence. This makes answer B incorrect. Answer C is incorrect as the offence under s. 62 is committed when the first offence is committed with the required intention. Answer D is incorrect as although FEARING has committed an offence, taking photographs of children (contrary to s. 1 of the Protection of Children Act 1978) is not a 'relevant offence' for the purposes of s. 62. A 'relevant offence' means a sexual offence under Part 1 of the Sexual Offences Act 2003.

Investigators' Manual, para. 4.7.2

Answer 36.2

Answer **C** — Answer A is incorrect as MILLENSTED intends to commit a 'relevant sexual offence' (i.e. an offence under Part 1 of the Sexual Offences Act 2003). Answer D is incorrect as this is an offence of intention rather than consequence, therefore there is no need to prove that the substantive sexual offence took place. The term 'premises' for the purposes of this offence is far wider than that which relates to burglary under the Theft Act 1968. Section 63(2) of the Sexual Offences Act 2003 defines 'premises' as including a structure or part of a structure and this will include a tent, a vehicle or vessel or other temporary or movable structure. This makes answer B incorrect.

Investigators' Manual, para. 4.7.3

Answer 36.3

Answer **C** — Answer A is incorrect as at this stage, DIX has not trespassed on any premises even though he has the intention of doing so. Answer B is incorrect as the defendant must intend to commit the relevant sexual offence on the premises where he/she is a trespasser. Unless DIX intends to commit a relevant sexual offence in LAMBURN's house he does not commit the offence (although he would be guilty of aggravated burglary at this stage). The offence is therefore committed at point C (making answer D incorrect).

Investigators' Manual, para. 4.7.3

Answer 36.4

Answer **D** — Section 61(1) of the Act states that a person is guilty of an offence if he administers a substance to, or causes a substance to be taken by, another person (B), knowing that (B) does not consent and with the intention of stupefying or overpowering (B) so as to enable *any person* to engage in sexual activity that involves (B). Answer A is incorrect as it does not matter that McMANUS is not the person who will engage in sexual activity if he is administering the substance. Answer B is incorrect as the fact that sexual activity did not take place is immaterial if the substance is administered with that intent. 'Administering' or 'causing to be taken by' cover a broad range of conduct and would include a set of circumstances where PEACH persuades McMANUS to administer a drug to WRIGHT so that PEACH could have sex with WRIGHT, making answer C incorrect.

Investigators' Manual, para. 4.7.1

Answer 36.5

Answer **C** — This offence is aimed at the use of 'date rape' drugs administered without the victim's knowledge or consent, but would also cover the use of any other substance with the relevant intention. It would cover A spiking B's soft drink with alcohol where B did not know he/she was consuming alcohol, *but it would not cover A encouraging B to get drunk so that A could have sex with B, where B knew he/she was consuming alcohol* so CHRISTON would not commit the offence in these circumstances (making answers B and D incorrect). Answer A is incorrect as the offence requires an intention to enable any person to engage in sexual activity with the victim which may or may not involve penetration.

Investigators' Manual, para. 4.7.1

Answer 36.6

Answer **A** — The Sexual Offences Act 2003, s. 63 states:

(1) A person commits an offence if—
  (a) he is a trespasser on any premises,

(b) he intends to commit a relevant sexual offence on the premises, and
(c) he knows that, or is reckless as to whether, he is a trespasser.

A person is a trespasser if they are on the premises without the owner's or occupier's consent, whether express or implied, or they are there without a power at law to be there. Generally, defendants ought to know whether or not they are trespassing and recklessness will be enough in that regard. Premises here will include a structure or part of a structure (including a tent, vehicle or vessel or other temporary or movable structure (s. 63(2))). This offence is intended to capture, for example, the situation where A enters a building owned by B, or goes into *B's garden* or garage without B's consent, and he/she intends to commit a relevant sexual offence against the occupier or other person on the premises. So as soon as SAMSON enters the garden the offence is complete, making answers B, C and D incorrect.

Investigators' Manual, para. 4.7.3

Answer 36.7

Answer **D** — Although ARCHER and BARNARD are brother and sister and are therefore 'relatives' for the purposes of s. 64 of the Act, the offence under s. 64 can only be committed when the relative knows (or could reasonably be expected to know) that he/she is related to the other. If this knowledge is not present, then the offence cannot be committed, making answers A, B and C incorrect. If the two were knowingly related, then the offence would take place at point B as masturbation is not included in the *actus reus* of the offence.

Investigators' Manual, para. 4.8.1

Answer 36.8

Answer **C** — The offence under s. 63 is committed when a person is in possession of an extreme pornographic image. There are three elements to the offence. They are:

- that the image is pornographic;
- that the image is grossly offensive, disgusting or otherwise of an obscene character;
- and that the image portrays in an explicit and realistic way one of a number of extreme acts.

Necrophilia and bestiality are included but so are acts which threaten a person's life, e.g. a sexual assault involving a threat with a weapon or an act which results in or is likely to result in serious injury to a person's anus, breasts or genitals (including the insertion of sharp objects). So the nature of the images that LAWSON shows to ANDERSON all appear to be covered, making answer B incorrect. The type of images covered include still images and moving images, making answer A incorrect. However, a major requirement in relation to the images is that a reasonable person looking at the image would think that the people and animals portrayed were real. Therefore, the cartoon and any animated images, regardless of what they are based on, would not be covered, making answer D incorrect.

Investigators' Manual, para. 4.8.2

Question Checklist

The following checklist is designed to help you keep track of your progress when answering the multiple-choice questions. If you fill this in after one attempt at each question, you will be able to check how many you have got right and which questions you need to revisit a second time.

	First attempt Correct (✓)	Second attempt Correct (✓)
1 *Mens Rea* (State of Mind)		
1.1		
1.2		
1.3		
1.4		
1.5		
1.6		
1.7		
2 *Actus Reus* (Criminal Conduct)		
2.1		
2.2		
2.3		
2.4		
2.5		
2.6		

	First attempt Correct (✓)	Second attempt Correct (✓)
2.7		
2.8		
2.9		
2.10		
2.11		
3 Incomplete Offences		
3.1		
3.2		
3.3		
3.4		
3.5		
3.6		
3.7		
3.8		
3.9		
3.10		

	First attempt Correct (✓)	Second attempt Correct (✓)
4 General Defences and Issues in Evidence		
4.1		
4.2		
4.3		
4.4		
4.5		
4.6		
4.7		
4.8		
5 Entry, Search and Seizure		
5.1		
5.2		
5.3		
5.4		
5.5		
5.6		
5.7		
5.8		
5.9		
5.10		
5.11		
5.12		
5.13		
5.14		
5.15		
5.16		

	First attempt Correct (✓)	Second attempt Correct (✓)
6 Detention and Treatment of Persons by Police Officers		
6.1		
6.2		
6.3		
6.4		
6.5		
6.6		
6.7		
6.8		
6.9		
6.10		
6.11		
6.12		
6.13		
6.14		
6.15		
6.16		
6.17		
6.18		
6.19		
6.20		
6.21		
6.22		
6.23		
6.24		
6.25		
6.26		

	First attempt Correct (✓)	Second attempt Correct (✓)
6.27		
6.28		
6.29		
6.30		
6.31		
6.32		
7 Identification		
7.1		
7.2		
7.3		
7.4		
7.5		
7.6		
7.7		
7.8		
7.9		
7.10		
7.11		
7.12		
7.13		
7.14		
7.15		
7.16		
7.17		
7.18		
7.19		
7.20		

	First attempt Correct (✓)	Second attempt Correct (✓)
7.21		
7.22		
8 Interviews		
8.1		
8.2		
8.3		
8.4		
8.5		
8.6		
8.7		
8.8		
8.9		
8.10		
8.11		
8.12		
8.13		
8.14		
9 Release of Person Arrested		
9.1		
9.2		
9.3		
9.4		
9.5		
9.6		
9.7		
9.8		
9.9		

	First attempt Correct (✓)	Second attempt Correct (✓)
9.10		
9.11		
9.12		
9.13		
9.14		
9.15		
9.16		
10 Disclosure of Evidence		
10.1		
10.2		
10.3		
10.4		
10.5		
10.6		
10.7		
10.8		
10.9		
11 Regulation of Investigatory Powers Act 2000		
11.1		
11.2		
11.3		
11.4		
11.5		
11.6		
11.7		
11.8		

	First attempt Correct (✓)	Second attempt Correct (✓)
11.9		
11.10		
12 Homicide		
12.1		
12.2		
12.3		
12.4		
12.5		
12.6		
12.7		
12.8		
12.9		
13 Misuse of Drugs		
13.1		
13.2		
13.3		
13.4		
13.5		
13.6		
13.7		
13.8		
13.9		
13.10		
13.11		
13.12		
13.13		
13.14		

	First attempt Correct (✓)	Second attempt Correct (✓)
13.15		
13.16		
13.17		
14 Firearms and Gun Crime		
14.1		
14.2		
14.3		
14.4		
14.5		
14.6		
14.7		
14.8		
14.9		
14.10		
14.11		
14.12		
14.13		
14.14		
14.15		
14.16		
14.17		
15 Terrorism and Associated Offences		
15.1		
15.2		
15.3		
15.4		

	First attempt Correct (✓)	Second attempt Correct (✓)
15.5		
15.6		
15.7		
15.8		
15.9		
15.10		
15.11		
15.12		
15.13		
16 Cybercrime		
16.1		
16.2		
16.3		
16.4		
16.5		
16.6		
16.7		
16.8		
16.9		
16.10		
16.11		
17 Racially and Religiously Aggravated Offences		
17.1		
17.2		
17.3		
17.4		

	First attempt Correct (✓)	Second attempt Correct (✓)
18 Non-Fatal Offences Against the Person		
18.1		
18.2		
18.3		
18.4		
18.5		
18.6		
18.7		
18.8		
18.9		
18.10		
18.11		
18.12		
18.13		
18.14		
18.15		
19 Hatred and Harassment Offences		
19.1		
19.2		
19.3		
19.4		
20 Child Protection		
20.1		
20.2		
20.3		
20.4		

	First attempt Correct (✓)	Second attempt Correct (✓)
20.5		
20.6		
20.7		
20.8		
21 Offences Involving the Deprivation of Liberty		
21.1		
21.2		
21.3		
21.4		
21.5		
21.6		
21.7		
21.8		
22 Theft		
22.1		
22.2		
22.3		
22.4		
22.5		
22.6		
22.7		
22.8		
22.9		
22.10		
22.11		
22.12		

	First attempt Correct (✓)	Second attempt Correct (✓)
22.13		
22.14		
22.15		
22.16		
22.17		
23 Robbery		
23.1		
23.2		
23.3		
23.4		
23.5		
23.6		
23.7		
23.8		
23.9		
23.10		
24 Blackmail		
24.1		
24.2		
24.3		
24.4		
24.5		
24.6		
24.7		
25 Burglary		
25.1		
25.2		

	First attempt Correct (✓)	Second attempt Correct (✓)
25.3		
25.4		
25.5		
25.6		
25.7		
25.8		
25.9		
25.10		
25.11		
25.12		
25.13		
26 Aggravated Burglary		
26.1		
26.2		
26.3		
26.4		
26.5		
26.6		
26.7		
26.8		
26.9		
26.10		
27 Taking a Conveyance Without Consent		
27.1		
27.2		
27.3		
27.4		

	First attempt Correct (✓)	Second attempt Correct (✓)
27.5		
27.6		
27.7		
28 Handling Stolen Goods		
28.1		
28.2		
28.3		
28.4		
28.5		
28.6		
28.7		
28.8		
29 Fraud		
29.1		
29.2		
29.3		
29.4		
29.5		
29.6		
29.7		
29.8		
29.9		
29.10		
29.11		
29.12		
29.13		

	First attempt Correct (✓)	Second attempt Correct (✓)
30 Proceeds of Crime		
30.1		
30.2		
30.3		
30.4		
30.5		
31 Criminal Damage		
31.1		
31.2		
31.3		
31.4		
31.5		
31.6		
31.7		
32 Sexual Offences, Rape and Sexual Assault		
32.1		
32.2		
32.3		
32.4		
32.5		
32.6		
32.7		
32.8		
32.9		
32.10		

	First attempt Correct (✓)	Second attempt Correct (✓)
32.11		
32.12		
32.13		
32.14		
32.15		
32.16		
32.17		
32.18		
32.19		
32.20		
32.21		
32.22		
32.23		
33 Sexual Offences Against Children		
33.1		
33.2		
33.3		
33.4		
33.5		
33.6		
33.7		
33.8		
33.9		
33.10		
33.11		
33.12		
33.13		
33.14		

	First attempt Correct (✓)	Second attempt Correct (✓)
33.15		
33.16		
33.17		
33.18		
33.19		
33.20		
33.21		
33.22		
33.23		
34 Sexual Offences Against People with a Mental Disorder		
34.1		
34.2		
34.3		
34.4		
34.5		
34.6		
34.7		
35 Offences Relating to Prostitution		
35.1		
35.2		
35.3		
35.4		
35.5		
35.6		
35.7		
35.8		

	First attempt Correct (✓)	Second attempt Correct (✓)
36 Preparatory Offences and Other Sexual Offences		
36.1		
36.2		
36.3		
36.4		
36.5		
36.6		
36.7		
36.8